Managing

Workplace Diversity

Selina A. Griswold

Alberta Educational Services, Inc.

Preface

A key competitive advantage for organizations in the future will be how to make the best use of their human resources. Traditional management methods and organizational structures will need to increasingly utilize the skills of women, people of color, immigrants, older workers, the disabled, and those with various lifestyles and religions. Diversity has replaced homogeneity as the business norm. Especially in private industry, where they are faced with reengineering, a more competitive marketplace, the global business environment and the changing way of conducting business, managing diversity is a critical issue that must be addressed effectively.

This textbook was developed to provide resources to help managers, students and employees (1) understand what it means to value diversity (2) effectively manage the diversity of their office/work areas and (3) integrate researched concepts and common sense ideas into their day-to-day business. Managers as well as employees can benefit from this text by expanding their knowledge on the range of topics that encompass difference and an understanding of Equal Employment Opportunity Laws. Managers and employees alike will gain a better understanding of self and others all while exploring answers to questions as it relates to valuing and managing diversity.

The textbook is able to accomplish the above through the wide-ranging list of topics addressed. The textbook is organized into three components: valuing difference, affirmative action and managing diversity with the focus on valuing difference. Valuing difference is critical because it seems much easier to manage what you value. Once able to "really" value difference then the mind becomes ready to handle and apply what the law says with a full understanding of why these laws exist. Within the text, each chapter begins with a famous proverb that starts the journey of critically thinking about the information to come. The conversational tone of each chapter will engage the reader to examine their own beliefs as well as begin to view issues through the lens of others. Through the extensive list of concepts covered, once done readers should be able to:

- Promote and support diversity initiatives; contribute to workplace diversity councils
- Serve as an advocate on EEO/diversity management issues; working to correct problems, eliminate social barriers, and replicate practices that positively impact diversity goals and objectives;
- Consider becoming a formal or informal mentor to support departmental diversity;
- Promote the creation of a work environment that reflects the mosaic of the communities we serve.

Acknowledgements

━━━

To the many students who have taken my Managing Diversity in the Workplace course over the last ten years, I appreciate the feedback and pre-test/post-test data (which often indicated that learning took place throughout the course). Many of these students have pointed out that the course should be required of all learners at the university. Thanks also to the expert reviewers whose comments have contributed to this text.

Additional thanks to the teachers at Children's Discovery Center (Ms. Nikki and Ms. Melissa) in Perrysburg, Ohio as without their care and attention given to my precious toddler this text would not be possible.

Special Thanks

━━━

To my loving husband, Aaron, son, Darius, daughter, Mia, parents, sister, nephew, and

other close family and friends, thank you so much for your support and unconditional

love as I spent many waking hours conducting research and writing this text.

"A united family eats from the same plate."- (Kiganda proverb)

Table of Contents

Managing Workplace Diversity

Chapter One

Introduction

The wise are as rare as eagles that fly high in the sky.

Bantu proverb

INTRODUCTION

Chapter Objectives

After reading this chapter, you should be able to:

- understand what it takes to manage change.

- explain how the right or wrong attitude affects managing change.

- clarify what it means to embrace diversity.

- identify the three approaches to diversity.

- describe what is required for cultural competence.

Introduction

What is Diversity? Organizations use definitions of diversity that are almost as diverse as the subject itself, but what is clear is that the central theme of 'valuing everyone as individuals – as employees, customers, and clients' extends diversity beyond what is legislated.

Business exists in competitive and changing markets, which means that all employees must make significant contributions to business success and add value in every conceivable manner, but everyone is different, so organizations will need to be able to harness individual workers' unique differences and convert them into competitive advantage.[1] When studying organizational phenomena, many Researchers implicitly assume that employees within an organization are homogeneous. They also assume that the phenomena being studied are unaffected by whether employees are different from each other. Diversity researchers reject both of these assumptions. Their work focuses on questions that arise when the workforce is acknowledged as a heterogeneous mix of people with different backgrounds, experiences, values, and identities.[2] A challenge of this type puts a premium on value systems that are inclusive, fair and ethical. We know from the essential characteristics of the psychological contract that employees expect their employers to value who they are.[3] This is why effective workplace diversity is so important to enhancing business performance and, as research evidence shows, is correlated with good people management.[4]

According to the change agenda, Managing Diversity: Linking Theory and Practice to Business Performance Conference foreward by Dianah Worman:

In the global market place of the twenty-first century, the pace of change in business practice is considered faster than ever before. Organizations are striving to keep one step ahead of competitors to gain and sustain market share and to appease the increasingly voracious appetites of customers regarding products and service delivery. Against this fluid background, the challenge organizations face is to be able to respond to change in ways that assure survival.[5]

While change is a constant factor in today's workplace, many of us perceive change to be burdensome. This indicates that there can be resistance to change which could result in a resistance to diversity efforts.

Managing Change

How well are you at managing change? To determine the response, let's start by answering the following questions:

1. If someone challenges your behaviors or beliefs, do you find yourself justifying, defending or rationalizing as a response?

2. Do you find yourself frustrated when you have to change your routine, change your plans, or change something as simple as your work route due to a detour?

3. Do you find that you are still dealing with the same problems you had 3, 6 or 9 months ago?

4. When confronted with a challenge regarding your character or work ethics do you find yourself giving excuses for why you are the way you are?

5. Do you find yourself complaining a lot about life, your job, your relationship or other significant areas in your life?

If you answered, "yes" to at least three out of the five questions, you may have some issues with managing change. Yet, if life is about growth then change is a natural part of the life cycle. But, so many people are resistant to change. Why? Because change often takes us out of our comfort zone.

Yet, as we start this discussion of workplace diversity you may find that you need to change your thoughts about others and/or open your mind to beliefs unlike your own. Part of managing change is being teachable where you are able to listen (not tune out, not argue with, not think of an answer before the person finishes speaking) to what others have to say. Listening does not require you to take the person's advice, but you must be able to respect what they have to say. If you are teachable, you will even ponder over what they have to say before making a judgment.

Being teachable also means that you realize that you have room for improvement (no matter the age or status) and you can, therefore, be more open to what others have to say. Having an open mind is imperative to being able to deal with change.[6] We must also understand that while having an open mind is an important ingredient to managing change, being cautious of what we put in our mind affects how we act toward change. We all know that our minds are power centers—the area where we store our thoughts, ideas, imaginings, and decisions. But, how does this power center control our behavior?

Read the following quote:

Watch your thoughts; they become words.
Watch your words; they become actions.
Watch your actions; they become habits.
Watch your habits; they become character.
Watch your character; it becomes your destiny.
Frank Outlaw[7]

If we really want to make a change that will affect who we are then it must start with the images, beliefs, values etc... that are a part of our thoughts. We must keep our minds open and be aware of our thoughts; just these two aspects alone can help us to make continual improvement in our character. While you may think that you are done improving your character, none of us are perfect and therefore we can all stand to make some changes. Managing diversity may require you to open your mind and challenge your ways of thinking.[8]

This can be done by first looking at our attitude toward change which can ultimately affect our ability to embrace diversity.

Managing Change Through our Attitudes

As we begin this journey of learning how to address workplace diversity, we will address a key ingredient that will determine how we adjust to change or difference—that is, our attitude. Your attitude is often one of the first things about your character that people will notice. So, what really is your attitude? It is the way in which we respond to our circumstances. According to the *American Heritage Dictionary* "attitude" is a state of mind or feeling with regard to some matter.[9] When choosing to deal with change or your circumstances you can respond negatively or positively or just simply shift into neutral. By shifting into neutral you may be choosing to ignore the situation, but how long will this be an effective response to change? You could also respond negatively to change by complaining, being sarcastic or even experiencing intense anger. But, does this type of response really make the circumstance go away?

Since none of us are perfect and don't always respond appropriately, we may find that our first response is a negative one. But if we can open our minds, reflect on the incident then maybe we can find a positive way to respond to the change. Even in the worst of conditions, if you look hard enough you can often find some positive way to view change. But is it really this simple?

Understanding why we respond to change unfavorably (that is with a negative attitude) goes a long way toward having a favorable response. Fear is often the most cited reason for people being unfavorable about change. Fear of the unknown, fear of a new way of thinking or doing and fear of failure are all fears that people experience when facing change.[10] But, fear is not the only reason people have a negative attitude toward change. Insecurity is another.

When a person's self-worth or what they thought made them who they are is being shaken, lost or questioned, change may not be welcomed.[11] We all have our comfort zones and when those are threatened we can often become uncomfortable. But, you cannot move ahead by holding on. You have to let go and understand that you will experience some discomfort. But this discomfort does not have to control you.

As you adapt to something new by having a positive attitude, you then give yourself the chance to feel the exhilaration surrounding this new experience.[12] Controlling our attitude is even more possible when we examine our various levels of thought. Researchers suggest that to bring order to the potentially chaotic landscape of the mind, it helps to think positively.[13] Positive thinking, the highest level of thinking breeds peace, love and creativity, and encourages harmony and happiness.[14]

Having positive thoughts may seem idealistic, but it is not as difficult to achieve as one might think. If we can first concentrate on and find the positives in ourselves, then maybe we can do this for others and for uncomfortable circumstances. To that end, I ask you to do the following exercise before moving forward in the chapter.

Positive Thinking Exercise

Take three to five minutes to complete the exercise. Please be honest and time yourself. List ten POSITIVE internal attributes (things that would define your character) about yourself such as "caring." Now list ten POSITIVE external attributes (things that make you physically attractive such as you have beautiful eyes). Please do not get ANY assistance (do not ask your spouse, partner, friends or family), all twenty answers must come from you alone.

Ten Positive Internal Characteristics About Me:

1. I'm intelligent
2. Nice person
3. caring
4. _____
5. _____
6. _____
7. _____
8. _____
9. _____
10. _____

Ten Positive External Characteristics About Me:

1. Nice hair
2. Pretty smile
3. Nice facial features
4. _____
5. _____
6. _____
7. _____
8. _____
9. _____
10. _____

Now that you have completed this Positive Thinking exercise, was it easy or difficult?

If you answered *easy*, were you able to come up with 20 answers or at least 16 in total? If yes, I applaud you. This is excellent and generally means that you have a great self image. Hopefully, if you feel this positive about yourself you should be able to see positive attributes in others as well as have a positive attitude toward change. According to psychologists, those who have healthy self-esteem feel less threatened by change and can therefore extend their positive thoughts to these difficult situations.

If you answered *difficult*, then maybe now is the time to ask others about your internal and external positive characteristics so that you can complete your list and add these positive thoughts to how you view yourself. Finding this exercise difficult could mean several things. For one, you may confuse being self-assured with being conceited and therefore have not allowed yourself to think these positive thoughts about yourself. Remember, thinking positively about ourselves does not indicate that we overvalue ourselves and have heads that can't fit into doors, it just means that we value who we are.

Additionally, if you found this exercise difficult it could mean that you need to work on valuing who you are. How can you expect others to value what you don't? How can you look for the positives in others and difficult circumstances when you can't do this for yourself? Unfortunately for many reasons, some of us have not built a healthy self-esteem based on realistic characteristics of self. Instead, we have a false sense of security because we don't value who we really are. If we can elevate our thoughts to positive from negative (especially our thoughts of self), then we should better be able to elevate how we respond to change. If we can be positive and allow creativity to permeate our attitudes then maybe we can have an open mind. With an open mind, positive attitude, and positive self-worth we can begin to see change as positive. This should go a long way toward starting the process of embracing diversity.

Embracing Diversity

People can be categorized in many ways, such as by gender, race, religion, ethnicity, language, income, age, ability or sexual orientation. Unfortunately, these categories are sometimes used to label people unfairly or to saddle them with stereotypes. Stereotypes are generalized assumptions concerning the traits or characteristics of all members of a particular group. They are frequently (although not always) negative and generally incorrect. Ironically, stereotypes discourage closer contact, preventing the perpetrator from discovering what the individual victims of these stereotypes are really like.[15]

Stereotypes often form the basis of prejudice, a premature judgment about a group or a member of that group made without sufficient knowledge or thought.[16] We can also develop prejudices towards a whole group based on a single emotional experience with one person. Prejudice demonstrates an unfair bias that does not allow for individual differences, good or bad. It violates the standards of reason, justice, and tolerance.

Many of today's prejudices have their roots in thousands of years of human history, such as the institution of slavery in America, the slaughter of European Jews by Christians en route to the Holy Land during the Crusades, and numerous religious wars between Catholics and Protestants. Other biases can be based on personal experiences and influences.

A number of sociologists attribute prejudice to modern social problems, including urban decay and overcrowding, unemployment, and competition between groups.[17] Research suggests that people of lower (but not the lowest) socio-economic status or who have lost status are more prejudiced because they seek scapegoats to blame for their misfortune.[18] Backlashes against minority groups are therefore more likely during periods of severe economic downturn and increased unemployment.[19]

Many of us recognize our own irrational prejudices (they may concern places, foods, ideas, etc., as well as people) and work to overcome them. In contrast, bigots are those persons who obstinately cling to their prejudices, displaying a degrading attitude towards others to whom they feel superior. Various groups have been and continue to be the victims of bigotry, including racial, ethnic and religious groups, women, persons with disabilities, and gays and lesbians amongst others.

We are intolerant if we reject or dislike people because they are different, e.g., of a different religion, different socio-economic status, or have a different set of values. When comparing different vs. normal in the United States culture, this has largely been based on white, heterosexual, able-bodied males, the norm against which to judge others. But, as we look around our jobs, our school systems and our communities at large, we will find more women, people of color, disabled, homosexuals/gay & lesbians and others that don't fit the above norm. It therefore becomes increasingly necessary that our environments acknowledge a

Three Approaches to Diversity

The rest of the text is broken down based on the three approaches to addressing workplace diversity. In order to embrace diversity and make equal opportunity a reality it is often necessary to understand and utilize all three approaches to diversity in the workplace. The following table explains (in very simple terms) the differences between the three approaches, using information from the following source: *Beyond Race and Gender: Unleashing the Power of Your Total Work Force by Managing Diversity*, author Thomas Roosevelt (1992).[23]

Valuing Differences	Affirmative Action	Managing Diversity
Emphasis here is on accepting, respecting and understanding differences.	Emphasis is on achieving equality of opportunity. Seeking to include those who were formerly excluded. Corrects recruitment, training and promotion tactics that have caused systematized discrimination.	Emphasis is on building specific skills and creating policies that get the best from all employees.
Necessary for any cultural change and can be ethnically driven.	Goals are outlined for achieving a multicultural workplace. Could be required if company is in prior violation of discrimination or seeks to be a contractor with the federal government. It can be legally driven or voluntary.	Once you've hired a multicultural workforce and learned to value differences, it is then necessary to have policies that are effective for all employees that is tied to rewards and results. Otherwise, you may start with diversity, but may end up with it being a revolving door. This step is often strategically driven.
Opens attitudes	**Opens doors**	**Opens the system**

different norm that is representative of all groups. Not only must the current norm based upon the dominant culture be altered, but so must our approach to embracing diversity. Let's start with the following myth:

MYTH: AMERICA IS A MELTING POT

While it may seem easier to have all cultures assimilate–that is, melt into the dominant culture, this is not a realistic or fair expectation. According to Holly Atkins in the December 2001 article: *An American 'tossed salad'* she indicates the melting pot is no more.[20] Today, many people from diverse backgrounds may blend together but never lose their cultural identity. Therefore, it makes more sense to change our mindset to the following theory:

FACT: AMERICA IS A TOSSED SALAD

We are all different (some of us could be cucumbers, some tomatoes, some cheese, etc...) one is not better than the other. But, just like each ingredient looks different and adds a different flavor to the salad, so can a diverse workplace produce a greater product if managed effectively. The nice thing about the tossed salad is that as each item is added it never loses its identity or flavor. As we begin to value diversity we should not expect those culturally or ethnically different from us to lose their identity or culture. Assimilation is not the goal in learning to value diversity but rather the goal is to learn to have an inclusive workplace where every person is valued for who they are.[21]

Once we see that different is not good or bad, it is just different then we can begin to understand that a salad with just lettuce would seem bland next to a salad with lettuce, cucumbers, tomatoes, olives etc... Requiring everyone to be just alike would cause America to be "bland." You know what they say: diversity adds spice to life. With diversity comes different types of music, food, customs, thought patterns, dress, etc... and each of these enriches the U.S. culture and workplace.

Despite this enrichment, some groups or individuals may find it more beneficial to assimilate rather than to hold onto their unique identity. This is when cabbage may want to change to lettuce. The lettuce may even welcome this assimilation but then we must remember that assimilation is not an over night process. It usually takes two or more generations for the members of a new group to become sufficiently absorbed into the life of a community so much so that they lose their separate identity.[22] This assimilation is easier and sometimes desirable when those groups assimilating are easily accepted into the group norm and are considered a valuable entity.

However, some ethnic groups—mainly those of dark skin colors—never achieve total assimilation. If we are in agreement with the tossed salad theory, total assimilation should no longer even be the expectation. But even still, those of dark skin have had a harder time due to the prejudices that society has exhibited towards people of color. Let's give a warning here, as some of you may be thinking, "Prejudices aren't an issue in today's world, I'm not prejudice."

People concerned about and committed to improving inter-group relations must guard against such clichés as: "I'm not prejudice." Even as you think about the tossed salad theory, I am sure that everyone can think of one item going into that salad that they don't care for due to one reason or another. But, if this does not fit you maybe you find that you like one item on the salad better than others, therefore you have a bias toward one ingredient. Just the same, people can be in general prejudiced for or against other people. However, there are many laws against discriminatory behaviors, but there are none against prejudicial attitudes.

However, the good news is if we can learn prejudices we can most certainly unlearn them. This begins with simple concepts and thought, such as viewing the world/workplace as a tossed salad where working together is the order of business. We must also know that of those who maintain their difference, no matter how different, we should not judge this person, hold prejudices against them but accept who they are. But, we can't get to this step if we don't fully recognize our prejudices. Once we recognize that we do have preconceptions toward others only then can we start to change our biased thoughts to unbiased thoughts.

The truth of the matter is where there are obvious differences due to skin color, accents, weight, height many in the U.S. society have more in common than they realize. This common ground supports the notion that while managing workplace diversity may not be simple; it is to the benefit of many. Learning to embrace diversity rather than have others try to fit into the norm or melt into the pot should be the goal of organizations.

There are three established diversity approaches that can assist us in embracing diversity.

In order to determine what approach to use for a given situation, it is necessary to review the factors that are taking place at your organization. Some companies will need to use all three approaches in a comprehensive diversity plan, while other organizations may have addressed certain issues and may need to use only one of the above approaches.[23] But no matter which approach is utilized, it is important for managers to understand what is going on in their workplace and what changes will need to take place in order to address the issue(s) effectively.

We begin this discussion of the three approaches with Valuing Differences (Affirmative Action and Managing Diversity will be discussed later in the text) because it is my belief that it is hard to manage what we don't value. It is very easy to mistreat those things and people that we don't value. Some people mistreat animals simply because they don't value their existence—this person's thinking is negative toward animals and comes out through their actions toward them.

Anthony Carnevale and Susan Carol Stone, authors of The *American Mosaic*, have emphasized that valuing diversity involves "recognizing that other people's standards and values are as valid as one's own," and note that for most organizations, valuing diversity requires nothing less than cultural transformation.[24] This is an extraordinary task, for it requires people—especially those of the dominant culture—to let go of their assumptions about the universal rightness of their own values and customary ways of doing things and to become receptive to other cultures.[25]

Valuing diversity requires respecting, understanding and accepting differences. It does not mean however that you must agree with the difference. But, if you choose to disagree, you must still show respect, and seek to understand and accept this difference. Respecting diversity starts by first expanding our *cultural knowledge* of "American history" to the point where it becomes inclusive of all groups that have contributed to our great society. Without this knowledge, it is easy to believe the negative media portrayals and news accounts that plague certain groups of people. Without cultural knowledge it becomes easy to believe the stereotypes and myths that can often be passed down from one generation to the next. Lack of knowledge can also result in lack of value where we don't treat those who are different with *cultural sensitivity* or respect.

Cultural Knowledge

Familiarization with selected cultural characteristics, history, values, belief systems, and behaviors of the members of another ethnic group (Adams, 1995).[26]

Cultural Awareness

Means developing sensitivity and understanding of another ethnic group. This usually involves internal changes in terms of attitudes and values. Awareness and sensitivity also refer to the qualities of openness and flexibility that people develop in relation to others. Cultural awareness must be supplemented with cultural knowledge (Adams, 1995).[27]

Cultural Sensitivity

Is knowing that cultural differences as well as similarities exist, without assigning values, i.e. better or worse, right or wrong, to those cultural differences (National Maternal and Child Health Center on Cultural Competency, 1997).[28]

Cultural knowledge + cultural awareness + cultural sensitivity
= Cultural Competence

Cultural Competence

Is the set of congruent behaviors, attitudes, and policies that come together in a system, agency or among professionals. It enables that system, agency, or those professionals to work effectively in cross-cultural situations (Cross, Bazron, Dennis, & Isaacs, 1989).[29]

Why is Cultural Competence Important?

Because without it the following can occur:
1. Lack of knowledge - resulting in an inability to recognize the differences.
2. Self-protection/denial - leading to an attitude that these differences are not significant, or that our common humanity transcends our differences.
3. Fear of the unknown or the new - because it is challenging and perhaps intimidating to get to understand something that is new, that does not fit into one's world view.
4. Feeling of pressure due to time constraints - which can lead to feeling rushed and unable to look in depth at an individual's needs.

End of Chapter Exercise

Take the Pretest/Posttest Challenge

Pretest

Directions: Answer questions 1-17 utilizing your "best" guess. The correct answers will be given after you have completed the post-test toward the end of the textbook.

True/False

1.   Thanksgiving is a celebration that everyone enjoys. Native-Americans especially enjoy this holiday because of the peace it represented to their community.

     _____

2.   Gay and lesbian people are a threat to the workplace and have few leaders who have contributed to our society.

     _____

3.   African-Americans even though they started as slaves in this country now have equal opportunity.

     _____

4.   Disabled employees can be a liability to a company due to missed work time.

     _____

5.   Caucasian men are accepted in Corporate America because they all belong to the "old boys network."

     _____

6.   For every job that a man can do, there is a woman able to do the same job.

     _____

7. Most people on welfare (a government transfer system where tax payer dollars are given to the poor for housing etc.) are Black and Hispanic women who live off the system forever.

    _____

8. Arabs come to this country and are given government subsidies (free money that is not to be paid back) this is why they are able to buy their own companies.

    _____

9. Asian-Americans have always been privileged minorities because of their higher intelligence and because they do not suffer from discrimination or illiteracy.

    _____

10. Hispanics are the poorest minority because they are lazy.

    _____

11. Cultural knowledge of various groups is not necessary to preventing discrimination in the workplace.

    _____

12. I believe that most people are treated fairly in the workplace and history plays no factor in how people treat each other.

    _____

13. It is not necessary to have diversity training in the workplace as most people understand diversity and its implications.

    _____

Multiple Choice

14. I belong to the following group: a. male or b. female

15.   I belong to the following group:
        a. Asian American
        b. African American/Black
        c. Caucasian
        d. Latino/Hispanic
        e. Native American
        f. Other

16.   I belong to the following age group:
        a. Under the age of 18
        b. age   18-25
        c. age   26-45
        d. age   46 and older

17.   The following is a true statement:
        a. I have had previous diversity training that relates to culture
        b. I have never had diversity training.
        c. I have had sexual harassment training only.
        d. I have had diversity training and sexual harassment training.

References

1. Worman, D. (2005). Managing Diversity: Linking Theory and Practice to Business Performance Conference. *Chartered Institute of Personnel and Development*. Retrieved from: http://www.cipd.co.uk/NR/rdonlyres/D4D2D911-FC8A-4FD2-A814-B80A55A60B87/0/mandivlink0405.pdf

2. Jackson, S.E. & Joshi, A. (n.d.). *Research on Domestic and International Diversity in Organizations: A Merger that Works?* Retrieved from: http://chrs.rutgers.edu/pub_documents/Jackson_5.pdf

3. Worman, D. (2005). Managing Diversity: Linking Theory and Practice to Business Performance Conference. *Chartered Institute of Personnel and Development*. Retrieved from: http://www.cipd.co.uk/NR/rdonlyres/D4D2D911-FC8A-4FD2-A814-B80A55A60B87/0/mandivlink0405.pdf

4. Ibid.

5. Ibid.

6. Austin, M. R. (1997, August). Managing Change. *Manage*, 49(1), 15-17.

7. Outlaw, F. (n.d.). Stubbleupon. Retrieved from http://www.uscg.mil/leadership/news/fall99/watch.htm

8. De Meuse, K. P. & McDaris, K. K. (1994, February). An Exercise in Managing Change. *Training & Development*, 48(2), 55-57.

9. The American Heritage Dictionary of the English Language. (n.d.). Retrieved from www.bartleby.com/61/64/S0946400.html

10. Costello, S. J. (1994). *Managing Change in the Workplace: Designing the Flexible, High Performing Organization*. New York: Wiley.

11. Ibid.

12. Decker, D. C. & Belohlav, J. A. (1997, April). Managing Transitions. *Quality Progress*, 30(4), 93-97.

13. Ibid.

14. Ibid.

15. Ponterotto, J. G. (1993). *Preventing Prejudice: A Guide for Counselors and Educators*. Newbury, CA: Sage Publishing.

16. Ibid.

17. Ibid.

18. Essed, P. (1991). *Understanding Everyday Racism: an Interdisciplinary Theory*. Newbury Park: Sage Publications.

19. Ibid.

20. Atkins, H. (2001, December). An American 'tossed' salad. *St. Petersburg Times*.

21. Thomas R. R. (1992). *Beyond Race and Gender: Unleashing the Power of Your Total Work Force by Managing Diversity*. New York: American Management Association.

22. Ahmed, N. R. (1993, December). Stirring the salad bowl: Diversity continues to increase. *Managers Magazine*, 68, 12.

23. Thomas R. R. (1992). *Beyond Race and Gender: Unleashing the Power of Your Total Work Force by Managing Diversity*. New York: American Management Association.

24. Carnevale, A. P. & Stone, S. C. (1995). *The American Mosaic: an In-Depth Report on the future of Diversity at Work*. New York: McGraw-Hill.

25. Ibid.

26. Adams, D. L. (1995). *Health issues for women of color: A cultural diversity perspective*. Thousand Oaks: SAGE Publications.

27. Ibid.

28. Texas Department of Health, National Maternal and Child Health Resource Center on Cultural Competency. (1997). *Journey towards cultural competency: Lessons learned*. Vienna, VA: Maternal and Children's Health Bureau Clearinghouse.

29. Cross T., Bazron, B., Dennis, K., & Isaacs, M. (1989). *Towards a Culturally Competent System of Care*, Volume I. Washington, D.C.: Georgetown University Child Development Center, CASSP Technical Assistance Center.

30. Maya Angelou quotes. (n.d.). ThinkExist.com. Retrieved from http://thinkexist.com/quotation/prejudice_is_a_burden_that_confuses_the_past/327559.html

Chapter Two

Ways of Thinking About & Across Difference

Your life is what your thoughts make it.

Unknown

WAYS OF THINKING ABOUT AND ACROSS DIFFERENCE

Chapter Objectives

After reading this chapter, you should be able to:

- understand how certain diversity questions relate to ways of thinking about difference.

- explain what is meant by "habitual ways of thinking about diversity."

- identify each of the nine reasoning models.

- clarify the use of the reasoning models and their impact on decision making.

- describe how to utilize the reasoning models to reframe diversity.

Ways of Thinking About and Across Difference*

*This entire chapter (except end of chapter questions/exercises) is an article from the following source: Ways of Thinking About and Across Difference, author Mary C. Gentile. Copyright © 1995 by the President and Fellows of Harvard College. Reprinted in entirety by permission Harvard Business School Publishing.[1]

This note begins with the hypothesis that many of us genuinely feel "stuck" when we engage in reflection and discussion about issues of "diversity." Over the last decade or so in the United States, the term "diversity" has become a kind of code word for issues triggered by the impacts of race and gender, and increasingly other types of difference—ethnicity, religion, national origin, sexual orientation, class, etc.—in businesses, schools, government, and other contexts. This note is written out of and refers to experience in the United States, but the reasoning model can be applied in other contexts as well.] At the level of explicit content, we generate limitless examples of seemingly insoluble dilemmas and untenable trade-offs: how do we respect another's point of view without devaluing our own, how can we be sensitive to the experiences and feelings of others without curtailing our own experience of fundamental personal liberty, and how can we address societal inequity toward some without imposing it upon others. At the level of implicit content and interpersonal reactions, we face another set of obstacles: a whole range of learned but unconscious assumptions about those who are different from us, as well as feelings of anxiety, fear, anger, guilt, mistrust and hopelessness that block communication and learning.

Most of us want to see ourselves as—and, in actuality, to be—fair, open-minded, intellectually honest, self-aware and even empathetic. In fact, most of us do see ourselves as all these things. But nevertheless, most of us would acknowledge the great and painful conflicts and inequities that wrack our personal relationships, businesses, governments, countries and our world—conflicts and inequities that often break down along lines of group differences (racial, ethnic, religious, gender, etc.).

So somewhere between all our individual good intentions on the one hand, and our interpersonal and group behaviors or impacts on the other, the equation breaks down. It seems that the way we think and talk about our interactions with difference limits the responses we can generate. Psychologists tell us that when we are considering change, we can target three levels: our beliefs, our feelings, and our actions. They will further explain that the most difficult target is the first, and that the most feasible approach to change is through actions (or behavior), where changes will in turn affect our feelings and finally our beliefs.

Therefore, in this note we have targeted reasoning behaviors, our cognitive strategies—not the thoughts and beliefs themselves but rather the way we put them together. By changing our thinking habits (and consequently the conclusions we act upon), we can begin to have an impact on feelings and beliefs.

The purpose of this note is to examine some of the habitual ways of thinking that are applied to so-called "diversity" questions, to reveal the commonalities and limitations of these models—the ways they can reinforce unexamined assumptions and destructive emotional reactions, and to suggest an alternative way of framing such questions that opens up the possibility for creativity and new learning.

Diversity Questions

Before we look at some of our mental models and ways of reasoning about diversity questions, let's define just what these questions are. The term "diversity" has come to refer to any number of issues and concerns, and although you or I may be thinking of very different things, we will often talk about diversity as if we mean the same thing. In fact, one of the barriers to fresh and unbiased thinking about diversity that we will discuss below is our tendency to present equivocal concepts as if they are clear, solid and single in their meaning. [Chris Argyris, "Teaching Smart People How to Learn," Harvard Business Review (May-June 1991), p. 103.]

To avoid this pitfall and to facilitate our discussion here, it may be useful to identify several of the types of questions that are often subsumed under this rubric of diversity:

• How and why we, as individuals, perceive, feel about, and behave toward other individuals whom we characterize as "different" from ourselves. We may attribute these differences to individual traits or to membership in a particular "group."

• How and why we, as individuals, perceive, feel about, and behave toward groups to which we do not belong.

• How and why institutions (families, businesses, schools, churches, governments) reflect, operationalize and perpetuate these perceptions, feelings and behaviors by rendering them invisible and/or "undiscussable."

• How and why these perceptions, feelings and behaviors might be changed.

These are questions of efficiency, productivity, equity, social harmony, group and individual survival, legality, public policy and morality. And as this note will eventually argue, they are fundamentally questions about the human potential, drive and need for learning and growth.

Habitual Ways of Thinking About Difference
Patterns of Duality and Oppositionality

From psychologist Carl Jung to anthropologist Edward T. Hall, from philosopher Simone de Beauvoir to linguist Saussure, many scholars have noted the ubiquity, across varied times and cultures, of certain patterns of duality, dichotomy, and binary opposition in human language and thought. Dichotomies in themselves are not a problem: they are simply a pattern of perception.

However, the tendency to oversimplify our observations by limiting them to binary oppositions as opposed to more complex and multiple perceptions, and the tendency to value one term of the dichotomy over another, whether appropriate or not, creates difficulties. If we require ourselves to self-consciously critique the very reasoning and critical thinking processes that we bring to bear upon questions of diversity, we will see a consistent application of these patterns, a consistency that restricts our answers for such questions to either/or, right/wrong, you/me choices.

In the following pages, we will examine nine descriptions of ways we typically think about difference, in an effort to reveal the dichotomies that shape and constrain our reasoning. Although some of the authors and approaches described below focus exclusively on race or gender or on the United States, the conceptual tendencies they discuss extend to other forms of difference. The objective here is not to explain the origins of racism or sexism or any other form of oppression, but rather to make visible the habitual but often unconscious patterns of thinking that keep us from thinking and acting our ways out of inefficient and destructive behaviors.

Mary Ann Glendon and Rights Talk
In *Rights Talk: The Impoverishment of Political Discourse*, Harvard Law professor Mary Ann Glendon examines the distinctive way in which thinking and talking about rights has developed in America. In particular, she observes an emphasis upon "absolute" rights: that is, there is a tendency to view rights as an "all or nothing" affair. People say that they have the "right to do and live as they choose," and any attempt to place limits around that statement is seen as a "slippery slope," a dangerous assault on freedom that will result in repression. For

example, people who themselves would never wish to offend a colleague will bristle at discussions of sexual harassment, arguing that their right to free speech is in jeopardy.

Glendon also observes a tendency in the United States to emphasize the protection of individual rights, but without a balancing emphasis upon responsibilities. She argues that these characteristics are not universal when one looks at other nations' official statements toward human liberties, providing historical and contemporary examples from other countries of a balancing language of duty and commitment to community.

Glendon argues that this emphasis on "absolute" rights and the omission of a balancing emphasis upon responsibilities compromise the United States' ability to move toward reasonable and equitable solutions to inevitable conflicts: Our rights talk, in its absoluteness, promotes unrealistic expectations, heightens social conflict, and inhibits dialogue that might lead toward consensus, accommodation, or at least the discovery of common ground. In its silence concerning responsibilities, it seems to condone acceptance of the benefits of living in a democratic social welfare state, without accepting the corresponding personal and civic obligations. In its relentless individualism, it fosters a climate that is inhospitable to society's losers, and that systematically disadvantages caretakers and dependents, young and old. In its neglect of civil society, it undermines the principal seedbeds of civic and personal virtue. In its insularity, it shuts out potentially important aids to the process of self-correcting learning. All of these traits promote mere assertion over reason-giving. [Mary Ann Glendon, *Rights Talk: The Impoverishment of Political Discourse*. (New York: The Free Press, 1991), p. 14.]

Thus, the tendency toward dichotomous thinking which Glendon observes in American discourse on rights feeds divisiveness and limits our reasoning and problem-solving repertoire.

Self-Definition through Oppositionality
In the introduction to her classic text, *The Second Sex,* Simone de Beauvoir writes about the human tendency to perceive and understand experience as dualities or binary oppositions:

Things become clear, . . . if, following Hegel, we find in consciousness itself a fundamental hostility toward every other consciousness; the subject can be posed only in being opposed—he sets himself up as the essential, as opposed to the other, the inessential, the object. [Simone de Beauvoir, "Introduction to *The Second Sex," New French Feminisms*, ed., Elaine Marks and Isabelle de Courtivron (New York: Schocken Books, 1981), p. 45.]

In other words, we define ourselves, our identity, in opposition to, or as distinct from, others: I know who I am because I am not you. This self-definition through oppositionality can be problematic as it sets up a chain reaction: my sense of myself is built upon my ability to distinguish myself from you; therefore I value the ways in which I am different from you; therefore I begin to devalue the traits that make you distinct from me.

Michelle Fine, a psychologist who has written extensively on gender and race in education and social policy, provides us with an example of how this process of self-definition through oppositionality works. She was asked to research and testify in the 1993/1994 legal proceedings considering whether or not The Citadel, an all male military college in South Carolina, was constitutionally bound to admit women students. In her observations and interviews at the school, she noticed that male students were regularly exhorted to behave in ways that would prove their masculinity, their strength, their courage, rather than behaving "like a woman." She concluded that the institution was organized around a concept of "oppositional identity," arguing that despite their official exclusion, women were in fact, "omnipresent at the school as (entities) to be reacted against," and that the institution reinforced a "fragile sense of masculinity perched on opposition to women, as 'the other.'" [Keynote address to Columbia University Teachers College Winter "Roundtable on Cross-Cultural Counseling and Psychotherapy: Race and Gender," February 18, 1994, New York.]

Fine pointed out that "as they are currently constituted, whiteness and maleness are about denigration of 'the other,' (and what is needed, therefore,) is to give whites and males other ways to see their identity than through oppositionality." Fine has put her finger on one of the ways in which "self-definition through oppositionality" is self-perpetuating and resistant to change: if I begin to see those different from myself in a more positive light does that mean that I will begin to see myself more negatively? Where is the appeal, or the motivation, in that? It seems that I need to begin to be able to define myself in a more complex way, and not simply in opposition to others along some dimension of difference, be it gender, religion, race, sexual orientation, or something else.

Cultural Generalizations: Dichotomy or Continuum
Deborah Tannen, linguistics scholar and author of the national bestseller, *You Just Don't Understand: Women and Men in Conversation*, has argued that women and

men tend to develop and use communication skills for different purposes, often resulting in misunderstanding:

Intimacy is key in a world of connection where individuals negotiate complex networks of friendship, minimize differences, try to reach consensus, and avoid the appearance of superiority, which would highlight differences. In a world of status, *independence* is key, because a primary means of establishing status is to tell others what to do, and taking orders is a marker of low status. Though all humans need both intimacy and independence, women tend to focus on the first and men on the second....If women speak and hear a language of connection and intimacy, while men speak and hear a language of status and independence, then communication between men and women can be like cross-cultural communication, prey to a clash of conversational styles. [Deborah Tannen, *You Just Don't Understand: Women and Men in Conversation* (New York: Ballentine Books, 1990), pp. 26, 42.]

Studies like Tannen's can be very useful in helping us to put ourselves in the shoes of others,to see the world through a different lens. But Tannen herself is among the first to caution against the dangers of generalizing about the behavior of an entire group. She understands that the tendency to value one pole of a dichotomy over another can result in prejudices reinforced: for example, if she describes differences in the conversational styles of men and women, men's style may tend to be valued over women's. Nevertheless, she fears even more the mutual understanding that will be lost if such concerns stop us from trying to understand the degree to which patterns of difference do seem to exist between the genders. [Deborah Tannen, *You Just Don't Understand: Women and Men in Conversation* (New York: Ballentine Books, 1990), pp. 14-16.

Interestingly, if we take this debate to either extreme, understanding is sacrificed. If we affirm that there *are* differences between identity groups (in this case, between genders), we can get lost in generalizations and stereotypes that keep us from seeing the distinctiveness of individuals and the commonalities between these same groups, and that can reinforce discrimination. On the other hand, if in our efforts to insure equal treatment and opportunity, we assert that there are no generalizable differences, that men and women differ only as individuals differ, we sacrifice the insights of work like Tannen's, or Carol Gilligan's, or that of any number of anthropologists who study cultural patterns.

In casual conversation about Tannen's work, we are likely to hear variations on the following: "I *did* recognize the patterns she writes about in my male/female friends' behavior. She really had them down. But, you know, I don't think I really fit the pattern she describes for *my* gender." In this instinctive response, we can see the crux of the issue: it is much easier and appealing to generalize about others than to be generalized about ourselves. Similarly, we tend to assume that others will be unaware of and thus bound by their gender or cultural conditioning, while being perfectly willing to believe in our ability to see through and therefore escape our own. Both of these tendencies can block true understanding and communication.

Shelby Steele and "Seeing for Innocence"
In his 1990 book of essays, *The Content of Our Character: A New Vision of Race in America*, Shelby Steele offers an analysis of racial dynamics built upon the concepts of power and innocence. He argues that the conflict between races is a conflict over power, and that this pursuit of power is rationalized by an appeal to innocence:

Your difference from me makes you bad, and your badness justifies, even demands, my pursuit of power over you . . . the human animal almost never pursues power without first convincing himself that he is *entitled* to it. And this feeling of entitlement has its own precondition: to be entitled one must first believe in one's innocence, at least in the area where one wishes to be entitled. By innocence I mean a feeling of essential goodness in relation to others and, therefore, superiority to others. [Shelby Steele, *The Content of Our Character: A New Vision of Race In America*, (New York: St. Martin's Press, 1990), p. 5.]

Steele goes on to explain that while whites in America have historically defended their subjugation of blacks with claims of innocence, blacks in the sixties began to use this equation to their own advantage. Blacks claimed the innocence that derives from being the victims of white racism, thereby gaining some power of their own. Thus, both blacks and whites are invested in seeing themselves as innocent, and since their innocence is based on the other's guilt, this means that they are unconsciously motivated to see the other in ways that preserve conflict, racial disharmony and prejudice. Ironically, each group claims the status of "victim," a status that disempowers them with regard to dismantling racism, discouraging individual initiative to get past these issues. [Shelby Steele, *The Content of Our Character: A New Vision of Race In America*, (New York: St. Martin's Press, 1990), pp. 8, 14.]

There are several dichotomous thought patterns embedded in this model of behavior. First, individuals are seen and see themselves in terms of a single identification, black or white, as opposed to possessing multiple identities.

Second, individuals are seen and see themselves as existing in a state of guilt or innocence, thereby limiting their options for learning, change and complexity. Although Steele's analysis focuses on American race relations, the fundamental model aptly describes a pattern of self-defeating dichotomization that can apply to other types of difference as well. His model can shed light on many of the counter-productive behaviors we observe around diversity. For example, sometimes individuals will resist behaving in a more supportive manner toward those different from themselves because such a change implies, in their minds, that they were somehow at fault or "guilty" in the past. Or sometimes individuals will look for ways to maintain their criticisms, even stereotypes, of those who are different from them in an effort to preserve a sense of innocence. And sometimes individuals will resist acknowledging and embracing the successes of other members of their own "identity group" (race, gender, etc.) for fear that such success casts doubt upon their own righteous experience of oppression—their "innocence" in Steele's terms.

Cornel West and "Racial Reasoning"

In his 1994 book, *Race Matters*, philosopher and theologian Cornel West describes a particular way of thinking he finds all too prevalent among black leadership in America today. "Racial reasoning," as he names it, is a way of thinking about black progress that tries to promote the race as a whole at the expense of many within its ranks.

The basic line of reasoning that West observes goes like this: since "America's will to racial justice is weak . . . black people must close ranks for survival in a hostile country;" this "closing ranks mentality" depends upon individuals' ability to lay claim to "racial authenticity" because if one is not "really black," or "black enough," he or she would be a threat to the group as a whole (in Steele's terms, they would not possess the entitlement that goes with "innocence"); as soon as one's sense of security and legitimacy is based upon racial authenticity, numerous reasons for exclusion emerge, and before we know it, black progress or "black social order" seems to rest upon the subordination and control of certain other blacks. [Cornel West, *Race Matters* (New York: Vintage Books, 1994), pp. 37, 38.]

West argues that:

The claims to black authenticity that feed on the closing-ranks mentality of black people are dangerous precisely because this closing of ranks is usually done at the expense of black women. It also tends to ignore the divisions of class and sexual orientation in black America—divisions that require attention if all black interests, individuals, and communities are to be taken into consideration. [Cornel West, *Race Matters* (New York: Vintage Books, 1994), p. 41.]

He calls for a corrective to this limiting and separatist form of thinking that attempts to correct one form of oppression while participating in another. His antidote is a new form of reasoning that bases its claims to moral authority not on "black authenticity" but on a "mature black self-love and self-respect...[based] on the moral quality of black responses" to the experience of racism. This reasoning would replace exclusivity and closed ranks with a "coalition strategy," welcoming the support of those genuinely committed to combating racism regardless of their color or ethnicity, and it would embrace truly democratic ideals rather than justifying the subordination of some blacks in the service of others. [Cornel West, *Race Matters* (New York: Vintage Books, 1994), pp. 43, 44.]

As with Steele's concept of "seeing for innocence," West's model of "racial reasoning" holds lessons for our thinking about other forms of difference as well. It underscores the diversity that exists within identity groups as well as between them. And it illustrates the ubiquity and limitations of dichotomous, us/them patterns of thinking.

Chris Argyris and "Defensive Reasoning"

In his research on organizational behavior, Harvard professor Chris Argyris has observed a pattern of behavior among managers that effectively, if unintentionally, blocks learning, and he calls this pattern "defensive reasoning." Argyris observes that in all his studies, across nation, gender, age, education, race and so forth, there seem to be four values that guide people's action:

1. to remain in unilateral control;
2. to maximize "winning" and minimize "losing";
3. to suppress negative feelings; and
4. to be as "rational" as possible—by which people mean defining clear objectives and evaluating their behavior in terms of whether or not they have achieved them. The purpose in all of these values is to avoid embarrassment or threat, feeling vulnerable or incompetent. In this respect, the master program that most people use is profoundly defensive.

Defensive reasoning encourages individuals to keep private the premises, inferences, and conclusions that shape their behavior and to avoid testing them in a truly independent, objective fashion. Because the attributes that go into defensive reasoning are never really tested, it is a closed loop, remarkably impervious to conflicting points of view. [Chris Argyris, "Teaching Smart People How to Learn," *Harvard Business Review* (May-June 1991), p. 103.]

In numerous case examples, Argyris demonstrates how this dichotomous approach to our role and functioning in organizations—winner or loser, in control or controlled—makes us fearful of new information and new perspectives, solidifying into a profoundly anti-learning stance. His antidote is to propose an alternative approach to action that is based upon making our premises and inferences transparent and discussable, and pursuing free choice rather than control in relation to others. [Chris Argyris, *Strategy, Change and Defensive Routines* (Marshfield, Mass.: Pitman Publishing, Inc., 1985), p. 261.]

In the service of learning and growth, what was once perceived as a threatening or embarrassing contradiction can then be seen as the source of innovation and new insight. Argyris's observations have obvious relevance for thinking about differences of identity. Without the willingness to reveal the sources of and assumptions behind our conclusions, we unwittingly reinforce others' tendencies to hear and understand us in terms of their preexisting stereotypes.

Thomas Gilovich and How We Know What Isn't So
In his highly readable 1991 book, *How We Know What Isn't So: The Fallibility of Human Reason in Everyday Life,* social scientist Thomas Gilovich describes and illustrates a series of reasoning errors, both common in human thinking processes and remarkably resistant to corrective factual data. If we examine these frequent reasoning flaws, we readily recognize how they can help to generate and reinforce counterproductive ways of thinking about diversity.

Gilovich examines the following cognitive tendencies:

• Our preference for clear dichotomies when considering options: yes/no, right/wrong, all/nothing. We tend to oversimplify experience in an effort to categorize it into these dualities, and then to hang onto our analysis with excessive confidence.

• Our preference for believing that all experience is controllable, a preference that may lead us to attribute causality or personal choice in situations where there is none.

• Our preference to see structure and consistency in experience rather than pure randomness.

• Our "tendency to be more impressed by what *has* happened than by what has *failed* to happen, and the temptation to draw conclusions from what has occurred under present circumstances without comparing it to what would have occurred under alternative circumstances". [Thomas Gilovich. *How We Know What isn't So: The Fallibility of Human Reason in Everyday Life*. (New York: The Free Press, 1991), p. 186.]

He then suggests a set of corrective cognitive tactics in order to minimize the frequency of reasoning errors:

• Focus not only on the foolishness of basing conclusions upon "incomplete and unrepresentative evidence," but also on the frequency with which "our everyday experience presents us with biased samples of information." We need to ask ourselves, "what do the other three cells look like?" In other words, what are the counter examples, the contradicting evidence that we have not considered, or even attempted to gather?

• Recognize our tendency to ignore the frequency with which our status, position, identity can cut us off from certain kinds of data or overexpose us to others.

• Recognize our "talent for *ad hoc* explanation . . . the facility with which we can explain a vast range of outcomes in terms of our pre-existing theories and beliefs. . . . Our beliefs thus appear to receive too much support from equivocal evidence, and they are too seldom discredited by truly antagonistic results." Gilovich suggests we counter this tendency by using" consider the opposite" strategies: "Suppose the exact opposite had occurred. Would I consider that outcome to be supportive of my belief as well?. . . How would someone who does not believe the way I do explain this result?. . . What alternative theory could account for it?"

• Recognize the "uncertainties and distortions of secondhand information."

• Ask ourselves "whether our beliefs are really as widely shared as they appear. The absence of explicit disagreement should not automatically be taken as evidence of agreement." [Thomas Gilovich, *How We Know What isn't So: The Fallibility of Human Reason in Everyday Life*. (New York: The Free Press, 1991), pp. 186-189.]

Although Gilovich is writing about cognitive behavior in general, it is easy to see how these various tendencies can contribute to an adversariality, a resistance to change and to trust, and a closed mind when dealing with questions of difference. Although diversity issues involve emotional, political, historical and economic levels as well, an understanding of these reasoning errors can aid us in our attempts to unravel their complexity.

Pareto Optimality/Scarcity Thinking

In many cultures, modes of reasoning borrowed from economics have penetrated deeply into our patterns of thinking about other areas of experience. Several of these mental paradigms can constrain our thinking about questions of diversity. There is a sort of "all or nothing," "me or you" quality to these reasoning patterns that can predefine the range of options we might conceive for a particular dilemma.

For example, microeconomic equilibrium models of optimal resource allocation assume as a minimal requirement the condition of *pareto optimality*: "a situation where no one in the economy can be made better off without someone else... being made worse off. [Stanley Fischer and Rudiger Dornbusch, *Economics* (New York: McGraw-Hill, Inc., 1983), p. 521.]

Although intended only as a descriptor, we can observe a tendency to evaluate the desirability of action choices in terms of this condition. In other words, if a particular course of action betters the position of some at the expense of worsening the position of others, it is considered sub-optimal. This seems sensible enough until we consider the situation where the privilege of some may be a direct result of the exclusion of others.

As in the economic markets from which this concept derives, it all comes down to the initial resource distribution. Adhering to this pattern of thinking precludes change.

A preoccupation with resource scarcity, the assumption of a "limited pie" to be divided among all comers, is another example of an economics-based approach to thinking about the choices diversity presents. The point is not that scarcity does not exist, but rather that the *assumption* of scarcity limits our creativity and sense of possibility, and ill positions us for the redefinition of goods and resources that such choices require.

Masking and Overdetermined Terminology

Questions triggered by diversity in the workplace go to the heart of some of our most cherished assumptions about our organizations and perceptions about ourselves: meritocracy, equal opportunity, fair treatment, unbiased standards of performance, and so forth. And painfully, these questions point out seeming contradictions and inconsistencies in those assumptions and perceptions.

These contradictions and inconsistencies are often the result of the way certain concepts and terminology acquire meanings over time, through repeated use and misuse and through association. The concept of meritocracy, for example, is firmly held and valued by many as the preferred and only truly fair, efficient standard by which to evaluate performance. We will often argue about the importance of *continuing* to reward individuals according to their merit, slipping in the assumed premise that this has been the case in the past. Yet we fail to examine the ways and reasons by which individuals are and have been rewarded in actuality.

"Merit" is, first of all, a subjective term. The indicators that cause us to *see* merit are multiple and are based upon many factors besides observable talent: familiarity, comfort, prior relationship, recommendation by a friend, association with familiar schools and institutions, prior commitments or a sense of obligation/guilt/gratitude, and so forth. All of these factors can be masked by the term "merit."

Even with these distorting factors put aside, how do we define "merit"? A candidate may exhibit ability along many criteria and a decision, often subjective, is made about how to prioritize these criteria. And once a few abilities have been defined as primary, how reliable are our measures?

This discussion is not intended to argue against the usefulness of attempts to evaluate "merit," but rather to point out the ways such concepts seem to take on a solidity, a clarity in our rhetoric which they often lack in actual experience.

REFRAMING DIVERSITY

In all nine of these reasoning models, we have seen that a tendency toward dualism in our thinking can restrict the way we frame and answer questions of diversity. And the most fundamental expression of that dualism is in our self-definition: I define myself as either male or female, gay or straight, right or wrong, and so on. In our earlier discussion of "oppositionalidentity," we said that I know who I am because I am not you. This is not an affirmation of my own identity or even an understanding of differences, but rather an exploitation of them as a "short-cut" to self-insight and self-esteem.

But let us consider an alternate approach to self-definition and to the consideration of and interaction with others. Rather than defining ourselves "in opposition to" someone else, let us incorporate opposition into ourselves. Let us adopt a "multiple perspective" rather than an oppositional and dualistic one—a multiple perspective that can comprehend alternate viewpoints not so as to excuse oppression but rather to clarify it, to expose the pain of one individual group without denying that of another. For ultimately, understanding and *experiencing* "the compelling quality of contradictory realities is the only way, short of violence, to resolve their differences." [Mary C. Gentile, *Film Feminisms* (Westport, Conn.: Greenwood Press, 1985), p. 8.]

What we are talking about here is a new way to approach and address the conflicts and the dilemmas posed by our encounters with differences, based upon a new way of defining ourselves and our own point of view. By defining ourselves multiply, by perceiving others multiply, by generating multiple hypotheses in response to seeming trade-offs, by seeking out and embracing disconfirming data and complexity, we open up the potential for new growth and learning, for creativity, and for breaking the cycle of reductionist dichotomies that keep us locked in a mutually self-destructive pattern of separation, discrimination, oppression, anger and guilt.

To this end, let us examine the following model for reframing diversity [Excerpts from Introduction to *Differences That Work: Organizational Excellence Through Diversity*, ed. And introduction by Mary Gentile (Boston: Harvard Business School Press, 1994.) pp. XV-XVII reprinted by permission.] (see **Exhibit 1**), first in terms of our own identity and then in relation to others, both individuals and groups. This model is really a set of observations, insights and acknowledgments that can serve as tools for promoting understanding of and conversation about diversity.

Our framework consists of the following six observations:

I. *Multiple Identities:*
We all have multiple identities, one or another of which we may identify with more strongly at different moments in our lives and in different contexts.

For example, we all have our gender, race, ethnic origins, religion, age, sexual orientation, class, educational background, etc. Sometimes we may stress one of these identities over others, and sometimes these identities may be in conflict. For example, we may feel discomfort expressing some of our views in a context where they might feed stereotypes about one of our identities. For example, when I am with a group of women, I may be more cognizant of the commonalities of our experience based upon gender, whereas when I am with a mixed gender group of colleagues at work, I may identify more strongly as an individual with a particular educational and professional experience held in common with my peers in that context.

From these multiple identities, we can begin to recognize that we each have experienced positions of relative privilege and relative exclusion in different contexts. Nevertheless, we negotiate more or less coherent, if complex, personalities. [C.D. Alderfer, "Intergroup Relations and Organizations," in J.R. Hackman, E.E. Lawler, and L.W. Porter (eds.) *Perspectives on Behavior in Organizations*. (New York: McGraw-Hill, 1983), p. 410.] This internal negotiation of identity can be a model for understanding the negotiation of a group identity and interactions, in social contexts or in business settings. And seeing our own identities multiply can be the beginning of seeing others in more complex, less stereotypical, and ultimately more realistic ways. We will not view women, African Americans, or white men as all alike because we will see ourselves and each other as so much more than just our gender or race.

II. *Salience:* We often experience contradictory urges or needs for a sense of belonging or "fitting in" on the one hand, and for a feeling of uniqueness or "specialness" on the other. [Mary C. Waters, *Ethnic Options: Choosing Identities in America*. (Berkeley, Calif.: University of California Press, 1990), p. 147.] **Thus in a particular situation, one of our multiple identities may feel more salient to us than others.**

In some contexts, we may tend to emphasize our ethnic identities, for example, in order to feel special or unique. In other contexts—family gatherings for instance—we may emphasize the same ethnicity as a means to feel part of the group. These conflicting urges can trigger complicated reactions of loyalty, rejection, pride, and guilt within the same individual and between different individuals.

Understanding our own mixed desires around a sense of belonging and a feeling of uniqueness can give insight into what may sometimes appear as the desire of other individuals or groups to "have it both ways," to have their particular history of achievement and perhaps oppression recognized as well as to be treated "just like everybody else." But as this second observation suggests, in a sense everyone wants it "both ways," and that may not be such a bad thing if we are self-aware and realistic about it.

III. *Costs and Benefits:* Some identities exact a higher and/or different cost (or provide greater and/or different benefits) for the bearer in a particular societal, historical, or even situational context than others.

In the United States, for example, the historical experience of African Americans has had very real implications generally speaking, for access to education, information, and financial resources. In a group of African Americans, however, the lone white individual may experience a temporary situational cost for being/feeling different that, if understood and explored, can serve as a foundation for empathy for all present.

Treating this lone white's experience as if it is "the same" as or somehow equivalent to the experience of African Americans is not accurate, but it is also inaccurate and counter-productive to insist that this individual has never experienced the pain of exclusion. It is certainly a different pain, without the historical and institutional and cultural weight of the African American's experience of racism, but it may serve as the beginning of shared insight. It suggests an appeal to empathy rather than merely guilt.

IV. *Choice:* Sometimes individuals have a choice of becoming recognized as members of a particular identity group in a particular setting, and that choice brings certain costs and benefits, as well.

Some identities, such as gender, race, and age, *tend* to be immediately evident. Other identities, such as religion or sexual orientation, can be less evident. It is useful to understand the potential advantages and disadvantages of so-called invisible diversity. For example, as a gay or lesbian person, often one can choose to "pass." This choice gives gay/lesbian people greater control over the impression they make on others at the same time that it creates personal and political dilemmas.

On the one hand, they may judge that to be open about their sexual orientation could be unsafe, either professionally, socially or even physically. But on the other hand, they may wonder if their discretion is actually a manifestation of internalized homophobia and a lack of self confidence.

Or is it a betrayal of gays and lesbians more generally because it allows others to assume they are not working with and depending upon homosexuals in their daily lives?

Understanding the advantages and the burdens of having a "choice" about how one's identity is perceived is critical to thinking about and addressing questions of diversity.

V. _Redefinition and Change_: Our individual identities are always developing, we are continually negotiating, defining, and redefining the internal coherence of our original values, our new experiences, and our multiple identities.

Individual identities—and group identities—are not static. If we remain aware of our own process of self-definition which involves a continual reconciliation of the multiple aspects of our identities, we can be more open to the same process in those with whom we learn and work. We need not be "frozen" in a single role or stance, nor need we "freeze" others. We are more than the sum of our "identities," and our behavior is not predetermined or fixed because of them.

VI. _Shared Goals_: Identity differences do not preclude the development and pursuit of "shared goals" among and across identities.

Effective response to diversity is dependent upon the acceptance of some primary objectives to which we all are willing to commit. In the workplace, such objectives might include survival of the firm, and therefore a commitment to the productivity and innovation necessary for that survival. This does not imply that a respect for and sensitivity to individual and group differences are not important—after all, the shared objective is _not_ the survival of the firm at _any_ cost —but rather this suggests that there are at least a few areas where our commonalities are as salient as our differences.

The preceding model—its insights and acknowledgments—can serve as the foundation and the impetus for both internal and external dialogue and inquiry about diversity. It gives us a way to think and talk about diversity as a learning process in which we all are or can be engaged, thereby providing a powerful _motivation_ for these discussions.

The model defines diversity _inclusively,_ indicating that it is about all of us. It offers a way to understand the behaviors and dynamics of both groups and individuals within them that is _descriptive, rather than judgmental._ Nevertheless it is based upon certain clear values, primarily the value of learning, the desirability of pursuing knowledge about oneself and others, and the acknowledgment that in a diverse and interdependent world, one of the most valuable kinds of knowledge is about understanding and communicating across differences.

Confronting a Decision

With this model in mind, what are some of the key questions we might bring to framing and addressing questions of diversity?

How does this model have an impact on our decision-making?

How does it address the sub-optimal patterns of thinking described earlier in this note? [See **Exhibit 2** for a checklist of questions that reveals when we are falling victim to the reasoning "traps" described earlier, and that suggests alternate responses to the same decision, based on the model above.]

Let's take a look at an example of the different ways we can approach the same issue, depending upon what types of reasoning frameworks we are using. We will take up an example that is frequently raised as a diversity dilemma and pose it in the words we are likely to hear:

If you have two candidates for a job—a member of the majority identity group in your organization (let's say a white man) and a member of a group "under represented" in your organization (let's say a white woman)—and the man is better qualified, whom do you hire?

Some of the responses to this question we are likely to hear or offer ourselves include:

• *You always have to hire the "more qualified candidate." If you don't, you are putting the effectiveness, perhaps even the survival, of the organization in jeopardy.*

This argument, and the dilemma itself, are posed using the "masking and over-determined terminology" discussed earlier. This confident assertion of "who is best qualified" serves to disguise any number of prior choices and unconscious assumptions. It asserts as unambiguous an evaluation that is often sublimely subjective. It assumes a clarity about what constitutes qualification for this job, when that conclusion itself is also often based upon tradition rather than science. And it begs the question of whether decision makers are able to perceive the relative qualifications of the candidates objectively, denying the impacts of stereotyping, historical oppression, and the documented perceptual effects when individuals make judgments about members of a group other than their own. This argument also illustrates the tendency to analyze and argue only one side of an oversimplified dichotomy that Gilovich describes in *How We Know What Isn't So.* Has the respondent asked him or herself, "in this case, what are the potential *positive* impacts of hiring the woman, and what are the potential *negative* impacts of hiring the man?"

• *If you don't hire the man, you are trying to right past injustices with current ones. You are trying to counteract discrimination with another form of discrimination, for the only thing working against the man is his gender.*

Aside from continuing to repeat the assumptions about qualification noted above, this argument illustrates Gilovich's concerns about our tendency to oversimplify events into either/or choices and to ignore unstated data. For example, the argument takes as an assumption that in any other situation, the only data considered in making a hiring or promotion decision is this unexplained criteria of "qualification." It ignores the fact that such decisions always involve weighing a number of considerations, such as seniority against targeted experience, depth of expertise against breadth, familiarity with the project against outside experience, and a candidate who brings significant experience in areas that are already represented in the project team against a candidate who brings less experience but in an unrepresented area. Might gender be just another set of criteria in this mix?

This argument also reflects a version of Steele's "seeing for innocence," where somehow "being qualified" is equated with having a right to a particular job and not getting that job is seen as a form of undeserved punishment. Thus, the male candidate's "innocence" is implied, while the female candidate is therefore "guilty" of obtaining a job unfairly. As noted above, this formulation contains all sorts of blurred distinctions and unconscious assumptions, but nevertheless carries an emotional weight that feeds a divisive "us against them" perspective on this dilemma.

Finally this argument (reminiscent of pareto optimality) blurs individual perspectives, experience and accountability with group perspectives, experience and accountability. It asserts that accumulated injustices toward and by groups in the past are being paid for with an individual injustice in the present, ignoring the fact that discrimination was and is always an individual *and* a group experience. We can address discrimination effectively only if we address it at both levels. This realization does not necessarily suggest that either candidate should be hired in this case; it merely suggests that the fact that both individuals and groups are affected by any actions taken is unavoidable.

• *If you hire the man, you are passing up the opportunity to begin to make a change in the demographic mix of the department/organization—a change that will be necessary in order to attract and best support other women and minority members in the firm.*

This argument, like the first one we examined, illustrates the tendency to analyze and argue only one side of an oversimplified dichotomy...only it is a different side. It ignores the importance of trying to make a decision that will result in a *successful* hire, regardless of gender, not only for the firm's benefit but also for the benefit of the other women and minorities in the firm now and to come.

Additionally this argument, and the dilemma itself, beg the question of why we are concerned with "representation" in the first place. There are legal arguments, moral arguments and "business" arguments that may underlie this concern [See *Managerial Effectiveness and Diversity: Organizational Choices*, HBS No. 395-020, for a discussion of these arguments, or "motivations."] However, if organizational decision makers do not adequately think through this question, their judgments risk superficiality, cynicism and self-contradiction -- or at least accusations of the same.

• *If you hire the man, you will demonstrate that the organization is not really interested in "diversity."*

Once again, this argument raises only one side of an oversimplified dichotomy; it ignores other data about the company's policies and actions around diversity. The more sophisticated argument might be that "if you hire the man, the organization will *appear* to not really be interested in 'diversity.'" This argument suggests something about the kind of consistency and trust the organization needs to build in order to be free to make difficult decisions as it sees fit.

• *If you hire the woman, you are not doing her any service for she will experience negative reinforcement around her performance.*
This argument illustrates our readiness to interpret evidence about an employee's performance in ways that support prior conclusions, what Gilovich refers to as our "talent for *ad hoc* explanation." This tendency can result in self-fulfilling prophecies.

• *If you hire the "less qualified candidate," you are not doing other women any service for you are reinforcing the perception that their successes may be based on identity rather than merit.*

The problem with this argument is that it ignores the fact that this perception can be caused by decisions to hire a woman or "minority" candidate, regardless of their qualifications. It also embodies an unstated and unexamined assumption that other hiring decisions are always based purely on objective qualifications, that this is the desired state of affairs, and that we can and do know what these objective qualifications are. "Merit" in this statement is an instance of "masking terminology."

However, this argument does surface the importance of thinking through and communicating decision criteria clearly. Differing perceptions ought to be respected, considered and addressed, but they ought not be a source of tyranny for they always cut both ways.

The point of these observations is not to suggest that any or all of these responses are necessarily wrong, but rather to suggest that each of them is incomplete. The original dilemma, as posed, asks for an either/or choice, when the real take-away from such a decision is the learning, the relationship and the process created by communicating about it. Ultimately there will be times when the hiring decision will go one way and times when it will go the other, for good reasons, but the test of the decision-making process is whether all parties can keep talking and working together afterward toward shared goals.

Applying the Model for Reframing Diversity

In order to achieve this objective, we need other ways of posing the dilemma that will shed new light on the question. After all, each of us has heard the arguments listed above before and yet many of us are no closer to a comfortable answer to the dilemma.

So let's revisit the original question in light of our model for reframing diversity:

If you have two candidates for a job—a member of the majority identity group in your organization (let's say a white man) and a member of a group "under represented" in your organization (let's say a white woman)—and the man is better qualified, whom do you hire?

First of all, the way this question is framed tends to discourage multiple identities, within ourselves, others or our organizations. Rather we may experience the question as requiring us to define ourselves oppositionally—that is, as for or against "merit" as a basis for hiring decisions.

What's more, the oppositional self-definition gets worse, because we may experience this choice as pitting a commitment to "merit" against a commitment to diversifying an admittedly "unrepresentative" or skewed employee pool. Finally, one more link in this chain of dualities aligns white males with a commitment to merit and a disregard for diversity, while white women are aligned with a commitment to diversity and a disregard for merit.

Thus we can see that without an attempt to reveal and unpack the assumed alignments within the framing of this question, the respondent feels him or herself torn, forced into an artificial choice that fails to reflect the true complexity of any of the parties. Because the choice is framed as a static dichotomy, using masking rhetoric and built upon a denial of shared goals, it literally pushes us into many of the reasoning pitfalls described above.

Now, of course, people and experience present us with challenges and dilemmas on a regular basis, and they are often posed in less than constructive ways. We cannot control the ways in which others identify and frame the questions they ask us. We can, however, restructure these choices in order to avoid some of the impasses we found in the responses above. We can do so by reflecting upon the decisions we face and asking the following questions derived from our proposed model for reframing diversity. With practice, this process of examining and reposing the choices we encounter will enable us to approach all such decisions in a new manner, designed to maximize learning and our openness to innovation and unexpected insights.

I. Multiple Identities

• *What are the aspects of ourselves (of others, of the organization) that are engaged in addressing this decision?*

In other words, are we bringing the full range of our multiple identities to this question? Are we openly addressing the potential conflicts or contradictory responses these different aspects trigger in us, or are we prematurely aligning with a single "side" of ourselves? The goal is not to define ourselves oppositionally, but rather to internalize the oppositionality, to acknowledge and name our internal conflicts, thereby reducing the defensiveness in ourselves and

others. That defensiveness blocks openness to new and potentially conflicting ideas, and reducing it allows for the generation of multiple perspectives and multiple hypotheses that boost our ability to see through masking terminology.
In the sample decision presented above, I might ask myself if I feel free to explore all my possible reactions, or if I feel pressure to foreclose my exploration and avoid entertaining a response that might feel as if it positions me as "anti-merit" or as "anti-diversity." If I feel discomfort around examining all aspects of my response, that's a pretty good signal that there is something to examine.

In particular, I would ask myself if I feel as if I have ever been awarded opportunities on any basis other than merit. If so, how do I feel about that? Do I feel I proved the decision sound? Do I feel as if someone else had a "right" to my opportunity, or do I think it is appropriate that other criteria enter into these decisions sometimes?

I might also ask myself if I feel as if others have been awarded opportunities on bases other than merit, particularly when I felt I had a claim on the opportunity. How have I reconciled these experiences of relative privilege and relative exclusion within myself?

Running myself through this exercise of getting in touch with multiple perspectives within myself makes it easier for me to imagine a similar range of responses in others, and in the organization. Such thinking discourages the painting of my own or others' points of view with a single brush. It allows me to consider this decision as both an individual situation facing specific managers, as well as a representative action on the part of the organization— rather than as just one or the other.

II. Salience

• *What aspect of our (others', the organization's) multiple identities feels most salient in this situation?*

To which aspect of our identity do we feel the desire/need to belong or "fit in"? Around which aspect of our identity do we feel the desire/need to "stand out" and be unique? And consequently, which aspects of ourselves are we suppressing? And why? What would be the cost of standing out in one way, or not fitting in another?

In the sample decision presented above, I might ask myself whose approval is most important to me here? Whom do I want to stand with, and why? And how do I want to be recognized around this issue? Once I recognize this experience of "salience" around some specific aspect of my identity, I free myself to stand apart from it, to question it, and to try on other points of view—and, of course, to see the same kind of tendencies operating in the others involved in this decision.

III. Costs and Benefits
• *What are the costs and benefits associated with engaging each aspect of our (others', the organization's) identities in response to this decision?*

By addressing this question, we can begin to unpack the baggage of history (culture and ideology, the experience of dominance and oppression) that comes along with different aspects of our identities. The fact is that not all experiences of relative privilege or relative exclusion are equal. In the sample decision above, for instance, one might ask whether or not the cost of a single career move to the white man is balanced against the range of career opportunities to which he has and will be exposed. Further, one might ask whether this position may represent one of the relatively few opportunities to which the other candidate has or will have access without the additional experience available in the new opening.

IV. Choice
• *To what extent do we (others, the organization) have a choice about how we will be perceived in this situation?*

In addition to the forms of "invisible diversity" mentioned above, there tends to be a greater range of possible images available to those who are in the numerical majority and/or the "higher power" group in a particular context. Understanding the abundance or scarcity of choices available to ourselves and others enables us to better gauge the impact of our decisions.

In the sample decision above, it appears that the woman has no good choice. She will either be perceived as unqualified for hire and therefore be passed over, or she will be perceived as unqualified for hire and taken on anyway. If she is to be hired, clearly the managers involved and the organization need to communicate about their criteria and goals in such a way as to offer her a fighting chance.

V. Redefinition and Change
• *How might we (others, the organization) redefine our identities so as to facilitate new learning and greater effectiveness within and among our multiple identities?*

For example, since I now have access to that aspect of myself that acknowledges that not all my accomplishments have been solely due to my autonomous effort, I can begin to question and redefine the concept of merit qualification in my organization. I can talk more openly about the variety of criteria I now do, and always have, sought out in candidates for hire. I am not locked into an Argyrean pattern of defensive reasoning that effectively precludes learning and change.

VI. Shared Goals
• *What shared goals can we identify among all parties to this decision?*
For example, all parties can be committed to the hiring organization's efforts to more fully understand their hiring criteria and to their enhanced ability to select candidates who can function effectively to the betterment of the firm and their own careers—in other words, to maximize productive learning and growth.

Conclusion

So finally, we are trying to reframe this question in such a way as to:
• encourage exploration of all perspectives, both between and within each party to the decision.
• avoid denying/suppressing aspects of each party. Address and balance the different costs/benefits associated with the identities of each party.
• maximize choice for all parties.
• allow change within each party.
• identify and pursue shared goals among all parties.
Instead of the dilemma as originally posed, we might ask:

How do we assess and communicate merit criteria and representation goals in our organization? What action plan can we develop to ensure meeting both these criteria and goals? When evaluating two candidates for possible hire (one white man, one white woman), how might we position the decision within the context of this plan?

This revised question allows us to position the decision within a history that extends both backward (allowing us to address past inequities) and into the future (allowing us to place each action step within a projected stream of actions, and avoiding the over-weighting of any single choice). It acknowledges at least two agendas for the organization and requires an integrated approach to design an action plan, rather than assuming a contest between them. It positions the actual hiring decision within a context that acknowledges issues that go beyond either candidate, creating the opportunity/necessity to communicate about the choice in ways that depersonalize the issues and preventing candidates from being dubbed as qualified or not, deserving or not, and so forth.

Thus we have attempted to both understand the ways in which our habitual ways of naming and reasoning about questions of diversity limit the responses we generate, as well as the ways in which we can begin to break out of those constraints. With practice, this type of analysis becomes a habit as well, and it allows us to think about these challenging issues in fresh ways, it begins to shift our emotional responses to these questions from the realms of frustration, anger, guilt and blame to those of openness and excitement about the possibility for new understanding.

Exhibits

Exhibit 1   Reframing Diversity: A Model

I. Multiple Identities
• We all have multiple identities, one or another of which we may identify with more strongly at different moments in our lives and in different contexts.

II. Salience
• We often experience contradictory urges or needs for a sense of belonging or "fitting in" on the one hand, and for a feeling of uniqueness or "specialness" on the other.

III. Costs and Benefits
• Some identities exact a higher and/or different cost (or provide greater and/or different benefits) for the bearer in a particular societal, historical, or even situational context than others.

IV. Choice
• Some individuals have a choice of becoming recognized as members of a particular identity group in a particular setting, and that choice brings certain costs and benefits, as well.

V. Redefinition and Change
• Our individual identities are always developing, we are continually negotiating, defining, and redefining the internal coherence of our original values, our new experiences, and our multiple identities.

VI. Shared Goals
• Identity differences do not preclude the development and pursuit of "shared goals" among and across identities.

Exhibit 2   Interrogating Our Thinking

The following checklist of questions can help us to recognize when we are falling into restrictive patterns of reasoning and to push ourselves beyond these common "traps."

Mary Ann Glendon and Rights Talk

TRAPS	ESCAPES
Does my thinking reflect a fearfulness or insecurity about inadvertently "giving away" my rights?	Am I more interested in understanding the reasons why others may feel that insecurity? and Does my thinking reflect a security in my own identity and an openness to new ideas that is born of the awareness that my identity is multiple and dynamic, and that change does not necessarily mean loss?
Am I focused only on preserving my own privileges, rather than also understanding my appropriate and necessary responsibilities to the community I inhabit?	Am I trying to understand the different costs and benefits associated with differing identities and positions in that community, including my own?

Self-Definition Through Oppositionality

TRAPS	ESCAPE
Do I define myself by the ways in which I am different from others, or in terms of "the ways I am not" (i.e., not ignorant, not guilty, not a failure, not weak)?	Do I define myself more complexly, recognizing the differing and even conflicting aspects of my own multiple identities? Can I admit that I have things in common with the people I most admire as well as with those of whom I am most critical?

Cultural Generalizations: Dichotomy or Continuum

TRAP	ESCAPE
Do I tend to see people either as representative of and somewhat determined by their group identities, or as distinct individuals completely free of any group identity determination?	Am I able to recognize the conflicting needs for both a sense of uniqueness and also a sense of belonging to a particular group, in myself and others?

Shelby Steele and "Seeing for Innocence"

TRAPS	ESCAPES
Does my argument focus on justifying the blame or innocence assigned to a group and its individual representatives?	Am I focused on understanding the differential costs and benefits of individual and group identities, and trying to find shared objectives?
Am I locking myself or others into one aspect only of my/their identities?	Am I trying to see the multiple aspects of my own and others' identities, and perhaps finding shared ground by so doing?
Am I invested in proving or holding on to a sense of oppression or a victim status?	Am I open to the changing, dynamic aspects of individual and group identity?

Cornel West and "Racial Reasoning"

TRAP	ESCAPE
Does my argument reflect a defensive, "closing ranks mentality," requiring others to prove their group "authenticity" if they are to stand with me? Am I setting up ever new tests or thresholds of legitimacy for those who "deserve" to share my position?	Am I interested in finding ways to embrace multiple perspectives and ever wider circles of participation, building a "coalition strategy," to address conflicts and to enable true learning?^

^Catherine Bateson talks about this practice as learning skills for changing times, arguing that when we experience discomfort with new information or unexpected reactions, we should recognize that discomfort as a cue to try to learn something, and the very process of trying to learn cures the discomfort. (From a reading and lecture on Peripheral Visions at the Brattle Theatre, sponsored by Wordsworth Books, Cambridge, Massachusetts, June 21, 1994.)

Chris Argyris and "Defensive Reasoning"

TRAPS	ESCAPES
Am I more interested in being "right" than in learning?	Am I open to, or even appreciative of, the potential to change one's mind, to see things in a new way?
Do I present my point of view in a way that discourages negative feedback and questioning?	Do I embrace disconfirming data and multiple perspectives as an opportunity for learning?

Thomas Gilovich and How We Know What Isn't So

TRAPS	ESCAPES
Do I tend to frame my decisions as dichotomous, either/or choices?	Am I able to hold multiple options, not all necessarily mutually exclusive, in my mind? Do I think in terms of dynamic and transitional solutions, as opposed to permanent answers?
Do I habitually look for someone to blame or praise for any outcome?	Can I recognize the limits of my own, and others', control?
Do I cut myself off from the conflicting and multiple aspects of my own experience and perceptions, tending to allow only one of my inner voices to dominate?	Do I try to remain in touch with differing perspectives within, as well as those from outside?

Pareto Optimality/Scarcity Thinking

TRAP	ESCAPE
Do I approach any attempt to improve conditions for some, from a defensive stance of "as long as it doesn't affect me . . ." ?	Am I willing to redefine the terms of cost and benefit? Am I willing to consider that some aspects of myself may benefit from a choice that costs other aspects of myself?

Masking and Overdetermined Terminology

TRAP	ESCAPE
Are my arguments built upon rhetorical appeals to loaded concepts that I do not question and "unpack"?	Am I able to see that the same concept or term may look and feel very different from various perspectives: i.e., the historical perspective vs. the eternal present, the individual perspective vs. the organizational, or your perspective vs. mine?

End of Chapter Questions

a. Explain how model of reasoning/thinking "rights talk" illustrates a person who refuses to change their viewpoint that a stereotypical mascot should not be changed even if it harms the group it is depicting.

b. Explain how someone who views difference through the model of reasoning/thinking "self-definition of oppositionality" can be a dangerous way to think in a diverse work environment.

c. Describe an instance in History where the people in power were thinking like the model of reasoning/thinking "seeing for innocence."

d. "Racial Reasoning" is the model of reasoning/thinking that occurs within a race not between races. Explain why this thinking occurs within the race and not between racial groups.

Internet Exercise

Go to the following website: http://www.adl.org/prejudice/default.asp or using www.google.com and type in: anti defamation league prejudice and click on the following book "101 ways to combat prejudice." Now select 10 of those ideas and explain how it fits with having multiple identities or salience as discussed in the chapter.

End of Chapter Exercise

In the following chapters the text will provide some cultural knowledge that should enhance one's ability to better "value diversity." Some of these issues such as: racism and it's negative impact, sexism in the workplace, gays and homosexual's right to work from discrimination, etc. may not affect you.

There is a trap of Pareto Optimality/Scarcity Thinking where the question becomes: Do I approach any attempt to improve conditions for some, from a defensive stance of "as long as it doesn't affect me . . ." What is your plan of attack, to prevent this type of thinking—that is what will be your escape?

Reference

1. Gentile, M. C. (1995). *Ways of Thinking about and across Difference*. Boston: Harvard Business School Publishing.

Chapter Three

Why Value Diversity

No one can make you feel inferior without your consent.

Eleanor Roosevelt

WHY VALUE DIVERSITY

Chapter Objectives

After reading this chapter, you should be able to:

- explain how U.S. demographics shifts affect workplace diversity.

- understand the melting pot myth.

- defend the business case for valuing diversity.

- put in plain words the EEO Laws.

- describe sexual harassment types and requirements.

Diversity is about recognizing, respecting and valuing differences based on primary differences such as ethnicity, gender, color, age, race, religion, disability, national origin and sexual orientation. It also includes an infinite range of individual unique characteristics and experiences, such as communication style, career path, life experience, educational background, geographic location, income level, marital status, military experience, parental status and other variables that influence personal perspectives.

These life experiences and personal perspectives make us react and think differently, approach challenges and solve problems differently, make suggestions and decisions differently, and see different opportunities. An organization can minimize the costs that are associated with a lack of managing diversity comprehension by understanding what diversity is, why it matters, and how to effectively manage a business in terms of diversity.[1] The first approach addressed in the text to effectively manage those primary differences listed above is valuing diversity (accepting, understanding and respecting diversity).

Valuing diversity is necessary because of the demographic shifts that affect the workplace, because it makes good business sense to do so and also because of the laws created to promote equal opportunity despite race, religion, age, sex and physical or mental ability.[2] As we continue considering why we should value diversity in the workplace, let's look further at the demographic trends and changes affecting the U.S. population and thus the U.S. workplace.

Demographics Say We Should Value Diversity

According to the 2006 *Changing Demographic Profile of the United States* created by Laura B. Shrestha, a Specialist in Demography the United States is the third most populous country globally and accounts for about 4.6% of the world's population.[3] Within the next few years, the U.S. population — currently estimated at 299 million persons — is expected to reach twice its 1950 level of 152 million. More than just being double in size, the population has become qualitatively different from what it was in 1950. "As noted by the *Population Reference Bureau*, The U.S. is getting bigger, older, and more diverse."[4]

Sex/Gender Change*

Despite a small decline in the growth of females in the United States, females still make up 50% of the U.S. population.

	1980	1990	Change from 1980 to 1990	2000	Change from 1990 to 2000
Population	224,811,135	248,710,012	10.6%	281,421,906	13.2%
Percent Female	51.5%	51.3%	10.2%	50.9%	12.5%
Percent Male	48.5%	48.7%	11.1%	49.1%	13.9%

Race/Ethnicity Change*

The U.S. population of color surpassed the 100-million mark in May 2007. Today, one in every three Americans is a person of color. According to the Census 2000 data the U.S. population has made the following changes.

U.S. POPULATION – 1996	U.S. POPULATION – 2000
73.6% White	69.5% White
10.2% Hispanics/Latino	12.5% Hispanics/Latino
12.0% Black	12.7% Black
3.3% Asian	3.8% Asian
.7% Native Americans	.9% Native Americans
Total Population: 262.8 million	Total Population: 281.4 million

*Source: adapted from Congressional Research Service ~ The Library of Congress, titled: *The Changing Demographic Profile of the United States*, updated May 5, 2006.[5]

It is important to understand as we discuss racial and ethnic categories, "who" actually are represented by each group.

Racial Designations
Source: Census 2000 Special EEO Tabulation Files[6]

"White" refers to people having origins in any of the original peoples of Europe, the Middle East, or North Africa. It also includes people who indicated their race as "White" or wrote in entries such as Irish, German, Italian, Lebanese, Middle Easterner, Arab, or Polish.

"Black or African American" refers to people having origins in any of the Black racial groups of Africa. It includes people who indicated their race or races as "Black, African American, or Negro" or wrote in entries such as Nigerian, or Haitian.

"Asian" refers to people having origins in any of the originals peoples of the Far East, Southeast Asia, or the Indian subcontinent.

"Native Americans" category includes Native Americans, Hawaiians and other Pacific Islanders. This group refers to people having origins in any of the original peoples of Hawaii, Guam, Samoa, or other Pacific Islander groups such as Tahitian, Mariana Islander, or Chuukese.

All of the above groups (Whites, Blacks, Asians, Native-Americans) represent racial categories, where as those who belong to the Hispanic population represent an ethnicity not a race. In the census questioning, you either are of Hispanic descent or not of Hispanic descent. So, you can be White and of Hispanic descent or Black and of Hispanic descent etc. and all of these numbers are represented by the Hispanic/Latino category.

There is considerable variation in the ethnic mix across the country. For example, California's population is 51 per cent non-Hispanic white, while New Hampshire's is 97 per cent.[7] The states with the highest proportion of Hispanics are mostly in the west and southwest, while those with the highest proportion of African Americans are mostly in the east and southeast. About 56 per cent of the people in Hawaii are Asian or Polynesian.[8] Rural and suburban areas are more likely to be inhabited by whites, while people of color more often live in large urban areas.

There are 552 federally recognized Native American groups in the US, of which about 285 have reservations (or regional or village corporations in Alaska) that are recognized by the state or federal government.[9] These lands total more than 20 million hectares (50 million acres).[10] The US government has recognized the political sovereignty of many of these organizations through treaties, statutes, court decisions, and executive orders.

Other Demographic Facts

Language

English is the predominant language of the US and is spoken by most of the population. US English sometimes differs from British English in spelling, pronunciation, punctuation, and even meaning in some cases. For example, in US English, a lift is an "elevator" and the bonnet of a car is the "hood." Spoken English is very flexible, and idioms and accents differ from one part of the US to another, while written English is more standardized. Many first-, second-, or even third-generation immigrants also speak their native language. In fact, one of every seven Americans speaks a language other than English in the home. Spanish is spoken in many Hispanic communities, and Native Americans speak a variety of Amerindian languages. Many secondary and some elementary schools teach one or more foreign languages, such as Spanish, French, and Japanese.

Religion

Although the US has never had an official state church, about 90 per cent of the population has some religious affiliation, mostly with Christian churches. As early European settlers were predominantly Christian, the Constitution and the Bill of Rights are based, in part, on Christian values and principles. However, the Constitution dictates that church and state remain separate. There are dozens of different Christian churches throughout the country. About 26 per cent of the population is Roman Catholic. Baptists, Methodists, and Lutherans are the largest Protestant groups.[11] Between 40 and 55 per cent of Christians attend services on a weekly basis.[12] There are also substantial numbers of Jews, Muslims, Hindus, and Buddhists in the US. In addition, some Americans practice alternative or non-traditional religions, and many consider themselves to be atheists or are otherwise non-religious.

All of these statistics show that America is becoming more and more diverse not just in the overall society but in the workplace as well. In looking at the job market, about half of the U.S. market will be Latino/Hispanic, African-American and Asian populations.[13] Another high growth group that is not represented above is people over the age of 55. From 1990 to 2000 this group was growing at a forty percent growth rate.[14] The baby boom generation is getting older and there will be a large number of people in their 50's–according to the U.S Census Bureau 2000.[15] Many in this group will be seeking employment and participating actively in the workplace.

The Census Bureau also forecasted that immigration would be approaching 820,000 people per year, of which 225,000 will be undocumented. This all indicates that the workplace of today will look very different than yester years.

Forty to Fifty Years Ago, The Average Worker:

Source: *Workforce 2000-Hudson Institute: Opportunity 2000, U.S.P.O.L. & American Demographics*[16]

- was white
- was male and able-bodied
- was about 29
- had less than 12 years of education
- was married to a woman who became a homemaker
- had children
- worked in a region of his birth
- was conservative politically
- held beliefs about work, the role of men and women, minorities, authority and family that were similar to those of other workers
- was loyal to his employer and obeyed authority

As Far As Other Workers, Forty to Fifty Years Ago:

Source: *Workforce 2000-Hudson Institute: Opportunity 2000, U.S.P.O.L. & American Demographics*[17]

- only certain jobs (mostly labor intensive) were open to ethnic minorities
- older workers were considered smarter because they were more experienced
- people with disabilities were not found in the workplace
- women generally worked in the home or worked part-time
- working women were teachers, nurses or support staff

Today, In The Workplace:

There is an increasing influence of women

- Close to 48% of today's workforce is female. (DOL)[18]

- The 48% is made up of 8% African American women, 5% of Hispanic/Latino women, 2% of Asian women and 0.3% of Native American women and the rest are Caucasian women. (EEOC-8/03)[19]

- 49.5% of lower level managers and professionals are women, which is up from 29% in 1970. Of the 49.5%, white women comprise 77%. (BLS)[20]

- 15.7% of corporate officers are female in 2002, which is up from 8.7% in 1995. Of this 15.7%, white women comprise 88%. (Workforce 2020)[21]

- One in three wives out-earn their husbands, compared to one in five wives in 1980. For MBAs, six out of ten women out-earn their husbands.[22]

- The percentage of employed women who provide half or more of their household's total income is: 48% of all women in a married couple, 55% of all working women, 91% of women who are separated, divorced or widowed, 90% of women in a single-parent household.[23]

There are more people of color

- By the year 2050, nonwhites will represent ½ of the U.S. population. (Census Projections 2050)[24]

- Beginning in the third quarter of 2001, Latinos made up more than 50% of all California births.[25]

- The Asian American population grew by 63% during the 1990s, making it the fastest growing minority group.[26]

There is more religious diversity and people with disabilities in the workforce

- There are more than 1500 different types of religious bodies in the U.S. making the U.S. the most religiously diverse country in the world. (ACLU)[27]

- People with disabilities comprise 11.7% of the U.S. workforce.[28]

Once a largely homogeneous group, the faces of customers, claimants, producers, employees and suppliers have been transformed into a dynamic mix of people comprised of various races, cultures and backgrounds. "Minorities" are now the majority in six out of the eight largest metropolitan areas of the United States.[29]

Clearly, the U.S. population is changing dramatically. Forward-thinking companies that recognize and understand the implications of these demographic shifts accordingly will want to alter their customer focus, employee base and business practices to better manage the needs of current and future customers and employees.

Business Case Says We Should Value Diversity

Those who perceive diversity as exclusively a moral imperative or societal goal are missing the larger point. Workforce diversity needs to be viewed as a competitive advantage and a business opportunity.[30] It is well-proven that diverse, heterogeneous teams and work groups promote creativity, innovation and product development. Only by fully embracing diversity and maximizing the well-being and contributions of all people can an organization fully maximize the strength and competitiveness of their company. Organizations must therefore encourage individuals to reach their full potential, in pursuit of organizational objectives, without anyone being advantaged or disadvantaged by their difference.

Valuing diversity is also important because the inability to manage diversity in the workplace can be extremely harmful and can cost an organization in many ways. It is important to value diversity due to the costs associated with not doing so **BECAUSE**:

- there is a marketplace of diverse customers with significant purchasing power and unmet needs = $

- as our work environments become increasingly culturally and ethnically diverse, we must maintain a productive, efficient and harmonious workplace. A non-productive workforce is costly = $

- business owners need to effectively serve, negotiate with, sell to and manage culturally different people. Lack of this ability results in high turnover, loss training costs, etc... = $

- companies are tapping into international markets where delayed or failed business transactions can result from ignorance of cultural variations

  = $

- unnecessary employee terminations and inappropriate behavior toward difference in the workplace can turn into costly discrimination suits. The following are several discrimination suits that resulted in companies paying millions of dollars to settle: Shoney's at $132.5 million, Texaco at $176.1 million and Coca-Cola at $192.5 million = $

So, valuing diversity is not just the moral thing to do. It is also makes good business sense. Let's just look at a few companies who have lost valuable profits because they were convicted of discriminatory actions (they were not valuing difference). A secret tape catches Texaco executives belittling blacks. In 1996, it was the year's most dramatic case that began with a tape recorder secretly slipped into a Texaco executive's pocket.[31] The recording caught executives at the country's 14th-largest corporation ridiculing blacks and plotting to destroy papers pertinent to a long-running racial discrimination lawsuit.

Days after the tape's release, Texaco agreed to a $176 million settlement, the largest ever at that time for a race discrimination case. Civil rights leaders called a boycott and Chairman Peter Bijur publicly apologized.[32] This same year a defense contractor paid $13 million after showing older workers the door and in another case the government sues an automaker, saying men groped and insulted women at an Illinois plant.

In the year 2000, the Coca-Cola Company agreed to pay $192.5 million to settle a racial discrimination suit brought by black workers.[33] The settlement included $113 million in cash, $43.5 million to adjust salaries, and $36 million for oversight of the company's employment practices.[34] Coca-Cola also would pay $20 million in attorneys' fees and agreed to create an ombudsman post and have its employment practices reviewed by an outside group.

Even with the large settlement that Coca-Cola paid out Ben White, of the *Washington Post* in the April 18, 2002 issue says that "despite 2000 Legal Settlement--Protesters Say Little Has Changed - Protesters lined Seventh Avenue outside Madison Square Garden today to press criticisms of Coca-Cola Co., which was holding its annual shareholders meeting inside. With labor and environmental activists were dozens of African American Coca-Cola employees who said conditions have not improved at the Atlanta-based company since it agreed in November 2000 to pay $192.5 million to settle a class-action race-discrimination lawsuit and promised to change the way it manages, promotes and treats minority employees."[35]

But, has the rest of Corporate America learned its lesson from these companies example? No, a Google search today of discrimination lawsuits still finds a litany of gloomy headlines about discrimination in the workplace.

Injustices occur from the factory floor to the executive suite. On just February 6, 2007, the Ninth Circuit Court affirmed class certification in the Wal-Mart sex discrimination case (representing all female employees of Wal-Mart) making it the largest civil rights class action ever certified *Dukes v. Wal-Mart Stores, Inc.* (N.D. Cal. No C-01-2252).[36] The suit charges that Wal-Mart discriminates against its female retail employees in pay and promotions. The class in this case includes more than 1.6 million current and former female employees of Wal-Mart retail stores in America, including Wal-Mart discount stores, super centers, neighborhood stores, and Sam's Clubs. Certification of this class shows that no employer, not even the world's largest employer, is above the law.

Profiting in America's Multicultural/Ethnic Marketplace begins with an awareness that it can be lucrative if done correctly and costly if not. Therefore, market economic forces should not be ignored but taken very seriously. If we disregard the data on changing demographics, we also disregard the substantial growth in buying power of diverse markets. Not only are these diverse minority groups increasing as a percentage of the U.S. population, but so too is the buying power they wield.

From 1990 to 2005, minority group market share and purchasing power doubled and in some cases tripled. By 2009, that buying power is expected to increase by another 50%.[37] This economic clout is not limited to minorities. Gay and lesbian consumers will control a 6.1% market share, or $608 billion, and the annual buying power of women is estimated to be $3.3 trillion.[38] The present and future monetary power of diverse markets is more apparent each year. Take the Diversity Marketplace Quiz found below, to get an idea of how diversity really impacts the marketplace.

Diversity Marketplace Quiz

Directions: Take an educated guess for each question below. Circle the correct answer.

1. Which is the fastest growing group in the U.S., increasing at a rate eight times as fast as the general population, where their buying power is approximately $100B (Billion) per year? Which is the second, with buying power of approximately $170B (Billion) per year and growing five times as fast as the general population?
    a. Asian-American, Hispanic/Latino
    b. Native-American, Asian-American
    c. African-American, Caucasian
    d. Caucasian, African-American

2. Which market segment opens the largest number of new businesses?
    a. Asian-American
    b. Native-American
    c. African-American
    d. Women

3. Which ethnic market currently has the greatest amount of purchasing power and it is approximately how much per year?
    a. Asian-American, $350B
    b. African-American, $300B
    c. Hispanic/Latino, $250B
    d. Native-American, $200B

4. Which market segment showed the greatest growth in advertising spending?
    a. Women
    b. African-American
    c. Homosexual/Gay & Lesbian
    d. Hispanic/Latino

After taking the quiz, you may be wondering some of the following thoughts:

- If there are populations growing faster than the national average wouldn't it be safe to assume that emphasis should be placed on the needs of these populations?

- If ethnic purchasing power is in the billions per year (not pocket change) isn't this worthy of a company's interest?

- Is it possible that these targeted ethnic consumers may be more inclined to buy from companies where they see people who look like them working at all levels of the organizations?

Researchers have indicated that the evidence that diversity can deliver a business benefit is complex, arguing that many workforces are diverse in a range of both invisible and established categories.[39] But despite the complexity, managing workplace diversity effectively should be a common ground that all can agree is necessary.

The authors above recognize the importance of diversity management, commenting that without appropriate management and organizational culture, benefits of diversity may not be realized and disbenefits may occur.[40] The 'disbenefits of diversity' are identified as including increased conflict within the workforce; poorer internal communications; and increased management costs. Diversity can be considered an expression of difference, which, if successfully managed, should reduce the costs associated with the disbenefits of diversity.[41]

The current experience of diversity management demonstrates at least four main ways in which diversity can contribute to business performance according to the research on *The Diversity Scorecard*.[42]

1. Diversity in employment promotes cost-effective employment relations.
2. Diversity enhances customer relations.
3. Diversity enhances creativity, flexibility and innovation in organizations.
4. Diversity promotes sustainable development and competitive advantage.

Summary

There is no denying the mounting empirical and anecdotal evidence that good diversity management can lead to improved business performance when the business contexts and market conditions are taken into account appropriately. Conversely, poorly developed and poorly matched diversity practices can be detrimental to business, creating conflict without gain, raising expectation without delivery, and increasing cost without benefit.

The key is the sensible adoption of good practices, tailored to reflect good diversity practice and specific business goals. Even without these good diversity practices there still exist laws that govern discrimination and equal treatment. Yet, another reason why valuing diversity becomes an important workplace issue today.

Equal Employment Laws Say We Should Value Diversity

The foundation for Equal Employment Opportunity (EEO) Laws can be traced back to the U.S. Constitution. However, significant progress in shaping current laws was made between 1941 and 1991. Executive Orders barring discrimination, passage of the Title VII of the Civil Rights Act of 1964 and the Equal Employment Act of 1972 are often cited as the cornerstones for eliminating employment discrimination.

The above laws are enforced by the Equal Employment Opportunity Commission (EEOC). The Commission is composed of five Commissioners and a General Counsel appointed by the President and confirmed by the Senate. Commissioners are appointed for five-year staggered terms; the General Counsel's term is four years.[43] The President designates a Chair and a Vice-Chair and the Chair is the chief executive officer of the Commission.[44] The Commission has authority to establish equal employment policy and to approve litigation. The General Counsel is responsible for conducting litigation.

EEOC carries out its enforcement, education and technical assistance activities through 50 field offices serving every part of the nation. EEOC is an independent federal agency originally created by Congress in 1964 to enforce Title VII of the Civil Rights Act of 1964.[45] In addition the EEOC enforces the following federal statutes prohibiting employment discrimination, including: the Age Discrimination in Employment Act of 1967, Title I of the Americans with Disabilities Act of 1990, and the Equal Pay Act of 1963.[46] The descriptions following provide a brief summary of these laws.

EEO Laws

Source: EEO Laws and Regulations found at http://www.eeolaw.org/law.html[47]

Title VII of the Civil Rights Act of 1964

Prohibits employment discrimination because of race, color, sex, national origin, and religion. Prohibits retaliation for opposing discrimination, filing a complaint, or participating in a related proceeding.

Age Discrimination in Employment Act of 1967

Prohibits employment discrimination because of age against persons age 40 and older. Prohibits retaliation for opposing age discrimination, filing a complaint, or participating in a related proceeding. This law was amended by the Older Workers Benefit Protection Act which sets minimum criteria that must be satisfied before a waiver of any ADEA right is considered a "knowing and voluntary" waiver.

Americans With Disabilities Act of 1990, Titles I and V

Prohibits employment discrimination because of: mental and physical disabilities that substantially limit a major life activity; or having a record of a disability; or being regarded as having a disability. Requires reasonable accommodation of mental and physical disabilities.

Equal Pay Act of 1963

Prohibits wage differentials based on sex for jobs that require equal skill, effort, and responsibility, and are performed under similar working conditions in the same establishment ("equal pay for equal work").

The following information: Title VII of the Civil Rights Act of 1964 is reprinted with permission from the U.S. Equal Employment Opportunity Commission and clearly explains what constitutes discrimination according to the previous discussed laws.

Title VII of the Civil Rights Act of 1964*[47]

Race & Color Discrimination

As this Act relates to Race, it is unlawful to discriminate against any employee or applicant for employment because of his/her race or color in regard to hiring, termination, promotion, compensation, job training, or any other term, condition, or privilege of employment. It also prohibits discrimination on the basis of an immutable characteristic associated with race, such as skin color, hair texture, or certain facial features. Even though not all members of the race share the same characteristic, there would still be a violation of Title VII based on the previous elements.

Title VII also prohibits employment decisions based on stereotypes and assumptions about abilities, traits, or the performance of individuals of certain racial groups. Title VII prohibits both intentional discrimination and neutral job policies that disproportionately exclude minorities and that are not job related.

Equal Employment opportunity cannot be denied because of marriage to or association with an individual of a different race; membership in or association with ethnic based organizations or groups; or attendance or participation in schools or places of worship generally associated with certain minority groups. Title VII also prohibits discrimination on the basis of a condition, which predominantly affects one race, unless the practice is job related and consistent with business necessity.

Furthermore, harassment on the basis of race and/or color such as ethnic slurs, racial "jokes," offensive or derogatory comments, or other verbal or physical conduct based on an individual's race or color constitutes unlawful harassment if the conduct creates an intimidating, hostile, or offensive working environment, or interferes with the individual's work performance. Title VII also states that when you isolate employees on the basis of race or color from other employees or from customer contact this is a violation. It also prohibits assigning mostly people of color to predominantly minority establishments or geographic areas. It is also illegal to exclude minorities from certain positions or to group or categorize employees or jobs so that minorities generally hold certain jobs. Coding applications/resumes to designate an applicant's race, by either an employer or employment agency, constitutes evidence of discrimination where minorities are excluded from employment or from certain positions.

As it relates to color discrimination this discrimination while categorized with race is slightly different. This slowly emerging form of workplace discrimination is based on color or skin tone. The unlawful conduct is predicated not on a person's specific race or nationality, but on the shade of his or her skin, often involving disputes between people of the same race and among individuals who act on cultural biases based on whether a person's skin tone is lighter or darker.

Vice-Chair Naomi Earp of the Equal Employment Opportunity Commission told a recent meeting of the American Bar Association that "colorism" represents a potential emerging trend in workplace discrimination claims. Color claims over the past year have risen from 1,400 in fiscal year 2002 to 1,555 in fiscal year 2003, Ms. Earp reported. She noted the increase may signal a trend attributable, in part, to the changing demographics of the American workplace, as more claims of colorism are included along with charges of race discrimination – the most prevalent charge year after year -- under Title VII of the 1964 Civil Rights Act.

Complaints of color discrimination go both ways, although more complaints are brought by individuals with darker skin than those with lighter skin. Ms. Earp reported the majority of charges alleging color discrimination were brought in the EEOC district offices in the cities of New York, Boston, Miami, Chicago, and Houston. She observed that color discrimination is inherent in some cultures, such as in India, Pakistan, and South America. As the United States becomes more culturally and ethnically diverse, awareness of colorism issues grow in importance, Ms. Earp emphasized.

Skin tone bias is not unique among people of color; whites also can equate darker skin with a "negative cultural stereotype." Yet, there is a great deal of uncertainty over whether discrimination based on skin tone is even illegal, although the EEOC clearly takes the position it is.

In August, 2003, the EEOC's Atlanta district office announced a $40,000 settlement in a "black on black" discrimination case against a franchisee of a large restaurant chain. The plaintiff was a dark skinned male waiter at the restaurant in Georgia when a light skinned black man began working as the general manager. The manager almost immediately began harassing the plaintiff, continuously making offensive and embarrassing comments about the dark color of his skin, the EEOC said in its complaint. Co-workers and some customers witnessed the harassment, the EEOC said. Despite the plaintiff's protests, the harassment continued, and the plaintiff eventually threatened to call corporate headquarters. Shortly thereafter, he received the first of four written reprimands for "minor" offenses, EEOC said, followed by his firing. Although the plaintiff did call the restaurant chain's hotline to complain about his treatment before being terminated, allegedly he got no response from his call.

Beyond the monetary settlement in which the employer admitted no wrongdoing, the restaurant agreed to provide anti-discrimination training to its employees and to report any complaints at its Georgia restaurants directly to EEOC. The restaurant also added a written policy prohibiting discrimination based on color.

Shortly after the restaurant case settlement, a federal judge in New York ruled that a black employee, who was fired after a darker skinned supervisor allegedly branded her a white "wannabe," can pursue a race discrimination law suit against her employer. However, despite these and other cases in recent years, claims of color discrimination still represent a very small amount of total employment complaints.

The EEOC received 1,382 charges of color bias in 2002, representing just 2% of all agency claims. Back in 1987, the EEOC received only 459 complaints of color discrimination. By 1999, color bias charges were up to 1,304, and they have held steady ever since. Although the most typical scenario of color discrimination involves lighter skinned African Americans discriminating against darker skinned African Americans, color bias cases also have been brought within other groups, including Native Americans and Arabs.

National Origin Discrimination

No one can be denied equal employment opportunity because of birthplace, ancestry, culture, or linguistic characteristics common to a specific ethnic group. Equal employment cannot be denied because of marriage or association with persons of a national origin group; membership or association with specific ethnic groups, attendance or participation in schools, churches, temples or mosques generally associated with a national origin group; or a surname associated with a national origin group.

A rule requiring employees to speak only English at all times on the job may violate Title VII, unless an employer shows it is necessary for conducting business. If an employer believes the English-only rule is critical for business purposes, employees have to be told when they must speak English and the consequences for violating the rule. Any negative employment decision based on breaking the English-only rule will be considered evidence of discrimination if the employer did not tell employees of the rule.

Furthermore, an employer must show a legitimate nondiscriminatory reason for the denial of employment opportunity because of an individual's accent or manner of speaking. Investigations will focus on the qualifications of the person and whether his or her accent or manner of speaking had a detrimental effect on job performance. Requiring employees or applicants to be fluent in English may violate Title VII if the rule is adopted to exclude individuals of a particular national origin and is not related to job performance. In addition, an ethnic slur or other verbal or physical conduct because of an individual's nationality constitute harassment if they create an intimidating, hostile or offensive working environment that unreasonably interferes with work performance or negatively affect an individual's employment opportunities.

Title VII also covers immigration-related practices that may be discriminatory. The Immigration Reform and Control Act of 1986 (IRCA) requires employers to prove all employees hired after November 6, 1986, are legally authorized to work in the United States. IRCA also prohibits discrimination based on national origin or citizenship. An employer who singles out individuals of a particular national origin or individuals who appear to be foreign to provide employment verification may have violated both IRCA and Title VII. Employers who impose citizenship requirements or give preference to U.S. citizens in hiring or employment opportunities may have violated IRCA, unless these are legal or contractual requirements for particular jobs. Employers also may have violated Title VII if a requirement or preference has the purpose or effect of discriminating against individuals of a particular national origin.

Sex Discrimination

Sex discrimination is discrimination based on gender. Title VII's broad prohibitions against sex discrimination also cover:

- Sexual Harassment which includes practices ranging from direct requests for sexual favors to workplace conditions that, create a hostile environment for persons of either gender.

- Pregnancy Based Discrimination which includes pregnancy, childbirth, and related medical conditions and must be treated in the same way as other temporary illnesses or conditions.

Sexual Harassment

There are basically two requirements for sexual harassment to be prevalent, unwelcome conduct and incidents of a sexual nature.

Unwelcome Conduct
This conduct is unsolicited meaning the victim has done nothing to incite it and the victim views the conduct as undesirable or offensive. By undesirable, the courts have declared that there is a clear distinction between conduct that is voluntary and that which is unwelcome.

A central inquiry of investigations should be whether the alleged harassing activity was unwelcome rather than involuntary and how the parties should have known that. A party may voluntarily be involved in sexual acts even though they don't want to be, solely out of fear of losing their job. This would be an example of unwelcome behavior.

Sexual Nature
Some common examples of sexually harassing conduct that's of a sexual nature are:

- Sexual propositions
- Comments on the sexual areas of a body
- Dirty pictures or jokes of nude or sexually suggestive individuals
- Sexually oriented cartoons
- Other physical or verbal conduct

The requirement can also be fulfilled through nonsexual verbal and physical behavior caused by the gender of the individual being harassed. An example of this is in the case of *Hall v. Leus Construction Co.* Here, three female plaintiffs were subjected to conduct designed to make their work life difficult and to let them know that women were not welcome on the job site. A few of these acts were as follows: the men involved in the suit urinated in the gas tank of one of the plaintiffs car, they had locked the door of the restroom at the job site and had refused to stop on the road so the plaintiff could go to the bathroom letting a dangerous condition persist in the plaintiff's truck until a male employee needed to stop to use the restroom. While these acts were not sexual comments or nude displays, they were still sexual in nature because they were based upon the gender of the victim.

When someone has a potential sexual harassment case, there are two ways to make the claim:

1) Quid Pro Quo
2) Hostile Environment

Quid Pro Quo
This claim requires showing of unwelcome activity of a sexual nature in exchange for tangible job benefits ("this for that") or it is also the loss of tangible job benefits owing to the rejection of such activity. This is fundamentally, an abuse of supervisory power.

To establish quid pro quo sexual harassment it is necessary to prove:

1. The person was a member of a protected class (group named in a law as protected from discrimination.) Some protected classes include race, gender, age and religion.
2. The person was subjected to unwelcome harassment.
3. The harassment was based on sex.
4. The person's reaction to the harassment affected tangible aspects of her or his compensation, terms, conditions, or privileges of employment.

Hostile Environment
This claim requires showing of frequent, nontrivial acts of a sexual nature that have created the effect of a hostile, offensive or intimidating working atmosphere. No money damages are required to be shown. To prove this, it is necessary to show the following:

1. The harassment was unwelcome.
2. The harassment was based on membership in a protected class.
3. The harassment was sufficiently severe or pervasive to create an abusive working environment.

4. The employer had actual knowledge or constructive knowledge of the environment but took no prompt and remedial action.

The Supreme Court has set two conditions as the standard for evaluating whether or not a working environment is "hostile":

1. A reasonable person* would find the environment hostile or abusive.
2. The victim subjectively perceives the environment to be abusive.

*In its decision on hostile environment sexual harassment cases, the Supreme Court has not directly addressed the question of whose viewpoint should be used in assessing the work environment. The Court has not ruled that decisions should be made from the perspective of the victim or the accused. Instead, they have the used the reasonable person viewpoint.

Men & Sexual Harassment

According to Julie Crane, a California Attorney at Law, more men are suing for sexual harassment. Based on cases taken to trial there have been situations where male employees cite sexual harassment because their male co-workers use vulgar language constantly, make lewd jokes and sometimes teasingly grab at their genitals. To you this may sound like the kind of horseplay that goes on in a typical high school locker room, and therefore as a manager you may just chose to ignore it. Well, this employee could (as some have done) file a claim for sexual harassment with the Equal Employment Opportunity Commission (EEOC), and if he is as successful as the claimants in one recent case, he could receive a settlement of $500,000.

The EEOC in the year 2000 stated that men filed 13.5 percent of all the sexual harassment claims, twice as many as they filed in 1992. The majority of these charges involve harassment by other men. The U.S. Supreme Court ruled a few years ago that men could file for sexual harassment. But, some federal courts have thrown out cases where the victim was gay because sexual orientation is not protected under federal law and therefore is not a basis for sexual harassment on the federal level.

Pregnancy Discrimination

The Pregnancy Discrimination Act is an amendment to Title VII of the Civil Rights Act of 1964. It states that women affected by pregnancy or related conditions must be treated in the same manner as other applicants or employees with similar abilities or limitations.

An employer cannot refuse to hire a woman because of her pregnancy related condition as long as she is able to perform the major functions of her job. An employer cannot refuse to hire her because of its prejudices against pregnant workers or the prejudices of co-workers, clients or customers.

An employer may not also single out pregnancy related conditions for special procedures to determine an employee's ability to work. However, an employer may use any procedure used to screen other employees' ability to work. In addition, pregnant employees must be permitted to work as long as they are able to perform their jobs. Employers must hold open a job for the same length of time for a pregnancy related absence as jobs are held open for employees on sick or disability leave.

Religious Discrimination

Title VII prohibits employers from discriminating against individuals because of their religion in hiring, firing, and other terms and conditions of employment. The Act also requires employers to reasonably accommodate the religious practices of an employee or prospective employee, unless to do so would create an undue hardship upon the employer. Flexible scheduling, voluntary substitutions or swaps, job reassignments and lateral transfer are examples of accommodating an employee's religious beliefs.

Employers cannot schedule examinations or other selection activities in conflict with a current or prospective employee's religious needs, inquire about an applicant's future availability at certain times, maintain a restrictive dress code, or refuse to allow observance of a Sabbath or religious holiday, unless the employer can prove that not doing so would cause an undue hardship.

An employer can claim undue hardship when accommodating an employee's religious practices if allowing such practices requires more than ordinary administrative costs. Undue hardship also may be shown if changing a bona fide seniority system to accommodate one employee's religious practices denies another employee the job or shift preference guaranteed by the seniority system.

An employee whose religious practices prohibit payment of union dues to a labor organization cannot be required to pay the dues, but may pay an equal sum to a charitable organization. Mandatory "new age" training programs, designed to improve employee motivation, cooperation or productivity through meditation, yoga, biofeedback or other practices, may conflict with the non-discriminatory provisions of Title VII. Employers must accommodate any employee who gives notice that these programs are inconsistent with the employee's religious beliefs, whether or not the employer believes there is a religious basis for the employee's objection.

As you have seen Title VII guarantees protection against discrimination in employment on the basis of race and ethnicity, religion, gender, sex and national origin. It then was later amended to include disability. When the first civil rights bill to follow the U.S. civil war was debated in Congress, it was criticized for granting "special rights" to African Americans. When the Civil Rights Act was debated in 1964, it was criticized on the basis that it would destroy the economic viability of companies and attack individual freedom of choice in hiring. It passed anyway and applies to companies with more than 15 employees.

The Age Discrimination in Employment Act of 1967 (ADEA)

Age Discrimination

ADEA protects individuals who are 40 years of age or older from employment discrimination based on age. The ADEA's protections apply to both employees and job applicants. Under the ADEA, it is unlawful to discriminate against a person because of his/her age with respect to any term, condition, or privilege of employment -- including, but not limited to, hiring, firing, promotion, layoff, compensation, benefits, job assignments, and training.

It is also unlawful to retaliate against an individual for opposing employment practices that discriminate based on age or for filing an age discrimination charge, testifying, or participating in any way in an investigation, proceeding, or litigation under the ADEA.

The ADEA applies to employers with 20 or more employees, including state and local governments. It also applies to employment agencies and to labor organizations, as well as to the federal government.

APPRENTICESHIP PROGRAMS

It is generally unlawful for apprenticeship programs, including joint labor-management apprenticeship programs, to discriminate on the basis of an individual's age. Age limitations in apprenticeship programs are valid only if they fall within certain specific exceptions under the ADEA or if the EEOC grants a specific exemption.

JOB NOTICES AND ADVERTISEMENTS

The ADEA makes it unlawful to include age preferences, limitations, or specifications in job notices or advertisements. As a narrow exception to that general rule, a job notice or advertisement may specify an age limit in the rare circumstances where age is shown to be a "bona fide occupational qualification" (BFOQ) reasonably necessary to the essence of the business.

PRE-EMPLOYMENT INQUIRIES

The ADEA does not specifically prohibit an employer from asking an applicant's age or date of birth. However, because such inquiries may deter older workers from applying for employment or may otherwise indicate possible intent to discriminate based on age, requests for age information will be closely scrutinized to make sure that the inquiry was made for a lawful purpose, rather than for a purpose prohibited by the ADEA.

BENEFITS

The Older Workers Benefit Protection Act of 1990 (OWBPA) amended the ADEA to specifically prohibit employers from denying benefits to older employees. An employer may reduce benefits based on age only if the cost of providing the reduced benefits to older workers is the same as the cost of providing benefits to younger workers.

WAIVERS OF ADEA RIGHTS

At an employer's request, an individual may agree to waive his/her rights or claims under the ADEA. However, the ADEA, as amended by OWBPA, sets out specific minimum standards that must be met in order for a waiver to be considered knowing and voluntary and, therefore, valid. Among other requirements, a valid ADEA waiver: (1) must be in writing and be understandable; (2) must specifically refer to ADEA rights or claims; (3) may not waive rights or claims that may arise in the future; (4) must be in exchange for valuable consideration; (5) must advise the individual in writing to consult an attorney before signing the waiver; and (6) must provide the individual at least 21 days to consider the agreement and at least 7 days to revoke the agreement after signing it. In addition, if an employer requests an ADEA waiver in connection with an exit incentive program or other employment termination program, the minimum requirements for a valid waiver are more extensive.

Titles I and V of the Americans with Disabilities Act (ADA)

Disabled Discrimination

The ADA prohibits discrimination on the basis of disability in all employment practices. It is necessary to understand several important ADA definitions to know who is protected by the law and what constitutes illegal discrimination:

Individual with a Disability
> An individual with a disability under the ADA is a person who has a physical or mental impairment that substantially limits one or more major life activities, has a record of such an impairment, or is regarded as having such an impairment. Major life activities are activities that an average person can perform with little or no difficulty such as walking, breathing, seeing, hearing, speaking, learning, and working.

Qualified Individual with a Disability
> A qualified employee or applicant with a disability is someone who satisfies skill, experience, education, and other job-related requirements of the position held or desired, and who, with or without reasonable accommodation, can perform the essential functions of that position.

Reasonable Accommodation
> Reasonable accommodation may include, but is not limited to, making existing facilities used by employees readily accessible to and usable by persons with disabilities; job restructuring; modification of work schedules; providing additional unpaid leave; reassignment to a vacant position; acquiring or modifying equipment or devices; adjusting or modifying examinations, training materials, or policies; and providing qualified readers or interpreters. Reasonable accommodation may be necessary to

apply for a job, to perform job functions, or to enjoy the benefits and privileges of employment that are enjoyed by people without disabilities. An employer is not required to lower production standards to make an accommodation. An employer generally is not obligated to provide personal use items such as eyeglasses or hearing aids.

Undue Hardship

An employer is required to make a reasonable accommodation to a qualified individual with a disability unless doing so would impose an undue hardship on the operation of the employer's business. Undue hardship means an action that requires significant difficulty or expense when considered in relation to factors such as a business' size, financial resources, and the nature and structure of its operation.

Prohibited Inquiries and Examinations

Before making an offer of employment, an employer may not ask job applicants about the existence, nature, or severity of a disability. Applicants may be asked about their ability to perform job functions. A job offer may be conditioned on the results of a medical examination, but only if the examination is required for all entering employees in the same job category. Medical examinations of employees must be job-related and consistent with business necessity.

Drug and Alcohol Use

Employees and applicants currently engaging in the illegal use of drugs are not protected by the ADA when an employer acts on the basis of such use. Tests for illegal use of drugs are not considered medical examinations and, therefore, are not subject to the ADA's restrictions on medical examinations. Employers may hold individuals who are illegally using drugs and individuals with alcoholism to the same standards of performance as other employees.

Equal Pay Act of 1963

Unequal Pay

The Equal Pay Act requires that men and women be given equal pay for equal work in the same establishment. The jobs need not be identical, but they must be substantially equal. It is job content, not job titles, that determines whether jobs are substantially equal. Specifically, the EPA provides:

Employers may not pay unequal wages to men and women who perform jobs that require substantially equal skill, effort and responsibility, and that are performed under similar working conditions within the same establishment. Each of these factors is summarized below (taken from *The U.S. Equal Employment Opportunity Commission Website*):

Skill - Measured by factors such as the experience, ability, education, and training required to perform the job. The key issue is what skills are required for the job, not what skills the individual employees may have. For example, two bookkeeping jobs could be considered equal under the EPA even if one of the job holders has a master's degree in physics, since that degree would not be required for the job.

Effort - The amount of physical or mental exertion needed to perform the job. For example, suppose that men and women work side by side on a line assembling machine parts. The person at the end of the line must also lift the assembled product as he or she completes the work and place it on a board. That job requires more effort than the other assembly line jobs if the extra effort of lifting the assembled product off the line is substantial and is a regular part of the job. As a result, it would not be a violation to pay that person more, regardless of whether the job is held by a man or a woman.

Responsibility - The degree of accountability required in performing the job. For example, a salesperson who is delegated the duty of determining whether to accept customers' personal checks has more responsibility than other salespeople. On the other hand, a minor difference in responsibility, such as turning out the lights at the end of the day, would not justify a pay differential.

Working Conditions - This encompasses two factors: (1) physical surroundings like temperature, fumes, and ventilation; and (2) hazards.

Establishment - The prohibition against compensation discrimination under the EPA applies only to jobs within an establishment. An establishment is a distinct physical place of business rather than an entire business or enterprise consisting of several places of business. However, in some circumstances, physically separate places of business should be treated as one establishment. For example, if a central administrative unit hires employees, sets their compensation, and assigns them to work locations, the separate work sites can be considered part of one establishment.

Pay differentials are permitted when they are based on seniority, merit, quantity or quality of production, or a factor other than sex. These are known as "affirmative defenses" and it is the employer's burden to prove that they apply. Furthermore, in correcting a pay differential, no employee's pay may be reduced. Instead, the pay of the lower paid employee(s) must be increased.

Sexual Orientation Discrimination

Neither the civil rights act nor the federal EEO law provides protection on the basis of sexual orientation. However, Executive Order 11478, as amended; Department Administration Order 215-11; and the Department's non-discrimination policy prohibit such discrimination. It is also a prohibited personnel practice under the Civil Service Reform Act of 1978. The Department of Commerce has a complaint process for sexual orientation discrimination.

Furthermore, a bill was introduced into the US congress in the mid 1970's, which would do for gays and lesbians what various civil rights bills had done for African-Americans, women and others. It went nowhere.

In 1994, a stripped down version of the bill was introduced to Congress; it had limited range, guaranteeing only freedom from discrimination in employment. It was called the Employment Non-Discrimination Act or ENDA. President Clinton supported this bill in 1995 "who said that if the bill were passed, it would guarantee that all Americans, regardless of their sexual orientation, can find and keep their jobs based on their ability to work and the quality of their work." It was also supported by: the Leadership Conference on Civil Rights, by many large corporations (AT&T, Eastman Kodak, Microsoft, RJR Nabisco, Quaker Oats, and Xerox), and by many religious organizations, including the National Council of Churches, National Catholic Conference for Interracial Justice, Southern Christian Leadership Conference, and the Union of American Hebrew Congregations. Yet, despite the obvious support this bill still has not passed.

Concluding Thoughts

After reviewing the demographics, the costs of devaluing diversity and the laws surrounding equal opportunity it becomes increasingly apparent that focusing on diversity and looking for more ways to make full use of the contributions of all employees is necessary for today's competitive workplace. Valuing diversity can yield greater productivity, competitive advantage and market share. To manage diversity is to support this collective talent in ways that add a measurable difference to organizational and industrial performance.

End of Chapter Questions

1. For what reasons is it important to know the "why" behind valuing diversity in the workplace?

2. Indicate three of the demographic shifts in the last twenty years and state how this can impact the marketplace.

3. What is the difference between race and color discrimination?

4. Could the following examples be considered discrimination according to the EEO laws and why.

   a. Woman is fired after her supervisor finds out she is pregnant.
   b. White male is harassed at work for being married to an Asian woman.
   c. A disabled employee asks for days off for doctor visits and is denied this request, without any reason given.
   d. A female flight attendant who is Arab must wear religious headcovering, this is not part of the uniform and she is fired.

Internet Exercise

Part A: Using the Internet or www.google.com find five companies that have settled discrimination lawsuits recently and indicate why these companies were sued, how much they settled for and who were the plaintiffs.

Part B: Answer the following questions: (1) Why do the settlements tend to be large monetary amounts and (2) Do you think lawsuits are a viable option for handling discrimination in the workplace, why or why not.

Search Key Words: Discrimination lawsuits settled or Race discrimination lawsuits settled, Religious discrimination lawsuits settled, Age discrimination lawsuits settled or Sex discrimination lawsuits settled, etc.

End of Chapter Exercise

Media and valuing diversity

Search your local newspaper, a magazine, or watch a television program or commercials and find two examples of companies that are showing they value diverse groups of people based upon their depiction or representation and explain why you feel they are valuing diversity. Also find two examples of companies that are not showing they value diversity and explain what they could do better in order to respond to a diverse marketplace.

References

1. Magazines Publisher of America. (n.d.). *The Value of Diversity*. Retrieved from
http://www.magazine.org/diversity/Managing_Diversity_at_Work/

2. Copeland, L. (1988). Valuing Diversity, Part 2: Pioneers and Champions of Change. *Personnel*, 65,

3. Shrestha, L. B. (2006). *CRS Report for Congress: The Changing Demographic Profile of the United States*. Library of Congress.

4. Ibid.

5. Ibid.

6. *Census 2000 Special EEO Tabulation Files*. Retrieved from
http://www.census.gov/hhes/www/eeoindex/descrvar.pdf

7. Gordon, N. M. (2002). *The U.S. Census at the Beginning of a new millennium*. 20th Annual Meeting of the Population Census Conference.

8. Ibid.

9. Story, M., Evans, M., Fabsitz, R. R., Clay, T. E., Holy Rock, B. & Broussard, B. (1999, April). The epidemic of obesity in American Indian communities and the need for childhood obesity-prevention programs, *American Journal of Clinical Nutrition*, 69, 4. 747S-754S,.

10. Ibid.

11. *Major Religions of the World Ranked by Number of Adherents*. (n.d.). Retrieved from
http://www.adherents.com/Religions_By_Adherents.html

12. Ibid.

13. *Census 2000 Special EEO Tabulation Files*. (2000). Retrieved from
http://www.census.gov/hhes/www/eeoindex/descrvar.pdf

14. Ibid.

15. U.S. Census Bureau, Population Division. (n.d.). Age Data.

16. Johnston, W. B & Packer, A. H. (1987). *Workforce 2000*. Indianapolis: Hudson Institute.

17. Ibid.

18. *America's Dynamic Workforce*. (2007, August). U.S. Department of Labor.

19. Occupational Employment in Private Industry by Race/Ethnic Group/Sex and by Industry, United States. (2003). The U.S. Equal Employment Opportunity Commission.

20. *Employed persons by detailed occupation, sex, race, and Hispanic or Latino ethnicity*. (2006). U.S. Department of Labor, Bureau of Labor Statistics, Employment and Earnings, Annual Averages.

21. Judy, R. & D'Amico, C. (1997). *Workforce 2020: Work and Workers in the 21st Century*. Indianapolis, IN: Hudson Institute.

22. Winkler, A. E., McBride, Timothy, D. & Andrews, C. (2005, August). Wives Who Outearn Their Husbands: A Transitory or Persistent Phenomenon for Couples? *Demography*, 42(3), 523-535.

23. Ibid.

24. *U.S. Interim Projections by Age, Sex, Race, and Hispanic Origin*. (2004, March). Population Projections U.S. Government.

25. *Census 2000 Special EEO Tabulation Files*. (2000). Retrieved from http://www.census.gov/hhes/www/eeoindex/descrvar.pdf

26. Ibid.

27. American Civil Liberties Union. (2003, Fall). *ACLU Reporter*.

28. Resources for cultural diversity at work. (n.d.). Diversity Central. Retrieved from http://www.diversitycentral.com/business/diversity_statistics.html

29. Ibid.

30. Gore, Al (Vice President). (1999). Best Practices in Achieving Workforce Diversity. *U.S. Department of Commerce*.

31. Jackson, M. (1996, December 26). Texaco leads 1996 parade of discrimination news. *The Oklahoma City Associated Press*.

32. Ibid.

33. *Satisfaction in Corporate America – Timeline*. (n.d.). Black Enterprise.com Retrieved from http://www.blackenterprise.com/cms/exclusivesopen.aspx?id=123

34. Ibid.

35. White, B. (2002, April 18). Black Coca-Cola Workers Still Angry Despite 2000 Legal Settlement, Protesters Say Little Has Changed. *Washington Post*.

36. Dukes v. Wal-Mart Stores, Inc. (N.D. Cal. No C-01-2252). (2009). Retrieved from: http://law.bepress.com/cgi/viewcontent.cgi?article=1193&context=uvalwps

37. Bush, I., Damminger, R., Daniels, L. M., & Laoye, E. (n.d.). Communication Strategies: Marketing to the 'Majority Minority'. *Villanova*, PA: Villanova University.

38. Ibid.

39. Worman, D. (2005). Managing Diversity: Linking Theory and Practice to Business Performance Conference. *Chartered Institute of Personnel and Development*. Retrieved from: http://www.cipd.co.uk/NR/rdonlyres/D4D2D911-FC8A-4FD2-A814-B80A55A60B87/0/mandivlink0405.pdf

40. Ibid.

41. Ibid.

42. Hubbard, Edward E. (2004). *The Diversity Scorecard: Evaluating the impact of diversity on organizational performance*. Boston: Butterworth-Heinemann.

43. United States Government Agencies and Organizations. (n.d.). Retrieved from http://www.west.asu.edu/jbuenke/government/

44. Ibid.

45. Equal Employment Opportunity Commission website. (n.d.). Retrieved from http://www.eeoc.gov/

46. Ibid.

47. EEO Laws and Regulations. (n.d.). Retrieved from http://www.eeolaw.org/law.html

Chapter Four

Understanding the White Male Culture

What you think is not always what is.

Unknown

UNDERSTANDING THE WHITE MALE CULTURE

Chapter Objectives

After reading this chapter, you should be able to:

- define what it means to be "white" in America.

- explain the Caucasian historical perspective.

- determine what is meant by WASP.

- list ways in which white males have been discriminated in the U.S.

- rationalize why it is important for especially white males to be a part of the diversity discussion.

In 1850, it was relatively simple to describe a White American. In all probability he or she was of Anglo-Saxon background and Protestant. However, after the Civil War, immigrants began coming from Southern and Central Europe. They were not Protestant, not Anglo-Saxon, and had different languages and cultures from those who preceded them. Despite the fact that each still maintains some of its uniqueness and has a different historical perspective, many have assimilated into what is known as the American way or the dominant culture that influences many U.S. workplace cultures.

Historical Perspective*

In 1980, approximately 200 million White Americans could trace some of their ancestry back to the following groups (in descending size order): English, German, Irish, French, Italian, Scottish, Polish, Dutch, Swedish, Norwegian, Russian, Czechoslovakian, Hungarian, Welsh, Danish, and Portuguese.

The White-American experience from its colonial beginnings is fairly short. It covers a period of approximately 400 years, a period that can be spanned by the overlapping lifetimes of a half-dozen individuals. Yet the roots of the White-American experience go deep into the human past. These roots are traced mostly to the Old World, but not the New.

Individuals who make-up the original White-American people, came to America from three areas of the world. They were:

a. North Africa related to the Berbers. A Caucasian people, the Berbers are related in physical type to the Mediterranean subgroup of southern Europe. They form the base population of Morocco, Algeria, Tunisia, and Libya. Today they are mostly Muslims and much of their culture is "Arabized."

b. Northwestern Europe. Belgium, Denmark, England, France, Germany, Ireland, the Netherlands, Northern Ireland, Norway, Scotland, Sweden, Switzerland, and Wales.

c. Southeastern Europe. Austria, Czechoslovakia, Greece, Hungary, Italy, Poland, Portugal, Rumania, Spain, USSR, and Yugoslavia.

But despite these varying cultures of what we call White it was the Anglo-Saxon and White Anglo-Saxon Protestant (WASP) who defined much of what we know today as the American workplace culture. An Anglo-Saxon and White Anglo-

Saxon Protestant (WASP) male is a person of Caucasoid, northern European, largely Protestant stock whose members constitute one of the most privileged and influential groups in U.S. society. In the New World, they were usually the landlord and their culture and values, with rare exception, were those that defined the culture.

Their culture and values were normally based on:

- Handwork.
- Perseverance.
- Self-Reliance.
- Puritanism.
- Missionary spirit.
- Abstract rule of law.

The White colonists prior to the Revolutionary War though immigrants by one definition, did not consider themselves immigrants. Rather, approximately 78% of the English population conceived themselves as Founders, Settlers, and Planters. As the formative population of those colonial societies, theirs were the policy, the language, the pattern of work, settlement, and many of the mental habits to which the post-Revolutionary War "immigrants" would have to adjust.

Even though an immigrant is defined as one who settles permanently in a foreign country or region in colonial America, ONLY those who arrived in America following the Revolutionary War were considered immigrants.

In 1607, the first permanent English settlement in America was established in Jamestown, Virginia. The Pilgrims arrived at Plymouth, Massachusetts, in 1620. In 1629, the Puritans came to Massachusetts Bay. Puritan settlers to the New England area differed from the inhabitants of other colonies. Nearly all other colonies were settled without education, driven by poverty or misconduct out of their homeland. Puritan settlers were British families with respectable social positions. They were educated and financially secure. They came to America so they could live according to their own principles and worship God in freedom.

The unique background of these early Puritan settlers established a foundation for many U.S. cultural norms. The words of the Bible were the origin of many Puritan cultural ideals, especially regarding the roles of men and women in the community. While both sexes carried the stain of original sin, for a girl, original sin suggested more than the roster of Puritan character flaws. Eve's corruption, in Puritan eyes, extended to all women, and justified marginalizing them within churches' hierarchical structures. An example is the different ways that men and women were made to express their conversion experiences.

According to Puritan belief, the order of creation was simple: the world was created for man, and man was created for God. If God had created the world with some beings subordinate to others, he applied the same principle to his construction of human society. Thus the Puritans honored hierarchy among men as divine order; this order presupposed God's "appointment of mankind to live in Societies, first of Family, secondly Church, thirdly, Common-wealth." Order in the family, then, was a fundamentally structured Puritan belief. Puritans usually migrated to New England as a family unit, a pattern different from other colonies where young, single men often came on their own. Puritan men of the generation of the Great Migration (1630–1640) believed that a good Puritan wife did not linger in Britain but encouraged her husband in his great service to God.

The essence of social order lay in the superiority of husband over wife, parents over children, and masters over servants in the family. Puritans in colonial America were among the most radical Puritans and their social experiment took the form of a Calvinist theocracy. Since, the British had been applying pressure on the Puritans for a while to conform to English customs it is no wonder that so many British Puritans ended up in the new land. The 1790 census indicated that 78 percent of the 2.75 million Americans were of British background. In July 1831, Dr. S.F. Smith took the music of the British national anthem and changed the words to create "America." The British had taken the tune from the Germans.

During WWI, millions of people living in the U.S. were seemingly more interested in their former homeland than their newly adopted country. The public labeled such people "hyphenated" Americans, German-Americans, Polish-Americans, and Irish-Americans. But despite the previous hypens, all of these people eventually melted into the pot and are no longer referred to by their hyphenated homeland but are just considered white.

Caucasians/Whites in America

The term white or Caucasian is represented of many people from various cultures whose common denominator is the lightness of their skin color. But, when we talk about "white" who are we referring to? If you look at the U.S. census definition of "white" discussed in chapter two we find that "White" refers to people having origins in any of the original peoples of Europe, the Middle East, or North Africa. But, if you asked people in the U.S. if a Middle Eastern was considered white the answer most often would be? "No." The following groups of people who migrated to the New Land (the United States) would have been considered "white" as long as they maintained the dominant culture along with having "white" skin (these are the largest groups some smaller groups are excluded):

Canadian-Americans.
The history of Canada is closely tied to that of the United States. The "Cajun" residents of Louisiana trace their roots back to French Catholic settlements in the provinces of Nova Scotia and New Brunswick. Run out by the English in 1775, they settled in Louisiana in places like Lafayette and New Orleans. With them they brought a unique French influence to the region. Over 4 million Canadians have immigrated to the United States since 1820. The peak for Canadian immigration to the United States was in the 1920s when 920,000 Canadians crossed the border looking for a new way of life. In the 1960's this number decreased to 413,000 and in the last decade, 100,000. Canada is made up of persons primarily of British (45%) or French (29%) descent. Since Canada is a bilingual country, most Canadian immigrants, regardless of French background, assimilate easily into American communities.

French-Americans.
The influence upon American life is disproportionately greater than their actual numbers in the United States. French explorers (e.g., Cartier, Champlain, Marquette, Joliet, LaSalle) were the first to "discover" based upon the definition of discoverer (covered in chapter four) areas in the heartland of America (e.g., the Mississippi River and all lands drained by it); the Great Lakes; the St. Lawrence River; Lake Champlain; Chicago, and Detroit. In 1562, the first group of French Protestants (Huguenots) came to America because of religious persecution and settled in South Carolina. The French fought alongside the colonists in the American Revolution; Rochambeau and Lafayette were great military minds.

Dutch-Americans.
In 1609, Henry Hudson set out to find a Northeast Passage to the East Indies and landed in which is now New York. The first Dutch settlement in America was in Fort Nassau, near Albany, New York. In 1621, the Dutch West Indies Company was formed. It promoted trade and settlement in America. The first group of permanent Dutch settlers came to America seeking religious freedom in America. The Patroonship System was established in 1629. Land plus ownership rights were given to anyone settling 50 people on their land within four years. To qualify as a patroon, a person had to be a major stockholder in the Dutch West Indies Company since its founding. Although six patroonships were registered, only one was successfully settled.

In 1640, in a renewed effort to bring more settlers to New Netherland, the Dutch West Indies Company developed a charter encouraging persons of limited economic means to settle there. As an early Governor of New Netherland, Peter Stuyvesant changed it from a trading post to a permanent settlement, which permitted a large degree of religious freedom. In 1663, a Dutch Mennonite named Pieter Cornelis Plockhoy established the first socialist community in North America. In 1668, the Dutch Quakers established the first declaration against slavery in the United States. In 1758, they expelled from their membership anyone who bought or sold slaves. The attitudes and behaviors of early settlers to this area (much of what is present-day New York) greatly influenced the current culture and characteristics that are distinctive to this part of America. Unrest in the Netherlands increased immigration between 1829 and 1865. Immigrants settled in Wisconsin, Michigan, Iowa, New Jersey, Indiana, and South Dakota.

German-Americans.
The first German immigrants to this country founded Germantown, Pennsylvania, in 1683. By 1766, one-third of Pennsylvania was inhabited by Germans. Most were poor farmers who settled along the frontier from Georgia to the New England colonies. The Pennsylvania Dutch were industrious and excellent farmers. They developed the Kentucky rifle and Conestoga wagon. Although many religious sects existed in Pennsylvania, there was a strong belief in religious tolerance and separation of church and state. John Peter Zenger established the concept of "Freedom of the Press." Von Steuben introduced a concept of military discipline during the Revolutionary War, which was instituted throughout the Army. During the first half of the 19th century, German immigration exceeded all other. Germans settled all over the country, especially in Rochester and Buffalo, New York; Cincinnati and Cleveland, Ohio, St. Louis, Missouri; and Milwaukee, Wisconsin. German artisans and craft persons established businesses and helped industrial expansion. German guilds marked the beginning of trade unions in this country.

Irish-Americans.
The first Irish person to come to America was William Ayers, who was one of Columbus' crew. Francis Maguire was one of the original inhabitants of Jamestown in 1607. John Dunlap, an Irish-American in Philadelphia, printed the Declaration of Independence. During and after the potato blight in Ireland (1846-48), immigration to the United States increased.

Italian-Americans.
Italians were among the earliest explorers of the country -- Christopher Columbus; Amerigo Vespecci (America was named after him); Verrazano missionaries Marcos de Niza and Eusebio Chino. Philip Mazzei, in 1773, established a plantation next to Thomas Jefferson's in Virginia, where he introduced grapes and olives to America. He also aided the colonists during the Revolution. Italian immigration increased after the failing of a great political uprising in Italy in 1848. The peak of Italian immigration was reached during 1900-1920. The majority of Italians coming were poor and settled in New England, the Great Lakes Region, Florida, and California. Most who could not get work in their specialties concentrated in the heavily urbanized states along the Northeast Seaboard.

Polish-Americans.
Several Poles accompanied the British when they landed in Jamestown, Virginia, in 1608. They were experts and instructors in the manufacture of glass, pitch, tar, and other products England imported from Poland. They did so well that other Poles were invited to come. However, they were not allowed privileges equal to those of the English. As a result of this inequity, the Poles organized the first American popular assembly and labor walkout in 1619 in Jamestown. Many Polish helped in the fight for American independence. Thaddeus Kosciuszko and Count Casimir Pulaski (father of American cavalry) organized some decisive victories. When Kosciuszko left America, he left his will in the custody of Thomas Jefferson. He designated that the proceeds from his estate be used to purchase Black slaves and give them freedom in his name.

Prior to 1865, Poles who came to this country were political exiles. Those who came after 1865 were poor peasants. They settled in Chicago, Buffalo, Detroit, Cleveland, Pittsburgh, and Milwaukee. Even though they came from rural backgrounds, they became involved in industry, working in the local and iron fields. Dr. Marie Elizabeth Zakrzewska, a medical pioneer, was active in women's suffrage and the abolition of slavery. She founded the New England Hospital for Women and Children. Caroline Still, one of the earliest Black women doctors, did her internship at the hospital. It was also one of the few White nursing schools to admit Blacks. Twelve percent of Americans who lost their lives in World War I were of Polish background, even though at no time did the number of Poles in this country exceed four percent of the total population.

Middle-Eastern-Americans.
Middle-Eastern-Americans are estimated to number 2.5 to 3.0 million in the United States where their religious affiliation is both Christian and Islamic. This

ethnic group is not closely tracked in the U.S. census and the trail of their immigration to the United States is sketchy. Many Syrians and Lebanese who immigrated to the United States in the last century came under Turkish passports. Although the number of Islamic-Americans is on the rise, there is a large number of the Middle-Eastern population in the U.S. that is made up of Maronite and Melkite Christians of Lebanese descent. The first Lebanese immigrant to the United States on record was Anthony Bishallany in 1854. The first Arabic newspaper in the United States was founded in 1892 as Kawab Amerika (The Star of America).

Early immigration of the Arabs to the U.S. took place between 1886 and 1914. Most were of Syrian and Lebanese descent and most lived in New York City. Historically, Syria included Lebanon, Palestine, Jordan, and occasionally Iran. In 1919, there were 400,000 recorded Middle-Eastern-Americans living in the United States. The majority were poor, under educated, and had a distaste for indoor factory work.

There were many thousands of them working as slaves on plantations. Others were primarily traders, peddlers, industrial workers and farmers. Later some enterprises grew into large businesses such as Haggar and Farah. These early communities, cut off from their heritage and families, inevitably lost their Islamic identity as time went by.

Immigration slowed during the period between W.W.I and W.W.II (1915 - 1945) due to immigration laws. Immigration quotas imposed in 1921 and 1924 reduced the allowable number of Middle-Eastern immigrants to less than 1,000. These restrictions were later repealed, but the flow of these immigrants into the United States has still remained at a trickle.

Arabs who immigrated to the U.S. after 1945 were more educated, professional, and mainly of the Muslim faith. Most came from Egypt, Iran and Palestine. This group has been able to retain more of their culture than the earlier group. Those who arrived during the first group attempted to distance themselves from some of the Arab world by adopting western culture and language.

Many of American English words have been borrowed from the Arabs such as algebra, alcohol, alkali and alcove. The word "al" means "the" in Arabic. Some of the name of foods in American are also Arabic such as apricot, sherbet, coffee, sesame and ginger.

*The source of this historical perspective is reprinted with permission from the Defense Equal Opportunity Management Institute through the Fort Gordon Equal Opportunity Office website.[1]

Why Migrate to America?

In early times many European settlers came to this land to avoid religious persecution. However, this was not the only reason to come to this new land: political oppression, economic opportunity, and dreams of freedom and opportunity. However, when they came to America how much freedom did these Europeans really experience?

America's servitude

During the seventeenth and eighteenth centuries a variety of labor market institutions developed to facilitate the movement of labor in response to the opportunities created by American factor proportions.[2] While some immigrants migrated on their own, many of the immigrants were indentured servants whose journey to the new land was a business exchange. The travel was paid by the "Master" who was the Lord to the indentured servant once they arrived on American soil. One half to two thirds of all immigrants to Colonial America arrived as indentured servants.[3] At times, as many as 75% of the population of some colonies were under terms of indenture.[4]

Indentured servitude first appeared in America a little over a decade after the settlement of Jamestown in 1607.[5] Labor was scarce; land was abundant and transportation costs to America were high compared to wages in England. An early economist noted that ... industry is limited by capital; but, through lack of labor, its limit is not always reached in older communities and seldom if ever in newer countries.[6] Indentured servitude appeared to have arisen from a combination of the terms of two other types of labor contract widely used in England at the time: service in husbandry and apprenticeship (Galenson, 1981).[7] In other cases, migrants borrowed money for their passage and committed to repay merchants by pledging to sell themselves as servants in America, a practice known as "redemptioner servitude.[8]

More often than not, the indentured servants were shocked by their new conditions. Rather than finding venues in which they could practice their profession, like gardens and orchards, overseers marched servants out to the fields. Many died, attempted to return, or ran away. In addition to mistreatment, many servants also encountered contract extension, a popular punishment of planters for rowdy indentures.

Indentured Servant Contract
(Courtesy of Northumberland County Virginia Records of Indentured Servants 1650-1795)

Master's Name:

Servant's Name(s):

Items:

1. The contract stated that the servant was to work for a set term, usually four years, during which time they would receive room, board, and clothing in addition to passage to America.

2. At the end of the term the individual was awarded "freedom dues," in the combination of money, tools, clothes, and/or land.

3. Skilled workmen sometimes added a clause exempting them from field work. Children's indentures, which were usually bound until the age of 21, specified that they be taught a trade or given an elementary education.

4. Many German indentures often entered into servitude on the condition that they be taught to read the Bible in English.

5. Servants were then assembled on deck so planters could interview them and/or feel their muscles. Then they were auctioned to the highest bidder.

6. Soul drivers were those individuals who would buy in mass and then walk the servants from town to town, reselling them.

7. In the early years, masters often drove their servants so hard that the backbreaking regime combined with crude living conditions caused over 50% of the servants to die.

8. Women indentured servants in some colonies had to serve an extra year if they became pregnant. Once their time of service was over, women did not receive land, as did men, and only rarely were given money.

Married couples were rarely indentured, and contract records normally listed each woman who signed on for indentured servitude as either a "singlewoman," a "spinster," or a "widow." [9] Contract holders were referred to as "master" or "mistress," while the indentured woman was called a "bondswoman" or "bound woman." For both men and women, though, the indenture period was strict and highly regulated, with laws protecting each side of the contract. The law specified, for example, the clothing that was due to a servant when his or her term was completed.

On the other hand, women who became pregnant while indentured could have their terms extended to reimburse the master for the loss of time the servant was unable to work and for the economic burden of her child.[10] Because servants were not allowed to marry, some women used this situation to deliberately become pregnant, hoping that the father of her child would buy out her contract. Indentured servant was a way for people to emigrate but did not often lead to the life of economic prosperity that was eventually hoped for.[11]

Throughout some history books Whites may not have been shown to start in America as servants, as religiously persecuted or as political refuges coming to seek freedom. Yet, this is exactly how many got their start in America.

White Male Perspective

As we look at the systems in the workplace, they most often are based upon the white male culture (those who created and controlled the systems). Women including white women very rarely participated in the workplace and people of color had no power to determine the direction of the workplace. But as we talk about "white males" this is done without ever really stating who is considered part of the white male group. So, how can we understand the systems they created without understanding the architects?

Over the course of time, the term "White Male" has come to refer to a group of people who espouse all of the following characteristics: (taken from the source: Addressing the Concerns of the White Man as Full Diversity Partners by Erik Oosterwal)[12]

- Northern/Western European descent (although males of southern and eastern European heritage are commonly included)

- Heterosexual, Male and Not Handicapped

- Middle class (more often upper middle class)

- Mainly Christian (Some Jews are now included)

If any of the characteristics are not met, then that person is often grouped with the associated subordinated group, such as gay, disabled, Arab, etc. White males who have the above characteristics in common also tend to have the same value system. This value system is based upon individualistic culture. Individualistic cultures generally value self-reliance and autonomy of the individual.[13]

Believing in fairness and equal opportunities for everyone is critical in more individualistic cultures that often equate hierarchy with rigidity, even if equality is more of a societal ideal than a reality.[14] Furthermore, this individualistic approach tends to value action, efficiency, getting to "the bottom line," while often downplaying social interactions in the interests of achieving goals.[15]

People in individualistic cultures emphasize their success/achievements in job or private wealth and are often aiming up to reach more and/or a better job position.[16] In business they try to improve their connections and to gain more value out of them, not for establishing a good relationship but just to be involved in a calculative way. Employees are expected to defend their interests and to promote themselves whenever possible. Ultimately, individualism stands for a society in which the ties between individuals are loose: everyone is expected to look after himself or herself and his or her immediate family only.[17]

This individualistic value system has also transferred to the workplace culture that many participate in. According to the article, *White Men and Diversity: An Oxymoron?* by Bill Proudman, White men in the United States work in organizational cultures that have been created by other white men therefore, the prevailing business culture often looks "normal"-it's the way business has always been done.[18] Common characteristics to be found in organizational cultures based upon those white males who created the organizations years and years ago are as follows: the individual is the most important societal unit and people should take care of themselves because individual achievement is most valued; time is perceived as a quantity and people are expected to save time, spend time, and perform on time; people must dress and be accepted by resembling the European ideal of beauty and status (limited use of color--blues, blacks, gray), smaller sized women, authority in men represents a suit and tie therefore Ethnic hairstyles and religious dress is often seen as unprofessional; also, the workplace's resources belong to the best where access to goods/jobs is determined by competition (the best) as reflected in test scores, etc.[19]

But why all the hype you may be asking: is there a problem with those values?

That depends on who you ask.

For those whose values differ—it requires assimilation if the culture of the workplace is based upon those values.

For instance, many people of color such as, African-Americans, Native Americans, Hispanic/Latino and most Asian cultures identify with Collectivism.[20] Collectivism stands for a society in which people from birth onwards are integrated into strong cohesive ingroups (family, neighborhood or tribe), which throughout people's lifetime continue to protect them in exchange for unquestioning loyalty.[21] What is known about collectivism verse individualism is that these cultures are often at opposite extremes.

Look at some workplace differences on the following page that are based upon race generalizations.

Normative Styles & Values for Cross-Cultural Collaboration

(Adapted from Candia Elliott, Diversity Training Associates, R. Jerry Adams, Ph.D., Evaluation and Development Institute and Suganya Sockalingam, Ph.D., Office of Multicultural Health, Department of Human Resources, Oregon.)[22]

Work Style (Focus Group)	Very Little	Little	Medium	Much	Very Much
Task Focused vs. Relationship	Native Am. Hispanic Asian Am.	African Am.			White
Long term history between groups important	White				Native Am. Hispanic African Am. Asian Am.
Perceived right to set rules	Native Am. Hispanic Asian Am.	African Am.			White
Perceived right to speak freely at meetings	Native Am. Hispanic Asian Am.	African Am.			White
Concern with clock time	Native Am. Hispanic	African Am.		Asian Am.	White
Perceived right to represent or speak for group	Native Am. Asian Am.	African Am. Hispanic			White
Collaborators must have community respect and support	White				Native Am. Hispanic Asian Am. African Am.

The chart above titled, *Normative Styles & Values for Cross-Cultural Collaboration* is BY NO MEANS representative of every person in the identified group. These are norms that researchers have found to be common elements of many in the associated groups. But if individuals in the workplace follow these cultural aspects then you can see why the systems that are based upon some aspects of white male culture don't work for everyone.

So, what does this mean? It often means that the challenge with white male culture is not the individual qualities of the culture, but the fact that some assimilate far more easily into the culture than others. White women, people of color, and openly gay, lesbian, bisexual, and transgender individuals often have to be bi-cultural. They must learn to consciously be seen as competent in the white male heterosexual culture. What complicates the issues is that often times, white heterosexual men are not even aware that such assimilation is part of their colleagues' everyday work experience. This "not knowing" can create difficulties, strained work relationships, and charges of "He just doesn't get it."

Many White men never have to leave their culture; thus they are often unaware of the systemic advantages they receive-from being white and/or male-and how this impacts their partnerships at work with white women, people of color, and other white men. [23] Systemic advantages are often the unspoken and invisible benefits that are received by a person because of their group membership (being white, male, heterosexual, and so forth). These advantages are made to look normal and available to any person who desires them. Systemic advantage is not so much what a person has, but it's more what a person doesn't have to think about on a daily basis. However, receiving systemic advantage does not entirely prevent white men from being the recipients of mistreatment and discrimination. But, systematic advantage can leave people outside of this culture to believe that systems will never advantage those outside of it.

While the highest position in America, President is held by a black man President Barack Obama White males in many respects still have cultural dominance due to the powerful positions they hold in Corporate America. White males hold the majority of top management positions in these companies. These positions are often gained through two main vehicles: hard work and effort or through the *good old boys network*.

A *Wikipedia* entry explaining good ol' boy networks basically says it is a social network, or at least the perception of it, which heavily influences local business, government, and legal functions and it is said to be very informal and decentralized, there's no real 'list' or organization, it's just known who is influential and calls the shots locally. It is usually composed of white males that come from local religious or legal organizations that extend opportunities to those who are most like them.[24] This allows "the birds of a feather who flock together" to maintain their power structure.

So based upon this definition, does this mean that the good ol' boy network is negative? Who wouldn't extend favors to their friends, or to friends asking for their friends, or for family members? I've often heard the phrase, 'it's who you know not what you know that's important' spoken in relation to finding jobs and good deals. On the other hand, I've heard the phrase 'big fish in a small pond' used to describe people who like being the big dogs and block things/people that would take away their power, even if those things/people are better for the community or organization. It is this mentality of the power hungry that can make the good old boys' network seem harmful.

But power (if you have it) can be difficult to give up. Apparently if you're connected to the network, you can get perks and deals not offered to the normal population. Membership in the boys' club has some definite advantages for those who can be an associate (not all white males are invited). As a member, you're privy to important information, and many critical business decisions. Club meetings are often held in such places as private golf courses, men's rooms and smoke-filled cigar bars.[24] With its unwritten rule, "No women allowed," and the environment not necessarily inviting to men of color the informal good old boys' network continues to bar unapproved white males, women and men of color from top management positions (positions that hold the most power).[25]

Just as there are white males who have or have had considerable access to power and privilege and only spread that amongst those like themselves, there are also many white males who understand what it means to be white and male in America and have used their influence and power to extend opportunity to those unlike themselves. There have been people of all races, genders and religious groups that have been and are advocates for diversity—but white males are the group that some don't see in this light. Some think that every white male is a part of the good ol' boy network—this is indeed a myth. It is also a myth that white males are not advocates for the ills of society. To destroy these myths is the very reason why we address white male advocacy for diversity.

White Males as Advocates for Diversity

Just as there are white males who participate and benefit from their "whiteness and maleness" in America and from the good 'ol boy network, there are many more white males who have been and are advocates for diversity. Oftentimes, when we discuss the problems of America that transcend into the workplace (as we will later discuss in this text) it is the "white male" as a group who is seen as the perpetrator by women and people of color. This is unfortunate as this does not allow those white males who could be and are advocates for diversity to be viewed as such—instead there can be a preconceived notion by subordinate groups that ALL white males are against equality and diversity initiatives.

As far back as the development of this country, you will find white males who fought for justice and rights of all people. These white males did not believe in the privileges being bestowed upon landowning white men and fought to change this power structure. Even before the declaration of political independence on the part of the British North American colonies, slavery was under attack by a number of religious and political leaders for example, from the Quakers and Evangelicals, such as William Wilberforce (1759–1833), Thomas Clarkson (1760–1846), and Granville Sharp (1735–1813). Antislavery movements flourished both in the metropolis and in the colonies.[26] In 1787, Abbé Grégoire (1750–1831), Abbé Raynal (1713–1796), the Marquis de Lafayette (1757–1834), and others formed an antislavery committee in France called the Société des Amis des Noirs, which took up the issue in the convened Estates General in 1789 and later pushed for broadening the basis of citizenship in the National Assembly. Their benevolent proposals, however, were overtaken by other events.[27]

During the Civil Rights Era on August 4, 1964, in Neshoba Country, Mississippi, the bodies of three civil-rights workers—two white men and one black male—are found in an earthen dam, six weeks into a federal investigation backed by President Johnson.[28] James E. Chaney, 21; Andrew Goodman, 21; and Michael Schwerner, 24, had been working together to register black voters in Mississippi, and, on June 21, had gone to investigate the burning of a black church. They were arrested by the police on speeding charges, incarcerated for several hours, and then released after dark into the hands of the Ku Klux Klan, who murdered not just the black man but all the men.[29]

Then there is Oliver Hill, a Roanoke-raised civil rights lawyer/pioneer. As one of the architects of the Brown v. Board of Education desegregation case he recently died at the age of 100 in Richmond, Virginia. Governor Tim Kaine of Virginia spoke of Hill and was quoted as saying "Few individuals in Virginia's rich history have worked as tirelessly as Oliver Hill to make life better for all of our citizens," "His life's work was predicated on the simple truth that all men and women truly are created equal."[30]

These are just a few white males who fought for the rights of equality, there are so many many more. There are also a substantial number of white males who fight today against discrimination and for workplace diversity initiatives. In May 2003, a group of white males known as Angry White Males for Affirmative Action led by Paul Kivel marched on behalf of Affirmative Action. This issue was being addressed at the University of Michigan. Paul Kivel created this group of white males because he states in many of his speeches that he became involved in the struggle to end racism as a college student more than thirty years ago.[31] It is then that he began to see the visible and devastating impact that racism had on people of color. He is the founder of the nationally recognized Oakland's Men's Project and has conducted hundreds of workshops on racism and anti-violence for teens and men all over the country.[32] He sees affirmative action and diversity programs as one way to address the racism that has benefited some and disadvantaged others.

The bottom-line is that in order to fight the isms, we need all people—white males, women, and people of color, etc. to work against the systems that perpetuate injustice and harm diversity. Yet it is frequently assumed that diversity initiatives should involve only women and people of color. This belief that white males should not participate with diversity is not only false, but also damaging. It keeps white men, who gain just like others from the benefits that diversity provides and white male leaders who represent the largest power base in our culture, from participating in diversity initiatives.[33]

So what can white men who are not aligned with diversity initiatives do to aid in the struggle for equality in the workplace?

Cultivate a hunger for new learning. By learning about other points of view, other cultures, even differences in gender perspectives, white males provide themselves a basis for being effective at fostering diversity and gaining for themselves, and others, the benefits diversity provide.[34]

Learn to speak out about what they've learned. White men should talk to others including other white men on diversity issues instead of leaving it to those people most directly impacted by workplace inequities. White males may need to recognize that speaking out demonstrates publicly their commitment to the value of diversity and helps to diminish the view that diversity is just about women and people of color.[35]

Recognize that they must be equal partners with members of subordinated groups. Partnering in an organization's diversity activities and initiatives lets it be known that not only does everyone have something to gain by diversity but everyone has something to contribute.[36]

Recognize that many in their group have not been subjected to the same experiences of discrimination. Subordinated group members have different experiences and views toward equality, thus leaving differing views toward workplace injustice and perceived opportunity.[37]

Support diversity initiatives. Change occurs much more easily when it comes from the top down, not bottom up.[38]

These are a few suggestions that can help address difference in a positive manner. But the real point is that—the building of successful diversity partnerships requires commitment not just from women and people of color but also from white men.

Discrimination against White Males

Just like other groups, many Whites came to America without freedom but the difference is they could eventually buy their freedom. Unlike the institution of slavery that was imposed on many blacks, Native Americans and other people of color—there was never to be any freedom—EVER. But does this mean that whites were without discrimination? We know that white women just like many other women were not given equal rights, as they could not vote, own land or be in control of their own destiny by many respects (which will be discussed in a later chapter). But what about white men? As we discuss this history of discrimination in White America, we will challenge the thought that white males are the sole group that has not experienced discrimination.

A generation ago, the major labor pool in the U.S. was White males, and jobs were designed to meet the needs of these workers. Seven out of ten American workers were men and fathers of families. As a rule, wives did not work outside the home. So, Caucasian men were the "traditional" workers. In 1990, they represented about 75 percent of the labor force. Back then life was so much simpler for management because most in this group held the same values. They held a belief in Christianity, family, were able bodied and adhered to a heterosexual lifestyle. However, today with the increase in diversity in the workplace and lifestyles, we will find that there are more white males as well as others who do not fit the mode of this traditional worker.

Some White males are parts of groups in society who experience discrimination in the workplace. These include older workers, disabled workers, non-Christian workers and homosexuals. But, this is only half of the story, as these aren't the only accounts of discrimination against White males in America.

The Irish

The Penal Laws, a series of ferocious enactments, dating from 1695, and not repealed in their entirety until Catholic emancipation in 1829, were aimed at the destruction of Catholicism in Ireland.[39] These laws were provoked by Irish support of the Stuarts after the Protestant William of Orange was invited to ascend the English throne in 1689, and England faced the greatest Catholic power in Europe – France. At this critical moment the Catholic Irish took up arms in support of the Stuarts.[40] James the II's standards was raised in Ireland, and he, with an Irish Catholic army, was defeated on Irish soil, at the battle of the Boyne, near Drogheda, on July 1, 1690.[41]

This threat to England had been alarming, and vengeance followed. Irish intervention on behalf of the Stuarts was to be made impossible forever by reducing the Catholic Irish to helpless impotence. They were, in the words of a contemporary, to become 'insignificant slaves, fit for nothing but to hew wood and draw water', and to achieve this object the Penal Laws were devised. These laws barred Catholics from the army, navy, the law, and commerce and from every civic activity. Catholics could not vote, hold any office under the Crown, or purchase land, and Catholic estates were dismembered.[42] Education was made almost impossible especially since Catholics could not attend schools, keep or run schools, nor send their children to be educated in Ireland or abroad.[43] They could not purchase land, lease land, keep arms or even receive a gift of land. These Penal Laws even allowed the Protestants to hunt Catholic priests as a sport.[44]

The Penal Laws caused material damage that was great; ruin was widespread, old families disappeared and old estates were broken up; but the most disastrous effects were moral. The Penal Laws brought lawlessness, dissimulation and revenge. The Irish character, above all the character of peasantry, did become degraded and debased. The basis of religion was used to divide the Irish from the English.

The next occurrence, the Great Potato Famine, caused destruction of the Irish and forced them to seek refuge in the Americas. The great potato famines of 1845-51 reduced the population of Irish from 8 million to 6.6 million through starvation, disease and emigration to Britain and America.[45] The potato was the Irish's agricultural base and their main food product. When the potato crop was destroyed by blight, the result was devastating: the people's only source of food was gone.[46]

Irish Catholics came to this country as an oppressed race. When they were back home these "native Irish or papists" suffered something similar but not as devastating as American slavery under English Penal Laws. Because of this the Irish and African Americans had a lot in common and a lot of contact when the Irish first arrived in America.[47] They lived side-by-side and shared workspaces. In the early years of immigration the poor Irish and Blacks were thrown together, very much part of the same class competing for the same jobs. In the census of 1850, the term "mulatto" appears for the first time due primarily to inter-marriage between Irish and African Americans.[48]

Furthermore, there was a custom of marrying White (Irish) servants to Black slaves in order to produce slave offspring. The offspring would be slaves because anyone who had more than 1/8 or so of African blood was considered a "Negro".[49] Many Irish children became slaves through this custom. If a servant is forced to mate with a slave in order to produce slave children for her slave master, is she not a slave?

At this point, you may be wondering what happened that allowed the Irish to finally be accepted into society. Many historians say they gave up their greenness for whiteness. An article by a Black writer in an 1860 edition of the *Liberator* explained how the Irish ultimately attained acceptance into this White protestant world that they were outsiders to.[50] A Catholic priest in Philadelphia said to the Irish people in that city, 'You are all poor, and chiefly laborers, the blacks are poor laborers; many of the native Whites are laborers; now, if you wish to succeed, you must do everything that the White natives do, no matter how degrading, and do it for less than they can afford to do it for.' The Irish adopted this plan; they lived on less than the White Americans could live upon, and worked for less, and the result is, that nearly all the menial employments was monopolized by the Irish.[51] There were other avenues open to other American white men, and so the threat of the Irish was not taken so harshly.

Once the Irish secured themselves in those jobs, they made sure blacks were kept out.[52] They realized that as long as they continued to work alongside Blacks, they would be considered no different. Later the Irish became prominent in the Labor movement, free Blacks were excluded from participation.

Now you may be wondering: I have never heard this story told this way. Unfortunately, this is not a myth it is the truth. Many historical accounts of this time however play little significance to race and have presented a biased picture of the events of this time leaving out very important facts. Race was of such importance in America that one oppressed race, Irish Catholics, learned how to collaborate in the oppression of another race, African Americans, in order to secure their place in the White republic. Was this wrong? Do you think they knew of any other options to change their status in this new land?

In an individualistic society it is often necessary for people to do what is best for them rather than what is good for others. So, the Irish melted into the pot. By giving up a lot of their Irish cultural heritage and the legacy of oppression and discrimination back home, they thus gained acceptance. The Irish came to the U.S. with nothing and were not seen as valuable and so they did what was necessary in their eyes to gain acceptance and value and to end the discrimination they felt here in America. The point is that, in a society where difference is appreciated this would not have been necessary.

German American Wartime Mistreatment

Thanks to federal legislation and effective activism by their ethnic group, U.S. government mistreatment of the 120,000 Japanese & Japanese Americans is well known. Many even know that an additional 2,000 Japanese from Latin America were picked up so that the United States would have prisoners to exchange with families in this country and in Latin America. But, after almost 60 years, the German American experience remains buried. The few surviving, aged internees remember their experiences well, despite years of trying to forget. Many say that these memories haunt them. Mostly, because they are Americans who revere freedom and they want the dreadful saga of their wartime mistreatment told so it will never happen again.

While their numbers are much smaller, the stories are virtually the same. In the days after the Dec. 7, 1941, bombing of Pearl Harbor, some 31,000 "enemy aliens" were swept up—ostensibly because of possible alliances to the Axis forces.[51] Among them were about 10,000 Germans and 3,000 Italians, and the rest were Japanese and smatterings of other European groups. These enemy aliens lost everything.

The 1918 Codification of Alien Enemy Act of 1798, 50 USC 21-24, permitted the apprehension and internment of aliens of "enemy ancestry" by US government upon declaration of war or threat of invasion.[52] The President was given blanket authority as to "enemy alien" treatment. Civil liberties could be completely ignored because enemy aliens had no protection under this 202-year old law. Government oppression is likely during wartime, but is it appropriate?

Due to this act, after the bombing of Pearl Harbor Roosevelt issued identical Presidential Proclamations 2525, 2526 and 2527 branding German, Italian and Japanese nationals as enemy aliens, authorizing internment, and travel and property ownership restrictions.[53] A blanket presidential warrants authorized U.S. Attorney General Francis Biddle to have the FBI arrest a large number of "dangerous enemy aliens" based on the CDI.[54] Hundreds of German aliens were arrested by the end of the day. The FBI raided many homes and hundreds more were detained before war was even declared on Germany.

From 1942 till 1945 thousands of German aliens and German Americans were arrested, interned, excluded, paroled, exchanged and generally harassed and discriminated against by a suspicious country.[55] Many of the Germans left Germany because of the Nazis, and then came to the U.S. and were considered Nazis. According to Joseph Fallon, co-author of the five-volume *German Americans in the World Wars*, writes on his Website: "The majority of the best-selling collegiate and secondary school history texts in the United States claim that, unlike Japanese Americans, the German and Italian Americans were not arrested and interned; and both the print and electronic media have propagated this myth. He further states, "that for the most part, the history of internment has been either quieted or distorted."[56]

Italian American Wartime Mistreatment

In November of 1999, Senator Robert G. Torricelli introduced the following bill, "Wartime Violation of Italian American Civil Liberties Act" to provide for the preparation of a Government report detailing injustices suffered by Italian Americans during World War II, and a formal acknowledgement of such injustices by the President.[57]

Based on this bill, Congress has made the following findings[58]:

- The freedom of more than 600,000 Italian-born immigrants in the United States and their families was restricted during World War II by government measures that branded them "enemy aliens".

- During World War II more than 10,000 Italian Americans living on the West Coast were forced to leave their homes and prohibited from entering coastal zones. More than 50,000 were subjected to curfews.

- Thousands of Italian American immigrants were arrested, and hundreds were interned in military camps.

- The impact of the wartime experience was devastating to Italian American communities in the United States, and its effects are still being felt.

- A deliberate policy kept these measures from the public during the war. Even 50 years later much information is still classified, the full story remains unknown to the public, and the United States Government has never acknowledged it in any official capacity.

A particular section in the Act states[59]:

"It is the sense of the Congress that ... (1) the story of the treatment of Italian Americans during World War II needs to be told in order to acknowledge that these events happened, to remember those whose lives were unjustly disrupted and whose freedoms were violated, to help repair the damage to the Italian American community, and to discourage the occurrence of similar injustices and violations of civil liberties in the future."

The noted poet and philosopher, George Santayana, observed that those who cannot remember the past are condemned to repeat it. This is exactly what North Carolina Representative Melvin L. Watt was saying in the discussion of the bill: You need to confront the truth before you can deal with assuring that that sad chapter is not repeated.

So, have white males experienced discrimination? Yes. I conclude this section with the following myth and fact:

Myth: White males have not experienced discrimination in America

Fact: White males from various ethnicities and backgrounds have and do experience discrimination in America.

Concluding Thoughts

People of all races, genders, religions, etc. have much to gain by effectively managing workplace diversity. This starts with people of color not blaming white males as a group for the ills of the world and ethnic pathology. It starts with white males eliminating their suspicion that people of color and women excel for only "those" traits and not their work ethics, skills and ability. Both of these negative mindsets denude true collaboration and respect. It seems obvious that if White males still hold the majority of top management positions then for diversity initiatives to be successful, it must have white male leadership support.

End of Chapter Questions

1. Name groups of white males who have experienced discrimination and why.

2. How did white women and white men settlers opportunities differ?

3. In America, the Irish, Germans and Italians are no longer referred to as Irish-Americans, German-Americans and Italian-Americans—they are just White/Caucasians, so why are there still groups that have the hyphenation such as Arab-Americans and African-Americans? How does this relate to the melting pot theory from the previous chapter?

4. Why were some White Americans considered immigrants and others not considered immigrants?

Internet Exercise

Using the Internet or www.google.com find an article that addresses the role of white men and diversity. Summarize what the article says and state if you agree or disagree with its viewpoint.

Search Key Words: role of white males and diversity

End of Chapter Exercise

Do we have the same perspective?

Directions: Using the chart in the chapter that espouses the workplace style differences between races, answer the questions below. Then find a partner and compare your answers to see if your viewpoints are the same.

1. You are part of a team that has diverse races of individuals. Some people show up late to the meetings even though the times were agreed upon. Others socialize once at the meeting because they are not task oriented but relationship oriented. Who is right? How do you bridge the gap—of the extremes?

2. You are having a community fundraiser and trying to elect a leader of your group, do you elect someone with the same background as that community? Why or Why not?

3. There is a group meeting and an employee comes dressed informally. There is no dress code but you know that people are judging this employee by their personal appearance. You hired this person and know that they are more than qualified to do the job however by their appearance they are not convincing. You have read the chart in this chapter and realize that some cultures do not believe in the European style of formal dress for the workplace. What do you do?

Managing Workplace Diversity

References

1. Fort Gordon Equal Opportunity Office. (n.d.). *White American Experience*. Retrieved from http://www.gordon.army.mil/eoo/white.htm

2. Ballagh, J. C. (1895). *White Servitude in the Colony of Virginia*. Baltimore MD: John Hopkins University Press.

3. Binder, F. M. Binder & Reimers, D. M. (1992). The way we lived: Essays and Documents. *American Social History*, 1, 1607-1877.

4. Cunnington, P. (1974). *Costume of Household Servants from the Middle Ages to 1900*. London, UK; Harper and Row Publishers, Inc.

5. Ibid.

6. Ibid.

7. Galson, D. W. (1981). *White Servatude in Colonial America: An Economic Analysis*. Cambridge, UK: Cambridge University Press.

8. Haynie, W. P. (1996). *Northumberland County Virginia Records of Indentured Servants 1650-1795*. Westminster, MA: Heritage Books, Inc.

9. Smith, A. E. (1947). *Colonists in Bondage: White Servitude and Convict Labor in America, 1607-1776*. Chapel Hill, NC.: University of North Carolina.

10. Ibid.

11. Ibid.

12. Oosterwal, E. (n.d.). *Addressing the Concerns of the White Man as Full Diversity Partners*. Retrieved from http://www.geocities.com/oosterwal/works/whitediversity.html

13. Black, R. S., Mrasek, K. D. & Ballinger, R. (2003, Spring). Individualist and Collectivist Values in Transition Planning for Culturally Diverse Students with Special Needs. *Journal of Psychology*, 25(2)(3).

14. Ziegahn, L. (2001). *Considering Culture in the Selection of Teaching Approaches for Adults*. Columbus, OH: ERIC Clearinghouse on Adult Career and Vocational Education.

15. Ibid.

16. Hofstede, G. (1994). *Cultures and Organizations - Intercultural Cooperation and its importance for survival*. London: HarperCollins.

17. Ibid.

18. Proudman, B. (2005, January/February). *White Men and Diversity: An Oxymoron?* Retrieved from http://www.mcca.com/index.cfm?fuseaction=page.viewpage&pageid=809

Managing Workplace Diversity

19. Helms, J. E. (1992). *A Race Is a Nice Thing to Have: A Guide to Being A White Person or Understanding the White Persons in your life.* Topeka, KS: Content Communications.

20. Ziegahn, L. (2001). *Considering Culture in the Selection of Teaching Approaches for Adults, Columbus.* OH: ERIC Clearinghouse on Adult Career and Vocational Education.

21. Hofstede, G. (1994). *Cultures and Organizations - Intercultural Cooperation and its importance for survival.* London: HarperCollins.

22. Elliott, C., Adams, R. J., & Sockalingam, S. (n.d.). Office of Multicultural Health, Department of Human Resources, Oregon Retrieved from http://www.vdh.state.va.us/ohpp/clasact/documents/clasact/general/normative.pdf

23. Proudman, B. (2005, January/February). *White Men and Diversity: An Oxymoron?* Retrieved from http://www.mcca.com/index.cfm?fuseaction=page.viewpage&pageid=809

24. Wikipedia. (n.d.). *Good ol' boy network.* Retrieved from http://en.wikipedia.org/wiki/Good_ol'_boy_network

25. Roediger, D. (1991). *The Wages of Whiteness: Race and the Making of the American Working Class.* New York, NY: Verso.

26. Knight, F. W. (2005, Fall). The Haitian Revolution and the Notion of Human Rights. *The Journal of the Historical Society*, (5)3, 391-416.

27. Ibid

28. Linder, D. O. (2002, Winter). *Bending Toward Justice: John Doar and the Mississippi Burning Trial.* Mississippi Law Journal, (72)2.

29. Ibid.

30. *Sorenson Institute for Political Leadership.* (n.d.). University of Virginia. Retrieved from http://www.sorenseninstitute.org/newsroom/entry/memoriam-oliver-hill

31. Kivel, P. (2002). *Uprooting Racism: How White people can work for racial justice.* Canada: New Society Publishers.

32. Ibid.

33. Atkinson, W. (2001, September). Bringing diversity to White Men, *HR Magazine*, 46(9), 76-83.

34. Helms, J. E. (1992). *A Race is a Nice Thing to Have: A Guide to Being a White Person or Understanding the White Persons in Your Life.* Topeka, KS: Content Communications.

35. Lester, J. S. (1994). *The Future of White Men and Other Diversity Dilemmas.* Berkeley, CA: Conari Press.

36. Oosterwal, E. (n.d.). Addressing the Concerns of the White Man as Full Diversity Partners. Retrieved from http://www.geocities.com/oosterwal/works/whitediversity.html

37. Katznelson, I. (2005). *When Affirmative Action Was White*. New York, NY: W.W. Norton & Company.

38. Henry, W., III. (1990, April 9). Beyond the Melting Pot. *Time*.

39. Dunn, J. (2004). *The Glories of Ireland*. Retrieved from http://www.gutenberg.org/files/12111/12111-8.txt

40. Ibid.

41. Ibid.

42. Nyland, C., Dimand, R. W. (2003). *The Status of Women in Classical Economic Thought*. Vermont: Edward Elgar Publishing.

43. Ibid.

44. Ibid.

45. Goodbody, R. (1996). *Transactions of the Central Relief Committee of the Society of Friends during the Famine in Ireland*. Dublin: Edmund Burke Publisher, 1852.

46. Dunn, J. (2004). *The Glories of Ireland*. Retrieved from http://www.gutenberg.org/files/12111/12111-8.txt

47. Dooley, B. (1998). *Black and Green. The Fight for Civil Rights in Northern Ireland and Black America*. Pluto Press: London, 1998.

48. Ibid.

49. Ibid.

50. Hodges, G. R. (1998). *Slavery, Freedom & Culture Among Early American Workers*. New York: M.E. Sharpe.

51. Ebel, K. E. (2003, February 24). *WWII Violations of German American Civil Liberties by the US Government*. Retrieved from: http://www.ams.org/bookpages/hmath-34/PioneeringWomen2.pdf

52. Ibid.

53. German American Internee Coalition. Retrieved from http://www.gaic.info/history.html

54. Ibid.

55. Ibid.

56. Earle, S. M. (2000, January 23). Germans, too, were imprisoned in WWII. *Concord Monitor*. Retrieved from http://www.foitimes.com/internment/Ebelcm.htm

57. U.S. Congressional Bibliographies. (n.d.). Retrieved from http://www.lib.ncsu.edu/congbibs/house/106hdgst1.html

58. 106th Congress. PUBLIC LAW 106–451—NOV. 7, 2000 114 STAT. 1947 Public Law 106–451

59. Ibid.

Chapter Five

Understanding Women & Work

Equality is difficult, but superiority is painful.

Serere proverb

Chapter Five

UNDERSTANDING WOMEN & WORK

Chapter Objectives

After reading this chapter, you should be able to:

- define what some refer to as "women's work."

- identify how women's work changed after industrialization.

- discuss women and physically demanding jobs.

- describe stereotypes that plague various cultures of women.

- understand the difference between the glass and concrete ceiling.

- argue equal pay issues.

What would the world be like without women? Based upon the theory of procreation, the world and its population as we know it would be extinct. But, is procreation the only type of work women are good for? This brings us to the topic of women's work—or is there such a thing? In addressing women as a diverse entity in the workplace it is essential that we address this topic of "women's work."

In order for there to be women's work there must also be men's work. But, when we go back to the days when people bartered for a living and everyone worked at home there wasn't this designation. Everyone worked the farm, did chores, cared for the family and participated in a skill or craft that provided a living for the family. Women chopped wood, worked in the fields, brought kids into the world and then went back to working. Everyone was paid equally by bartering for what the family needed, as there was no one "breadwinner." Yet, somehow working at home meaning domestic work, family maintenance, the reproduction and socialization of children became "women's work." This work typically earns no pay whereas working outside the home, a "man's job" earns pay.

Industrialization Changes Women's Participation in the Workforce

This term "women's work" was quite common prior to the Industrial Revolution as the free American born women performed their work tasks in the home and rarely worked outside the home. In pre-industrial America, women and girls not only performed much of the labor necessary for family survival but participated in the household manufacture of yarn, cloth, candles, and food. But, this simple definition of work life soon ended as the industrial revolution transformed many women's lives. By 1790, the availability of water-powered machinery such as spinning frames and carding machines enabled businessmen to substitute power tools for women's hand labor in the manufacture of cloth.[1] In December of 1790, the first water-powered spinning mill opened its doors in Pawtucket, Rhode Island.[2] By 1813, 175 other cotton and wool spinning mills, employing entire families, punctuated the river rich New England landscape.[3] This was the beginning of women working in factories.

Until the immigration wave of the 1840s many of the female factory workers were single, native-born Caucasian women recruited from middle-class farms.[4] During this time, many of these women worked over seventy hours a week at substandard wages.

Managing Workplace Diversity

As more women were recruited to work in the factories, the women's experiences as factory workers varied according to their ethnicity, race, and class, and differed from those of men. An occupational hierarchy among women prevailed in which Yankee women enjoyed the greatest access to the best-paying women's jobs; daughters of immigrants concentrated in semiskilled positions; and immigrant women worked in the least skilled, most poorly paid occupations. As a rule, free African American women were excluded from factory employment and were kept mainly as poorly paid domestic workers.[5]

Rigid gender-based occupational segregation ensured that even the highest-paid, most senior female factory worker could expect to receive less than a man employed in the same establishment. Furthermore, by the 1840s women represented 50 percent of factory workers in the shoe and textile industries but even with these numbers they rarely worked alongside men; instead, they held jobs whose low wages affirmed the belief that women's work was less skilled than men's and less important to family survival.[6]

Most women holding factory jobs in the first decades of industrialization were single and could therefore participate as factory labor. Immigrant and working-class wives and mothers were more likely to participate in the wage-based labor market as outworkers. In New York City, the foremost manufacturing center of the antebellum period, outwork was the dominant form of female employment and it was also one of the most exploitive.[7]

Outwork enabled women confined to their homes to contribute to the family economy while still performing tasks as wives and mothers. But merchants took advantage of the women's limited mobility and bargaining power by withholding and cutting wages. Already doubly burdened by society's expectations of them as wives and wage earners, female outworkers coped with their precarious financial status by accepting more contracted jobs to make ends meet.

Although upper- and middle-class white women were typically spared the long hours and low wages that characterized both factory labor and outwork, they were nevertheless forced to contend with the ideological devaluation of housework that industrialization spawned.[8] As "real" labor became more closely identified with work that had a concrete market value, women lost out.

Childbearing, child rearing, cooking, cleaning, and other traditionally female tasks, whether performed by elite women, working-class women, or a growing number of domestic servants, were demeaned. The household, increasingly perceived in opposition to a male-dominated market as a feminized space, came to be viewed as a site of leisure and consumption rather than labor and production. This left women's work out as a variable to be considered when determining the pay associated with these types of duties.

The Economic System & Women's Work

Would you believe that our economic system in the U.S. (capitalism) has set the tone for the wage-labor system (pay vs. no pay) used for men and women? Capitalism operates as a system where prices and wages are often set by demand and supply, thus making certain items valuable and other's not so valuable which is determined by the desired demand for the item and the price paid for it. For example, we value a Mercedes more than a Pontiac not just because the Mercedes is a good car but also because it is pricey and that often denotes value. So when we put women's work into this context, we find that women's work is not valuable since there is no set price paid for it. Meaning women aren't paid for their work so it must not be valuable.

Whether you buy this argument or not, it is true that this women's work continues to be seen by some people as natural functions, instinctive and of little importance when compared with men's work. This downgrading of what is known to many as women's work has been the cause of many myths surrounding women and their value to the workplace.

Up until World War II, most White married women living with their husbands worked outside their homes only if they were extremely poor or if a hardship was experienced, such as the husband was unable to pay the bills or unable to work.[9] If this occurred the family was shamed and this often negatively affected the man's self esteem because he was unable to fill this societal expectation of men.

But, does the above example prove that women were unable to work or do the same job as men in the workplace or was it that they were expected not to? Trust me, there is a difference. If we knew more about women's history we would know that being able to do a job is more a factor of an individual's personality, skills, heredity, learning ability, etc... than just a factor of one's gender. For every job that a man can do you will find a woman that is capable of doing that same job.

Women and physically demanding jobs

If you look at the physical challenges as it relates to male and female Firefighters, they often don't have to meet the same standards: while men must be able to bench-press 200 lbs., women are asked only to bench-press 150.[10] Does this make it obvious that men are stronger than women and women therefore can't cut it when it comes to a physically demanding job.

Karen Messing has a book entitled One-Eyed Science (1998) which deals with occupational health. Some of the ideas she presents in this book can help explain why differential strength requirements exist for male and female workers in such jobs as firefighting (though the argument has also been raised for construction work, police work, certain areas of the military, and other traditionally male occupations.

According to her chapter "Are Women Biologically fit for Jobs? Are Jobs Fit for Women?" (Ch 3) she indicates that tests of this sort are based on average abilities.[11] Of course, some women will be able to lift the same heavy weight that some men will not be able to lift and vice-versa. What may make a difference in a woman's ability to lift the object is how she is being told to lift it.

If workers are told that there is one appropriate way to lift an object (like a person in a fire), and that lifting procedure was developed using men who were the traditional workers in that field, then the procedure will most likely make the most of men's upper body strength.[12] What Messing and her colleagues found was that if women are allowed to develop their own techniques to lift heavy objects, then they will most likely shift the burden toward their lower-body strength and perform the task successfully; women will use their hips.[13]

For instance, when women hold babies for long periods of time - they balance the baby on their hips. This is a practical solution to the problem of holding and/or lifting heavy objects whether these objects are babies or adults caught in a fire. When given some freedom to structure how women will perform certain tasks on the job, women are much more likely to be able to perform on par with men than when women are told "this is how it needs to be done."[14] The argument Messing makes is that jobs traditionally held by men (such as firefighting) developed tests (such as strength tests) specifically with men's bodies in mind.[15]

Managing Workplace Diversity

In studying the history of various cultures, we find several examples of different ethnic groups that prove that women were valued or given the work responsibilities of men. There were also times in history where little distinction was given to the work for men vs. women. During the enslavement of Blacks, was it only the men that worked the fields from sunrise to sunset? No, the price of slaves was often based upon how healthy and stocky they were—men or women. The women worked in the field right along with the men and they sometimes did this with their babies on their back. These enslaved women also were beaten just like the men and put back in the field to carry on as their male counterparts.

Furthermore, in Messing's book she uses an example of a baker - also a traditionally male job. The baker must carry sacks of sugar which could be of any weight – the decision to make sacks of sugar 40 pounds each instead of 20 pounds each is a political decision which takes for granted the strength of the "average" (male) baker who will be required to lift the bag.[15] But such sacks of sugar could just as easily have been made 20 pounds a piece. Eventhough some women could likely lift the 40 lb. bag of if she is allowed to develop a technique suited to her own body, the average woman may not be able to.

Messing's main point is that jobs are adaptable. They have usually been adapted to men because men were the traditional workers in those jobs. When women come along and ask that the job be adapted to their average capabilities, however, this strikes people as being unfair, as somehow lowering the standards of the job, or as admitting that women are not as capable as men, or in creating "double standards". In fact, the job itself, the techniques, and the equipment used were designed to "fit" with men's average capabilities (they were and many still are – male standards) and so are biased in favor of male workers.

Again, this is not to say that some women will not be able to perform the job or that some men won't. But, too often the equipment and techniques used in a particular job are not suited to the average woman, but then this is used to justify the notion that the average woman is not suited for the job. However, Messing suggests we think of it differently:"Fitness for a job must be considered as an interaction between individuals (with all their possibilities for change) and a plastic, adaptable work environment.[16] As long as the job gets done does it matter if you carry two 20 pound bags or one 40 pound bag?

In studying Native Americans, we will find many tribes not only shared the work between men and women (even when it was physically demanding) but many gave women power over the family and the tribes. If only the pilgrims could have learned more than just to survive from the Native Americans we would not have had to fight for rights for women. Rights that already existed in many of the tribes structure. If we go back and revisit the Thanksgiving Dinner that occurred at Plymouth Rock we will find that the Puritan women stood and waited as expected as there men were seated and ate whereas the Indian women ate right alongside their men because they were considered equal and were valued. Unfortunately, this country was founded not on the Native American's values but on the early settlers who believed women were second class citizens.

Furthermore, numerous rationalizations have been used by employees for not employing women in certain fields or for not paying women as much as men. Many women were and still are excluded from skilled jobs (opportunities to learn trades). They were and are often forced to accept low wages and poor working conditions. Basically, in prior times when there was enough men to meet the demands of the labor force the women who were free to work for wages could be treated with less favor.

Stereotypes of Women

The above treatment of women in the workplace is not just attributed to the culture that the pilgrims brought with them to start the new world but is also a result of stereotypes and sexism. Sexism results in the process of assigning life roles according to gender, which is passed down from one generation to the next. Instead of these beliefs about women and their ability being unlearned they continue to be learned.[17] Sexism is conditioning that can start very early in a female's life. But, even worse than this are the stereotypes that follow many women throughout their adult years. These stereotypes interact closely with racial and class stereotypes and they tend to form many representations of women in the media.

For example, the "Jewish American Princess" concept dominates the film *Clueless* (1995). Black and Latina women often fill the roles of domestics, as in films such as *Forrest Gump* (1994) and *The First Wives Club* (1996). In some rap music, the stereotype of the Black woman as emasculating and manipulative is central to the message. Even though as you watch the Miss America pageant you won't find the women gyrating across the stage (as in the rap videos) but is it any less demeaning to have women parading around in high heels and bathing suits to prove you can be Miss or Mrs. America?

Lesbians have had to watch as the pendulum of popular culture swings from the stereotype of man hating and masculine, to chic and fashionable, going from one extreme to another. Stereotypes have been used both to define women and to control them. They limit the possibilities women envision for themselves and therefore damage women's self esteem and deprive society of women's potential. The following have been some stereotypes that refer to women in our society. Many of these are sexual stereotypes of women that are currently in operation and were formed in the past century under racist and classist ideologies. Read below and see if you identify with any of the images that have been placed on women.

Anglo-American Stereotype

Anglo-American women of the upper and middle classes, as we have already discussed, were generally confined to the following roles: wife, mother, and one not discussed— also as a mistress. This class of woman was considered to be the White man's ideal companion and thus the mother of his children. The White woman was considered to be the "true woman." [18] As the true woman she was often expected to have the following four virtues: piety, purity, submissiveness, and domesticity. The external physical signs of true womanhood were delicacy, softness, and weakness.

This true woman was placed on a pedestal especially during the antebellum and post-Civil War South periods. This true woman was to be protected by White men.[19] We will later read of laws that were imparted to not just protect White women but to protect them from the evils of interracial relationships. But, what we must remember is that this true woman image did not often extend itself to the working-class poor White woman. The working class White woman while her image was tainted; she still was not viewed as a woman of color.

Native American Stereotype

These women have been stereotyped as strong, spiritual "earth mothers". During the period where the pilgrims took over the land as well as control of the Native people, the Native woman was not seen as a threat. She still is not often seen as a threat and therefore has not been subjected to some of the more rigorous stereotyping that other women have seen in recent years. In fact, she along with the males of her ethnicity has been deemed invisible and really not an important entity in this society.[20]

However, this has not always been the case. During the period of colonization and the westward expansion of the United States, two dominant stereotypes of Native women existed. The first was a variant of the mammy stereotype who was loyal, trusting and trustworthy and therefore redeemed themselves as being useful to White men of power.[21]

The second stereotype was as a "squaw", in which they were just seen as servants to men--be it sexual servitude or domestic; they were also seen as maintaining the Natives' culture while their men hunted and acted as warriors.[22]

African American Stereotype

In the nineteenth century, enslaved women of African descent were expected to be physically strong—able to bear fatigue and reproduce "property" for the White master.[23] African American women became the very image that the "true" woman was not.[24] She was often viewed as promiscuous and overtly sexual and after emancipation, the stereotype of the strong, Black woman turned into the controlling image of the mammy—who was a faithful servant to the affluent White family.[25] Often in the workplace, Black women have complained of being treated like a mammy where she is expected to appear warm and nurturing at all times.

Other images exist such as matriarch and welfare mother. Where the welfare mother is characterized as having a lot of children and this concept goes back to the breeder role that was expected of Black women during slavery.[26] This same welfare mother with all of her children produced out of wedlock is also categorized as a bad mother who is content to sit around and live off the government. The last stereotype of jezebel is another way to view black women. The common theme of all these stereotypes revolves around the issues of race, gender and class oppression.

Asian American Stereotype

Asian women of all nationalities are most often stereotyped as quiet, delicate and submissive, especially to men's desires. The two most common sexual stereotypes are as a geisha or mail order bride.[27] While there have been instances in past history that used some Asian women as mail order brides, it is not a characteristic that is attributable to all Asian women. The sexual stereotype that prevails around Asian women is one where they lack aggressive behaviors appealing to the weak characteristic that the "true" woman was to exhibit.[28] According to the stereotypes of submissiveness and weakness, Asian women make ideal wives because they make few demands, never complain and exist only to serve. These stereotypes that limit the roles and opportunities for Asian women are as controlling as the role of weakness for Anglo women and welfare mother for Black women.

Latina/Hispanic American Stereotype

Oftentimes we find some overlap in these stereotypes as they apply to the various women discussed. The mammy stereotype is one not just used for Black women but also for the Latina as well.[29] Not only is she viewed as a domestic help to the white family but has also often been stereotyped to lack intelligence due to the incorrect English spoken.[30] Latinas are also seen as sexually aggressive in response to the cultural stereotype of machismo and sexually repressive, strict Roman Catholicism.[31] They are seen as welfare dependent as well.

Now after reading the above I ask you, do you think these stereotypes influence the way women are seen in the workplace? Do they contribute to the sexual harassment of women in the workplace? Do they impact the advancement of women in the workplace? Well, if you aren't yet convinced that there may be a correlation between our view of women and their equality in the workplace then read on to see if any of the following myths grab your attention.

Myths vs. Facts

MYTH ONE
Women can't be both good homemakers and workers outside the home.
FACT ONE
Throughout history when given an opportunity women have participated successfully in both the workplace and as homemakers.

MYTH TWO
Women are too emotional to be good managers.

FACT TWO
Women and men may have learned different approaches to dealing with emotions. Even though a woman's ways of expressing emotions are different, women and men—both express them.

MYTH THREE
Women have a low commitment to the world of work.

FACT THREE
Studies show that men job hop more than women.[32] The perceived lack of commitment may be due to the fact that disproportionately more women are in dead end jobs than men.

MYTH FOUR
Women lack education and work experience.

FACT FOUR
As a whole, female employees possess more education than males, their major problem is getting promotions.[33]

MYTH FIVE
Women are not interested in certain phases of business.

FACT FIVE
This may be partly true but only because women have been socialized different than men and therefore lack this type of business exposure.

MYTH SIX
Women are poor economic risks because they are frequently sick and quit work when they have children.

FACT SIX
There is no statistically significant difference in the absenteeism of men and of women employees.[34] Some women who leave the workforce to have children reenter when the children reach school age but many mothers take just a brief leave and return after several weeks.

MYTH SEVEN
Women have equality in the workplace.

FACT SEVEN
Women have made substantial strides in the workplace, in large part due to Affirmative Action.[35] But, there is still a glass ceiling.

Now that we've addressed the above myths, it is necessary to review some other issues that significantly impact women in the workplace. One such issue is the glass and concrete ceiling that women face.

Glass Ceiling*
*The statistics found in this section is courtesy of The Business and Professional Women's Foundation (2005), "101 facts on the status of workingwomen."[36]

The "glass ceiling" is a commonly used term today that implies that while many women can see the next step up the hierarchy of management, there is a ceiling/barrier there preventing them from getting there. This is based on the fact that White males still hold over 90% of all top management positions. Only 6 of the Fortune 500's CEOs were women in 2002. There were 2 in 1995 and only 11 in the Fortune 1000 in 2002. Only 3 of the Fortune 500's CEOs are African American. Among all Fortune 500 Companies, 393 have no women among their top 5 executives.

Women still comprise less than 5% of firefighters, less than 10% of state and local police officers, less than 3 % of construction workers, less than 15% of college presidents, and less than 10% of the senior-level jobs in major companies. In private industry, white men comprise 65% of officials and managers, with white women holding 24.8 %, men of color 6.5% and women of color 3.8% of these positions.

In trying to think of a rational reason for women to be so poorly represented in these male dominated fields your thought may be that women don't have these jobs because they don't want them. Sorry, but while this sounds good it is just not the case. Many studies show that women have been traditionally denied access to nontraditional jobs despite their qualifications.

The question then becomes: Why in this century do we still have these types of problems? Well I will offer you one possible explanation—leading psychologists would tell you that what we think about people, we often act out so if women are not perceived as "able" to do certain types of jobs then don't you think this mindset will impact their employment in these fields? Since what we think of people often turns into how we act against them, having stereotypes and myths can prove to be very damaging as it relates to the progression of women in the workplace.

A new study was recently published that took this concept of the glass ceiling a bit further. The study revealed that the difficult but breakable glass ceiling really refers to the experience of White women in top management but there is another ceiling that women of color must break through—the concrete ceiling.

Women of Color and the Concrete Ceiling*
*The information in this section is an excerpt reprinted with permission from Catalyst Women of Color Report: A 'Concrete Ceiling' Barring Their Advancement in Corporate America. (July 1999).[37]

In July 1999, the Catalyst *Women of Color Report* states that there is a "concrete ceiling" barring women of color from advancement in Corporate America. *Women of Color* is a three year study that has been the largest and most comprehensive examination of African American, Asian American and Hispanic women managers in professional and managerial positions in the U.S. The study is based on a survey of 1735 minority women, 300 in-depth interviews and a one-year study of 15 major companies.

"The metaphor of a concrete ceiling stands in sharp contrast to that of the glass ceiling. Not only is the concrete ceiling reported to be more difficult to penetrate, women of color say they cannot see through it to glimpse the corner office," says Catalyst President Sheila Wellington. "This study is ground breaking. It adds facts and hard data to the anecdotal information that has dominated the discussion of women of color in the workplace thus far."

The data reveals that of those companies that do have diversity programs, the diversity initiatives are not as effective as they could be or were intended to be for women of color. Seventy five percent of the women surveyed are aware of training in their corporation to address race and gender issues, but only 22 percent say their managers receive adequate training in managing a diverse workforce.   More than half (53 percent) of the women feel their companies' diversity programs are ineffective in dealing with issues of subtle racism, 26 per cent of the women say that career development is an important part of their companies' diversity programs, and only 17 percent believe their managers are held accountable for advancing women of their racial/ethnic group. And in evaluating their work environments, many women, particularly African American women, cite pervasive stereotypes.

"People assume that all women and people of color benefit from diversity initiatives," said Katherine Giscombe, PhD, Catalyst's project director for *Women of Color,* "But this simply is not true. In fact, many women in our study feel that they are overlooked in these programs. In order to make change for women of color, companies must zero in on these women and tailor programs to fit their particular needs. In this case, one size does not fit all." Some examples of companies taking this initiative seriously are:

Motorola, who has realized in its quest to advance women to the level of vice president, few of the women were women of color. Now, the company is making sure that its diversity initiatives successfully target women of color. There are currently 54 women vice-presidents and 11 are women of color.

IBM, which has a Women's Task Force suggested they focus more closely on women of color. A subcommittee of executive women of color concluded that the corporation needed to provide developmental programs as well as role models and mentorship programs for women of color. This recommendation not only aided their company but others have followed in their footsteps increasing the number of women of color executives in the U.S. from 1.3% (17 of 1,261) in 1995 to 2.3% (42 of 1,802) in 1998.

Breaking the Glass and Concrete Ceilings

While some companies, are making moves to penetrate these ceilings. There are also things that females can do early in the educational process to prepare for these obstacles.

> *According to Donna Lopiano, of the Women's Sports Foundation, "Much of what women need to know to become successful entrepreneurs and businesswomen within large organizations can be learned on the playing field. In many successful women's view—they feel every girl should learn team sports because many corporations are modeled "exactly" after sports teams. One example of this is the phrase "team player". So, if you don't know how they work, if you don't know that language, you are at a tremendous disadvantage.*[38]

Another glass/concrete breaker is when women learn to build professional networks and relationships. One way this can be done is by finding a mentor. Women in the workplace just like entrepreneurs, even those women carving a path within a large organization tend to spend so much time fighting for their project to succeed that they rarely have time to come up for air. Yet networks and mentors are essential for long-term success; they are also unbeatable sources of advice at key moments. But, what if your company does not have a formal mentoring program? Well, I say create your own mentoring relationship. How? Seek out an experienced player (executive, manager, etc) who knows the rules of the game and is willing with encouragement from you to coach you through the process.

But what else can help women transition into these higher powerful positions? Money Smarts. It is necessary for women to have "money smarts" if they are to break that ceiling. Furthermore, the notion that there needs to be tension between making money and doing good is a false one that many boys are not usually burdened with, said Godfrey in *Witness*. He states that even Mother Teresa was a powerhouse fundraiser, a fact not often recognized. Because she had people to feed, she understood the power of money and how to use it to make social change.[39]

There is no "one" solution that can be offered to break the glass or penetrate the concrete ceiling but with the rise of women as CEOs, board directors and prominence in politics this illustrates it can be done. While the glass/concrete ceiling is a very serious issue impacting the promotion of women in the workplace, there is yet another issue that seriously affects a woman's ability to be compensated for their work. This is the issue of equal pay, which can directly impact a women's opportunity to financial gain.

Equal Pay Act

Since the early days of women working, they have often been paid substantially less money for their skill level. Also, as more women participated in male dominant jobs they have been paid less for doing the same work. You may think that this is not an issue in the twenty-first century especially with the passing of the Equal Pay Act of 1963.

But today, 40 years later, women still are paid less than men—even when they do similar work and have similar education, skills and experience. In 2002, women were paid 78 cents for every dollar men received. That's $22 less to spend on groceries, housing, child care and other expenses for every $100 worth of work women do.

Because women are paid less now, women have less to spend on their families and less to save for their futures. And when women retire, they'll earn smaller pensions than men. Half of all older women with income from a private pension received less than $5,600 per year, compared with $10,340 per year for older men. Sure, women have made progress, but not nearly enough and not fast enough.[40] In the 40 years since the Equal Pay Act passed, the pay gap between men and women has narrowed by less than half, from 41 cents per dollar to 22 cents. And most of the recent change is because men's real wages have been falling, not because women's have risen. But even at this current rate of change, it is estimated that women won't achieve equal pay with men until the year 2050.

Equal Pay Is an Issue for All Working Women

Over the past few decades, laws barring discrimination in education and employment have helped give working women opportunities their mothers never had. Today, women work in many different fields each requiring different skills and experience and paying different wages. But opening doors for working women has not closed the door on pay discrimination. Equal pay is a problem for all working women, just to cite a few statistics—based on 2003 data taken from *101 facts on working women*[41]:

- For women lawyers, their median weekly earnings are nearly $373 less than those of male attorneys, and for women administrative support and clericals, they generally receive about $100 a week less than male administrative support and clericals;
- For women doctors, their median earnings are nearly $679 less each week than men's—or 58.3 percent of what male doctors earn—and for the 95 percent of nurses who are women they still earn $90 less each week than the 5 percent of nurses who are men;
- For women professors, their median pay is more than $244 less each week than men's, and for women elementary school teachers, they receive $86 less a week than men teachers;
- For women food service supervisors, who are paid $60 less each week than men in the same job, and for waitresses, whose weekly earnings are about $46 less than male waiters' earnings.

It's an Issue for Children and Families and for MEN, Too

Equal pay is not just a working woman's issue, it's a family issue. If we ended pay discrimination against women, family incomes would rise.[42] Working parents would have more to spend on household needs and more to save for their children's education or their own retirement security; working parents might be able to spend less time at work and more time with their families, a change that many families would welcome.[43]

Ending pay discrimination would directly help men. When an employer ends discrimination by raising pay for jobs traditionally done by women (teachers, for example), men in those jobs get raises as well. If we had equal pay for work of equal value, the IWPR (Institute for Women's Policy Research at www. iwpr.org) estimates, women's pay would be 13 percent higher and men's pay would go up 1 percent. Furthermore, the law bars employers from lowering men's pay to correct discrimination against women.

Women Get Paid Less Because Employers Still Discriminate in Several Ways

Jobs usually held by women pay less than jobs traditionally held by men even if they require the same education, skills and responsibilities. For example, stock and inventory clerks, who are mostly men, earn about $520 a week. General office clerks, on the other hand, are mostly women and they earn only $474 a week.

Women still don't have equal job opportunities. A newly hired woman may get a lower paying assignment than a man starting work at the same time for the same employer. That first job starts her career path and can lead to a lifetime of lower pay.

Women still don't have an equal chance at promotions, training and apprenticeships. Because all these opportunities affect pay, women don't move up the earnings ladder as quickly as men do.

For instance in 2000, Ford Motor Company agreed to pay $3.8 million to women and minority applicants who claimed they were denied jobs as entry-level assemblers because of their gender and race. (Michigan Employment Law Letter, 2000)

In 2000, CBS Broadcasting Inc. agreed to pay $8 million to 200 female technical workers who were discriminated against in salary, promotions and training, as well as harassed and retaliated against for complaining about discrimination. (EEOC, 2000)

In 2002, American Express Financials Advisors Inc. agreed to pay $31 million to settle a sex discrimination suit alleging that female professionals were paid less and unfairly denied promotions. (Daily Labor Report, Bureau of National Affairs, Feb. 22, 2002)

Discrimination Is Against the Law

An employer who pays women less than men or denies them job opportunities just because they are women is guilty of sex discrimination. Two federal laws, an executive order and some state and local laws prohibit pay discrimination against women. These cases can be brought to court as shown above and are often with an appropriate level of evidence brought to justice.

- The Equal Pay Act: Under the Equal Pay Act, which covers most workplaces states the following: it is unlawful to pay women less than men for work that is "substantially equal"—that is, almost identical unless the pay difference is based on seniority, experience or other legitimate factors.

- Title VII: Title VII of the Civil Rights Act of 1964, which covers employers with 15 or more workers, prohibits a range of discrimination, including paying women less than men even when their jobs are different if the reason for the pay difference is gender. Title VII also bars discrimination against women in hiring, promotion, training, discipline and other job aspects and makes sexual harassment against workers illegal.

- Executive Order 11246: A third measure, Executive Order 11246, is a long-standing presidential directive (which has the effect of law) that applies the protections of the Equal Pay Act and Title VII to companies that receive federal contracts.

- State and Local Laws: Many states and communities have their own fair employment laws and agencies that enforce equal pay protections and other prohibitions against sex discrimination on the job. These laws are similar to and sometimes stronger than federal laws.

How Do We Fix Pay Discrimination?

The laws that bar pay discrimination include "remedies." Proving discrimination can be hard and can take a long time. But women who win often get back pay, new job opportunities and repayment of lawyer fees and other money they spent to have their rights enforced.

Managing Workplace Diversity

What Can You Do if You Believe Your Rights Have Been Violated?

(Source: EEOC Website found at http://www.eeoc.gov/charge/overview_charge_filing.html)

1. File a discrimination charge with a federal or state anti- discrimination agency.

   If you believe you have been denied a job, paid less, passed over for promotions or discriminated against in other ways because you're a woman, you can file a complaint with the EEOC office in your area. Generally, you must file your complaint within 180 days of the discriminatory action. You don't need a lawyer; the EEOC will help you prepare the case and advise you of additional rights you may have or steps you should take (including any requirements for filing complaints with state agencies). To be connected with the EEOC office in your area, call 1-800-669-4000. The EEOC also can give you information about state or local fair employment agencies in your area. You may also contact your state's Civil Right's Commission.

2. If you belong to a union, talk to your shop steward.

   The steward can give you advice about your rights and help you file a grievance under the collective bargaining agreement. The steward may also be able to help you file a complaint with the EEOC office in your area.

So Your Question May Be: Why Sue the Company?

My answer is why not?

What else can you do when you have been discriminated against and the company won't rectify it? These companies almost always have a chance to fix the problem before it goes to court. It is this unwillingness that often prompts many judges to make the company pay. This is the United State's way to rectify justice. Fighting for rights is not about greed but about making companies do the right thing. What will force a company's hand? An individual employee, most often not. A court that mandates proper treatment, of course.

What Else Can You (whether you are a man or woman) Do About Equal Pay?

- **Support efforts to bring "pay equity" to your workplace.** "Pay equity" means paying equal wages for jobs of equal value to a company. You and your co-workers (or your union) can encourage your employer to implement a pay equity policy, including a job evaluation system that reviews and compares the education, skills and experience needed to perform different jobs. Your employer then may adjust pay rates so that jobs of equal value to the company are paid equally regardless of who holds them. In addition, your union can include pay equity among its bargaining demands. Unions have won hundreds of millions of dollars for women and men by bargaining for pay equity.

- **Support new federal and state laws designed to strengthen protections against pay discrimination and bring pay equity to the workplace.** Organize your friends and co-workers to urge your U.S. senators and House members to vote for the Fair Pay Act or other proposals that may be introduced in Congress to require employers to end pay discrimination against women. And push your state legislature to enact similar pay equity protections. In 2003, 23 states introduced 50 bills regarding equal pay.

- **If you work for a state or city government, find out whether efforts have been made to end pay bias against public employees.** Many have. If your state or city hasn't taken action to end pay bias against its own employees, tell your state and local officials that you want your tax dollars to go to equal pay for working women!

These issues of the glass/concrete ceiling and unequal pay can be discouraging—but women have continued to persevere forward and beat the odds. Women not only have fought for equal rights in the workplace but have fully participated in making this country great.

In many countries, you will even find that women have held the highest position of the land proving to be powerful leaders for their countries. But rather than I go on, how about I ask you to name 15 significant women who have contributed greatly to their countries well being. Can you?

Well, like many people I would assume you probably had a hard time rattling off names unless they were of athletes or entertainers. But if significant women in other fields exist, why aren't we taught about their contributions?

If you were taught, at what point in your education did you learn these things. Many people educated in the United States would answer college. Yet, isn't it important for all people to learn about the contributions of both men and women?

Even if a few women names have been thrown out there how often has this information been repeated in your educational process? Remember, learning is repetition. For learning to take place a permanent change or knowledge must be gained and remembered. That is why we often learn over and over again about this country's forefathers. I would ask you to name five men who are or were presidents/leaders of countries? Could you do it? Sure. What about five women presidents/leaders of various countries?

The political contributions of men have been a concentrated area of learning for many while the significant contributions of women in politics has rarely been taught. Throughout history, women were excluded both by law and often by custom from active participation in the affairs of the state. But, does this mean that women have not been represented in the political arena?

In the beginning of the 20th century women around the world demanded the right to vote. It has taken nearly 100 years, but women have achieved political rights in nearly every country of the world. The fight for these political rights as well as the leadership that women have exhibited is enough to be noted in history books.

But women's contributions often are not included in history books; I bet you could name 10 significant Caucasian men who contributed to history, but can you can you name 10 women? Even if you can't name the 10 men, I would bet if you were educated in your early years in the U.S., you were taught about significant men in history. While not knowing women's history (assuming that you don't) is no reason to feel incompetent and respond on the defense. I say don't GET ON THE DEFENSE because history is written by the victors. Women were not the victors and therefore in many cases were left out of the history books. But this by no means indicates that women were insignificant, weak or contributed nothing to their societies.

Political Dignitaries*

*Source: The information found in this section is courtesy of Wikipedia: The Free Encyclopedia found at http://en.wikipedia.org/

Let me share with you a few stories of women who have excelled in the political field despite the unseemingly odds and the incredible risks to their lives. There are so many women in U.S history and World history that I could discuss, but I will limit the discussion that follows to a few of the most respected women world leaders.

ELLEN JOHNSON-SIRLEAF OF LIBERIA

Born in 1938, Ellen Johnson-Sirleaf a widowed mother-of-four in 2006, was sworn in as Liberia's president, making her Africa's first elected female leader. Mrs Johnson-Sirleaf becomes Liberia's first elected head of state since the end of the war in 2003. The 67-year-old grandmother won 59% of the vote in a November run-off election, beating Liberian football star George Weah. A former World Bank economist and veteran politician, Mrs Johnson-Sirleaf is nicknamed the Iron Lady but has promised to show a new, softer side as president. Mrs Johnson-Sirleaf drew much of her support from women voters, and from Liberia's small educated elite. She faces the twin challenges of trying to rebuild the country and of fostering reconciliation. One of her priorities is to reintegrate into society former child soldiers. She has declared a "zero tolerance" of corruption. Mrs Johnson-Sirleaf said her top challenge is to maintain peace, law and order after 14 years of civil war.

INDIRA GANDHI OF INDIA

Indira Nehru was born in Allahabad, India in 1917. During her early years she organized a Monkey Brigade, attended Somerville College at Oxford University, joined the National Congress Party and was eventually jailed by the British. In 1947, Indira's father became prime minister. In 1959, she was elected president of the National Congress Party then that next year her husband passes away. After this, Indira resigns her post with the party to take the place of her husband who had assisted her father. In 1964, Indira Gandhi's father dies and she gets appointed minister of information. In 1966, she was appointed as interim prime minister then five years later she was elected prime minister. Indira served two separate terms as prime minister of India helping to lead her country to a premier position among the developing countries of the world.

QUEEN HATSHEPSUT OF EGYPT

Born in the 15th century B.C., Hatshepshut was the daughter of Tuthmose I and Aahmes, both of royal lineages. She was the favorite of their three children. When her two brothers died she was in the unique position to gain the throne upon the death of her father. To have a female pharaoh was unprecedented. As a favorite daughter of a popular pharaoh, and as a charismatic and beautiful Black (as defined today) woman in her own right, she was able to command enough of a following to actually take control as pharaoh before the reign was to be given to her nephew. She ruled for about 15 years during the New Kingdom, 18th Dynasty, until her death in 1458 BC.

She left behind more monuments and works of art than any Egyptian queen to come. Even though Hatshepsut's name was erased from many images and from her country's ruling timeline, historians have proven that she accomplished what no women had before her. She successfully ruled the most powerful, advanced civilization in the world. Even if there were some who resented her success, her success stands for all time.

BENAZIR BHUTTO OF PAKISTAN

She was born Benazir Bhutto in Karachi, Pakistan in 1953. Bhutto's father, Zulfikar Ali Bhutto was elected prime minister a few years after she entered Radcliffe. After her Radcliffe graduation, she attended and graduated from Oxford University. After this, she returned to Pakistan in 1977. During this same year, a military coup ousts her father and she herself was jailed numerous times. Her father was hung in 1979 and in 1984 she returned to England. In 1987, she married and then a year later she not only gave birth to her first son but also was elected prime minister. In 1993, she was reelected for a second term as prime minister. Both of these times, she was forced out of office, before the end of her terms.

WILMA MANKILLER OF THE CHEROKEE NATION

Wilma Mankiller was born in Tahlequah, Oklahoma in 1945. In 1957, the Mankiller family moved to San Francisco where she met and married her husband and birthed two daughters. In 1969, Wilma assisted in the Alactraz takeover protest. In 1975, she divorced her husband and then moved back to Oklahoma. In 1977, she took her first job for the Cherokee Nation. She continued to develop and implement community projects on the Nations behalf. In 1983, she was appointed Interim Deputy Chief then elected Deputy Chief. In 1985, she was elected as principal chief, the first woman to hold this position for the Cherokee Nation. In 1986, she remarried and then the next year was re-elected to a second term as principal chief. She finally retired as principal chief in 1995.

GOLDA MEIR OF ISRAEL

Born as Golda Mabovitch in Kiev, Russia in 1898, Golda migrated to Milwaukee, Wisconsin as a small child. There she lived out her youth. Many of her adult years were spent in Palestine where she helped to smuggle Jewish refugees as well as start her political career. In 1949 when Golda's sons were five and three, Golda Meir served as Israel's first minister of labor till 1956 when she then began to serve as Israel's foreign minister. In 1969, she was elected as Israel's fourth prime minister. She saw this as an opportunity to have her dream of a new homeland for the Jewish people come true. But she knew the establishment of the state was only the beginning of a long struggle for peace with its Arab neighbors.

MARGARET THATCHER OF BRITAIN

Born Margaret Hilda Roberts in Grantham, England in the 1925 she attended Somerville College at Oxford. After graduation Margaret ran for a member of parliament for Dartford. In 1953 she gave birth to twins as well as began her law practice. In 1959, she was elected as a Member of Parliament for Finchley. After having several leadership positions for her party and country, Margaret became prime minister of Britain from 1979 till 1990. She was the first woman to head a major Western country. She was also the longest serving British prime minister in the 20th century.

VIOLETA CHAMORRO OF NICARAGUA

Violeta Barrios born in Rivas, Nicaragua in 1929 played a significant leadership role in her country as she helped to rid Nicaragua of two repressive regimes. She served as her country's first democratically elected president form 1990 to 1996. She had previously taken over the paper, *La Prensa,* after her husband who was the publisher was assassinated. His assassination had to do with opposition of the Somoza government. However, his untimely death did not prevent Violeta from continuing opposition and in 1979 Somoza fled the country. In 1986 prior to being elected president, Sandinista government shuts down *La Prensa.*

CORAZON AQUINO OF THE PHILIPPINES

Born Maria Corazon Cojuangco in Tarlac Province of the Philipines in 1933. She attended both high school and college in the United States. In 1954, she married Benigno S. (Ninoy) Aquino, Jr. who was imprisoned 18 years later when martial law was declared. In 1978, Corazon spoke out for her jailed husband. In 1983, her husband was assassinated at the Manilla Airport. The following year, Corazon urged people to vote despite corruption of the government. In 1986, she became President of the Republic of the Philippines restoring democracy to her country after helping to oust dictator Ferdinand Marcos. Her presidency lasted till 1992.

Concluding Thoughts

The political contributions of women are only one area in which women have excelled despite the odds. Despite the fight, women continue to excel in all areas of life and the workplace.

End of Chapter Questions

1. Why was there a change for women and work after industrialization?

2. What makes women able to do physically demanding jobs?

3. Define glass ceiling and concrete ceiling.

4. Why should men support equal pay for women?

5. Why are stereotypes of women dangerous in the workplace and what stereotypes have you noticed in the media or in the workplace?

Internet Exercise

Using the Internet going to the following website, http://www.now.org/press/04-02/04-16.html and reading the article found along with the article you find at the bottom that is called "pay equity fact sheet" or go to www.google.com and find an article on equal pay. Now summarize what the article says and state if you agree or disagree with its viewpoint.

End of Chapter Exercise

Take the Women's History Quiz

Do not use an encyclopedia, the Internet or any other resource to determine the answers to the questions 1-14 below. The knowledge MUST come from your own mind, and if you don't know the answer just leave the question blank.

1. First woman to receive a medical degree in the U.S.?

   _____

2. First Black woman to become a millionaire?

   _____

3. Led the first revolt in Southeast Asia against the Chinese?

   _____

4. First U.S. woman foreign correspondent?

   _____

5. First African American and first woman of a southern state to serve in congress?

   _____

6. First woman to travel in space?

   _____

7. First woman to rule as emperor in Chinese history?

   _____

8. First woman to receive the Distinguished Flying Cross?

   _____

9. First woman member of a U.S. Cabinet?

   _____

10. Considered the first modern novelist?

_____

11. First published poet in American history?

_____

12. Warrior Queen who fought against the Roman conquerors of Britain?

_____

13. First woman and first Latino surgeon general of the United States?

_____

14. What month is women's history month?

_____

Did you find it difficult to answer the questions above? If yes, why? If no, why? What does this say about what we learn regarding significant women in society?

References

1. Foner, P. S. (1979). *Women and the American Labor Movement*. New York, NY: Free Press.

2. Ibid.

3. Ibid.

4. Abramovitz. M. (1996). *Regulating the Lives of Women, Social Welfare Policy from Colonial Times to the Present*. Boston: South End Press.

5. Harlan, S. L. & O'Farrell, Brigit. (1982). After the Pioneers: Prospects for Women in Non-Traditional Blue-Collar Jobs. *Work and Occupations*, 9, 363-386.

6. Ibid.

7. Weiner, L. Y. (1985). *From Working Girl to Working Mother: The Female Labor Force in the United States, 1820-1980*. Chapel Hill: University of North Carolina.

8. Ibid.

9. Abramovitz, M. (1986). Social Policy and the Female Pauper: The Family Ethic and the U.S. Welfare State. *Feminist Visions For Social Work*, 211-228.

10. Craig, J. M. & Jacobs, R. R. (1985). The Effect of Working With Women on Male Attitudes Toward Female Firefighters, *Basic and Applied Social Psychology*, (6).

11. Messing, K. (1998). *One-eyed Science: Occupational health and women workers*. Philadelphia: Temple University Press.

12. Ibid.

13. Ibid.

14. Messing, K., Lippel, K., Demers, D. L. & Mergler, D. (2000, Fall). Equality and Difference in the Workplace: Physical Job Demands, Occupational Illnesses, and Sex Differences. *NWSA Journal* (12)3, 21-49.

15. Ibid.

16. Messing, K. (1998). *One-eyed Science: Occupational health and women workers*. Philadelphia: Temple University Press.

17. Duley, M. & Edwards, M. (1986). *The Cross-Cultural Study of Women*. New York, NY: The Feminist Press.

18. Hoganson, K. (1993, December). Garrisonian Abolitionists and the Rhetoric of Gender, 1850-1860. *American Quarterly*, (45)4, 558-595.

19. Ibid.

20. Jordan, W. (1974). *The White Man's Burden*. London, Great Britain: Oxford University Press.

21. Stedman, R. W. (1982). *Shadows of the Indian: Stereotypes in American Culture*. Norman: University of Oklahoma Press.

22. Ibid.

23. King, W. (1996). *Suffer with them till death: Slave women and their children in nineteenth-century America*. In David Barry Gaspar & Darlene Clark Hine (Eds.), More than chattel: Black women and slavery in the Americas, 147-168. Bloomington, IN: Indiana University Press.

24. Welter, B. (1976). *Dimity Convictions: The American Woman in the Nineteenth Century*. Athens, Ohio: Ohio University Press.

25. Yarbrough, M., Bennett, C. (Spring 2000). Cassandra and the "Sistahs": the Peculiar Treatment of African American Women in the Myth of Women as Liars. *Journal of Gender, Race and Justice*.

26. Ibid.

27. Lott, J. T. & Pian, C. (1979). *Beyond Stereotypes and Statistics: Emergence of Asian and Pacific American Women*. Washington, DC: Organization of Pan. Asian. American.

28. Ibid.

29. Karamarae, C & Spender, D. (2000). Routledge International Encyclopedia of Women: Global Women's Issues.

30. Keller, G. D. (1994). *Hispanics and United States Film: An Overview and Handbook*. Tempe: Bilingual Press/Editorial Bilingual.

31. Ibid.

32. Lipman, H. (2001, May 31). Unbalanced Pay Scales. *The Chronicle of Philanthropy*.

33. Burke, P. (1996). *Gender shock: exploding the myths of male and female*. New York: Anchor Books.

34. Sujata, S.V. (1992). *Struggles of Women at Work*. New Delhi: Vikas Publishing House.

35. Bergmann, B. R. (1996). *In Defense of Affirmative Action*. New York: Basic Books.

36. The Business and Professional Women's Foundation. (2005). *101 facts on the status of workingwomen.* Retrieved from http://www.bpwusa.org/files/public/101FactsonWorkingwomen2005.pdf.pdf

37. Women of Color Report: A 'Concrete Ceiling' Barring Their Advancement in Corporate America. (1999, July). *Catalyst*.

38. Lagace, M. (2002, November 11). Women Entrepreneurs Usher in the Next Generation, *Harvard Business School*.

39. Means, G. (n.d.). Retrieved from http://www.independentmeans.com/imi/press/index.php

40. The Business and Professional Women's Foundation. (2005). *101 facts on the status of workingwomen.* Retrieved from http://www.bpwusa.org/files/public/101FactsonWorkingwomen2005.pdf.pdf

41. Lockyer, S. E. (2005, April 4). Equal pay still a battle of the sexes: 40 years after the pay act was signed into law, women still make less than men. *Nation's Restaurant News.*

42. Ibid.

43. Ibid.

Chapter Six

Understanding the Native American Experience

A lie would have no sense unless the truth were felt as dangerous.

Alfred Adler

UNDERSTANDING THE NATIVE AMERICAN EXPERIENCE

Chapter Objectives

After reading this chapter, you should be able to:

- understand why Native Americans are not savages.

- explain how Native American women were equal and in some cases more powerful than men.

- state the exploitation of Native American values used to gain land by European settlers.

- identify specific treatment of Native Americans in the U.S. today.

- describe why mascots that stereotypically depict Native American culture is culturally insensitive.

What is your view of Indians/Native Americans?

- Do you think of savages running around half naked?
- Do you think of a people incapable of maintaining their land which is why they no longer have it?
- Is it of a defeated people?
- Groups who live on reservations in tepees because they know of no other way to live or survive the land?
- A stubborn people who disrespect America?

If any of these are your views of Indians/Native Americans then you have a viewpoint full of untruths. None of the above depicts Native Americans, their history or their story. To know the truth about Native Americans is to understand the indigenous people of this land known as America and how far removed America is from this great people's values.

Native Americans are the indigenous people of this country. According to researchers, the indigenous people of "America" have been here for at least 12,000 years where some even believe that these people first started living here much earlier than that.

It is estimated, based on archaeological data and written records from European settlers, that up to a possible 30 to 100 million indigenous people lived in the Americas when the 1492 voyage of Christopher Columbus began a historical period of large-scale European interaction with the Americas.[1]

Native American Living

Before the Europeans came, there were no people here that called themselves "Indians." Instead, there were and still are Navajo or Menominee or Hopi, or Dakota, or Nisqually, or Tlingit, or Apache, etc. They refer to themselves by their specific nation. They received the name "Indian" from Christopher Columbus because he thought he landed in India. That is why we sometimes use the nation name or the term Native American to refer to the original inhabitants of America.

The natural environment of the Great West provided life to Native Americans. It also took life. People learned that working together, and hunting together, was extremely important. Living alone on especially the plains meant certain death. It could be a hard life, taught by Nature. The power of a tornado, a thunderstorm and its lightning, the pressing heat of a summer day, or the sweeping cold air made everyone very observant of the Earth. The native people learned from the Earth, the animals and plants. Everything fit together in this Universe as many tribes understood it, and everyone and everything had its role and responsibility.

Instead of often being taught the many viewpoints of Native Americans-- one story has often been told. This story involves tepees, war paint and the savage image.

But, when it came to their lifestyle and homes there were many different types of Native American houses that would fit their lifestyle and their climate. Since North America is a continent of various land types and conditions, different tribes had varying degrees of weather to contend with. In the Arizona deserts, temperatures can hit 120 degrees Fahrenheit, and in the Alaskan tundra, -50 is not unusual. Naturally, Native Americans developed different types of dwellings to survive in these different environments as they were a cunning and skillful people.[2]

Native American tribes also had different traditional lifestyles. Some tribes were agricultural-- they lived in settled villages and farmed the land for corn and vegetables. They wanted houses that would last a long time. Once such group, the Eastern Woodland Indians had homes called longhouses. Like the homes of the Northwest Culture, these were rectangular homes with barrel shaped roofs. As their name states, these homes were very long.[3] Families shared these homes, as many could hold up to 60 people. The insides had a long hallway with rooms for each family on either side.

Not all tribes were agricultural, some tribes were more nomadic, moving frequently from place to place as they hunted and gathered food and resources. They needed houses that were portable or easy to build, such as a tent. The tribes of the Southwest Culture lived in apartment-style buildings. These buildings were made of adobe, clay and vegetables dried in the sun. This type of home was especially good for areas that had very little rainfall and a hot desert climate.[4] Many families lived in each apartment and as families grew, rooms were added on top of the rooms that were already there.

If you have ever traveled to the Red Mountains in Sedona, Arizona, you would find mansions that Native Americans built within the structure of these mountains. Many of these homes had 10 or more rooms and are still standing inside these mountains today. It is spectacular to view the architecture and modern day building of these homes by a people who lived in them many years ago.

No matter what the conditions on the land, the Native Americans survived by gathering all the things they needed from the natural world around them. They built structures that fit the environment while also preserving the Earth.

Native American Respect for Women

Native American women traditionally belonged to a culture that gave them respect, power, autonomy and equality. In the Iroquois tribes of New York, women had the political right to nominate and recall civil chiefs, they controlled and managed their families, they had the right to divorce and could determine how many children they would raise.[5]

In Blackfoot society, a woman owned the products of her labor including the tipi that her family lived in.[6] A woman was judged by the quality of her work and treated with respect in reference to her good work.[7] Women were seen as powerful due to their ability to give life.[8] The female was so powerful that it was she who unwrapped and rewrapped holy bundles because a man would not be able to handle this power directly, without her intercession.[9] A woman's superior spiritual power was seen in her ability alone to hold the Sun Dance ceremony.[10] Women were Shaman's (acting as a medium between the visible and spirit worlds; practices used for healing or divination) as often as men were and brought blessings to the people showing that Blackfoot women had power, freedom and autonomy.

It was understood in most Native cultures that men and women's work was of equal value and is complimentary. Men hunted and women processed the fruit of his hunts. One did not function well without the other. Each person worked for and counted the possessions one had that they would then give away, because the giving of gifts was seen as a powerful and prestigious act.[11]

In addition, unlike the culture of Americans where relationships are based on a patriarchal structure with the man as the head many Native societies including the Iroquois, Cherokee and Navajo men took the name of the women. These families operated under either matriarchal (a form of social organization in which a female is the family head and title is traced through the female line) or matrilocal (a form of marriage in which, after the wedding, the bridegroom moves to his new wife's family home) structures.[12]

Exploitation of Native American Values

The First Nation's Peoples had a great value system. There were normally only four commandments and they were as follows[13]:

1. Respect Mother Earth
2. Respect the Great Spirit
3. Respect our fellow man and woman
4. Respect for individual freedom

Native Americans respected the earth but did not feel ownership of it. But with this viewpoint does this mean thet the original inhabitants or indigenous people of the U.S. did not have any rights to the land they occupied?

The historical antecedents of the legal rights of indigenous people were found centuries prior to the European arrival in the Western hemisphere.[14] So, yes they did have rights. However, after the establishment of the Holy Roman Empire, but prior to the colonial travels of Europeans, distinctions were being made between the various people of the known world. These distinctions were in terms of Christians and "infidels" where infidels was a term given to people who were not Christians.[15] If you were not a Christian, then you were viewed as a savage-- someone seen as wild and menacing; who would attack brutally and fiercely as a member of an uncivilized people. This superior/inferior religious attitude continued despite the similarities between Christianity and the Native's religions.

Laws that governed everyone but were only agreed upon by a few countries, the law of nation, allowed the expansion of Christianity, by acquiring territory from newly discovered peoples (such as those in Asia and Africa) or from familiar peoples (particularly the Saracens and Turks) who were unwilling to accept Christian doctrines.[16] Under these laws, a "discoverer" could legally occupy a territory that was already inhabited (by "infidels") and extend Christian sovereignty over it.[17]

This may answer the question as to how Christopher Columbus who was working on behalf of the Spaniards could be labeled the discoverer of America when many had previously traveled here, and the Native Americans were living here when he arrived.

But, how exactly did the Native Americans get exploited?

When the English started to come to the Americas from Europe, they didn't particularly care who was already living on the land and they certainly didn't have any regards for the Native Americans way of life as the Natives were infidels or plainly put just savages. Europeans looked at their discovery as a new way of starting over and due to the law of nations they felt they complete rights to conquering land from infidels. The English wanted the land and they did whatever was necessary to take it from "these savages" as they referred to them.

But, why would you take unfamiliar land from those who are familiar with how to live and survive on this new territory? This taking of the land was done after the Europeans knew how to live off the land. Living off the land was only possible because the Native Americans showed the newcomers how to starve off disease and survive on a soil that they themselves had lived on for thousands of years. The Natives respected individual freedom and it was their culture to provide this assistance. Therefore, instead of trying to force these newcomers (the pilgrims) off the land they gave them all the assistance they needed to survive and thrive on it.

As more settlers came they began to expand. But did they honor the "Indians" for helping them to survive the land or for allowing them to occupy it no instead they (the pilgrims and early settlers) not only treated the Natives poorly but many tried to kill them altogether. These settlers even brought with them disease that they purposely gave to the Natives because they knew the Natives had no cures.

Genocide of Native Americans

Throughout decades of English immigrants and the formation of the United States, Native Americans were continually mistreated. They were looked at as "savages" and were even made slaves. The English had no tolerance of them and many wanted them dead. This was mostly because they did not share religious beliefs and they did not share the same way of living. Natives were killed by attack after attack. Their crops were destroyed by settlers, leaving them dying of starvation. The settlers had the advantage since a bow and arrow could not beat a gun.

In his book, *American Holocaust*, David Stannard argues that the destruction of the aboriginal peoples of the Americas, Native Americans, in a "string of genocide campaigns" by Europeans and their descendants, was the most massive act of genocide in the history of the world and he further states:[18]

During the course of four centuries - from the 1490s to the 1890s - Europeans and white Americans engaged in an unbroken string of genocide campaigns against the native peoples of the Americas. [It] was, far and away, the most massive act of genocide in the history of the world.
(p. 147)"

In 2003, Venezuelan President Hugo Chavez urged Latin Americans to not celebrate the Columbus Day holiday. Chavez blamed Columbus for leading the way in the mass genocide of the Native Americans by the Spanish.[19]

So, now you may be wondering why did the English/Pilgrims or Puritans as they were called do this?

Puritan Values

The Pilgrims who settled in America were not innocent exiles who unjustly had been banished from their country as some historians put it. Instead, they were "political revolutionist" belonging to the Puritan movement, which was seen as unorthodox and intolerable by the King of the Church of England.[20]

The Puritans exemplified this in what many would consider was extreme. There was a two-fold ideology about them, 1) They knew their Bible well and consequently wrote deeply, and passionately about it, and 2) They put their knowledge about Christ into action.[21] Compared to the 21st century church, they were biblically intellectual and spiritual giants and they longed so intensely for holiness of saintly living that they strove for the quality of that life through Jesus Christ constantly. This yearning and desire for pure spiritual experience, or an experimental Calvinism, was so overwhelming that they were religiously zealous for the Kingdom of God and for purity of doctrine in every area of life and nothing held them back from attempting to attain this.[22]

Puritans also had some beliefs that became a part of the culture of this "new" America. The essence of Puritan social order lay in the authority of husband over wife, parents over children, and masters over servants. Puritan marriage choices were influenced by young people's inclination, by parents, and by the social rank of the persons involved. Upon finding a suitable match, husband and wife in America followed the steps needed to legitimize their marriage.[23]

Contrary to popular belief, slavery was not established in America by uneducated Southern whites as the origin of American slavery sprang from the minds of Northeastern Puritan colonists, who through a twisted interpretation of the Bible and a corrupted practice of Europeanized Christianity, delegated black people to sub-human status, fit only to serve whites and to submit to their every whim under the threat of the most cruel reprisals and penalties.[24]

Unlike the Southern slavers and plantation owners, Northern Puritans prided themselves on their culture, intellectualism, religious piety and moral purity allowing them to inflict some of the most atrocious crimes against Native Americans and people of African descent. These Puritans on the new land considered themselves blessed in the sight of God even while committing the most evil of acts against the dark skinned people they encountered.[25]

Pilgrims were "seeing for innocence" in their way of thinking. Since they were God's chosen elect, they felt this gave them the right to treat women second to men and to believe that "white" skin was superior to dark skin and that Native Americans were infidels/savages who could be exposed of--killed off. These are the value systems upon which this country was founded--is there any wonder why we have sexism, racism and religious intolerance toward certain groups who appear different?

But does this mean that certain groups aren't entitled to their beliefs? When is power in the wrong hands dangerous to those who are different?

What about Thanksgiving?

Given this terrible history between Native Americans and Pilgrims, why is there a celebration of Thanksgiving?

Rather than give you my perspective, I'll give you the perspective of a Native American and her view of Thanksgiving. Jacqueline Keeler, a member of the Dineh Nation and the Yankton Dakota Sioux works with the American Indian Child Resource Center in Oakland, California. Her work has appeared in *Winds of Change*, an American Indian journal. She writes the following in an article titled,

"Thanksgiving: A Native American View" excerpt below taken from the website found at http://www.alternet.org/story/4391/:

> *I celebrate the holiday of Thanksgiving...Thanksgiving to me has never been about Pilgrims. When I was six, my mother, a woman of the Dineh nation, told my sister and me not to sing "Land of the Pilgrim's pride" in "America the Beautiful" but "Land of the Indian's pride" instead.... Bigotry, hatred, greed, self-righteousness... We have seen the evil that it caused in the 350 years since. Genocide, environmental devastation, poverty, world wars, racism... when I give thanks this Thursday...I will be thinking of ...how my ancestors survived the evil it caused.[26]*

Manifest Destiny

After killing the Native Americans, taking their land they still was conquering to be done by the settlers here in North America. War with the Native Americans or other nations was not of moral or ethical concern for the European settlers as they made it their right to continue seizing land. With all the settlers means (guns and technology) by which to conquer land it became a philosophy that white America had the "manifest destiny" which is the right to dominate the North American continent.[27]

This is where there became a clear distinction not just in religious beliefs but also in color differences, as now only White settlers had the right to occupy and possess these lands. Based on this accepted philosophy of the settlers, the early 1800s were years of extraordinary territorial growth for free White settlers of the United States.[28] During a four year period, the national domain increased by 1.2 million square miles. Yet, this expansionist agenda was never a clearly defined movement or one that enjoyed broad support due to lost rights of the indigenous people and the fact that this was also a racist philosophy.

Native American Myths

The image that has been presented to so many of us regarding the founders of this land brings humility to a group of people who deserve our utmost respect. Bias about American Indians is often the result of inaccurate information. The realities of American Indian life are often oversimplified and distorted. Stylized classroom accounts of Indian life reinforce the "buckskin and feather" and the

"Eskimo and igloo" stereotypes. With such instruction, students are certain to develop misguided impressions of Native Americans.

In textbooks, movies, and TV programs, American Indians and Alaska Natives have been treated in ways that tend both to overlook their dignity and to disgrace their heritage. For example, Indians who defended their homeland from invaders (and who today seek to preserve their languages and culture) have often been viewed as enemies of progress. In the context of history, White people are portrayed as having viewed the Native Americans as barriers to the settlement of the frontier. In the present, Native Americans have been viewed as a "social problem", a drain on national resources. In order to value the contributions of this indigenous people we must challenge the distortions, stereotypes, myths and racist information that have been commonplace.

Explanation of Laws Passed to Control Native Americans

When the Constitution was written, it included a provision that implied federal authority over the conduct of Indian relations. Thereafter, the federal government - not state governments - was empowered to deal directly with Indian nations.

The Dawes Act
On February 8, 1887, Congress passed the Dawes Act, named for its author, Senator Henry Dawes of Massachusetts. Also known as the General Allotment Act, this law allowed the president to break up reservation land, which was held in common by the members of a tribe, into small allotments to be parceled out to individuals. Thus, Native Americans registering on a tribal "roll" were granted allotments of reservation land. Each head of family would receive one-quarter of a section (120 acres); each single person over 18 or orphan child under 18 would receive one-eighth of a section (60 acres); and other single persons under 18 would receive one-sixteenth of a section (30 acres).[29]

While this may seem like a lot of land, let's first remember that the land was the Native Americans' to begin with. Between 1887 and 1934, the U.S. Government took over 90 million acres, nearly 2/3 of reservation lands from the tribes without compensation and gave it to the settlers.[30] Then once the best lands were given to the settlers they gave back to the Indians desert land or near-desert lands unsuitable for farming. Many Indians did not want to take up farming anyway as the techniques of self-sufficient farming were much different from their tribal way of life. But, of the Indians who were willing to give this a try they could not afford the tools, animals, seed, and other supplies necessary to get started.

So, they were left with land that was worthless and could not provide them a means by which to live.

The Indian Reorganization Act

The Indian Reorganization Act is legislation that passed in 1934 in an attempt to secure new rights for Native Americans on reservations. Its main provisions were to restore to Native Americans management of their assets (mostly land); to prevent further depletion of reservation resources; to build a sound economic foundation for the people of the reservations; and to return to the Native Americans local self-government on a tribal basis.[31] The objectives of the bill were vigorously pursued until the outbreak of World War II. While the act seems to restore some dignity to Native Americans, many Native Americans questioned its purpose which seemed more of gradual assimilation. Their opposition to the act reflects their efforts to reduce federal condescension in the treatment of Native Americans and their cultures.[32]

1924 Citizenship Acts

By the act of June 2, 1924 (43 Stat. 253, ante, 420), Congress conferred citizenship upon all noncitizen Indians born within the territorial limits of the United States. The text of the act follows:

Be it enacted by the Senate and House of Representatives of the United States of America in Congress assembled, That all noncitizen Indians born within the territorial limits of the United States be, and they are hereby, declared to be citizens of the United States: *Provided*, That the granting of such citizenship shall not in any manner impair or otherwise affect the right of any Indian to tribal or other property and prior to the passage of the act of June 2, 1924, about two-thirds of the Indians of the United States were already citizens. There were a number of different provisions of law by which or under which Indians became citizens previous to June 2, 1924.[33] But, why did they need citizenship when they were here first?

The participation of American Indians in the Great War probably accelerated the granting, by an Act of Congress in 1924, of American citizenship to all American Indians born in the United States.[34] But, while it may appear a great gesture this citizenship act did not grant Native Americans the right to be both a citizen and live according to their culture only the right to be a citizen and be governed by the rules of the "White man."[35]

Treatment of Native Americans Today

Despite broken treaties and numerous laws created to control American Indians, the indigenous people of America have never stopped fighting for self-determination-- government of a political unit by its own people.

Given the track record between the U.S. and Native Americans, one would hope that the dismal treatment was over. However, Native Americans must still face very racist symbols and defamation that is often accepted by mainstream America. From the racially derived "Washington Redskins" to the war-like "Florida Seminoles", American Indian mascots are found at the professional sports level as well as the elementary, high school and college levels. Far from honoring Native Americans, many of these mascots are a national insult, and represent the last vestiges of a time thought to have long passed when such stereotypes were commonplace. Just as "Sambo" served to perpetuate racism and bigotry toward the African-American community, these "Indian" mascots and team names that are depicted stereotypically serve to keep Native Americans in a similar position. How much more insult should Native Americans take?

Indian Mascots--politically incorrect or horrifically defaming

While some people are tired of being told how to think and act politically correct, it is important to note that being politically correct is not just the moral thing to do but makes good business sense. The big issue right now is Indian mascots. Many State School Boards have taken a strong stand against the mascot and team names; in many cases, people have strong emotional attachments to these names but if they are perceived as being culturally insensitive then shouldn't they be changed?[36]

Why is Native people the only *race* of people that are permitted to be used as mascots? Interchange the name of any race with the Indians and it immediately becomes clear that we cannot have teams called The Negroes, or The Asians.[37]

There is a lot of debate over Indian mascots. But how do you debate the appropriateness of using racist terms like redskin or using cultural artifacts in a disrespectful manner? Would there be a debate if it was customary to go a U.S. baseball game and burn the American flag?

The controversy over the Washington Redskins trademark has brought this debate to the mainstream. It began with a petition by seven American Indian activists led by Suzan Harjo in 1992 to the Trademark Trial and Appeal Board of the US Department of Commerce requesting cancellation of the trademark on the grounds that the word *redskin* was and is a pejorative, derogatory, denigrating, offensive, scandalous, contemptuous, disreputable, disparaging and racist designation for a Native American person

It becomes clear that valuing diversity is not as simple as we would like to make it. It becomes an issue when asked to give up something you may value because it devalues someone else. Issues like the Indian mascots really test our commitment to diversity, why? It is simple, revisit the definition of cultural sensitivity and you will see why it is an issue for valuing diversity. Cultural sensitivity does not mean that a person need only be *aware* of the differences. But, to interact effectively with people from other cultures we must move beyond cultural biases, symbols, language etc. that creates a barrier.

A document titled "What's Wrong With Indian Mascots, Anyway?" (found at http://www.racismagainstindians.org/UnderstandingMascots.htm tries to answer the question it poses)[38]:

> *"Because virtually the only image that non-native children view of Native people are of the mascots, most children assume that Native people are dead or were war-like people. This stereotype diminishes the Native culture and is hurtful to Native people. Our myths and legends that the Native people were bloodthirsty killers are perpetuated by the mascot. These myths are what psychologists deem as "dehumanization," which is necessary in any war to justify the killing of people. In other wars, we can remember the names used for Germans, "krauts," Japanese were "Nips," etc. But when wars are over we drop those names and show respect once again for people who are not our enemies. We have never dropped those names and perpetuate a war like attitude towards Native people by the continuance of those names."*

If you believe the claim of being called war-like is an "honor," read Smashing People: The "Honor" of Being an Athlete that can be found at www.google.com.

In an interview with CBSNews.com, on March 20, 2001, author Sherman Alexie (Spokane/Coeur d'Alene) adds another important point:

"The mascot thing gets me really mad" Alexie says. "Don't think about it in terms of race. Think about it in terms of religion. Those are our religious imagery up there. Feather, the paint, the sun that's our religious imagery. You couldn't have a Catholic priest running around the floor with a basketball throwing communion wafers. You couldn't have a rabbi running around..."[39]

I could keep providing examples of how the mascot issue is culturally insensitive and in some cases downright disrespectful but instead I ask you—Is having a mascot (depicted stereotypically) really worth the continued racist, culturally inconsiderate actions that it represents? Do you think it is politically incorrect to take into account the treatment of Native Americans in this country as it relates to how sensitive we should be today?

If according to your answers you still don't see anything wrong with Indian mascots or at best you see no need to argue against keeping the mascots, then I leave you the following words:

"In Germany they came first for the communists,
and I didn't speak up because I wasn't a communist.

Then they came for the Jews,
and I didn't speak up because I wasn't a Jew.

Then they came for the trade unionists,
and I didn't speak up because I wasn't a trade unionist.

Then they came for the Catholics,
and I didn't speak up because I was a protestant.

Then they came for me,
and by that time no one was left to speak up."

--- Said by Rev. Martin J. Niemoller in 1945

Native American Contributions and Inventions*

*Information below is copied with permission from various encyclopedias.

Foods   Edible plants domesticated by Indians have become major staples in the diets of peoples all around the world. Such foods include corn (maize), manioc, potatoes, sweet potatoes, peanuts, squashes and pumpkins, tomatoes, papayas, avocados, pineapples, guavas, chili peppers, chocolate (cacao), and many species of beans.

Animals   Indians were the first to raise turkeys, llamas, guinea pigs, and honeybees for food.

Non-edible plants   Other plants of great importance developed by Indians include cotton, rubber, and tobacco.

Medicines   Indians discovered the medicinal use for quinine. Also, Canadian Indians knew how to prevent scurvy by eating plants rich in vitamin C, and they passed this information along to the Europeans.

Mathematics   The Maya of Mexico appear to have been the first to use the zero in mathematics. Scholars believe that Asians traveled across the Pacific Ocean and learned about the zero from the Maya.

Government   Indian governments in eastern North America, particularly the League of the Iroquois, served as models of federated representative democracy to the Europeans and the American colonists. The United States government is based on such a system, whereby power is distributed between a central authority (the federal government) and smaller political units (the states).

Economy   Indian contributions to the modern world's economy have been enormous. In the 1500's, Indian labor produced the gold and other valuable metals that helped bring the Spanish Empire to the height of its power. In the following centuries, Indian labor in the North American fur trade contributed significantly to the wealth of England, France, the Netherlands, and Russia. In addition, for hundreds of years the agrarian economies of the Latin American nations have been based on Indian labor on plantations.

Partial List of Inventions

abstract art- Abstract art was used by nearly all tribes and civilizations of North and South America. Native American art was believed to be primitive until the 1990s, when it served as inspiration for the modern American abstract art movement.

adobe- Adobe was used by the peoples from South America, Mesoamerica, and up to Southwestern tribes of the U.S. It is estimated that it was developed around the year 3000 B.C.

almanacs- Almanacs were invented independently by the Maya. Their culture arose and they began using them around 3,500 years ago, while Europeans are known to have created written almanacs only after 1150 A.D. Almanacs are books containing meteorological and astronomical information, which the Maya used in various aspects of their life.

anesthetics- American Indians used coca, peyote, datura and other plants for partial or total loss of sensation or conscious during surgery. Non-Indian doctors had effective anesthetics only after the mid 1800s. Before this, they either had to perform surgery while the patient felt pain or knock the patient out.

balls, rubber- The Olmec produced rubber balls around 1700 B.C. They were the first people to develop and play with rubber balls as well as manufacture other objects of rubber.

basketball- Basketball was played by the Olmec 3,000 years ago. The game followed the Olmec's creation of the rubber ball. See Mesoamerican ballgame for more information on this ancient sport.

calendars- Were developed by throughout North America, Mesoamerica, and South America. They are known to have been in used since 600 B.C. American Indian calendars were so precise that by the 5th century B.C. they were only 19 minutes off.

chewing gum- American Indians in New England introduced the settlers to chewing gum made from the spruce tree. The Mayans, on the other hand, were the first people to use latex gum; better known to them as chicle.

chocolate- The Mayans were the first to drink cocoa. This tradition was later passed on to the Aztec's who called the beverage xocalatl. Natives in mesoamerica introduced it to the Spanish and Portuguese, but they kept the beloved xocalatl from the rest of Europe for nearly a century.

corn (maize) - The domestication of maize, now cultivated throughout the world, is one of the most influential technological contributions of Mesoamericans.

dog breeds- Dog breeds believed to have been bred by Native Americans are the xochiocoyotl (coyote), xoloitzcuintli (known as xolo or Mexican hairless), chihuahua, the Carolina dog, and the Alaskan malamute.

electricity- The Moche invented electricity through chemical means somewhere between 200 B.C. and 600 A.D. Electrical current was produced by dipping copper into an acid solution.

embalming- Egyptians are known for mummification which began around 2000 B.C. In what is know Chile however, the Chinchoro are known to have been embalming and mummifying their dead since 5000 B.C. which would make them the world's earliest embalmers. Embalming is using preservatives to prevent decay of the body.

Geographical Names- Native Americans have had a major impact in names of locations and places commonly used today. There are 26 states in the United States alone whose names derive from Native Americans. Most notable however, are the countries of Canada and Mexico. Names do not limit themselves to political states; there are also mountains, rivers, cities, lakes, and counties deriving from indigenous terms. For a full list see Native American Geographical Names.

hammocks- Hammocks were commonly used in the Caribbean, South and Central America at first contact with Europeans. The Spanish liked the comfortable way of sleeping and adopted them. Europeans eventually used them as the primary way of sleeping on ships.

hockey- Both field hockey and ice hockey are based on a game called shinny. This American Indian stickball game was played throughout North America well before the European arrival.

llamas- Indigenous people from Peru domesticated llamas in around 5000 B.C.

rubber balloons- The Olmec were the first people to use rubber balloons. Their civilization arose in B.C 1700 in the Yucatan Peninsula.

spinning top- North American Indians invented the spinning top. A device used as a toy and made out of wood.

tipi- A cone shaped, portable dwelling popularized by Native Americans of the Great Plains. Tipis were warm, durable and comfortable and could be easily broken down and packed. A settlement could be ready to move in about one hour.

tortillas- this staple food well known today was used throughout Mesoamerican and Southwestern cultures. Although they were mainly made of corn, squash and amaranth were also popular among the natives. The tortillas were wrapped around different fillings such as avocado. Today this has resulted in the creation of the modern taco, burrito, and enchilada.

Concluding Thoughts

As we close with this chapter, one thing should be clear—America has treated the Natives of this country with disdain, disrespect and in some cases dishonor toward their humanity and culture. This can make some feel ashamed, embarrassed and even guilty for this treatment. It is okay to feel this, but what becomes more important is what we do with these feelings.

If you feel ashamed, don't—feel empowered. Make it a point to teach your children, friends and family the truth about the Natives of this country—this can go a long way toward erasing the many myths that exist. If you feel embarrassed, don't—feel empathy. Celebrate Thanksgiving in a different manner not as a victory toward the pilgrims but as respect and honor toward the Natives of this country for their suffering and loss. If you feel guilty, don't—instead feel responsible. Use this accountability to work toward restoring honor to this culture as it relates to the mascot issue, Native American sovereignty, and other issues that Native Americans still must fight for. Remember, strength lies in numbers and we all need to use our voices to speak up for this most honorable race of people.

End of Chapter Questions

1. Define the following terms and indicate how they relate to Native Americans:
   a. Indigenous People
   b. Discoverer
   c. Infidels

2. Name and describe two laws that were implemented to control Native Americans.

3. What is manifest destiny and how does it relate to "who" could acquire land?

4. How does America explain the taking of Native American land or does it and what does continued disrespect say about how Native Americans are valued in U.S. society?

5. For each statement below, indicate if it is an appropriate way to show respect to Native Americans and indicate why or why not.
   a.   A company creates a new potato chip and names it "redskin" potato chips and on the bag shows a Native American in "red" face.
   b.   During a school pep rally, the school utilizes the religious symbols (such as the images of eagle feathers, symbols of clothing, song, dance) of Native Americans to get the crowd excited.
   c.   When someone at work takes back a gift they gave you, you refer to them as an "Indian Giver."
   d.   During the month of November your organization creates factual literature on the various cultures of Native Americans.

Internet Exercise

Using the Internet, look up the following address:
http://www.law.ou.edu/hist/iroquois.html or go to www.google.com and

search for "Iroquois Constitution". Once you have retrieved the document, skim it so that you can answer the two questions below.

        a.   What famous document in U.S. history sounds similar to the document on the above website?

        b.   What is this document's view on women, religious freedom, and the designation of power?

End of Chapter Exercise

What is the "real" Thanksgiving Story?

Using the Internet, look up the following address: http://www.manataka.org/page269.html or go to www.google.com and search for "The Real Thanksgiving Story." Once at the website *Teaching About Thanksgiving* read "Introduction for Teachers" and "The Plymouth Thanksgiving story." Now complete the following:

(1) Explain five things that you learned from this story.
(2) State if you were taught this version of the story and if yes what impact did this have on your view of Native Americans. If you were not taught this version of the story, indicate what impact did the story you were taught have on your view of Native Americans. If you did know about Thanksgiving, state what your views are regarding the U.S. treatment of Native Americans.

References

1. Wikipedia. (n.d.). *Population history of American indigenous peoples*. Retrieved from http://en.wikipedia.org/wiki/Population_history_of_American_indigenous_peoples

2. Anderson, K. (1993). *Before the Wilderness: Environmental Management by Native Californians*. Menlo Park, CA: Ballena Publishers.

3. Ibid.

4. Buskirk, W. (1987). *The Western Apache: Living with the Land before 1950*. Oklahoma: University of Oklahoma Press.

5. Buffalohead, P.K. (1983). *Farmers Warriors Traders: A Fresh Look at Ojibway Women*. (Doc No. 28).

6. Kehoe, A.B. (1995). *Blackfoot persons*. In L. F. Klein & L. A. Ackerman (Eds.), Women And Power in *Native North America*, 113-125. Oklahoma: University of Oklahoma Press.

7. Ibid.

8. Ibid.

9. Ibid.

10. Ibid.

11. Popick, J. (2006). Native American Women, Past, Present and Future. *Lethbridge Undergraduate Research Journal,* 1(1).

12. Ibid.

13. Native American Culture. (n.d.). Retrieved from http://www.greatdreams.com/native.htm

14. Jaimes, M. A. (2003, Spring). Patriarchal Colonialism and Indigenism: Implications for Native Feminist Spirituality and Native Womanism. *Hypatia*, (18)2, 58-69.

15. Ibid.

16. Morris, G. T. (1995). *International law and politics toward a right to self-determination for indigenous peoples*. Washington: Center for World Indigenous Studies.

17. Ibid.

18.   Stannard, D. (1993). *A review of American Holocaust: The Conquest of the New World*. England: Oxford University Press.

19.   Columbus 'sparked a genocide'. (2003, October 12). *BBC News.* Retrieved from http://news.bbc.co.uk/2/hi/americas/3184668.stm.

20.   The Pilgrim fathers; or, The journal of the Pilgrims at Plymouth, New England, in 1620. (n.d.). Retrieved from http://www.archive.org/stream/pilgrimfathersor00inchee/pilgrimfathersor00inchee_djvu.txt

21.   McMahon, C. M. (n.d.). A Puritan's Mind. Retrieved from http://www.apuritansmind.com/PuritanArticles/PuritanRoots.htm

22.   Ibid.

23.   Ibid.

24.   Shelton, S. M. (2004). *The Puritans, and The Myth of Democracy*. Retrieved from http://www.afromerica.com/columns/shelton/vantagepoint/mythofdemocracy.php

25.   Ibid.

26.   Keeler, J. (2000, January 1). Thanksgiving: A Native American View. *Pacific News Service*. Retrieved from http://www.purewatergazette.net/nativeamericanthanksgiving.htm

27.   Kluger, R. (2008). *Seizing Destiny: The Relentless Expansion of American Territory*. New York: Random House.

28.   Ibid.

29.   General Allotment Act or Dawes Act, Statutes at Large 24, 388-91, NADP Document A1887. (n.d.). Retrieved from http://www.Archives.gov

30.   Ibid.

31.   Wunder, J. R. (1985). *No More Treaties: The Resolution of 1871 and the Alteration of Indian Rights to their Homelands*. In Working the Range: Essays on the History of Western Land Management and the Environment. Westport, CT: Greenwood Press, pp. 39-58.

32.   d'Errico, P. (2000). *Sovereignty: A brief history in the context of U.S. Indian law*. Phoenix: The Encyclopedia of Minorities in American Politics.

33.   Kappler, C. J. (1927, March 4). *Indian Affairs: Laws and Treaties*. Government Printing Office, 1V, laws.

34. Camurat, D. (1993). *The American Indian in the Great War: Real and Imagined*. Retrieved from http://net.lib.byu.edu/estu/wwi/comment/Cmrts/Cmrt8.html.

35. Ibid.

36. Rabbit, W. (2009, February 7). Indian Mascots and death threats to a 15 yr. old. *Daily Kos*.

37. Rose, C. (2002). *The STAR - Students and Teachers Against Racism*. Retrieved from http://www.racismagainstindians.org/UnderstandingMascots.htm

38. Ibid.

39. Team Names and Mascots. (n.d.). Retrieved from http://www.bluecorncomics.com/mascots.htm

Chapter Seven

Understanding the African American/Black Experience

Not to know the past is to be in bondage to it, while to remember and to know is to be set free.

Dr. Sigmund Freud

UNDERSTANDING THE AFRICAN AMERICAN/BLACK EXPERIENCE

Chapter Objectives

After reading this chapter, you should be able to:

- define chattel slavery.

- identify several slave revolutions.

- describe the slaves impact on the American Revolution.

- understand why slavery was worse in America than other countries.

- discuss the Willie Lynch Speech and Jim Crow Laws.

- provide examples of the treatment of Blacks today.

Managing Workplace Diversity

According to George Henderson in *Cultural Diversity in the Workplace: Issues and Strategies*:

> "Ethnicity and race are often confused in the United States. For example, Hispanics from the Americas and Puerto Rico with African ancestors, even though they tend to identify with their native country, are frequently and erroneously labeled African Americans in the U.S. workplace. The terms blacks, African Americans, and people of color are popular. Some writers use them interchangeably without understanding that African Americans do not include peoples of African descent who are not American citizens; and people of color refers to minorities that have darker skin tone such as: Hispanics, Asians, Native Americans and the like--not just African Americans."[1]

So in order not to confuse you, we are going to be addressing the plight of a race of people who have been called many things from Negroes to colored to Blacks and now African American. Today, terms like "Negro," and colored are considered derogatory in many quarters (due to political overtones). The term "Black" still has some currency because not all those with brown skin has a homeland of Africa which is assumption if referring to someone as African-American.

The term "African American" (aka Afro-American, Black American, or Black) is generally used for Americans with at least partial Sub-Saharan African ancestry. Many African Americans are the direct descendants of captive Africans who survived the slavery era within the boundaries of the present United States, although some are—or are descended from—voluntary immigrants from African, Caribbean, Central American or South American nations.

According to 2007 U.S. Census Data there are about 40 million Blacks or African Americans in the United States including those who indicate that they are more than one race. Black make up 13.5 percent of the total U.S. population.[2] This figure represents an increase of more than half a million residents from one year earlier. The projected black population of the United States (including those of more than one race) for July 1, 2050 is 67 million.[3] On that date, according to the projection, blacks would constitute 15 percent of the nation's total population.

We will begin this discussion with the experience of the first Blacks who arrived in America. Just like other immigrants, these free Blacks saw opportunity.

Managing Workplace Diversity

One example, of a free African looking for opportunities in America is Juan las Canerias, who sailed with Columbus on the first voyage. He was like many Africans in Europe at the time, in that they had achieved freedom and had spent several years in Spain as domestics, soldiers, clerks, and artisans.[4] According to Madeleine Burnside in *Marooned: Africans in the Americas 1500 - 1750*[5]:

Juan Garrido, another free man of African descent, joined Ponce de Leon's expeditions to the Caribbean and subsequently traveled to Mexico with Cortez. His experience appears to have been entirely similar to that of any   other Spaniard and, ironically to 20th century eyes, the wealth produced by these expeditions came from the sale of Native American slaves. Garrido was accustomed to this, as slavery was a way life for the conquered in Spain. For centuries, the Moors had been enslaved by Spanish Christians and Christians by Moors, and sub Saharans had been brought to the slave markets of Italy and Spain, along with the Slavs and other eastern Europeans.

Europeans enslaved each other as easily as Africans have ever been accused of doing. According to a new study, Europeans were even enslaved by White Africans (North Africa). This study indicates that a million or more European Christians were enslaved by Muslims in North Africa between 1530 and 1780 – a far greater number than had ever been estimated before.[6]

Why enslave others? Slavery was profitable. Free labor allows those in power to gain wealth at the expense of others. Slavery also existed as a means to utilize criminals. Those who were convicted of crimes instead of being punished by death or other means, they paid their debt to society by enslavement.

But enslaving individuals who would otherwise want their freedom meant isolation. Slaves who were "not" isolated could run away. Therefore it became common practice to look outside of your own country for slaves. This is one reason that many of the Native Americans did not end up as slaves in America but were instead killed or sent to other countries as slaves. Native Americans knew the land and therefore would not be easy to isolate. For slavery in America to flourish and exist with ease, the slaves needed to come from outside the land-- come to an unknown territory.

A prime area for slaves was on the west coast of Africa called the Sudan. This area was ruled by three major empires Ghana (790-1240), Mali (1240-1600), and Songhai (670-1591).[7] Other smaller nations were also canvassed by slavers along the west coast; they included among them: Benin, Dahomey, and Ashanti.

Africans were ideal for this isolated placement in the Americas, as they would recognize immediately that they had no hope of getting home. But this was not the only reason the people of Africa were enslaved. The peoples inhabiting those African nations were known for their skills in agriculture, farming, and mining.

The Africans of Ghana were well known for smelting iron ore, and the Benins were famous for their cast bronze art works.[8] African tribal wars produced captives which became a bartering resource in the European slave market. Other slaves were kidnapped by hunters. The main sources of barter used by the Europeans to secure African slaves were glass beads, whiskey and guns.[9]

Slavery as a form of free labor was on the rise as products like sugar, coffee, cotton, and tobacco became in great need. Many countries like Spain, France, the Dutch, and English wanted their colonial plantation system to work to produce these good and the most profitable means of doing this was by cheap or free labor through slaves. The slave trade was so profitable that, by 1672, the Royal African Company chartered by Charles II of England superseded the other traders and became the richest shipper of human slaves to the mainland of the Americas and the slaves were so valuable to the open market - they were eventually called "Black Gold."[10]

But, we know African slaves were valuable because of their skill level but to the Americas they also were valuable because the Native Americans were difficult to be used as slaves in their own land. Native Americans knew the land and could therefore easily escape. So, it would just be easier to kill off the Native Americans. Africans were also brought to the colonies to replace Native American labor as the Natives died out to the diseases they caught from the Europeans.

For those Native Americans who were not killed they would be bartered for African slaves and would become slaves elsewhere. After King Philip's War in 1697, thousands of Wampanoags were sent to the Caribbean in exchange for Africans.[11]

Slavery in America

Slavery in America has its own unique story but before this is discussed, one question: Why were the Africans chosen as slaves?

According to many researchers like Peter Wood, the Western Africans lived comfortable lives punctuated by the usual environmental and ecological problems that one would expect in the 6th century through the 19th century.[12]

Actually Wood states in his text: "it was because of their settled domestic situations that Africans made good targets for slavery and the slave trade. The very similarity of their material existence to the Europeans of that period made it possible for them to function in the plantation economy of the Americas. If they were wild people living in jungles they would not have made good workers so, they were plucked from their lands not only for their brawn, but for their skills as well."[13]

The number of Africans brought to the Americas has been hard to estimate. While records of the "official" trade are reliable, records of the early trade and smuggled slaves are non-existent. Estimates vary between 9 and 15 million. The slave trade began in the 1500s with only several thousand being bartered or stolen, then over the next 400 years there were tens of thousands being shipped.[14] However, the slave trade dramatically increased from the last quarter of the 17th century through the first quarter of the nineteenth, with more slaves being shipped in the trades last one hundred years than in the previous three hundred.[15] The total estimate of slaves shipped to the United States is more than 600,000.

What happened to make the slave trade grow? Sugar, which was a warm climate crop, created demand for hard working slave (free) labor. Then there were the plantations of tobacco and cotton. While slavery had been a profitable institution to many in the world, slavery in the United States took on a different meaning. Slaves in other areas often could work off their time or even buy their freedom, but slaves in the U.S. were considered a permanent fixture as they were not even considered humans worthy of rights and freedom.[16]

This inhumane treatment started from the point of transferring the slaves from Africa to this part of the world. This transference is known as the Middle Passage and it was an example of what the slave institution would be like in America. Brutal, disgusting, horrifying and frequently fatal was it for the Africans to live through the Middle Passage.[17] But it also showed the African's capacity for survival and fight as the rebellion of the slaves started at this point also. So upon arrival, the Europeans tried to lessen any further likelihood of slave rebellions by transporting people in mixed ethnic groups so that they could not communicate with other transported Africans or family members. This enslavement of blacks was not just about people working the fields and being treated as peasants. As stated earlier, many countries have enslaved people, even countries in Africa. But, it must be stated again that these institutions of slavery were quite different than the enslavement of Blacks in the U.S.

Imagine you, your children, and spouse arrive in an unknown country in a ship on which many people died during the voyage. They didn't just die trying to escape but died because women and children who were less valued were thrown off the ship to decrease the ship's weight. Now, you and your family are standing on an auction block with people flocking around you as though you are workhorses. Then, in a language you are not familiar with you hear words, then see your children and husband sent away each to different places. You are then tied up and gagged to keep the noise of your tremendous emotional outcry down. You arrive alone (without your family) on new land and are stripped, inspected, and raped. You are then given new clothing, tools and scraps that no one else wants to eat.

You are forced to work from sun up to sun down, working in the field and raising the White folks children. When there is the slightest bit of rebellion you are stripped and hung on a tree and beat till blood covers your body. You are taken down and given some time to heal and put right back to work. You are the possession of your master who has total control and will work you, beat you, rape you, and drink the milk out of your breast that's for your newborn baby, all at his desire. You have no rights and are not even considered human; you're just somebody's possession.

This is just one illustration that depicts the experience of slavery from a woman's perspective. There are so many other stories that also depict the horrific experience of slavery in the U.S. But, rather than bombard you with story after story of how the slaves were treated, it is necessary that you understand that slavery was not as depicted on the television production of "Gone with the Wind." Slaves were not out there in the fields singing because they were happy to be slaves.

The brutality of this slave institution was not accepted or tolerated by the slaves. These people who fathered the Civil Rights Movement or Black Freedom Movement as it is often called have a history consumed with a fight for equality. Their fight was unlike the immigrants who voluntarily came here and found discrimination and fought against it. The Africans and their generations of American born children were forced here into a situation where they were treated worse than the wild animals that walked the streets.

Therefore, the Africans had to fight to get back the dignity and rights they had lost. While there were many movements for this fight for dignity, the most well known is The Civil Rights Movement, which is a century long history rooted largely in Southern Black communities. This struggle was against the legally mandated structures of White supremacy.[18] The movement was mobilized and sustained with the mass protests of the 1960s. But, as important as this movement was, it would not have happened if the slaves had not mounted revolutions that forced the issue of freedom and then the issue of equal treatment. The slave revolutions started when they got off the boat and did not end until freedom was proclamated.[19]

Slave Revolutions

Slave revolutions took place because the African people never lost sight of their heritage or their freedom. They did not choose to immigrate here or leave their bountiful continent, which is one of the richest continents in the world. Africa also the first known civilization to man was years ahead (as it relates to intelligence and structure) of many other continents of the world. These great African ancient civilizations that the slaves came from were just as splendid and glorious as any on the face of the earth. These Africans came from greatness and were forced to leave it and would not be satisfied until they were free again.

While some history books and television shows would like to make you think that Africans were savages out in the wild--naked, hungry and illiterate--this is not the true picture of Africans at all. If we were to buy this image, it would make the enslavement of these people in the U.S. seem more like a favor than the brutality that it was. It would seem that there was no reason for the Africans to fight back and if there are no historical accounts of these people fighting back, then maybe people will believe there was some value to slavery in America.

But the truth is there was no value to slavery except to those White slave owners who amassed a fortune from the free labor. According to the 1860 U.S. census, nearly four million slaves were held in a total population of just over 12 million in the 15 states in which slavery was legal.[20] Of all free persons in the 15 slave states, 393,967 people (8%) held slaves.[21] The majority of slaves were held by planters, defined by historians as those who held 20 or more slaves.

So, from the time that the first African was captured until completion of the Emancipation, slaves struck out against the institution in one way or another. Actually, many Africans rebelled even before making it to the ship. Reports show that many Africans committed suicide before they would be taken from their homeland.[22] "Many more committed suicide while crossing the Atlantic. Some others revolted and/or plotted revolt during the voyage. Once subjected to American slavery, many Africans ran away, some found refuge with the Native Americans. Others lived in maroon camps."[23]

Runaways who banded together or who had joined with the Native Americans occupied these maroons. Their existence was fragile and although maroon communities provided a haven for the runaways, it was also an opportunity for new alliances or for flight to thinly populated lands where new life could be made. As the European conquest expanded it became harder for slaves to find anywhere to escape to. But, they never stopped looking for safe havens or stopped fighting for their freedom.

Herbert Aptheker, a famous historian and author, has recorded hundreds of insurrections. Many slave revolts in America were small and ineffective because the slaves did not have access to weapons or resources to fight against the plantation owners who had access to money and weapons.[24] However, three insurrections in particular chilled Southern hearts. These were led by Gabriel Prosser, Denmark Vesey, and Nat Turner and occurred within the short span between 1800 and 1831.[25]

In the spring of 1800, Gabriel, slave of Thomas H. Prosser, a 24 year old man who stood six feet two inches tall began laying plans for a slave revolt that would enlist between 2,000 and 50,000 slaves and field hands.[26] People of all races participated. The plan also enlisted the aid of such resident aliens as the radical Frenchman Charles Quersey and the probably German Alexander Bedeenhurst, and Lucas, a non-Black worker.[27]

Gabriel envisioned the conspiracy as the promised realization of the American Revolution, the struggle of oppressed workers of all races as well as slaves against the "merchants". This was not a war on race but on class.

At this time there were many oppressed white workers who were indentured servants, not free or able to take advantage of capitalism. Gabriel committed his followers (the oppressed) to his vision. They planned and organized for several months where they were able to assemble weapons. They collected clubs, swords, and other crude weapons. On the day of the insurrection, Gabriel and his followers had some bad luck--a severe storm hit Virginia which wiped out many roads and bridges.[28] There plans were then delayed. This delay hurt them though as word had gotten out about what was occurring.

After several masters on plantation knew of the details, they got the government of the United States involved. The government took swift action and 26 of the 35 organizers including Gabriel were hung, and the other nine were transported to Louisiana.[29] In September 1800, during the first weeks of the trials of Gabriel's comrades, the slaves of South Carolina were staging an uprising as well.

In Charleston, some 20 years before these trials of Gabriel's, a slave named Denmark Vesey won $1,500 in a lottery with which he purchased his freedom.[30] During the following years he worked as a carpenter. Originally from the island of St. Thomas, Denmark had been enslaved for a time in Haiti (around 1781).[31] While Denmark could have been satisfied with his own freedom, he was not. He was knew that others were enslaved and he could not just do nothing about this so he created a plan for an insurrection.[32] According to Author Norman Freedman, "he and other freedmen collected two hundred pike heads and bayonets as well as three hundred daggers to use in the revolt, but, before the plans could be put into motion in 1882, a slave informed on them."[33]

Most of the members of Denmark's group were from the "African Church" (the secessionist Methodist Episcopal Church). Over a hundred arrest were made, including four whites who had encouraged the project, and several other leaders including Denmark were executed.[34]

Some additional slave insurrections and conspiracies (these are just of few of the many) are discussed below[35]:

- In 1826, the people of Newbern, being informed that forty slaves were assembled in a swamp, surrounded it, and killed the whole party. Other citizens were discomforted in Hillsboro and Tarboro in North Carolina by these types of uprisings.

- In August of 1839, Joseph Cinque led an African revolt on the slave ship *Amistad* with 53 Africans aboard, killing the captain: "the vessel was then captured by a United States vessel and brought to Connecticut." "Defended before the Supreme Court by former President John Quincy Adams, and were awarded their freedom." This was the basis for the American Film, *Amistad*.

- On November 7, 1841 the slave ship *Creole* of Richmond, Virginia was transporting slaves to New Orleans, the crew mutinied and took her to

Nassau, British West Indies. "The slaves were freed and Great Britain refused indemnity."

Gabriel, Denmark, and their countless predecessors had been intelligent, cunning, rhetorical, and powerful Black figures, but in 1831 a truly charismatic leader emerged from the slave social order—Nat Turner. While Gabriel was a resistance leader, Denmark a preacher, Nat Turner was a prophet. Nat's warrant came from God and the Holy Spirit. Nat's African born parents read the marks on his head and breast as confirming that the child was a prophet who would be able to recount tales of events before they occurred as well as tell the future.[36] His grandmother told him that he would never be of any use to anyone as a slave. Nat proved these things to be true because as a child he had a thirst for knowledge and could give insight into things as a child. Nat soon knew that he was destined for great things.

Several years before an 1831 rebellion, Nat began to experience visions and inner voices.[37] He used these visions and inner voices to assemble slaves basing their plans on what was to occur—their eventual freedom. On August 22, sixty to eighty slaves and free Blacks rose up to join Nat.[37] For two days they ravaged Southampton, killing some fifty-five adults and children of the slave-holding classes. "Nat eluded capture for almost two months. While he was at large, a panic seized large parts of Virginia, North Carolina and Maryland . . . The panic rolled over a large part of the South. It was the barking of a dog that betrayed Nat. When he was finally captured, guns fired all over Southampton County. At his trial he pleaded not guilty, saying that he did not FEEL guilty. Nat Turner was found guilty and sentenced to hang until he was "dead! dead! dead!"[38]

There is documented evidence of conspiracies throughout the entire duration of chattel slavery. Few actually realized fruition, since most were discovered or betrayed by scared and or loyal servants. Moreover, there were plenty of individual acts of rebellion, including a refusal to work hard, poisoning, arson, killings, the breading of tools, faking sickness, and escape (e.g. the "Underground Railroad"). Native Americans often aided the slaves, and for various reasons, including retribution and conviction, some Whites too.

It is no doubt that during this time slave insurrections and the fear of their occurrence created great a need for alarm among the White general population. Because of this fear, they built shelters so they could escape if necessary, slept with guns and even a number of them had heart attacks which caused their death.

Due to this fear and the physical strength of the slaves the plantation owners had to seek various methods for trying to control the slaves. They often would use poor Whites to catch the slaves once they had run. They created slave patrols, which were enlisted groups who could enforce laws against the slaves.[39] state militias. Slave patrols were often equipped with guns and whips and would exert brutal and racially motivated control.[40] Militias were organized to handle revolts. White preachers were used to instill docility and the acceptance of the lot of slavery. Many bible verses were twisted to say that being Black was a curse and slavery was an accepted manner to handle these cursed people (many churches still preach that being black was a curse). They also told their congregations that if slaves were obedient, they would be rewarded in the hereafter.

Even with these resurrections and control methods those in the south did not want the news of what was going on to get back to the white populace. They censored reports and distorted just how amenable the slaves were to slavery. They did not want Whites outside of their areas and foreigners to learn of the warlike environment that had been created due to the Africans fighting back. They still felt that they could get the "Negroes" under control.[41]

Slaves and the American Revolution

While this unrest between slaves and their owners continued, the U.S. found themselves fighting the American Revolution for the same thing—freedom.

During this time of war, do you think the Africans stopped their fight? Would you (as a slave) have helped the U.S. fight for freedom? Did you read about the slaves' role during the American Revolution? If you heard of nothing regarding the slaves during the American Revolution was it because they just quietly sat back and watched?

Well, despite what you may have heard or not heard, Africans played a significant role in the American Revolution. They fought on the opposition's side in many roles because they were promised their freedom by the opposition. Those who did not fight in the war, continued to stage slave uprisings. Therefore, the American Revolution was not a solitary insurrection but several simultaneous upheavals. Yet, according to author and historian Cedric Johnson, in his book on slavery and the constitution, he notes few historians or others portray the Revolution preferring instead to follow George Bancroft (another historian) in staging the Revolution as a "culminating event" that transformed a complex colonial society "into a comfortable, democratic nineteenth-century society that was, after all, good enough for everyone."[41] The American Revolution was hardly anything of the kind, for it bequeathed civil rights on what Linda Grant DePauw, professor of history at George Washington University, estimates to be only 15 percent of the population, leaving poorer colonists, the slaves, all women, and Native Americans to the mercies of a few.[42]

This limited freedom was not what most Americans fought for—the poor whites, the Blacks, and the Native Americans possessed a radically different mission. There were also many uprisings that occurred before this time that forged the American Revolution. Many of these uprisings were that of Blacks (the enslaved and the free). This war of the Blacks, frequently allied with Native Americans and sometimes abolitionist colonials, provided the occasion for the liberation of what some estimate to be one hundred thousand slaves, a fifth of the Black population.[43] This constituted the largest emancipation of slaves in the Americas prior to the Haitian Revolution. But many historians have treated these events as though they did not happen because they are not recounted in many American history books.

Willie Lynch & Slavery

As the slaves fought back and died as punishment, the White slave owners continually sought out ways to keep control without losing their free labor. One example was the "Willie Lynch Chip." The "Willie Lynch Chip" was a controversial letter that some say did not exist, but if it did not exist it certainly was a system that was used to control slaves whether Willie Lynch was the author or not. Whether you accept that the Willie Lynch speech existed or not--isn't the issue (the method of control is). Kenneth Stampp in his important work on slavery in the American South, *The Peculiar Institution* (1956), uses the historical records to outline the five rules for making a slave[44]:

1. Maintain strict discipline.
2. Instill belief of personal inferiority.
3. Develop awe of master's power (instill fear).
4. Accept master's standards of "good conduct."
5. Develop a habit of perfect dependence.

The Willie Lynch speech follows these same rules of thumb. Willie Lynch Chip was named for a White slave owner named William "Willie" Lynch, who supposedly, in a speech delivered on the banks of the James River in 1712, said

Managing Workplace Diversity

there were many ways to maintain control over Black slaves.[45] His strategy of 287 years ago is still being used, in the view of many. The city Lynchburg, VA is named after this man's brother John Lynch. The word lynching was coined because of their family's practice of beating, tarring, feathering and hanging his Black victims coined as "Lynch law."[46]

A replica of the speech given in 1717 by William Lynch follows below[47]:

Gentlemen:

I greet you here on the banks of the James River in the year of our Lord 1712. First, I shall thank you, the gentlemen of the Colony of Virginia, for bringing me here. I am here to help you solve your problems with slaves. Your invitation reached me on my modest plantation in the West Indies where I have experimented with some of the newest and still the oldest methods for control of slaves. Ancient Rome would envy us if my program is implemented.

As our boat sailed south on the James River, named for our illustrious king, whose version of the Bible we cherish, I saw enough to know that your problem is not unique. While Rome used cords of wood as crosses for standing human bodies along its old highways in great numbers, you are here using the tree and rope on occasion.

I caught a whiff of a dead slave hanging from a tree a couple of miles back. You are not only losing valuable stock by hangings, you are having uprisings, slaves are running away, your crops are sometimes left in the field too long for maximum profit, you suffer occasional fires, your animals are killed.

Gentlemen, you know what your problems are; I do not need to elaborate. I am not here to enumerate your problems. I am here to introduce you to a method of solving them.

In my bag I have a foolproof method for controlling your black slaves. I guarantee that if installed correctly it will control the slaves for at least 300 years. My method is simple and members of your family or any overseer can use it.

I have outlined a number of differences among the slaves, and I take these differences and make them bigger. I use fear, distrust and envy for control purposes. These methods have worked on my modest plantation in the West Indies and will work throughout the South.

Take this simple list of differences, think about them. On top of my list "age" but it is there only because it starts with "a", the second is "color" (or shade); there is intelligence, size, sex, size of plantation, status of plantation, attitude of owner, whether the slave lives in the valley or on a hill, east, west, north, south, has fine hair or coarse hair, or is tall or short.

Now that you have a list of differences, I shall give you an outline of action, but before that, I shall assure you that distrust is stronger than trust, and envy is stronger than adulation, respect, or admiration. The Black slave after receiving this indoctrination shall carry on and will become self-refueling and self-generating for hundreds of years, maybe thousands.

Don't forget you must pit the old black vs. the young Black and the young Black male vs. the old Black male. You must use the dark skin slave vs. the light skin slave. You must also have your white servants and overseers distrust all Blacks, but it is necessary they trust and depend on us. They must love and respect and trust ONLY us.

Gentlemen, these kits are your control; use them. Have your wives and children use them, never miss an opportunity. My plan is guaranteed, and the good thing about this plan is that if used intensely for one year, the slaves themselves will remain perpetually distrustful.

Thank you, gentlemen.

It is believed that Willie's message or this type of system was passed around the South as an effective way of handling Black slaves. These new types of control worked through violence but also through a divide and conquer philosophy. Many White slave owners embraced this thinking in order to control their possessions (the slaves) and increase their profit.[48]

Cotton was the largest imported product during this time period and if the plantation owners did not have the slaves to pick the cotton and work for free they would lose a tremendous amount of money. Can you imagine having hundreds of workers who worked for free, were fed the scraps that your family would not eat, that you spent no amount of money on to take care and could work from sun up to sun down. Many families became wealthy as a result of this free labor. Additionally, the United States became a prosperous country on the backs of slaves.[49] These slave owners would do what they could to keep this free labor as long as possible. But, despite this huge incentive to keep control of slaves, slavery did not last.

The slaves ran, utilized the Underground Railroad, and fought for their freedom. This freedom was gained through their bravery, ability to survive the cruelest circumstances, intelligence to learn this new land and language through the desire to be as physically free as they were in their minds. But, in an environment where the slaves were against slave owners who had everything to lose if slavery was abolished, this was not a fight of all Whites against Blacks. Sure, Willie Lynch taught many White minds to distrust Blacks, a distrust that we still see today. But, there were other Whites who knew that slavery was an inhumane institution and they worked with the Africans to abolish it.

White & Black Abolitionists

By the 1840s those associated with the abolitionist movement had gained strength in American life. Abolitionists made slavery a moral issue and used the political process of citizen protest and actions to increase pressure for change. Though the abolitionist movement did not cause the Civil War, it clearly defined its moral principles.

The very first abolitionist demonstration in America took place in 1688. A group of brave Quakers gathered in Germantown, Pennsylvania, to voice their religious objections to the slave trade.[50] At first, few free Whites paid much attention to the Quakers' calls for an end to slavery. But, eventually those men and women of all races who participated in the abolitionist movement made their case through speeches, pamphlets, and journals. In these spoken and written words by individuals such as William Lloyd Garrison, Frederick Douglass, and Angelina Grimke Weld they captured the moral passion of their cause.

Many when they think of slavery see blacks verse whites. But, when you note that oppressed whites joined in the fight against slave owners (the merchants), that whites risked their own freedom in order to teach blacks the American language (a language very different from their native tongue), that whites joined forces to become abolitionist as well as walk along side blacks during the civil war—this African American experience cannot be blamed on "whites" as a group because not all whites bought into what was occurring to blacks in America.

The first abolitionist organization on record, the American Colonization Society, was founded in 1816 and focused on gradual emancipation by individual slaveowners.[51] Once the slaves were freed, some thought it best that they be returned to Africa. William Lloyd Garrison, a White man and reformer from Boston, directly challenged the claims of this mindset. He felt that such an approach was racist and focused more on returning slaves than on ending slavery.[52] He also challenged the central writers of the U.S. Constitution because it was the document that granted freedom to all.

On January 1, 1831 he published the first issue of *The Liberator*, which became one of the leading antislavery journals in the U.S.[53] In a church basement; he organized a new abolitionist group, the New England Anti-Slavery society that included Blacks and Whites. In 1833, he and 62 others established the American Anti-Slavery society. This organization became what many referred to as "militant in their views" because they started threatening all slave owners.[54]

Abolitionists used different tactics to persuade the nation to end slavery. The primary method was the moral appeal to do the right thing and to convince Christians that slavery was a sin. Other abolitionists used more direct methods such as bringing anti-slave petitions before Congress and by forming alternative political parties. Another approach was to boycott goods made by slave labor hoping this economic method would be felt through loss of profits.

Mob violence was following abolitionists wherever they took their message. When William Garrison wrote an editorial attacking mob violence for *The Liberator*, Amgelina Grimke, a White Quaker, wrote a private heartfelt response in support of Garrison but hesitated to send it.[55] After a few days she mailed it and without permission, Garrison published it in his paper. Many abolitionists believe that it forwarded the movement immensely, but it forced Angelina and her sister Sarah to repudiate the letter and remain Quakers in good standing or embrace the abolitionist movement.[56]

They decided to embrace the abolitionist movement and were met with the same violence that Garrison had spoken of in his letter. Many abolitionists welcomed them as women because as southern women they knew first hand of the horrors of slavery. The Grimke sisters helped the cause because they reached an untouched segment of society—southerners and women. Yet while they were welcomed by some abolitionists, some did not welcome them as they felt they were abandoning their God given role as women.[57] They came to understand that their sex would be used against them as another way of attacking the anti-slavery movement—as would be the case for thousands of women to come. The Grimke sisters became loyal feminists because they realized that if they did not create an environment in which women could operate, they would not be effective in the fight against slavery.

Furthermore, Angelina became the first American women to address the state legislature on behalf of slavery and women's rights.[58] Sarah Grimke addressed slavery but also addressed it from a woman's perspective. She also did a review of the bible to understand how it related to women. Through her study of the bible she offered one of the most coherent arguments for woman's equality of all races yet written by a woman in *Letters on the Equality of the Sexes*.[59] She identified and characterized the difference between sex and gender taking race and class into consideration. She tied the subordination of women both to educational deprivation and sexual oppression. She identified white males, individually and as a group, as having benefited from the subordination of women. These women worked twofold as they saw the connection between slavery of Africans and subordination of women.

These types of issues of course added to the complexity of the abolitionist movement. But there was a much further complicated issue that was addressed by Black abolitionist Frederick Douglass. Douglass and other Black abolitionists sharpened the view even more: they called attention to the effects of slavery and discrimination felt by Blacks.[60] This was different because White abolitionists tended to see slavery and freedom as absolute moral opposites, while African Americans knew that there were degrees of freedom. Many of the Black abolitionist experienced discrimination from some of their White abolitionist colleagues. The White abolitionist refused to hire Blacks. Due to this difference and Douglass speaking out against this discrimination, there was friction between Douglass and Garrison and they went their separate ways.[61]

While there were many issues that the abolitionists brought forth by addressing slavery, each had a different commitment to their view. But, despite their differences, both Black and White and male and female abolitionists agreed more than they disagreed and generally worked together. They supported each other's publications, worked together fighting discrimination as well as slavery, and united in defending themselves against attacks of people who regarded them as dangerous fanatics.

Jim Crow Laws

Once slavery was abolished, it was clear that the slaves were not the only ones who had been exposed to Willie Lynch's brainwashing methods. The White servants and family members of these slave owners had also been brought into Willie's ways of thinking, the distrust and fear of blacks that he so advocated still existed. Plus, there was still an air of White supremacy. Many Whites still felt that Blacks were inherently inferior and to supported this belief sought rationalization through religion and science—as some still attempt to do today.[62] During the 1880's, the U.S. Supreme Court was inclined to agree with the White supremacists judgment and began to strike down the foundations of the post-Civil War reconstruction.[63] It declared that the Civil Rights Act of 1875 was unconstitutional.

There were also many attempts made to keep Blacks and Whites separate. In 1896, the Supreme Court legitimized the principle of "separate but equal" in its ruling *Plessy v. Ferguson.* The high court ruling led to an explosion of "Jim Crow Laws" named after Jim Crow a Black character in minstrel shows. From the 1880s until the 1960s, a majority of American states and cities enforced segregation through these Jim Crow Laws. The following pages give some examples of Jim Crow laws from various states and are taken from *www.eastridgehigh.org/academics/departments/english_languageArts/documents/Jim_Crow_Webquest.doc*

Jim Crow Laws from Varying States

Nurses No person or corporation shall require any White female nurse to nurse in wards of rooms in hospitals, either public or private, in which Negro men are placed.

Buses All passenger stations in this state operated by any motor transportation company shall have separate waiting rooms or space and separate tickets windows for the White and Colored races.

Restaurants It shall be unlawful to conduct a restaurant or other place for the serving of food in the city, at which White and Colored people are served in the same room, unless such White and Colored persons are effectually separated by a solid partition extending from the floor upward to an instance of seven feet or higher, and unless a separate entrance from the street is provided for each compartment.

Pool and Billiard Rooms It shall be unlawful for a Negro and White person to play together or in company with each other at any game of pool or billiards.

Toilet Facilities, Male Every employer of White or Negro males shall provide for such White or Negro males reasonably accessible and separate toilet facilities.

Intermarriage the marriage of a person of Caucasian blood with a Negro, Mongolian, Malay, or Hindu shall be null and void.

Theaters Every person...operating . . . any public hall, theater, opera house, motion picture show or any place of public entertainment or public assemblage which is attended by both White and Colored persons shall separate the White race and the Colored race and shall set apart and designate... certain seats therein to be occupied by White persons and a portion thereof, or certain seats therein to be occupied by Colored persons.

Railroads the conductors or managers on all such railroads shall have power, and are hereby required, to assign to each White or Colored passenger his or her respective car, coach or compartment. If the passenger fails to disclose his race, the conductor and managers, acting in good faith, shall be the sole judges of his race.

Wine and Beer All persons licensed to conduct the business of selling beer or wine . . . shall serve either White people exclusively or Colored people exclusively and shall not sell to the two races within the same room at any time.

Reform Schools The children of White and Colored races committed to the houses of reform shall be kept entirely separate from each other.

Circus Tickets All circuses, shows, and tent exhibitions, to which the attendance of . . . more than one race is invited or expected to attend shall provide for the convenience of its patrons not less than two ticket offices with individual ticket takers and receivers, and in the case of outside tent performances, the said ticket offices shall not be less than twenty-five (25) feet apart.

Housing Any person . . . who shall rent any part of any such building to a Negro person or a Negro family when such building is already in whole or in part in occupancy by a White person or White family, or vice versa when the building is in occupancy by a Negro person or Negro family, shall be guilty of a misdemeanor and on conviction thereof shall be punished by a fine of not less than twenty-five ($25.00) nor more than one hundred ($100.00) dollars or be imprisoned not less than 10, or more than 60 days, or both such fine and imprisonment in the discretion of the court.

The Blind The board of trustees shall . . . maintain a separate building . . . on separate ground for the admission, care, instruction, and support of all blind persons of the Colored or Black race.

Intermarriage All marriages between a White person and a Negro, or between a White person and a person of Negro descent, to the third generation, inclusive, or between a White person and a member of the Malay race; or between the Negro and a member of the Malay race**; or between a person of Negro descent to the third generation, inclusive and a member of the Malay race, are forever prohibited, and shall be void.

**The Malays are the race of people who inhabit the Malay Peninsula (what is today Peninsular Malaysia) and portions of adjacent islands of Southeast Asia, including the east coast of Sumatra, the coast of Borneo, and smaller islands that lie between these areas.

Education Separate schools shall be maintained for the children of the White and Colored races.

Promotion of Equality Any person . . . who shall be guilty of printing, publishing or circulating printed, typewritten or written matter urging or presenting for public acceptance or general information, arguments or suggestions in favor of social equality or of intermarriage between Whites and Negroes, shall be guilty of a misdemeanor and subject to a fine of not exceeding five hundred ($500.00) dollars or imprisonment not exceeding six (6) months or both.

Intermarriage The marriage of a white person with a Negro or mulatto or person, who shall have one-eighth or more of Negro blood, shall be unlawful and void.

Hospital Entrance There shall be maintained by the governing authorities of every hospital maintained by the state for the treatment of White and Colored patients separate entrances for White and Colored patients and visitors, and such entrances shall be used by the race only for which they are prepared.

Prisons The warden shall see that the White convicts shall have separate apartments for both eating and sleeping from the Negro convicts.

Education Separate free schools shall be established for the education of children of African descent; and it shall be unlawful for any Colored child to attend any White school, or any white child to attend a Colored school.

Intermarriage All marriages between . . . White persons and Negroes or White persons and Mongolians . . . are prohibited and declared absolutely void . . . No person having one-eighth part or more of Negro blood shall be permitted to marry any White person, nor shall any White person be permitted to marry any Negro or person having one-eighth part or more Negro blood.

Education Separate rooms [shall] be provided for the teaching of pupils of African descent, and [when] said rooms are so provided such pupils may not be admitted to the school rooms occupied and used by pupils of Caucasian or other descent.

Textbooks Books shall not be interchangeable between the White and Colored schools, but shall continue to be used by the race first using them.

Libraries The state librarian is directed to fit up and maintain a separate place for the use of the Colored people who may come to the library for the purpose of reading books or periodicals

Militia The White and Colored militia shall be separately enrolled, and shall never be compelled to serve in the same organization. No organization of Colored troops shall be permitted where White troops are available, and while White troops are permitted to be organized, Colored troops shall be under the command of White officers.

Intermarriage All marriages between a White person and a Negro, or between a white person and a person of Negro descent to the fourth generation inclusive, are hereby forever prohibited.

Cohabitation Any Negro man and White woman, or any White man and Negro woman, who are not married to each other, who shall habitually live in and occupy in the nighttime the same room shall each be punished by imprisonment not exceeding twelve (12) months, or by fine not exceeding five hundred ($500.00) dollars.

Education The schools for White children and the schools for Negro children shall be conducted separately.

Juvenile Delinquents There shall be separate buildings, not nearer than one-fourth mile to each other, one for White boys and one for Negro boys. White boys and Negro boys shall not, in any manner, be associated together or work together.

Mental Hospitals. The Board of Control shall see that proper and distinct apartments are arranged for said patients, so that in no case shall Negroes and White persons be together.

Barbers No Colored barber shall server as a barber [to] White women or girls.

Burial The officer in charge shall not bury, or allow to be buried, any Colored persons upon ground set apart or used for the burial of White persons.

Restaurants All persons licensed to conduct a restaurant, shall serve either White people exclusively or Colored people exclusively and shall not sell to the two races within the same room or serve the two races anywhere under the same license.

Amateur Baseball It shall be unlawful for any amateur White baseball team to play baseball on any vacant lot or baseball diamond within two blocks of a playground devoted to the Negro race, and it shall be unlawful for any amateur Colored baseball team to play baseball in any vacant lot or baseball diamond within two blocks of any playground devoted to the White race.

Parks It shall be unlawful for Colored people to frequent any park owned or maintained by the city for the benefit, use and enjoyment of White persons . . . and unlawful for any White person to frequent any park owned or maintained by the city for the use and benefit of Colored persons.

Transportation The . . . Utilities Commission . . . is empowered and directed to require the establishment of separate waiting rooms at all stations for the White and Colored races.

Teaching Any instructor who shall teach in any school, college, or institution where members of the White and Colored race are received and enrolled as pupils for instruction shall be deemed guilty of a misdemeanor, and upon conviction thereof, shall be fined in any sum not less than ten dollars ($10.00) nor more than fifty dollars ($50.00) for each offense.

Fishing, Boating, and Bathing The [Conservation] Commission shall have the right to make segregation of the White and Colored races as to the exercise of rights of fishing, boating, and bathing.

Mining The baths and lockers for the Negroes shall be separated from the White race, but may be in the same building.

Telephone Booths The Corporation Commission is hereby vested with power and authority to require telephone companies . . . to maintain separate booths for White and Colored patrons when there is a demand for such separate booths. That the Corporation Commission shall determine the necessity for said separate booths only upon complaint of the people in the town and vicinity to be served after due hearing as now provided by law in other complaints filed with the Corporation Commission.

Lunch Counters No persons, firms, or corporations, who or which furnish meals to passengers at station restaurants or station eating houses, in times limited by common carriers of said passengers, shall furnish said meals to White and Colored passengers in the same room, or at the same table, or at the same counter.

Child Custody It shall be unlawful for any parent, relative, or other white person in this State, having the control of custody of any White child, by right of guardianship, natural or acquired, or otherwise, to dispose of, give or surrender such white child permanently into the custody, control, maintenance, or support, of a Negro.

Libraries Any White person of such county may use the county free library under the rules and regulations prescribed by the commissioner's court and may be entitled to all the privileges thereof. Said court shall make proper provision for the Negroes of said county to be served through separate branch or branches of the county free library, which shall be administered by [a] custodian of the Negro race under the supervision of the county librarian.

So, what does this mean regarding the **Treatment of Blacks Today?**

Race is a real part of black people's lives—so much so that it keeps them guessing about why they are being treated a certain way when situations occur. "Is it because I'm black or is it me?" "Was that an insult because I am black or just because...?"

As people, we might not be aware of it everyday but it only takes a look, a word, an inappropriate action, or an overt denial of basic rights or privileges to make race present, felt, and therefore real.

These are burdens of the past, that still affect many today and can become an everyday experience for Blacks. Race and inequality has been the cause that has united Blacks (despite attempts to divide and conquer). Fighting for the promise of mutual respect and a level playing field of economic opportunity. The struggle for many Blacks or Blacks as a group continues because after hundreds of years of mistreatment, forty years of equal rights laws and a Black President (President Obama) just is not enough to level the playing field and keep blacks from wondering "is it just me or is it because I am black."

Many blacks are just a few generations removed from their slave ancestors, so would slavery still bother them? Would confederacy symbolism and nooses that represent lynching's still bother them? Would words utilized during slavery (like boy, colored people, fetch this) still bother them? The answer in many cases is yes--as for many blacks the wounds are still open and have not healed.

But who should be responsible for this healing? Whites? This would make a complex problem seem simple. Majority of whites did not benefit from slavery, did not participate in slavery and have not directly done an injustice to blacks.

So then how does healing occur?

A start would be a serious apology for the brutal treatment of Africans in this country. This actually has begun when Rep. Steve Cohen, a Democrat from Tennessee, drafted the resolution and presented it to the House on July 29, 2008 indicating in his speech that a total of 120 lawmakers, including two Republicans, co-sponsored the resolution, Cohen said.[64]

In February, the Senate apologized for atrocities committed against Native Americans, and the body apologized in 2005 for standing by during a lynching campaign against African Americans throughout much of the past century. Twenty years ago, Congress apologized for interning Japanese Americans in concentration camps during World War II.[65]

While an apology for slavery has long been an issue for African Americans it is often stated that this apology was prolonged because of the issue of reparations. There has yet been any type of reparation and the apology continues as Iowa Democratic Senator Tom Harkin sponsored a resolution that passed on June 17, 2009 that "acknowledges the fundamental injustice, cruelty, brutality and inhumanity of slavery," and "apologizes to African Americans on behalf of the people of the United States for the wrongs committed against them and their ancestors who suffered under slavery and Jim Crow Laws."[66]

So now what?

- Reparations (repayment for all the hundreds of years of free labor that corporations and land owners had)?
- More laws and policies to stop racial profiling, an unfair criminal system targeted towards Blacks (read the sentencing project found on www.google.com) and enforcement of workplace policies that would level the playing field forcing equal treatment?
- History books in the K-12 curriculum that teaches the real story about people of color in the country?
- Media that is not focused on black violence which always makes the headline aside from other group's violence?

You think about what would it take. Most certainly an attack on Affirmative Action (the policy that seeks to level the playing the field) is probably not the answer. Politicians and big business (those) who have directly benefited from slavery have to recognize that America would not be the "powerhouse" it is today without those hundreds of years of free labor. So now that that was all done, do you just walk away and say oh well we, the U.S. are (in some eyes) okay now?

Unfortunately, still today you can find that "race" an obvious difference among people—perpetuates itself in many negative ways. Are there those who are afraid of Blacks because they have been portrayed as violent even though they were the ones taking the lynchings and not giving them? Is it not the case that blacks still disproportionately live separate from their suburban counterparts where acceptance and integration in certain neighborhoods is occurring very slowly? Is it not the case that Blacks get racially profiled when it comes to crimes, jobs, driving, and voting opportunities? The list could continue but you get the point.

There is still another disparaging fact—despite all of this oppression against blacks in this country, Blacks have and continue to make significant contributions to our U.S. society; yet, this has not been included in American history. Black history month is when you learn about African American contributions but you learn very little about the Black scientists, doctors and inventors (areas that are perceived as only for the intellectual best). We learn instead that blacks contributed when it benefited themselves during the Civil Rights Era. We hear about black athletes and entertainers. But is this all that Blacks in America have and continue to do? If you don't know the real answer then that is unfortunate.

If we are to continue in our quest for valuing diversity, it is not only necessary to understand the past and the struggles of different groups in our society, but it is just as important to understand each group's contributions. Otherwise, we wonder: why do "these people" deserve the respect and equal treatment they are always demanding.

Concluding Thoughts

Restoration of the rich history that slavery and segregation severed seems necessary if we are to understand why yet still today we are addressing various plights from social to systematic racism faced by blacks. Few would argue against the fact that nearly four decades of employment law have made a significant change to the face of the American workplace. But, after hundreds of years of racism toward Blacks, equal opportunity is not yet a realism for African Americans.

End of Chapter Questions

1. What is meant by chattel slavery? Why was slavery in America more brutal than other slave institutions?

2. In what manner did the slaves fight back against slavery?

3. How does the Willie Lynch speech still impact blacks and whites today?

4. Is equal opportunity a reality today for blacks, why or why not?

5. Is the following a true or false statement: All whites were in favor of slavery, explain your answer.

Internet Exercise

Using the Internet, go to (short list of inventions provided) http://www.phillyhiphop.com/_features/wedidittheyhidit1.html or http://www.black-collegian.com/african/inventions605.shtml or to the following site to look at a more extensive list of black inventors http://inventors.about.com/library/blblackinventors.htm or go to www.google.com and type: black inventors

- Now list eight to nine of the inventions that you use in a normal week.
- Now answer the following question: Blacks seem to be highlighted when it comes to sports and entertainment or civil rights—what is your view on sharing these important scientific contributions to U.S. society, how can this cultural knowledge (area of knowledge and contribution perceived as only for the intellectual best) change or enhance one's view of Blacks? How could it help Black children?

End of Chapter Exercise

Was this just a joke gone bad?

According to the January 2008 Press Release by the EEOC, from approximately 1998 through January 2006, African American employees at Henredon's High Point manufacturing plant were subjected to racial slurs and name calling -- including the "N-word" -- as well as threats by hangman's nooses that were displayed at the plant. The suit alleged that the harassment occurred almost daily. Henredon Furniture, a subsidiary of Furniture Brands International, operated a furniture plant in High Point, N.C., until January 2006. Furniture Brands International is America's largest home furnishings manufacturer.

"This case is the latest indicator that racial harassment in general, and nooses in particular, remain persistent problems at some job sites nationwide," said EEOC Chair Naomi C. Earp. "It's time for corporate America to be more proactive in preventing and eliminating racist behavior in the workplace. The EEOC intends to make clear that race and color discrimination in the workplace, whether verbal or behavioral, is unacceptable and will not be tolerated."

In addition to the $465,000 in compensatory damages to be divided among the seven class members, the three year consent decree resolving the case (*EEOC v. Henredon Furniture Industries Inc.*, Case No. 1:06CV00744, filed in the U.S. District Court for the Middle District of North Carolina), includes injunctive relief enjoining Henredon Furniture from engaging in racial harassment or retaliation.

Questions for Discussion

Why would some diminish this to just being a joke and blacks in the plant see this as a hostile work environment? How should this have been handled so it would not involve a lawsuit? What should be done by management to change the racial climate at the plant?

References

1. Henderson, G. (1994). *Cultural Diversity in the Workplace: Issues and Strategies*. Westport, Connecticut: Praegar Publishing.

2. U.S. Census Bureau. (n.d.). *African Americans by the Numbers*. Retrieved from http://www.infoplease.com/spot/bhmcensus1.html

3. Ibid.

4. Burnside, M. (n.d.).*Marooned: Africans in the Americas 1500 - 1750*. Mel Fisher Museum. Retrieved from http://www.kislakfoundation.org/millennium-exhibit/author1.htm

5. Ibid.

6. Davis, R. C. (2009). *White Slavery in the Mediterranean, the Barbary Coast and Italy, 1500-1800*. New York, NY: Palgrave Macmillan Ltd.

7. Klein, H. S. (1999). *The Atlantic slave trade*. New York: Cambridge University Press.

8. Ibid.

9. Ibid.

10. Thorton, J. (1997, November). The business of slavery. *New York Times Book Review*, 11.

11. Burnside, M. (n.d.). *Marooned: Africans in the Americas 1500 - 1750*. Mel Fisher Museum. Retrieved from http://www.kislakfoundation.org/millennium-exhibit/author1.htm

12. Wood, P. (1974). *Black Majority*. New York: Random House.

13. Ibid.

14. Burnside, M. (n.d.). *Marooned: Africans in the Americas 1500 - 1750*. Mel Fisher Museum. Retrieved from http://www.kislakfoundation.org/millennium-exhibit/author1.htm

15. Ibid.

16. Thomas, H. (1997). *The slave trade: the story of the Atlantic slave trade, 1440-1870*. New York: Simon & Schuster.

17. Howard, T. (1971). *Black voyage: eyewitness accounts of the Atlantic slave trade*. Boston: Little, Brown.

18. Bennett, L., Jr. (1966). *Before the Mayflower: a history of the Negro in America, 1619-1964*. Baltimore: Penguin Books.

19. Ibid.

20. 1860 Census Results. (n.d.). *The Civil War Home Page.* Retrieved from http://www.civil-war.net/pages/1860_census.html

21. American Civil War Census Data. (n.d.). Retrieved from http://www.civil-war.net/census.asp?census=Total

22. Howard, T. (1971). *Black voyage: eyewitness accounts of the Atlantic slave trade.* Boston: Little, Brown.

23. Dixon, L., Hynes, G. & Nelson, C. G. (n.d.). *A Black Perspective of American History.* Retrieved from http://www.duboislc.org/BlackPerspective/BlackPerspectivePart3.html

24. Aptheker, H. (1983). *American Negro Slave Revolts.* New York: International Publishers.

25. Genovese, E. D. (1992). *From Rebellion to Revolution: Afro-American Slave Revolts in the Making of the Modern World.* Baton Rouge: Louisiana State University Press.

26. Aptheker, H. (1983). *American Negro Slave Revolts.* New York: International Publishers.

27. Ibid.

28. Genovese, E. D. (1992). *From Rebellion to Revolution: Afro-American Slave Revolts in the Making of the Modern World.* Baton Rouge: Louisiana State University Press.

29. Ibid.

30. Wood, P. H. (1974). *Black Majority: Negroes in Colonial South Carolina from 1670 through the Stono Rebellion.* New York: Knopf.

31. Ibid.

32. Coombs, N. (1972). *The Immigrant Heritage of America.* New York: Twayne Press.

33. Ibid.

34. Ibid.

35. Katz, W. L. (1990). *Breaking the Chains: African-American Slave Resistance.* New York: Macmillan.

36. Ibid.

37. Robinson, C. J. (1997). *Black Movements in America.* New York: Routledge.

38. Oates, S. B. (1975). *The Fires of Jubilee: Nat Turner's Fierce Rebellion.* New York: Harper and Row.

39. Genovese, E. D. (1992). *From Rebellion to Revolution: Afro-American Slave Revolts in the Making of the Modern World.* Baton Rouge: Louisiana State University Press.

40. Ibid.

41. Johnson, C. (2007). *Revolutionaries to race leaders; Black power and the making of African American politics*. Minnesota: University of Minnesota Press.

42. Bennett, L., Jr. (1966). *Before the Mayflower: a history of the Negro in America, 1619-1964*. Baltimore: Penguin Books.

43. Ibid.

44. Stampp, K. (1989). *The Peculiar Institution: Slavery in the Ante-Bellum South.* London: Vintage Publishing.

45. Slave Chronicles. (2004, July). The Willie Lynch Letter and The Destruction of Black Unity. *Black Wallstreet*.

46. Wells, I. B. (1893). *Lynch law*. Retrieved from http://www.historyisaweapon.com/defcon1/wellslynchlaw.html

47. Slave Chronicles. (2004, July). The Willie Lynch Letter and The Destruction of Black Unity. *Black Wallstreet*.

48. Ibid.

49. Ibid.

50. The Northern Abolitionist Movement. (2005-2006). *American Civil War Reference Library*. New York: Thomson Learning, Inc.

51. *Sisterhood and Slavery: Transatlantic Antislavery and Women's Rights*. (2001). Retrieved from http://www.yale.edu/glc/conference/civin.pdf

52. *Means and Ends in American Abolitionism*. (1969). New York: Pantheon Books.

53. Ibid.

54. McPherson, J. M. (1964). *The Struggle for Equality*. Princeton, N.J.: Princeton University Press.

55. Lerner, G. (1971). *The Grimké Sisters from South Carolina*. New York: Schocken Books.

56. Ibid.

57. Ibid.

58. Ibid.

59. Ibid.

60. Taylor, K. H. (1996). *Black Abolitionists and Freedom Fighters*. West Bloomfield: Oliver Press.

Managing Workplace Diversity

61. Means and Ends in American Abolitionism. (1969). New York: Pantheon Books.

62. Jentz, J. B. (1977). *Artisans, Evangelicals, and the City: A Social History of the Labor and Abolitionist Movements in Jacksonian New York*. City University of New York: Ph.D. dissertation.

63. Franklin, J. H. & Moss, A. A. Jr. (1988). *From slavery to freedom: a history of Negro Americans*. New York: Knopf.

64. Fears, D. (2008, July 30). The Washington Post. Retrieved from: http://www.washingtonpost.com/wp-dyn/content/article/2008/07/29/AR2008072902279.htm

65. Ibid.

66. Hannah, D. C. (2009, June 19). *Congress Apologizes for Slavery*. Retrieved from: http://www.diversityinc.public/5995.efm

Chapter Eight

Understanding the Asian American & Latino Experience

A wise man makes his own decisions an ignorant man follows the public opinion.

Chinese Proverb

UNDERSTANDING THE ASIAN AMERICAN AND LATINO MIGRATION EXPERIENCE

Chapter Objectives

After reading this chapter, you should be able to:

- understand why the Chinese, Japanese and Filipino migrate(d) to the United States.

- identify laws that were created against the Chinese, Japanese and Filipino.

- understand why the Mexicans, Puerto Ricans and Cubans migrate(d) to the United States.

- identify laws created against the Mexicans, Puerto Ricans and Cubans.

- describe why the United States wanted the Asian and Latino populations in America.

- determine what caused these groups migration to be no longer wanted.

ASIAN AMERICAN MIGRATION EXPERIENCE

<u>Who are Asian Americans?</u>
Chinese, Japanese, Filipinos, Koreans, Vietnamese, Cambodians, ethnic Lao, Hmong, Thai, Samoans, Tongans, & Asian Indian are just a few of the ethnicities that are considered Asian American. Chinese, Filipinos, Japanese, Asian Indians, Koreans, and the Vietnamese constitute nearly 90% of all Asian Americans.

Many would also like to add Hawaiians, Samoans, & Guamanians to the above list however they should not be added, as they are Pacific Islanders. Pacific Islanders are qualitatively and culturally different from Asian Americans. They also make up smaller numbers as compared to the population of Asian Americans and therefore will not be discussed in this textbook.

Each Asian American group is very distinct with its own history, language and culture. The ancestral tongues of Asian Americans range from Tagalog to Japanese to Hindu to Korean. They also practice various religions such as: Hinduism, Buddhism, Jainism, Taoism and Roman Catholicism just to name a few. Any person of Asian descent, either native or foreign born, living in the U.S. is considered Asian American. But, many of Asian descent still identify strongly with their country of origin. They may often be more likely to refer to themselves as Japanese or Chinese American, etc... rather than just Asian American.

Many of Asian descent as well as other immigrants come to the U.S. seeking relief from their communistic economic systems and dictatorial leadership. In many communistic countries the government has control of all the land, labor and capital (money). They can therefore make it very difficult for the average citizen to have any freedom or wealth. If in a communistic country those in rule decide to take 90% of the wealth and divide it amongst 2% of the population it can and the other 98% of the country could live in extreme poverty. The people who leave these countries and migrate to the United States are often in search of the many freedoms and wealth that the U.S. has to offer.

CHINESE AMERICANS

The first significant immigration to America came about in the 1850s when gold was found in California. The Californians didn't seem to mind when more than 80,000 fortune seekers from every corner of the globe descended on the gold mines.[1] The Chinese (mainly men) were among these seekers whom California rolled out the welcome mat for.

While the Chinese may have come for gold, the U.S. wanted them here because they needed cheap labor to work in the fields, factories and on the railroads.[2] The word got out and more Chinese men came to assist the U.S. in building up its country. As the population of California continued to increase, by 1852, 10% of the 250,000 people were Chinese.[3] But, now they weren't welcomed. Some whites were becoming furious at their arrival as they felt they were a threat for their employment.[4] There were soon cries like, "California for Americans" that were heard across the state.[5]

The government, however, refused to pass laws forbidding foreigners to mine. Nor did the government limit immigration. This outraged many Whites because they were not only mad about the Chinese participation but also considered the Native Americans and Mexicans who lived in California foreigners as well.[6] Never mind the fact that the both the Native Americans and Mexicans lived in California and elsewhere in the U.S. centuries before the arrival of White settlers.

In these days of the California Gold Rush, the young American Republic was pursuing a dream of "Manifest Destiny."[7] That is, stretching its borders in every direction for the free development of multiplying millions. America needed strong, reliable workers and they found them in the Chinese. The Chinese were also in abundance and would work for minimal wages and the government did not want them to leave.[8]

Some whites in Congress, however, didn't just want to use the Asian Americans for cheap labor they wanted to secure citizenship rights for them by amending the Naturalization Law of 1790.[9] This Law specified that only "whites" were eligible for naturalized citizenship. However, this only received one-third of Congress' support and the fight against the Chinese did not end here.

Another very detrimental act towards the Chinese was passed. The Chinese Exclusion Act of 1882, which was a victory for those who wanted to rid the U.S. of Chinese immigrants. This Act was the first and only immigration law in American History to target a specific nationality as it prohibited the Chinese from entering the U.S.[10]

At the time of the Act there were 70,000 documented Chinese men and fewer than 4,000 Chinese women in the U.S.[11] These numbers posed a serious problem for the Chinese bachelors, because there were so few Chinese women and most non-Chinese women shunned their company. Furthermore, many of these men did not want non-Chinese women anyway because they did not want to jeopardize the ethnic purity of their lineage.

But over time, as the Chinese men assimilated to American life these aliens did marry American women who were citizens. They themselves were then able to achieve citizenship. But, the government felt that America's Anglo-Saxon way of life was in jeopardy and so they then passed the Draconian Cable Act in 1922.[12] This act punished American women for marrying these Chinese men. Their punishment was a loss of U.S. citizenship. This act was fought and repealed in 1936, but until then American women stayed clear of Chinese men.[13]

But those angry Whites with power did not stop there, there were other acts passed that were similar to the Cable Act, such as the Exclusion Act.[14] By 1943, the Exclusion Act was finally repealed and a statue was put into place that was to be completely colorblind. However, this new law only allowed an annual quota of 105 for naturalization (citizen by oath).[15] This law did not alleviate the obvious racism that had been targeted towards the Chinese all these years. For example, if there was a Chinese born in Canada they still fell into this category of naturalization, but if a person of European ancestry was born in Canada they could enter as a non-quota immigrant despite the fact that both of these individuals would have been Canadian citizens.

So even though the Chinese came for freedom and wealth once here they struggled for equality and dignity. Yet despite all these setbacks, there were still many Chinese Americans who contributed significantly to American history. The construction of the Central Pacific Railroad line was a feat accomplished mainly by the Chinese. Of the 10,000 laborers in the Central Pacific, 9000 were Chinese.[16] They worked extremely hard, clearing trees, blasting rocks with explosions, shoveling and carting away debris and laying tracks. A thousand of these Chinese workers lost their lives in this endeavor.[17]

But, when the railroad was done and the golden spike was driven to commemorate the momentous occasion, no Chinese were present. Despite their significant contributions, the Chinese had been purposely left out of the ceremonies as well as from the "famous" photograph of Americans who drove the golden spike.[18] As if this wasn't enough, to add insult to injury, the Central Pacific then laid-off almost all of the Chinese.

Rather than return home to an impoverished government controlled China, these now unemployed Chinese gathered in San Francisco where they joined with other Chinese ex-miners in the manufacturing fields. San Francisco, the 9th leading manufacturing city in America, may have not acquired this title had it not been for the Chinese. The Chinese were in low paying jobs in these manufacturing companies and even when they did the same work as Whites, their wages were less. The question is though, weren't the Whites immigrants as well? So, why was there differential treatment? This hostility toward the Chinese as well as Native-Americans, Mexicans and enslaved Blacks leads us to the issue of racism.

While every culture or ethnicity has the premise to be racist, in understanding racism, an important variable to understand is the presence of power. It is the power to enforce the "prejudgment" of superiority or inferiority that leads to racism. Author Judy Katz in studying "White" racism wrote, "Racism is perpetuated by Whites through their conscious and/or unconscious support of a climate and institutions that are founded on racist policies and practices."[19] The racial prejudice of these White people (those at the top of the wealth pyramid who have power) coupled with their political, economic, and social power allows them to be able to enforce discriminatory practices on every level of life and race of people (including other whites).

Racism can make it very difficult for those on the receiving end to achieve success, but it does not prevent it. In this climate of racism, the Chinese have continued to aid the U.S. For instance, the horticulturalist Ah Bing developed in Oregon the popular Bing Cherry and in Florida Lue Gim Gong bred oranges that were resistant to frost, thus enabling Florida's nascent citrus industry to get off the ground. In 1957, Tsung-dao Lee and Chen-nin Yang were awarded the prestigious Nobel Prize in physics for breaking the conservation-of-parity law.[20]

The Chinese also advanced their community, for example in 1852 in San Francisco the first Chinese theater was established in a building brought from China; then in 1854, to advance their own interest the San Francisco's first Chinese Newspaper was published.[21] A few years later an organization was formed later known as the Chinese Consolidated Benevolent Association which arbitrated on behalf of the Chinese, their social welfare and community interests.[22]

During this time of racial discourse directed toward the Chinese, it did prevent the Chinese for fighting for their rights. In one such case Yick Wo, who was convicted of operating a laundry without a license, took his case to the Supreme Court and they found that "the law was administered with an evil eye" to drive Chinese out of business; the law was struck down as discriminatory and this was a key case in defining the 14th Amendment.[23]

JAPANESE AMERICANS

In the 1880s the Japanese government lifted its ban on emigration. Thousands of Japanese, mostly from the countryside, came to Hawaii and later to the United States.[24] They came as many other immigrants did, because of the prospect of a brighter financial future. But, their difference was that while they came to work hard and save money, they also planned to return home. They were planning on being sojourners, that is, travelers. They just wanted to come, live and work for a while in this country, as they were only here temporarily.

As the Japanese came to the U.S., the Japanese government strictly supervised who came in order to protect their honor sending only healthy, strong and relatively well educated Japanese.[25] Many of these Japanese who came were from the rural areas of their country and they brought a wealth of agricultural skills. They utilized these skills in the U.S. and were successful farmers. But, the Japanese weren't comfortable working other's land. They wanted farm ownership for themselves. So, they started pooling their money to make this happen. Even though they owned less than 2% of all farmland in California, White landowners in the western states began to fear Japanese competition.[26] They had so much fear that they used their power to cause Congress to pass the Alien Land Act.[27]

The Alien Land Act of 1913 prohibited ownership of property by "aliens ineligible to citizenship" which due to the Naturalization Act included the Japanese.[28] But, the Japanese attempted to find a loophole in the law. They started purchasing land in the name of their children who were American citizens.[29] But, to keep the Japanese from being successful Congress then amended the Alien Act to exclude purchase of land by minors. This eliminated the Japanese from farm ownership.

Around the time of the Alien Land Act hatred toward the Japanese was widespread. Not only weren't they ineligible for citizenship and barred from owning land, but they often experienced the same Jim Crow like hostilities that were enforced on Blacks.[30] The Japanese were routinely segregated by Whites and refused service in barbershops, grocery stores, hotels and restaurants.

Roosevelt, president at the time, was worried that this treatment of the Japanese in the U.S. would get back to Japan and cause international chaos.

Therefore, Roosevelt signed a Gentlemen's Agreement with Japan.[31] This agreement halted Japanese immigration and legislation was designed to reduce the harassment of the Japanese. The agreement also allowed immigration of the parents, wives and children of the 90% male U.S. Japanese population.[32]

This last immigration arrangement angered the White exclusionists (Whites who felt access to America should only for Europeans) as the immigration of these men's family were more than many thought would come. Therefore, Congress appealing to the White male voting population passed the Immigration Act of 1924.[33] This Act prohibited foreigners ineligible for U.S. citizenship—by definition all Asians—from coming to American shores.

With all of this turmoil the Japanese Americans were experiencing, when the attack at Pearl Harbor occurred it just made it worse for the Japanese. Roosevelt had signed the Executive Order 9066. This order authorized and structured the relocation and internment of nearly 120,000 Japanese women, men and children.[34] Executive Order 9066 imparted a large dose of legitimacy to the wartime hysteria and racism rampant in America.[35]

Americans bought the propaganda they were fed about how the Japanese Americans on the West Coast were enemy aliens loyal to Japan. The U.S. public supported the government in its assault against Japanese Americans. Newspaper columnists commonly called Japanese Americans the following: nips, japs, and yellow vermin.[36] This just incited others into the hatred of the Japanese. However, the thing to remember is that this was not the first exhibition of hatred toward the Japanese. The war was just a more 'valid' reason to incite hatred.

FILIPINO AMERICANS

While the Philippines are an Asian country, some think due to its name that it is not. Confused because it has a Spanish name taken from Philip II, does not make it any less "Asian." While Japan and China have contributed to the shaping of the history of the Philippines, the country has also been impacted by Spain and later the United States. Despite the Filipinos resistance to foreign domination, the U.S. went there and enacted many of its ways of living. It setup a democratic government and American style schools, which enforced usage of the English language. The schools also taught American history and values instead of teaching Philippine history. This introduction to America inspired many to immigrate to America.

Managing Workplace Diversity

When the Filipinos arrived many were already accustomed to American culture. Because Americans wanted the Filipinos to come to America, Filipinos were exempt from the discriminatory legislation that virtually halted all Asian immigration for a period of time.[37] But just like the Chinese and Japanese aliens in America, Filipinos also did not have the right to vote, own land or attain U.S. citizenship.

When the Filipinos arrived in the U.S. many were men. But, unlike their Japanese and Chinese counterparts who either weren't comfortable around American women or wanted to preserve their lineage, the Filipinos had neither concern. In the absence of Filipino women, many married White women. At the time, however, anti-miscegenation laws only barred marriages between Whites and persons of African or Mongolian blood.[38] But, even though the marriages between Filipinos and Whites were allowable by law many still received harassment. The Caucasian women were often called "nigger lovers."[39] They called them this because of the brown skin tone of the Filipinos.

While this harassment dampened the experience of the Filipino immigrants, what really hurt them was the Great Depression. The Great Depression was a bad time for all, but it was even worse for people of color who were already being discriminated against. Desperate from the shortage of jobs across the country, racists blamed their misfortunes on these immigrants of color.[40] There was also rioting against Filipinos on the Pacific Coast. In October 1929, in White River Valley, Washington, White farm workers fought Filipino workers because the latter worked for less pay. By the summer of 1930 anti-Filipino activities had spread to Idaho and Utah.[41]

In addition, there were many attempts to exclude Filipinos from the mainland. Congressman Richard Welch of California introduced a bill with this aim. He received support from the states of Oregon and Washington, from labor unions, and from groups concerned about the ethnic composition of the United States population.

But even still during this time, the American government started making deals with the Philippines that was presented as a win-win that is, a win for the U.S as well as the Philippines. In 1932, the Cutting-Hare Bill passed which was the culmination of these dealings. Then in 1934, there was the Tydings-McDuffie Act. These acts were a triumph for those who wanted to end Filipino immigration.

The act stated that the Philippine Islands would become independent after a transition period of 15 years where the U.S would provide assistance and during those 15 years of commonwealth status, the annual quota was set at 50 immigrants to the mainland, U.S.[42] This also called for separate regulations for immigration to Hawaii. Filipinos in Hawaii were restricted from moving from Hawaii to the U.S. and they were reclassified as aliens rather than nationals. After successful lobbying, the Hawaiian Sugar Planter's Association convinced Congress to allot additional spaces for Filipino immigrants to Hawaii, where cheap labor was needed.[43]

The Tydings-McDuffie Act of 1934 still restricted immigration and it wasn't until The Immigration Act of 1965 which liberalized immigration from Asia did Filipino immigration pick back up.[44] While the previous immigrants were laborers, these new immigrants were White-collar professionals. But, many still couldn't meet stringent U.S. certification requirements.[45] For example, dentists from the Philippines were forced to work as dental aides in the U.S., unless they underwent more training. What was strange about this is that the U.S. set up the school systems in the Philippines and therefore it would be assumed that their quality of education wouldn't be questioned. But, was the quality of education the issue or more the issue of keeping these well paying jobs for those American's or immigrants who were more favored?

Furthermore, these new Filipino immigrants brought their wives who were educated as well and often worked outside the home in the one of the few fields open to women, nursing.[46] Because many American women weren't really working outside the home this opened this opportunity to the Filipino women and this economic opportunity helped the Filipinos preserve their heritage in America.

LATINO/HISPANIC MIGRATION EXPERIENCE

Who makes up the Hispanic/Latino population?
The term "Hispanic" is often used to refer to people of the Latin culture but according to the dictionary "Hispanic" only refers to the language, people and culture of Spain.[47] The term "Hispanic" is therefore not representative of all Latin ethnicities, such as: Africans of Cuba and Puerto Rico and Indians of Central America. It is therefore necessary to extend this definition to include people who live in the U.S. who came or whose ancestors came—not just from Spain—but also from other Spanish-speaking countries around the world. Many will refer to this grouping of people as Latinos. Insisting that Latinos not only includes the above groups but also those from other Latin areas like the Dominican Republic,

El Salvador, and Nicaragua. But, because the U.S. government recognizes Hispanic rather than Latino the terms are often used interchangeably.

As we discuss Latinos/Hispanics in the United States, a group that is estimated at 44.3 million (not including the 3.9 million residents of Puerto Rico) as of 2006 constituting 15 percent of the nation's total population and the nation's largest ethnic or race minority group, we will focus on the three largest of this ethnicity, which are: Mexican Americans, Puerto Rican Americans and Cuban Americans.[48]

Like many Americans, Latinos are the product of immigration from an old world to a new one. Yet they are unique. Through their history, Latinos bring together three great cultures: African, Native-American and European which explains their variation in color—from the light skin color of Jennifer Lopez (famous entertainer) to the darker skin color of Sammy Sosa (famous baseball star) both of whom consider themselves Latino.

The African influence of Latinos began through the first Africans who crossed the narrow Strait of Gibralter to the Iberian Peninsula in 2000 B.C.[49] These Iberians lived in Libya, Algeria and Morocco and they built their own villages and planted crops.[50] One thousand years later, they mixed with newcomers, the Celts, to create a new culture and about 500 B.C., a powerful city-state in northern Africa, Carthage, began to send armies and colonists across the Mediterranean to the Iberian Peninsula.[51] There, the Carthaginians created colonies that lasted almost 300 years until the Roman Empire moved in to take control.

Then in 711 A.D. a group of African Muslims invaded this Iberian Peninsula and forced the mixed European culture northward toward the Pyrenees. For the next 800 or so years, these Moors, as they became known, shaped the culture of the Iberian Peninsula.[52] Their mark can still be seen in the Mosques, gardens, and paved streets of Spanish cities.

In the late 1400s, Spain joined Portugal in the African slave trade.[53] This type of slavery was similar to the slavery that existed in a few countries in Africa where a person was enslaved for a time period and was required to work. However, once this period ended the slaves assumed all rights as free citizens. Over the next few centuries, Spain relied on the labor of Africans to build its empire in the New World. In Spanish America, Spain's African heritage joined with the heritage of slaved Africans. This heritage was passed on through the years to other Hispanic Americans.

The second cultural influence was from the Native Americans. About 7000 B.C. some ancient Native Americans turned from hunting and gathering to farming for food. Over the next 5000 years, farming brought these groups together and a village culture grew. By 1200 B.C., the Olmec culture had been founded.[54]

Elsewhere in the Americas other Native American civilizations grew and prospered. Among some of the most important were the Incas of Peru and the Pueblo culture of the American Southwest.[55] Others lived in South America, the Caribbean, and the American Southeast. These cultures influenced the Spaniards and Africans who traveled to the New World after 1492. This Native American heritage has also been passed on through Latinos/Hispanic Americans.

Beginning in 1492, there were the Spanish conquests that again brought together these different cultures. Christopher Columbus, born in Italy, but working for the Spaniards, sought new routes to the rich lands of Japan and China. But in 1492, he startled onto a different continent. In this growing of the Spanish empire—the Old World—Europeans and Africans came together and mixed with the New World—Native Americans.[56] These people of Spanish America created many of the cultures and traditions that we now view in the U.S. among Hispanic Americans.

The movement of Latinos to the Americas began at the start of the 20th century that found Cuba, Puerto Rico, and Mexico in turmoil. Spain's archaic rule of its Caribbean possessions was challenged successfully in 1898. The U.S. went into these countries trying to clean up what they considered to be neglect and mismanagement of these countries' resources.[57]

Hispanic Colonial History

According to the contributors of "AmericaUSA", out of the 50 U.S. states Hispanics explored and colonized at least 31 of the present states in the United States.[58] Spanish speaking America's far-reaching influence, and contributions, continues throughout the U.S. today. Spanish was spoken in the majority of the present states in our country from the early 1900's to the present, during which time English and Spanish have shared the status of dual languages in the present USA. In 1776 when the Declaration of Independence was signed, it was a toss up between several languages; even though Spanish continued to be the collective language of the majority in the "U.S." at the time of the American

Revolution.[59]

When new immigrants from Spanish speaking countries assimilate, they assimilate into the USA Spanish speaking community, which has been in existence collectively for 500 years. There are two collective (dual languages) throughout the present USA- Spanish and English. Within the Spanish and English languages, which are spoken collectively in the USA, there are also thousands of Indigenous Tribes, each with their own distinct languages. As the following facts illustrate, the Spanish language was/is not only confined to the American southwest, but is spread throughout the present USA. When it comes to pioneers, one fact was that these Spanish speaking people were very instrumental in spreading the Hispanic culture and the Spanish language; from Alabama, Alaska, Arkansas, Arizona, California (which is a Spanish word), Florida (a Spanish word meaning flowery) and Georgia which were traditionally Spanish speaking from the early 1500 as they colonized by the Hispanics.[60]

Also, during the 1500's, 1600's, 1700's the influence was provided to the United States through the Hispanics: Presidios (forts), Missions were established; in 1598 they created the 1st Cattlemen's Organization; in 1776's American Revolution the Hispanics or Spanish speaking people from New Mexico collected funds and fought British soldiers on behalf of the United States and 500,000 Hispanics fought in WWII.[61]

Mexicans in America

While Mexicans occupied western North America during manifest destiny, there was a time period in history that brought immigrant Mexicans to America. Dictator Porfiria Diaz, who had ruled for 30 years, had left lower classes poor and much of the country's wealth was in the hands of a few Mexicans and foreigners.[62] In 1910, this situation in Mexico got worse. The bloody Mexican Revolution that lasted several years made life unbearable for most. As Cuba, Puerto Rico and Mexico continued to experience the harsh life of many dictatorial rulers along with the remains of the war, these people began to head North in hopes of finding a better life in the U.S.

Based on the history of Mexico and many other countries (including the U.S.), it is easy to see how greed and the desire for wealth have caused those in power to do to undeserving acts to humans. The "freedom" that can be experienced through a capitalistic economy, for those who can migrate here believe they will be able to escape the poor conditions of their homelands.

The railroads enabled masses of Mexicans to reach the U. S. Once in the U.S., the railway also employed many of these immigrants. However, most Mexicans in the U.S. worked not only at the railroad as laborers but also as constructions workers or watchmen. Many others were employed in agriculture or mining. These occupations isolated Mexican Americans from the rest of the American population—creating separate Spanish speaking communities.[63] This separation also did nothing to increase the "American" education of the Mexican workers and their children. There was no access to schools in these remote locations, and because many of the children worked alongside their parents, this made formal "American" education and adaptation to the English language nonexistent for them. It was also during this era, that Mexican Americans developed the stereotype of being agricultural field hands.[64] This stereotype has existed for many decades.

This massive movement of people from Mexico to the U.S. was not intended to be a permanent emigration. Many came to stay for a season or for a few years to accumulate money as the wages were three to four times better than in Mexico. But, as circumstance would have it, many did not return back to Mexico. Like other groups of transient workers, labor contractors recruited these non-English speaking agricultural Mexican laborers. They worked in gangs under the contractor's direction and total control. While these Mexicans were working, they still were very poor and lived under such primitive conditions that it shocked other Americans.[65] This poverty that they had to accept, along with their folk culture, race and work patterns set them apart culturally. But not all were set apart as the lighter complexioned, acculturated and middle class portion of the Mexican-American population was more easily accepted.[66] They often could speak English and could therefore blend into the White society (melt into the pot).

But, as more Mexicans arrived there was increased prejudice felt from some of the Anglo-community. The result of this prejudice impacted the Mexican community in many ways. By the 1940s, the Mexican children, many who were born U.S. citizens, had grown dissatisfied with the bad housing, bad schools and bad jobs. To deal with their feelings of mistreatment, they formed gangs.[67] These gangs were largely concentrated in Los Angeles where there was a large Mexican population.

The Pachucos, one of these gangs, emphasized the difference in their culture and the rest of White society.[68] They dressed differently, wearing zoot suits consisting of high wasted baggy pants and long suit coats with very broad shoulders. These young people needed a way to express their feelings of frustration and bitterness, which is what they did through their clothing and hairstyles.

However, the LA police saw these gangs as more than just rebellious teenagers. They believed the Pachucos were a threat to public order. Also, at this time in LA, military men were on leave and also felt that these young men were "Un-American" and needed to be taught a lesson.[69] What began as street fights, turned into major race riots. Many say this was the ugliest mob action since the coolie (Chinese) race riots of the 1870s.

The race riots continued until the Mexican Ambassador in Washington asked the U.S. State Department to help stop the violence. U.S. Government officials stopped the riots by removing the military men.[70] While many Mexican Americans weren't easily accepted into the Anglo communities due to their differences, Mexican Americans still held strong to their own culture.

The family is central in Mexican American culture.[71] Family breakups are much less common among Mexican Americans than other immigrant groups. Spanish is also the language that is still spoken in more than half of Mexican American homes.[72] Language choices of all Latinos and proficiency in English have in recent years become ideological issues, rather than simply pragmatic questions related to functioning in an English speaking country.

Some believe that these families should use English more. But, many others in this debate don't see the value in this—even non-Latino intellectuals see this issue as an attempt to stigmatize Spanish as "inferior." But, what makes one language better than another? People who believe this about Spanish should remember that Spanish as well as the 300 or so Native tongues, were spoken on this continent long before English became the "first language" of the United States.

Columbus and the Spaniards

What do the following people/groups have in common that is related to the Latino experience:

- Christopher Columbus
- Puerto Rico
- Cuba
- Native Americans

- Blacks

The Crusades were responsible for bringing to Europe imported treasures that were coveted.[74] The nations tired of filling the pockets of the Italian city-states they were acting as middlemen. An alternate route was needed. Christopher Columbus devised a plan to reach the East by traveling West. The British decided to back Columbus, but it was too late, Spain had already signed an agreement with Columbus.[75]

With profit being the motivating factor of the journey, Columbus was unsuccessful. He sailed within twenty miles of the Mayan ruins and was just hairs from the pearl fisheries in Columbia.[76] His journeys did take him to both Puerto Rico and Cuba. Claimed by the Spanish, the islands were subsequently settled by people obsessed by the Three G's—Gold, Glory, and Gospel.[77] Neither Cuba nor Puerto Rico was initially as profitable as Mexico and certain parts of South America. In order to gain the most from these possessions agriculture was to be developed. The Spanish tradition of not sullying one's hands led to the use of "Indians" as laborers. To better facilitate this aim Queen Isabella issued an order on December 20, 1503.[78] In the document she compelled the governors of the possessions to 'compel and force' the Indians to do the labor.[79] Subsequently, literally millions of Indians were worked to death.

> "Bartolomé de las Casas (1474-1566), a Dominican monk, was appalled at the treatment the Spaniards bestowed on the Indians. He crusaded for the natives, pled their case to King Ferdinand (1515), wrote the Historia de las India, and was appointed the 'Protector of the Indians.' In his role as the latter, he suggested something he would regret for the rest of his life. He proposed that instead of Indians, Black slaves be used in the mines and plantations. African slaves were then imported in 1518. There emerged in the possessions a very rigid caste system. (Many Indians also had one.) The Spanish class system was triangular. At the top were the Peninsulares, those born on the Iberian Peninsula. They were the only ones who could hold top administrative positions. Next were the Criollos, sons and daughters of Europeans born in the possessions. They had status, gained wealth, but had no administrative power. Constituting the lower echelons were the Mestizos, half Indian half European; the Mulattos, half black half European; the Indians, the Negroes, and the Sambos, half black half Indian."[80]

America had designs on its southern neighbors for much of the nineteenth century. Jefferson saw them as Spanish daggers; the South saw them as potential slave states (slavery was abolished in Spain in 1870). Nothing really came of it until William Randolph Hearst went to New York, bought a newspaper, *The Journal*, and began a circulation war with his competitor, Joseph Pulitzer. Taking on the cause of the Cuban revolutionaries, he and his battalion of 'literary mercenaries,' the Yellow Journalists, began an all out effort to rally support for a war. Americans were also quite concerned over their investments involving sugar. In 1898 when the *Maine* was sunk, either accidentally or deliberately, the U.S. went to war with Spain. The "Splendid Little War," or "Hearst's Little War" was over quickly, cost few lives to the U.S., and reunited a nation that had not been cohesive since the Civil War. Spain had lost its entire empire. Spanish influence declined, relegating her to the position of a defeated mother. This marked the beginning of U.S. intervention in the islands. Cuba was granted independence under U.S. supervision. Puerto Rico became a possession of the U.S.

Puerto Ricans and America

Puerto Rico has had a relationship with the United States since the early 1900s when the United States starting intervening in the island. Why would the U.S. want this country so close to the border? Some would say that its prime location for enemies of the United States to take up location there if it is not controlled by the United States.

But for whatever the reason, the United States enacted several acts. The acts concluded with Puerto Rico being a possession of the United States and not a state as it had once desired.[81] While Puerto Rico is a possession and not a state the acts created a provision that provides U.S. citizenship to Puerto Ricans who live in Puerto Rico. But as citizens they do not pay federal income tax. Puerto Rico is also not provided the same services that would be offered through an income tax system. Puerto Rico was issued a Bill of Rights and governor who is selected through the United States political process in Washington which was later overturned.[82]

The governance and support of Puerto Rico through the United States has been strong and weak throughout the years. This strength of the Puerto Rican economy versus the United States economy has contributed to the waves or downfalls of Puerto Ricans migrating to the United States.[83] Since 1930, many Puerto Ricans in the U.S. have lived in New York City. The water access of New York (it being a port city) and boat travel created this access to migration.[84]

Puerto Ricans, like the Irish and many other migrants to this country came from environments that provided little or no access to formal education, limited exposure to U.S. language and culture. Like many others who have Spanish as their first language, Spanish is spoken in the homes of most Puerto Ricans. These language and cultural issues have become a complication in the life of Puerto Ricans living in the U.S.[85]

Color (for the darker skinned Puerto Ricans) is also an additional complication in an already difficult situation.[86] Individual color differences remain socially significant in a group that extends from pure Caucasian to pure African American. Studies show that those Puerto Ricans who have attained middle class status have tended to be lighter in skin color and may identify themselves as white in order to gain the unspoken privileges that many Whites in the U.S. have.[87]

Cuba

Just like Puerto Rico the United States has maintained some control over Cuba since the early 1900s until the 1950s where such control extended to the United States having power to intervene in as it related to Cuba's independence.[87] However, the U.S. did not exert much influence over Fulgencio Batista's regime allowing what called inhumane treatment to take place in this country.

Cuba has been no stranger to dictatorships, which like many countries who operate under these conditions pass poverty unto its citizens. Some chose to stay in their homeland and live under these conditions while others have sought a better life elsewhere.[88] This is what brought many of the well educated upper and middle class Cubans to America.

At the time they arrived, Miami was in decline and welcomed the Cuban refugees with open arms. These well-educated Cubans started new businesses and brought this once crumbling city back to life. Before long, Cuban Americans in Miami had higher average incomes than non-Latino Whites. They had created 18,000 new businesses many small and family run.[89] These new business ventures brought large investments from Latin American business people who had barely noticed Miami before.

By 1980, the next wave of refugees arrived to find Miami a bilingual community. These refugees arrived but were considered "social problems" in

Cuba, some were even criminals.[90] Many had maintained this criminal lifestyle in order to survive the communistic dictatorial regime in Cuba. The Soviet Union, who Cuba supplied massive amounts of financial aid to Cuba to help improve its economic situation. Cuba was having a difficult time supporting its citizens due to agricultural losses. So what better way to cut your cost than to get rid of some of your troubled citizen's?

Exclusionists in the Anglo/white community were not happy with the new Cubans arrival. But, Florida's Cuban community assisted these new Cubans in American living and finding jobs. Still, not all made successful transitions. Many of the Cubans were discouraged due to the bitterness and despair that life in America offered them. What we must remember, though, is that these new refugees had never experienced personal freedom. They had been told all their lives what to do, what they could have and how to do things. Arriving in a country where motivation and discipline are the keys to success was a true culture shock.

The Cubans because of their education and wealth were able to gain influence in the United States. They used this power to create the Torricelli Bill which was signed by President Bush to express what many considered was outrage of the treatment of their people in Cuba. This bill showed the power of the Cubans in America as it banned trade with Cuba by the United States and prohibited ships docking in U.S. ports if they had visited Cuba.[91] This bill however was not supported by the United Nations.

Other Legislation Affecting the Latino Population

Californians passed a measure designed to keep undocumented immigrants from receiving state-funded social services, including welfare and non-emergency treatment. It also forced undocumented schoolchildren out of California schools. A federal court order kept this law from passing but there was an increase in discrimination to the Latinos in California.[92]

The North American Free Trade Agreement (NAFTA) was another piece of legislation that has impacted the This agreement allowed Canada, Mexico and the U.S. to eliminate all tariffs between them till 2009. This is the first step towards an American common market, but there were also Northern Mexican farmers who protested by marches and sit-ins.

Concluding Thoughts

There is a central theme to this chapter—Asians and Latino/Hispanics migrated to this country in search of opportunity, a better life or to assist their government. Once here they were faced with racism from exclusionist whites who felt they did not belong. The fear of "these" immigrants taking jobs forced congress to enact laws that stifled these groups participation in American society. Just as the Native Americans gave America "free land", the Africans provided "free labor", poor whites provided "cheap labor" through indentured servitude, the Asians and Hispanic/Latino population provided more "cheap labor" as they were exploited work groups. Yet, despite this ill treatment it was still better in the United States for Asians and Latinos than in their home countries due to the dictatorial governments and the impoverished living conditions. While these groups just like many others have contributed significant accomplishments to American society— their recognition is just swept away. They are often not even recognized today as "full" citizens—just immigrants. But aren't most people in America immigrants?

End of Chapter Questions

1. Why did the Chinese, Japanese and Filipino each migrate to the United States? How were they each treated once here?

2. What is the Naturalization Act of 1790 and how did this impact nonwhite immigrants?

3. Why were the Filipinos encouraged to come to the U.S. over other groups?

4. Why did the Mexicans, Puerto Ricans and First group of Cubans migrate to the United States? Why were the Cubans treated better than the other groups?

5. What does cheap labor have to do with migration experiences of the Asian Americans and Latino/Hispanic groups?

Internet Exercise

Directions: Using the Internet or your library resources, answer the following three questions. Please site the website or textbook that you used for your answer.

(1) How have hate crimes impacted the lives of Asian Americans or Asian American college students? Why do you feel people have hatred toward these students?

Search Key Words: hate crimes Asian Americans

(2) Why are Asian Americans referred to as the model minority?

Search Key Words: model minority Asian Americans

(3) Is the above, considered a positive stereotype? Why or why not?

End of Chapter Exercise

Immigration Reform: Yes or No

After reading in the chapter about the various contributions of non-white immigrants to this country along with the passage of laws to hinder these immigrants success in America, read about the newest immigration reform, *The Family Reuniting Act* then answer the questions that follow.

The legislation would reinforce the historical emphasis on families in the immigration system and reduce current wait times in the family immigration system by:

* Helping an estimated 322,000 spouses and children under the age of 21 of lawful permanent residents who are waiting in line to reunite with their families by reclassifying them as immediate relatives

* Addressing the decades-long backlogs for certain countries by raising the per-country immigration limits from 7 percent to 10 percent of total admissions

* Protecting widows, widowers and orphans by allowing them to continue to wait in line for a visa after the death of the sponsoring relative.

* Utilizing an estimated 400,000 family-sponsored and employment-based visas that went unused

between 1992 and 2007.

* Respecting the contribution of Filipino World War II veterans by reducing their children's waiting times for an immigrant visa.

* Promoting family unity by allowing more people who are already eligible for an immigrant visa to efficiently use our legal family immigration system.

* Providing equal treatment for stepchildren and biological children by allowing stepchildren under the age of 21 to immigrate upon their parents' marriage (current age limit is 18).

Questions

1. Why haven't these types of issues of family been addressed before?

2. How would this impact the U.S. workplace and do you think there would be backlash as seen in previous times when favorable treatment was given to "certain" immigrants?

3. What is the purpose of passing this type of act?

4. What does it say about the value of immigrants in the country?

Managing Workplace Diversity

References

1.   Ping, C. (1963). *Chinese Labor in California.* Madison, Wisconsin: State Historical Society of Wisconsin for the Dept. of History, University of Wisconsin.

2.   Chu, G. (1970, March). Chinatowns in the Delta: The Chinese in the Sacramento-San Joaquin Delta, 1870-1960. *California Historical Society*, Quarterly 49:1, 21-37.

3.   Ping, C. (1963). *Chinese Labor in California.* Madison, Wisconsin: State Historical Society of Wisconsin for the Dept. of History, University of Wisconsin.

4.   Ibid.

5.   Alien Americans: a study of race relations. (n.d.). Retrieved from http://www.archive.org/stream/alienamericansst00schrrich/alienamericansst00schrrich_djvu.txt

6.   Ibid.

7.   Horsman, R. (1981). *Race and Manifest Destiny: Origins of American Racial Anglo-Saxonism.* Cambridge, Massachusetts: Harvard University Press.

8.   Coolidge, M. R. (1909). *Chinese Immigration.* New York: Henry Holt.

9.   Wikipedia. Retrieved from: http://en.wikipedia.org/wiki/Naturalization_Act_of_1790

10.   Coolidge, M. R. (1909). *Chinese Immigration.* New York: Henry Holt.

11.   Ibid.

12.   Ibid.

13.   Ibid.

14.   Coolidge, M. R. (1909). *Chinese Immigration.* New York: Henry Holt.

15.   Chinn, Thomas W., editor. (1969). *A History of the Chinese in California.* San Francisco: Chinese Historical Society of America.

16.   Central Pacific Railroad Photographic History Museum. (n.d.). Retrieved from http://cprr.org/Museum/Chinese.html

17.   Ibid.

18.   Ibid.

19. Katz, J. H. (2003). *White Awareness: Handbook for Anti-Racism Training*. Oklahoma: University of Oklahoma Press.

20. Commission on Asian American Pacific Affairs. (n.d.). Retrieved from http://www.capaa.wa.gov/community/history.shtml

21. Ibid.

22. Ibid.

23. Ibid.

24. Ichihashi, Y. (1969). *Japanese in the United States: A Critical Study of the Problems of the Japanese Immigrants and their Children*. Stanford: Stanford University Press.

25. Ito, K. (1973). *Issei: A History of Japanese Immigrants in North America*. Seattle: Executive Committee for the Publication of Issei.

26. Ibid.

27. U.S Supreme Court Oyama v. California [332 U.S. 633 (1948)] [332 U.S. 633 , 634]. Retrieved from: http://caselaw.lp.findlaw.com/scripts/getcase.pl?court=us&vol=332&invol=633

28. Ibid.

29. Higgs, R. (1978, March). *Landless by Law--Japanese Immigrants in California Agriculture to 1941*. Journal of Economic History, 38(1), 205-26.

30. Ito, H. (1966*). Japan's Outcastes in the United States*. Berkeley: University of California Press, pp. 200-21.

31. Hata, D. T. (1978). *'Undesirables': Early Immigrants and the Anti-Japanese Movement in San Francisco, 1892-1893: Prelude to Exclusion*. New York: Arno Press.

32. Ibid.

33. Chuman, F. F. (1976). *The Bamboo People: The Law and Japanese-Americans*. Del Mar, CA: Publisher's Inc.

34. Taylor, S. C. & Kitano, H. H. L. (1986). *Japanese Americans: From Relocation to Redress*. Salt Lake City: University of Utah Press.

35. Ibid.

36. *Prisoners Without Trial: Japanese Americans in World War II*. (1993). New York: Hill and Wang.

37. Constantino, R. *(1975). A History of the Philippines: from the Spanish colonization to the Second World War*. New York: Monthly Review Press.

38. Grunder, G. A., & Livezey, W. E. (1951). *The Philippines and the United States*. Norman: University of Oklahoma Press.

39. Walker, S. (1994). *Hate Speech: The History of an American Controversy*. Lincoln, NE: University of Nebraska Press.

40. *Pau Hana: Plantation Life and Labor in Hawaii, 1835-1920*. (1983). Honolulu: University of Hawaii Press.

41. Ibid.

42. Ninkovich, F. (2001). *The United States and Imperialism*. Malden, Massuchesetts: Blackwell.

43. Ibid.

44. Ibid.

45. Ibid.

47. Online Encyclopedia. Retrieved from: http://www.fact-archive.com/encyclopedia/Hispanic

48. U.S. Census Bureau. Retrieved from: http://www.census.gov/Press-Release/www/releases/archives/facts_for_features_special_editions/010327.html

49. Handlin, O. (1959). *The Newcomers: Negroes and Puerto Ricans in a Changing Metropolis*. Garden City, NY: Doubleday.

50. Brett, M. & Fentress, E. (1996). *The Berbers*. Cambridge, MA: Blackwell Publishers.

51. Ibid.

52. Hoyt, R. S. & Chodorow, S. (1976). *Europe in the Middle Ages*. Boston: Houghton Mifflin Harcourt.

53. Ibid.

54. Ibid.

55. Galens, J., Sheets, A., Young, Robyn V. & Vecoli, R. J. (1995). *Gale Encyclopedia of Multicultural America*. Detroit: Gale.

56. Ibid.

57. Kanellos, N. & Esteva-Febregat, C. (1993). *Handbook of Hispanic Cultures in the United States*. Houston: Arte Publico.

58. Ibid.

59. Ibid.

60. Republican National Hispanic Alliance. (n.d.). Retrieved from http://www.rnhacentralflorida.org/information.html.

61. *Hispanic Contributions State by State*. (1996). Hispanic America USA. Retrieved from http://www.neta.com/~1stbooks/colony9.htm

62. Meier, M. S. (1981). *Dictionary of Mexican American History.* Westport: Greenwood.

63. Ibid.

64. Ibid.

65. Meier, M. & Ribera, F. (1993). *Mexican Americans/American Mexicans: From Conquistadors to Chicanos.* New York, NY: Hill and Wang.

66. Ibid.

67. Daniels, R. & Olin, S. C. Jr. (1972). *Racism in California: A Reader in the History of Oppression.* New York: Macmillian.

68. Bookrags. *Pachucos.* Retrieved from: http://www.bookrags.com/history/pachucos-sjpc-04/

69. Ibid.

70. Mazón, M. (1984). *The Zoot Suit Riots.* Austin, University of Texas Press.

71. History of the Mexican Family. (n.d.). Retrieved from: http://family.jrank.org/pages/1163/Mexico-History-Mexican-Family.html

72. U.S. Census Bureau. (n.d.). Retrieved from: http://www.census.gov/Press-Release/www/releases/archives/facts_for_features_special_editions/010327.html

73. Simon, J. & Riley-Smith, C. (2002). *The Oxford History of the Crusades*. Oxford: Oxford University Press.

74. Ibid.

75. Ibid.

76. Wagenheim, O, J. & Wagenheim, K. (2002). *The Puerto Ricans: A Documentary History*. Princeton, NJ : Markus Wiener Publishers.

77. Ibid.

78. Ibid.

79. Ibid.

80. Coughlin, A. (1989). *The Heritage of Puerto Rico and Cuba*. Connecticut: Yale New-Haven Teacher Institute. Retrieved from:
http://www.yale.edu/ynhti/curriculum/units/1989/3/89.03.02.x.html

81. Ibid.

82. Ibid.

83. Sowell, T. (1997). *Ethnic America: A History*. Ashland, Oregon: Blackstone Audio Books.

84. Ibid

85. Ibid

86. Schaefer, R. T. (2006). *Racial and Ethnic Groups*. New Jersey: Prentice-Hall. Retrieved from http://studentoffortune.com/cgi/getfile/8574/5643/eth125_week1_reading1.pdf

87. Coughlin, A. (1989). *The Heritage of Puerto Rico and Cuba*. Connecticut: Yale New-Haven Teacher Institute. Retrieved from:
http://www.yale.edu/ynhti/curriculum/units/1989/3/89.03.02.x.html

88. Ibid.

89. Chabran, R. & Chabran, R. (1995). *The Latino Encyclopedia*. New York: Marshall Cavendish.

90. Ibid.

91. Ibid.

92. Texas Conservative Coalition Research Institute. (n.d.). Retrieved from
http://www.txccri.org/publications/Illegal_Immigration_Task_Force_Report.pdf

Chapter Nine

Understanding Religious Freedom & Work

Know from whence you came. If you know whence you came, there are absolutely no limitations to where you can go.

James Baldwin

UNDERSTANDING RELIGIOUS FREEDOM AND WORK

Chapter Objectives

After reading this chapter, you should be able to:

- understand various beliefs of the largest U.S. religions.

- know the practices of other religions that exist in the U.S.

- describe religious accommodation.

- identify various components of religions that may require accommodation in the workplace.

- respect religious difference.

The worlds three largest religions in order by size are: Christianity, Islam and Buddhism. We will discuss these groups as well as a few others to get a better understanding of the commonly practiced religions in U.S. society.

Christianity

Christians in America

Christians follow the teachings of Jesus Christ and his apostles.[1] Jesus is the Greek name for Yeshua where Yeshua has a hebrew meaning of salvation from despair, depression, hate, feeling empty inside, and death--you will never be alone again, but happy and fulfilled.[2] Yeshua of Nazareth was the name that was given to Jesus Christ when he was a child. The second part of his name, Christ is Greek and it means "the Messiah" or the "anointed one."[3]

Yeshua was a Jewish itinerant preacher who was born circa 4 to 7 BCE where BCE means "before the common era" (= Christian "BC" notation).[4] He was executed by the Roman occupying authorities in Palestine, perhaps on Friday, 30-APR-7 CE (i.e. in the spring of the year 30) where CE means "of the common era" (= Christian "AD" notation).[5] Most Christians regard him as the Son of God. They further believe that he is God, the second person in the Trinity (the Trinity consists of the Father, Son and Holy Spirit; three separate persons, all eternal, all omnipresent, who form a single, unified deity).

Most Christians believe that Jesus co-existed with God before the creation of the world, was born of a virgin, was resurrected three days after his death, and later ascended to Heaven. They believe in one God, prayer, in paying tithes or giving to the poor. Some believe in fasting as a ritual or for spiritual cleansing. They also attend services in a church (their holy place) on Saturday, Sunday etc... the day depends on the particular Christian denomination.

Christians have a holy book often referred to as the Bible. However, there are many versions of the Bible (over 50 in English alone). The most common differences is that some leave out entire verses or books, others disagree on whether Jesus should be called God's servant or God's Son.[6] Two of the more common English versions are the King James Version and the new International Version.

Of the common versions, the books of the Bible is divided into two parts: the 46 Books of the Old Testament primarily sourced from the Tanakh (with some variations), and the 27 Books of the New Testament containing books originally written primarily in Greek.[7] Some versions of the Christian Bible have a separate section for the books not considered by the publisher as canonical (of Canon law which is an internal ecclesiastical law governing the Roman Catholic Church, the Eastern Orthodox churches, and the Anglican Communion of churches).

Christian Holidays

A celebrated holiday of many Christians is Christmas. Christmas which is a holiday that celebrates the birth of Jesus Christ, has been a federal U.S. holiday since June 26, 1870 which means school systems and many workplaces in the U.S. celebrate this holiday as well. According to the History of Christmas, it indicates that:

> "In the early 17th century, a wave of religious reform changed the way Christmas was celebrated in Europe. When Oliver Cromwell and his Puritan forces took over England in 1645, they vowed to rid England of decadence and, as part of their effort, cancelled Christmas. By popular demand, Charles II was restored to the throne and, with him, came the return of the popular holiday. The pilgrims, English separatists that came to America in 1620, were even more orthodox in their Puritan beliefs than Cromwell. As a result, Christmas was not a holiday in early America. From 1659 to 1681, the celebration of Christmas was actually outlawed in Boston. Anyone exhibiting the Christmas spirit was fined five shillings. By contrast, in the Jamestown settlement, Captain John Smith reported that Christmas was enjoyed by all and passed without incident."[8]

Christmas is celebrated in many manners in the U.S. From trees being purchased and decorated, homes being lit with lights, big family dinners with Turkey to presents that can be opened on Christmas Eve or Christmas Day brought to kids by Santa Claus are all examples of Christmas merriment.

While many Christians celebrate Christmas in the above manner, some Christians believe that Christians should not observe Christmas at all.[9] Some object to the commercialism of the holiday; others object to its origins. But those that celebrate this holiday celebrate Jesus' birth on December 25th. Some also celebrate Jesus' resurrection (when Jesus' comes back from the dead to save all sinners) in April and call this Easter. Easter, though, is not a federal holiday.

Church History

'The followers of Yeshua formed the Jewish Christian movement, centered in Jerusalem, after his death. They regarded themselves as a reform movement within Judaism; they continued to sacrifice at the temple, circumcise their male children, follow Jewish kosher food laws, etc. Saul of Tarsus, originally a persecutor of the Jewish Christians, reported having a vision of the risen Christ. Adopting the new name of Paul, he became the greatest theologian of the early Christian movement. His writings, along with those of the author(s) of the Gospel of John, provided much of the theological foundation for Christianity, as we know it according to Christian history.[10]

This Christian religion was documented as a legitimate religion in 313 CE and the authority of the church converged among the five bishops or patriarchs located in Alexandria, Antioch, Constantinople, Jerusalem and Rome.[11] However, because Islam's religious power was spreading throughout the Middle East in the 7th century the power of the Christian base changed to Constantinople and Rome.[12] These two Christian centers gradually grew apart in belief, and practice. In 1054 CE, a split was formalized between the Roman Catholic and Eastern Orthodox churches; it remains in effect today.

The splitting of the Christian religion did not stop there as in the 16th century the Protestant was split within the western church which later split into thousands of individual denominations and groups of denominations. [13]

A Prime Belief: Life After Death

Christian beliefs about one's destination after death vary greatly[14]:

- Many conservative Protestant Christians believe that people are born and remain sinful; they will end up being eternally punished in Hell unless they are "saved" by trusting Jesus as Lord and Savior.

- Roman Catholics believe that salvation comes from God, and is channeled through church sacraments to sinful, repentant persons. Most people, at death, go to Purgatory, which is a type of temporary Hell; a few go directly to Heaven; others go permanently to Hell.

- Religious liberals generally interpret Hell symbolically, not as an actual place. They reject the concept of a loving God creating a place of eternal torment.

Current Status of Christianity

About 33% of the world's population regard themselves as Christian with Catholics being the largest group with at least 1.1 billion adherents.[15] Eighty-eight of American adults and a similar number of Canadians identify themselves as Christian. This number has been dropping very slowly in recent years, mainly due to[16]:

- An increase in non-theists, such as Agnostics, Atheists, Humanists, etc.
- An increase in the numbers of followers of minority religions, largely caused by immigration.
- The emergence of new spiritual/religious movements like New Age, Wicca and other Neopagan religions.

However, there are over 1,000 Christian groups in North America alone; each has their own set of beliefs, policies and practices. Like individual politicians, Christians can be classified as conservative, mainline and liberal. Like political parties, individual denominations can also be considered conservative, mainline and liberal. Within each faith group there can also exists a wide range of opinion; individual members hold a wide range of religious beliefs.

Christian denominations include but are not limited to: Orthodox/Eastern Christian, Conservative Protestant, Liberal Protestant, African Indigenous Sects, Pentecostal, Anglican, Assemblies of God, Jehovah's Witness, Latter Day Saints, New Thought--Unity, Christian Science, Friends (Quakers). Of these groups, many people within each group tends to view the Christian world in terms of "*us*". e.g. "*there is my denomination, and then there are all the other faith groups that consider themselves to be Christian.*"[17] For example, this could cause one denomination (a conservative Christian group) to believe they are the "true" faith and therefore denounce the validity of another Christian group that may be more liberal in their approach to Christianity.

Some of the differences among the three categories of Christianity are:

- Fundamentalists and other Evangelical Christians believe in order for someone to be a "real" Christian they must be saved. You must profess your belief in Jesus and live according to the principles of the Bible.[18]

- Mainline Christians are more wide-ranging in who they accept as Christian. If you believe in the teachings of Jesus Christ whether saved or not, then you are a Christian.[19]

- Liberal Christians are even more open to who is a Christian and they often have no set doctrine or set of beliefs that must be followed but this does not preclude them from having common beliefs with conservative or mainline Christians. They are liberal in the sense that they often interpret the scripture without any preconceived notions but use it to apply to life today.[20]

The most common method of arranging Christian denominations is from the most conservative to the most liberal. Unfortunately, not everyone agrees on the specific order. In 1979, author D.R. Hodge created a list that sorts Christian denominations from the most conservative to the most liberal according to the doctrine of the denominations at the time, the list is as follows[21]:

- *Assemblies of God* (the most conservative)
- *Seventh-Day Adventist*
- *Church of Jesus Christ of Latter-Day Saints (Mormons)*
- *Lutheran Church - Missouri Synod*
- *Church of the Nazarene*
- *Southern Baptist Convention*
- *Churches of Christ*
- *Presbyterian Church in the United States*
- *American Baptist Churches in the USA*
- *Evangelical Lutheran Church in America*
- *Christian Church (Disciples of Christ)*
- *United Presbyterian Church in the United States of America*
- *United Methodist Church*
- *Episcopal Church*
- *United Church of Christ* (the most liberal)

Islam

An Introduction to Islam

The second most popular religion is Islam. It is growing and is expected to become the dominant religion of the world during this century.[22] The word "Islam" in Arabic language means "submission" & "peace."[23] Religious followers of Islam are referred to as Muslims. A Muslim is a person who submits to the will of

Allah (which is the name for God in Arabic language) and finds therein peace.[24] The *Masjid* (Mosque) is the Muslims place of worship and found all around the world.

Islam is derived from the Arabic word "salaam" meaning peace. Islam originated with the teachings of Muhammad in the 7th century. Muslims believe Muhammad is the final of all religious prophets (beginning with Abraham) and that the Qu'ran, which is the Islamic scripture, was revealed to him by God.[25]

Who are the Muslims?

There are two major sects of Muslims throughout the world--Sunni and Shiite where about 92% of world's Muslims are Sunni and another 6% are Shiite leaving a very small percentage amongst the following groups: Sufi, Wahhabi, Maliki, Deobandi, the U.S.-based Nation of Islam (previously known as "Black Muslims"), and Ahmadiyya.[26] Shiites are found mainly in Iran and Azerbaijan where they make up about over 70% of each country's population. Shiites are also the majority in Iraq and are the second largest group in Lebanon. They also have a minority of followers in Yemen, Pakistan and Turkey.

Sunnis on the other hand are the majority in all other Muslim countries and they represent the majority of Muslims in non Muslim countries like China and the continent of Africa. One of the major difference between the two sects (Sunnis and Shiites) is their definition or interpretation of the Sunnah and the Hadith.[28] The Hadith is the recorded practice and teachings of Prophet Mohammad which were early regarded as his Sunnah, meaning 'path' or 'way.'[29] These traditions became powerful symbols for the Islamic religion, models of right belief and practice.

World's Major Branches of Islam
Taken From the CIA World Fact Book on Religion[27]

Islam claims about 22.5% of the World's Population

Branch	Number of Adherents
Sunni	1,140,000,000
Shiite	220,000,000
Ahmadiyya	10,000,000
Druze	450,000

It is estimated that there are over 1.5 billion Muslims around the world.[30] There is almost no country on earth without some groups of Muslims, and in such countries as Pakistan, Saudi Arabia or Turkey, the populations are almost wholly Muslim. Islam is also perhaps the fastest growing religion on the North American continent.[31] Most people however equate the term Muslims with Arabs. While many Arabs are Muslims, not all Muslims are Arabs. This confusion may come because its scriptures or holy book, the Holy Qur'an, must be recited in original Arabic form.

Muslims represent many races and socioeconomic classes. Due to the popularity of the Islamic faith in the United States some cities are rethinking the religious holidays that they offer as days off. For instance, the western Detroit suburb of Dearborn, Michigan has been a magnet for immigrants from the Mid East for decades and has one of the nation's largest concentrations of Arabs as they makeup one third of the population.[32]

This city also serves as a cultural and religious center for an estimated 300,000 members of the Arab-American community in southeastern Michigan.[33] The two major holidays that these cities with a large Arab-American population is considering as celebrated city holidays are Eid al-Fitr, which marks the end of the month long fast of Ramadan. The other holiday is Eid al-Adha, which marks the annual completion of the pilgrimage to Mecca. The dates of these holidays change every year though because they are determined by a lunar calendar.

Key Islamic Concepts*

In order to understand Islam, it is necessary to know the meaning of certain key terms and the identity of some proper names. Most of them are in the Arabic language, and there is often no equivalent in English or in other tongues.

*The concepts below are copied with permission from the website: Islam Answering found at http://www.islamanswering.com/subpage.php?s=cat_open&cid=46[34]

Allah

The true name for the creator of the Universe is called Allah.[34] He is merciful, the Beneficent, the Knowledgeable, the Protector, the Mighty, the God, the Provider, the Exalted, the Lord, the All-Knowing, the All-Hearing, the All-Seeing, the Magnificent, the Wise, the Loving, the First, the Last, and the Eternal. The Qur'an (the Muslims holy book) mentions 99 beautiful names for Allah through which Muslims do recognize Him, and His responsibilities for the whole Universe.[35]

Many people ask why the term "Allah" is used instead of "God" and assume its use implies that Muslims worship a separate God. There is only ONE GOD - a belief held by followers of each of the three main world religions: Islam, Christianity and Judaism.

Allah is the Supreme Being, the one and only God. Allah is the same God as is worshipped by the Jews and Christians, and Arabic-speaking Christians also use this name when referring to God.

Ayah

The Arabic meaning of Ayah is a miracle and a sign. The Qur'an is considered to be a miracle itself. Each verse or sentence is called an Ayah or a miracle. The plural of Ayah is called Ayat, which means miracles.

Azan

The call for the daily prayers are called Azan. The person who calls the Azan is called a Mu'azzin. A Mu'azzin calls the Azan five times a day before Muslims so as to perform their daily Salah (Prayer).

Birth

Muslims believe that people are born free of sin. It is only after they reach the age of puberty and it is only after they commit sins that they are to be charged for their mistakes. No one is responsible for or can take the responsibility for the sins of others. However, the door of forgiveness through true repentance is always open.

Festivities

Other than the two general feasts, there are few festivities that Muslims do enjoy. These are related to different activities or functions. Some of these activities are:

Aqiqah: It is a dinner reception to be made after a child is born. Relatives, friends, and neighbors are invited for such an occasion.

Walimah: It is a dinner reception to be made after a marriage is consummated. It is offered by the parents and/or by the married couple. Friends, relatives, and neighbors are also invited.

Islam

Islam is an Arabic word the root of which is Silm and Salam. It means among others: peace, greeting, salutation, obedience, loyalty, allegiance, and submission to the will of the Creator of the Universe. It is asserted by many that Islam is the last and final religion to all mankind and to all generations irrespective of color, race, nationality, ethnic background, language, or social position. It is incorrect and objectionable to call Muslims Muhammadans, as Muhammad is not worshipped in the way Christians worship Christ.

Jihad

It is an Arabic word the root of which is Jahada, which means to strive for a better way of life. The nouns are Juhd, Mujahid, Jihad, and Ijtihad. The other meanings are: endeavor, strain, exertion, effort, diligence, fighting to defend one's life, land, and religion. This word has been in frequent use in the Western press over the past several years, explained to mean a holy war. As a matter of fact the term "holy war" was coined in Europe during the Crusades, meaning the war against Muslims. It does not have a direct counterpart in Islamic glossary, and Jihad is certainly not its translation.

Jihad is not a war to force the faith on others, as many people think of it. It should never be interpreted as a way of compulsion of the belief on others, since there is an explicit verse in the Qur'an that says: "There is no compulsion in religion" Al-Qur'an: Al-Baqarah (2:256). Jihad is not a defensive war only, but a war against any unjust regime. If such a regime exists, a war is to be waged against the leaders, but not against the people of that country. People should be freed from the unjust regimes and influences so that they can freely choose to believe in Allah. Not only in peace but also in war Islam prohibits terrorism, kidnapping, and hijacking, when carried against civilians. Whoever commits such violations is considered a murderer in Islam, and is to be punished by the Islamic state. During wars, Islam prohibits Muslim soldiers from harming civilians, women, children, elderly, and the religious men like priests and rabies. It also prohibits cutting down trees and destroying civilian constructions. The term may be used for/by Muslims as well as non-Muslims.

Muhammad (s.a.w.)

The last and the final prophet and messenger of Allah to all mankind is called Muhammad (s.a.w.) and at the age of forty he received the message of Islam from Allah through angel Gabriel (Jibril). He was the last of a line of prophets like Nuh (Noah), Ibrahim (Abraham), Musa (Moses), and Isa (Jesus).

Muslim(s)

Also spelled Moslem is based on the same Arabic root as Islam (s-l-m) and means one who submits to God, that is, a believer in Islam. Any person who believes in the creed and the teachings of Islam is called a Muslim. More than one billion Muslims are found in different parts of the world. They are not to be confused with Arabs, as Arabs may include Christians, agnostics, or other non-Muslims.

Some Commonly Asked Questions about Muslims

Question: How do Muslims view death?

Muslims like Jews and Christians believe that there is life after death, believing that this life prepares us for this life after death. Basic articles of faith include: the Day of Judgment, resurrection, Heaven and Hell.[35] When a Muslim dies, the burial occurs very quickly if at all possible the same day. The body is prepared by being washed, usually by a family member, wrapped in a clean white cloth, and buried with a simple prayer.[36]

Question: Do Christianity and Islam have different origins?

"No. Together with Judaism, they go back to the patriarch Abraham, and their three prophets are directly descended from his sons Muhammad from the eldest, Ishmael, and Moses and Jesus from Isaac. Abraham established the settlement which today is the city of Makkah (Mecca), and built the Ka'abah towards which all Muslims turn when they pray. In fact, Christians and Jews are thus afforded a special, protected place in Islamic tradition and are known as "People of the Book."[37]

Question: Islam is a monolithic religion that does not allow debate or discussion on matters of faith. True or False?

False. There are more than one sect of Muslims due to different interpretations of Islamic law and unlike Catholicism there is no final doctrinal authority or pastor/clergy.[38]

What are some Muslim Customs?

- **SALAT (Prayer)**: "Performing daily prayers is an act of communication between humans and God. Five daily prayers are considered a duty for all Muslims, and on these occasions preparations in ritual purity are required. The prayers must be said while facing in the direction of Mecca. The congregational prayer of Friday afternoon is compulsory and must be said in the Mosque, Muslim's place of worship. There is a sermon and then the prayers are said in uniform rows."[39]

- **ZAKAT (Alms)**: Before the month of Muharram, the first month of the Islamic calendar Muslims are required to give 2.5% of wealth and assets to those who are less fortunate.[40] This is a yearly obligation. Giving the Zakat is considered an act of worship because it is a form of giving thanks to God for the means of material well being one has acquired.[41]

- **SAWM OR SIYAM (Fasting)**: Another form of offering thanks to God is fasting. It is required of all Muslims to fast during the ninth month of the

Islamic calendar, Ramadan. During this month, Muslims refrain from food and drink during daylight however this does not apply to all Muslims as exceptions are made to those who are elderly, ill, insane, pregnant and nursing women, and travelers.[42] But, they are to make up for this lost time at a later date. Many children complete the fast but is not absolutely required.[43]

What is RAMADAN?

Ramadan is a very important celebration of the Islamic faith. Ramadan is the ninth month of the Muslim calendar. The Month of Ramadan is also when it is believed the Holy Qur'an "was sent down from heaven, a guidance unto men, a declaration of direction, and a means of Salvation."[44]

Muslims fast during the month. This fast is an opportunity for Muslims to focus more on their faith and worship rather than the daily issues of life. During this month of fasting, Muslims do not eat or drink anything from true dawn until sunset.[45] Other restraints are placed on the life of Muslims during the fast such as no smoking or sexual relations. At the end of the day the fast is broken with prayer and a meal called the *iftar*.[46] Fasting is meant to teach patience, sacrifice and humility.

"Ramaḍān is a time to fast for the sake of Allah, and to offer more prayer than usual. Muslims also believed through good actions, they get rewarded twice than they normally can achieve. During Ramaḍān, Muslims ask forgiveness for past sins, pray for guidance and help in refraining from everyday evils, and try to purify themselves through self-restraint and good deeds."[47]

According to the Holy Qur'an:

One may eat and drink at any time during the night "until you can plainly distinguish a white thread from a black thread by the daylight: then keep the fast until night"[48]

The good that is acquired through the fast can be destroyed by five things[49]:

- the telling of a lie
- slander
- denouncing someone behind his back
- a false oath
- greed or covetousness

These are considered offensive at all times, but are most offensive during the Fast of Ramadan.

During Ramadan, in addition to the five daily prayers, there is the Taraweeh prayer (Night Prayer) that is said—some Muslims will pray all night. it is common for Muslims to go to the Mosque and spend many hours praying and studying the Qur'an.[50]

When the fast ends (the first day of the month of Shawwal) a holiday called Id-al-Fitr begins that lasts for three days. During this holiday some city fairs are held, family and friends gather to pray and gifts are exchanged celebrating the end of the Fast of Ramadan.

It is important to have a "true" understanding of the Islamic faith since Islam is the fastest growing religion in the world. It is also important to note that Muslims have made an impact on the evolution of American society. Historically, Muslims have made major contributions in the humanities, the sciences, art etc. They explored North America 300 years before the "discovery" of the New World by Christopher Columbus. They used the Mississippi river as their access route to and from the continent's interior.

Here are a few glimpses of Muslim life in American History as told by Fareed Numan (December 1992)[51]:

In **1178**, a Chinese document known as the Sung Document recorded the voyages of Muslim sailors to a land known as Mu-Lan-Pi (America).

In **1312**, African Muslims from Mandinga arrive in the Gulf of Mexico and explore the American interior via the Mississippi River.

In **1513**, Piri Reis completes his first world map, including the Americas, after researching maps from all over the world. The map is unsurpassed in its practicality and artistry.

In **1530**, African slaves arrive in America. Many of these slaves were sent to Mexico, Cuba, and South America. During the slave trade more than 10 million Africans were uprooted from their homes. More than 30 percent of these were Muslims.

In **1839**, Sayyid Sa'id, ruler of Oman, orders his ship The Sultana to set sail for America on a trade mission. The Sultana touched port in New York. Although the voyage was not a commercial success, it marked the point of successful friendly relations between the two countries that continue to this day.

In **1893**, Muslim immigrants from the Arab provinces of the Ottoman Empire, Syria, Lebanon, Jordan, etc. arrive in North America. They are mainly Turks, Kurds, Albanians, and Arabs.

In **1915**, Albanian Muslims build a Masjid in Maine and establish an Islamic association. By, 1919, they had established another Masjid in Connecticut. Theirs was one of the first associations for Muslims in the U.S.

In **1933**, The Nation of Islam, one of the significant Organizations in American Muslim history is founded. It is responsible for converting a high number of African Americans to Islam.

In **1952**, Muslims in the Armed Services sue the federal government in order to be allowed to identify themselves as Muslims. Until then, Islam was not recognized as a legitimate religion.

Buddhism

More than 300 Million people in the world today are practicing Buddhism. Buddhism has spread throughout Asia from its homeland in India. It has had a significant and lasting impact on India, China, Japan, Korea, Thailand, Tibet and other Asian nations.[52] Buddhism, however, is not confined solely to Asia. In the past century, it has won admirers and followers in Europe and the United States. Indeed, a large majority of people in one of the states of the U.S., Hawaii, are Buddhists.[53]

Definition of Buddhism

Buddhism is a path to spiritual discovery. Its founder Siddhartha Gautama, looked at the human condition, much as a doctor does and he found disease, decay and death.[54] He fully realized that joy and pleasure existed as well, but he recognized that those qualities did not last. All things in life were transient or temporary. So even in joy, the awareness of impermanence and death caused suffering.[55]

Siddhartha Gautama left his parents, lovely wife, and a child in Kapila Palace at the age of 29.[56] He denounced the luxurious life of the kingdom and became a monk with a homeless life. After six years of practice, he attained Enlightenment under a Bodhi tree, and then He became the Sakyamuni Buddha; he is the only historical Buddha, The Buddha that revealed the truth.[57]

Because of his Indian background, Siddhartha did not believe that death was a final release from suffering.[58] For in Indian religious tradition, the cycle of birth, death and rebirth goes on endlessly.[59] To solve and understand this problem of suffering, Siddhartha practiced severe self-denial and meditation. Once he gained "the answer or insight" he became known as the Buddha. This title means "the enlightened" or "the awakened."[60]

This truth is said to have both universality and adequacy. Buddhist believe that the Buddha's teachings that were revealed 2,000 years ago still apply to current daily life or the teachings would not be true.[61] If the Buddha's teachings that can be applied in only one location were not adequate in other locations, the teachings would not be true, either; because the Buddha Dharma is universal and adequate, Buddhists have respected the teachings.[62]

Since the truth is universal and adequate, Buddhist believe that the truth that the Sakyamuni Buddha has revealed must have existed even before His Enlightenment, just as gravity must have existed before Newton discovered it.[63] Buddhists believe that if the truth existed for millions, billions, trillions, or an infinite number of years ago, then many different Buddhas must have taught the truth in the past. A scripture of the religion says there were seven past Buddhas; Amida Buddha of the Nembutsu Sect is one of them; Dainichi Buddha of the

Shingon Sect is also one of the seven past Buddhas; Amida Buddha lives in the far west, and Dainichi Buddha lives throughout the universe; only Sakyamuni Buddha lives in this world, where we live.[64]

In Buddhism, the eternal past and future is imagined because there is no beginning and no end in time.[65] Since the Buddha Dharma is universal and adequate, a Buddha shall teach the same truth in the future and that Buddha is in the Tushita Heaven now as he is only Buddha in the future so far.[66] But there should be more Buddhas because time is limitless.

The future Buddha is practicing Buddha's teachings in the heaven now. He is not a Buddha yet, therefore he is called Bodhisattva Maitreya.[67] In a broad sense all that believe are Bodhisattvas because everyone seeks Enlightenment and has the desire to try to help others. Therefore everyone is a candidate to be a Buddha.

Like Christ and Muhammad, the founders of Christianity and Islam, the Buddha never wrote down his teachings. His disciples memorized his words, and their followers carried on the oral tradition. The first comprehensive written record of the Buddha's doctrine was not compiled until 500 years after his death.[68]

Buddhist Practices

The practice of Buddhism does not, strictly speaking, require a temple (place of worship) or the intercession of a monk. Anyone can follow the teachings of Buddhism in his or her daily life. The temples provide a refuge for those who wish to devote themselves more deeply to the teachings of the Buddha.[69] Members of the Sangha (an organized assembly of Buddhist monks), however, are frequently called on to participate in ceremonies marking important events in people's lives—birth, marriage, and death.[70]

It should be noted though that Buddhist customs vary from country to country. The study of Buddhism and its different forms are as follows:

East Asian Buddhism - by Country
Chinese
Korean
Japanese

East Asian - by Type
Nichiren
Pure Land
Shingon
Tendai
Zen

South and Southeast Asian
Theravada
Vietnamese
Tibet and the Himalayas
Tibetan

Buddhist Schools of Thought
Madhyamaka
Yogâcâra

Buddhist Religious Observances

Buddhists are not required to attend regular services at a temple, as Christians attend church on various days of the week or Jews go to the synagogue on Saturday. Nor do Buddhists have specified daily times of prayer as Muslims. However, in Theravada Buddhism (one type of Buddhism), devout laypeople may observe a "Sabbath" called the Uposatha. This falls on the 1st, 8th, 15th, and 23rd days of the lunar month.[71]

The faithful bring offerings to the temple on these days. Some may observe the day by remaining in seclusion to meditate, and use the temple for this purpose. Others may listen to religious sermons. On these days, the monks at the temple usually organize special rites that can include music, processions, and even fireworks displays.[72]

During the monsoon season that comes at differing times from June to October in Southeast Asia, Buddhists observe a time of penitence that is the equivalent of Christian Lent.[73] During the approximately three-month season, monks observe stricter religious duties. Lay people increase their donations to the Sangha, an organized assembly of Buddhist monks. They accumulate merit by meditating and listening to sutras which are scripture containing the teachings of Buddha.

This tradition may be the oldest one of the religion. For it dates from the time when Buddha himself, along with his disciples, wandered through northeastern India preaching the Dharma (the ultimate law or doctrine taught by Buddha.) The rainy season, which in the nations of Southeast Asia is severe, required that the Buddha and his followers seek a place of refuge while it lasted.[74]

The monsoon season is also the time for another important religious observance, called the vassa, or rain-retreat. This is the time when young people may choose to enter the Sangha, also in most Buddhist countries it is also common for adult males to enter the Sangha temporarily at this time to accumulate merit for themselves.[75]

Buddhism and God

When Buddhists use the word God, the word has nothing in common with God— the Creator of the Christian, Jewish or Islamic faith.[76] Buddhist do not believe that gods are supernatural but instead Buddhists believe that the supreme law of cause and effect governs all.[77] The existence of this absolute and ultimate law is proven over and over again with every new discovery of science. But, since everything that occurs in life cannot be explained through science, it is these unexplainable forces that Buddhists refer to as "gods."

Buddhist gods do not hold a controlling position like that of the Christian God.[78] On the contrary, Buddhist gods come out of life itself. They do not punish and they do not give deliverance. They respond to the sound of the ultimate law of the universe, Nam-Myoho-Renge-Kyo.[79] These "gods" are at the service of everyone who embraces the Gohonzon and its practices. This is a mandala, a symbolic representation of the ideal state of Buddhahood, or enlightenment, in which all the tendencies and impulses of life--from the most debased to the most noble--function in harmony toward happiness and creativity. The Gohonzon is not an "idol" or "god" to be supplicated or appeased but a means for reflection and a catalyst for inner change.[80]

Buddhism and Prayer

"Buddhist prayer may be thought of as a focused expression of the same sentiments of yearning, commitment and appreciation as of other religions. It is, however, distinguished by the fact that Buddhism locates the divine within the life of the individual practitioner. The purpose of Buddhist prayer is to awaken the innate inner capacities of strength, courage and wisdom rather than to petition external forces."[81]

Buddhist prayer is essentially the process by which a person's intensely felt desires and sufferings are transformed into compassion and wisdom. In this sense, it inevitably involves self-reflection, including a sometimes-painful confrontation with the person's own deeply rooted destructive tendencies. To quote Nichiren Daishonin, "Your practice of the Buddhist teachings will not relieve you of the sufferings of birth and death in the least, unless you perceive the true nature of your life." (*The Major Writings of Nichiren Daishonin,* "On Attaining Buddhahood in this Lifetime," page 3.)[82]

Buddhism: Dharma and Reincarnation

Dharma is the principle of righteousness. It is the principle of holiness. It is also the principle of unity whereby followers learn to be selfless by thinking of others first, being respectful of parents and elders, following divine law, and creating mental, emotional and physical non-injury to all beings.

Rebirth or reincarnation as it is often called is the doctrine that indicates when a person dies the new person could come back as identical to or totally different from the old person. Reincarnation is one of the central tenets of Tibetan Buddhism. Reincarnation is often misunderstood as Buddhism does not teach that the soul is reincarnated but that the energy produced by the mental and physical activities of a being that has died creates a new mental and physical energy.[83]

However, in Tibet as elsewhere, mainly of "the elite" understood the views of the philosophers to mean the following as it relates to rebirth: "all aggregates are impermanent; no 'ego' exists in the person, nor in anything," remain attached to the more simple belief in an undefined entity traveling from world to world, assuming various forms.[84]

Hinduism

Hinduism is India's indigenous religious and cultural system, followed today by nearly one billion adherents, mostly in India, but with large populations in many other countries. Hinduism is referred to as Sanatana Dharma, "eternal religion," and Vaidika Dharma, "religion of the Vedas."[85] Hinduism encompasses a broad spectrum of philosophies ranging from pluralistic theism to absolute monism. It is a family of myriad faiths with four primary denominations: Saivism, Vaishnavism, Shaktism and Smartism.[86] These four share the same culture and belief in karma, dharma, reincarnation, temple worship etc. even though they each have such very different views that they could be considered their own religion.[87]

This type of separatism allowed new religious traditions to form and among these were Jainism, Buddhism and Sikhism. These religions while similar in cultural values they still operate under different prisms.

Just like Christianity, Islam and Buddhism, Hinduism has no central headquarters. Hinduism has had many past founders there is no different in today's world. Hinduism is basically around a 5000-year-old faith. It has had many founders in the past and various teaching lineages headed by a pontiff (a title given to a religious leader). Hinduism's nearly three million swamis, gurus and sadhus work tirelessly within and upon themselves and then, when ready, serve others, leading them from darkness into light, from death to immortality.[88]

Unlike some other religions where you are born into them or accepted unto them (by being saved or accepting the faith) that does not necessarily apply to Hinduism. Hinduism is more than just a "religion" it is a way of life, a culture, both religious and secular.[89] Hindus don't see religion as one component or a separate system in their life, instead it encompasses all of life. Hindus can have this view because Hinduism in its practice accepts all forms of beliefs. There is not just one way of practicing this religion and lifestyle. Those who choose to live according to the basic beliefs (dharma, karma and reincarnation) and values are then Hindus.

Sri K. Navaratnam of Sri Lanka, devotee of Paramaguru Siva Yogaswami for some 40 years, in his book *Studies in Hinduism* quotes from the book, *Introduction to the Study of the Hindu Doctrines*, "Hindus are those who adhere to the Hindu tradition, on the understanding that they are duly qualified to do so really effectively, and not simply in an exterior and illusory way; non-Hindus, on the contrary, are those who, for any reason whatsoever, do not participate in the tradition in question."[90] Sri K. Navaratnam enumerates a set of basic beliefs held by Hindus[91]:

1. A belief in the existence of God.
2. A belief in the existence of a soul separate from the body.
3. A belief in the existence of the finitizing principle known as avidya or maya.
4. A belief in the principle of matter--prakriti or maya.

5. A belief in the theory of karma and reincarnation.
6. A belief in the indispensable guidance of a guru to guide the spiritual aspirant towards God Realization.
7. A belief in moksha, or liberation, as the goal of human existence.
8. A belief in the indispensable necessity of temple worship...in religious life.
9. A belief in graded forms of religious practices, both internal and external, until one realizes God.
10. A belief in ahimsa as the greatest dharma or virtue.
11. A belief in mental and physical purity as indispensable factors for spiritual progress.

Five Obligations of all Hindus[92]

Worship, upasana: Through chants, traditional dress, yogas and religious study in the family shrine or temple.

Holy days, utsava: Participation in festivals and holy days in the family home and temple on Monday and Friday and other holy days which can also include the act of fasting.

Virtuous living, dharma: Living a life of duty and good conduct by being selfless and thinking of others first. Being respectful of parents, elders and swamis, following divine law, especially ahimsa, mental, emotional and physical noninjury to all beings. Thus they resolve karmas.

Pilgrimage, tirthayatra: At least once a year worldly and secular activities are set aside for time with God at a temples or locations near or far.

Rites of passage, samskara: Observance and celebration of the rites of birth, name-giving, head-shaving, first feeding, ear-piercing, first learning, coming of age, marriage and death.

Jews in America

Before we discuss the plight of Jews in America, we must have a clear understanding of what it means to be Jew. Many people think of Jews as a race, but if you look at the U.S. Census data you will not find Jewish under the same category as Blacks, Whites, Asian or Native American because there is a Jewish faith not a racial category. A common ancestry or biological distinction is what makes up a race of people and this does not apply to Jews. There have been Jews of every racial group. The famous African American novelist Walter Mosley and the famous African American entertainers Sammy Davis, Jr. and Lisa Bonet are Jewish.[93]

Some also think of Jews as a nationality but, Jews are not central to Israel as Judaism can be found all over the world. People of many different nationalities are Jewish and part of this religious group.[94]

So, if anyone can be Jewish how does one join?

Many Jews become a part of this religious movement not because of anything they have done but through birth. If your mother is Jewish then you are Jewish and this affiliation stays with you all of your life even if you don't follow the religious practices--you would just be considered a non-religious Jew or secular Jew.[95]

Another way to become Jewish is by a conversion process. According to the website by Rabbi Celso Cukierkorn, "The rituals of conversion will formally mark your acceptance of your new Jewish identity and your commitment to Judaism. But the work of creating Jewish memories for yourself, of shaping the Jewish human being that you will become, is a much more subtle and long-term process."[96]

The conversion process has been a very important element of Judaism. But, over the years the different Jewish denominations of Orthodox, Conservative and Reform have disagreed about the content of the conversion process.[97] However one adaptation of the various denominations of the 20th century regarding who is a Jew is that children of Jewish fathers, as well as adopted children, don't have to be converted but are accepted as Jews.[98]

Jewish Immigrants

Now let's address the immigrant Jews that came to the United States. According to author Thomas Sowell, "this immigrant generation of Eastern European Jews flooded into the lower east side of Manhattan at the same time as the massive influx of Italian immigrants; helping to create one of the most crowded communities known to the United States. Unlike the German Jews before them, the eastern European immigrant Jews could not readily spread out across the nation or even across the city. Their observance of the Saturday Sabbath often prevented them from access to certain types of jobs. Factories often operated on Saturdays, the Sabbath—observed by Orthodox Jews. In addition, their language differences also made it difficult for them to work or live among other Americans, as did their need for kosher food and a synagogue."[99]

The German Jews and Europeans Jews (who arrived later) had many differences in culture. The German Jews who were more reformed in their interpretation of the Torah (the Jewish Holy book) allowed them to fit into mainstream America. However, the European Jews were required to follow the customs of their ancestors, and did not regard themselves as having the option of what beliefs to follow.[100] The differences between the German Jews culture and mainstream America which were mainly Christians caused anti-Semitism in the U.S. to grow at unprecedented proportions in the last quarter of the 19th century with the mass arrival of these eastern European Jews.[101] This anti-Semitism affected all Jews in America not just the Eurpoean Jews and a result the German Jews lost their privilege of social clubs, posh hotels, and other benefits and honors now denied them because they were Jewish.[102]

Soon, employment opportunities were closed to the Jews just as was closed to the Irish, free Blacks and Native Americans.[103]

Religious discrimination has therefore had its place in American society, so much so that the Civil Rights Act of 1964 Title VII prohibits religious discrimination. But even with religious discrimination being illegal, there are still many ways in which those who celebrate different holidays and customs are forced to make a choice between their religion and their job. Still today, many U.S. companies celebrate religious holidays and days off based upon Christianity.

Synagogues, Shuls and Temples

The Jewish religious place of worship is called a synagogue (called this by many conservative Jews) and it operates as a social center where Jewish prayer takes place, study and education of Judaism occurs, and where social work and charitable events happen. However, there are actually different terms utilized for this Jewish place of worship. Yiddish term of "shul" is what Orthodox and Chasidim Jews call it because it focuses on the synagogue's role as a place of study. This term can however, be unfamiliar to some modern Jews.[104]

Reformed Jews use the word "temple or The Temple," which focuses on the synagogue's role as a meeting place.[105] But, be aware that "temple" can offend some traditional Jews because according to this group it does not denote the full usage of this place of worship.[106] Last, Beit k'nesset meaning house of assembly is the Hebrew term for synagogue. According to the website, *Judaism 101*, the word "synagogue" is the best bet, because everyone knows what it means.[107]

<u>How are Synagogues structured?</u>
There is a board of directors made up of members of the church that run the synagogue who do not answer to a central authority. While there are central organizations for the various movements of Judaism, the individual synagogues do not report to these organizations. The board has the important role of managing the synagogue's activities as well as hiring the rabbi, which in Hebrew means "teacher."[108]

Rabbis can perform weddings but not to ordain the wedding just to make sure the civil law is followed. A rabbi more importantly provides leadership, guidance and education to the membership. However, a synagogue can exist without a rabbi where necessary religious services can be performed by synagogue members.[109]

When it comes to offering in the Christian religion, a collection plate or offering box takes the offering or tithe that members pay voluntarily. However in a Synagogue, members often pay annual dues to finance the synagogues operation. Members can also purchase reserved seats for services on Rosh Hashanah and Yom Kippur (two Jewish holidays) or purchase memorial plaques or provide voluntary donations which go towards the operation of the Synagogue.[110]

Worship at a Synagogue is also open to anyone. But, if you plan to worship or study regularly there then it is expected that you should cover your share of the synagogue's cost. The synagogue plays an important role in lives of Jews as it meets the educational, social and emotional needs of this religious community.

Jewish Beliefs

<u>Bar or Bat Mitzvah</u>
Bar Mitzvah is term utilized most often in Orthodox congregations and Bat Mitzvah in non-Orthodox congregations.[111] Bar and Bat Mitzvah is the coming of age where youth now become responsible for their actions and for boys this occurs at age 13 and age 12 for girls. Since girls typically mature physically and mentally earlier than boys their Bar and Bat Mitzvah occurs one year earlier.[112]

According to Jewish tradition, puberty which is occurring at this time means that boys and girls becoming bar and bat mitzvah, must now become morally aware of their actions and have a better understanding of the world and the people they want to be as participants in the world. Also, it is understood that these young people now can channel their energy to do good for others rather than submit to the natural desire of putting self first.[113]

Shabbat

The *Shabbat* is seventh day of the Jewish week and a day of rest in Judaism. *Shabbat* is observed from sundown Friday until the appearance of three stars in the sky on Saturday night. Depending on the time of sunset at the various locations this exact time could change from week to week.[114] Some Jews who celebrate the Sabbath would not be allowed to work from Sunset till Sundown on Saturday.

Jewish Calendar, Festivals and Holidays

The Jewish calendar must keep up with the civil year so festivals occur at the "correct" time therefore the Jewish calendar has 12 months. The Jewish calendar runs according to the Moon, rather than the Sun, as the civil calendar does. Each Jewish month has either 29 or 30 days and every Jewish year is about 11 days shorter than a civil year.[115]

Jewish festivals are celebrated on fixed dates. In order to do this, the calendar has leap years, with an extra month of Adar in January-February. The normal month of Adar (February-March) is then called Adar 2 and there are seven leap years every 19 years.[116] There is a celebration, *Rosh Chodesh*, for the beginning of each month.

The Jewish New Year, *Rosh Hashanah*, is on 1 and 2 Tishrei (September-October).[117] *Yom Kippur*, which is a 25-hour fast and a very formal festival, is on 10 Tishrei and the first ten days of Tishrei, which includes two festivals are known as the Ten Days of Penitence.[118]

At this point, you may be wondering, I am not Jewish so why do I need to know this? It is important again to understand differences. How do you respect another person's religion in the workplace if you know nothing about it?

To understand the basic aspects of Jewish beliefs you would need to read the Torah, which means teaching. The Torah (Jewish holy book) is the written word that explains how Jews should act, think and feel about life, and it contains over 613 commandments. The Torah is divided into two parts: the Written Torah called the Tenakh and the Oral Torah, which is the explanation of the written Torah that is passed down verbally from generation to generation.[119] After the destruction of the Temple in Jerusalem, it was decided the Oral Torah should be written down so it would not be forgotten. The Mishnah is the written outline of the Oral Torah.[120]

Whether you are Jewish, Christian, Muslim, Hindu, Buddhist, etc. religion is a personal matter. Religion is often passed down through our family beliefs and culture which means we typically only know about the religion that we practice. If you are agnostic, a person who believes that they cannot have true knowledge about the existence of God (but does not deny that God might exist) or an atheist, a person who denies the existence of God, then you may know little about religion. Lack of exposure to another's religion or the various religious beliefs that exist can create a workplace where religious discrimination occurs simply from lack of knowledge. Cultural knowledge as it applies to religion is key to allowing religious freedom in the workplace.

Wicca the Religion

Wicca is one of about 17 unrelated activities with more than 500,000 followers, which has been called Witchcraft.[121] Religious conservatives often link Witchcraft to Satanism, which relates Satan worship and Satanic Ritual Abuse. The problem here is that the single word "Witchcraft" has so many unrelated meanings. But the question is not so much, is it witchcraft and how is it utilized but is Wicca a religion?

According to the Civil rights Act of 1964, Title VII requires employers to accommodate only those religious beliefs that are "sincerely held."[122] If Wicca is not considered a bona fide religion, then it has no legal protection. Some say yes it is a bona fide religion and others say no. However, through a Michigan court case it was determined that Wicca was indeed a religion in this States consideration. The case was brought in 1983 in the U.S. District Court in Michigan and it was found that three employees of a prison had restricted an inmate in the performance of his Wiccan rituals. The court found that this "*deprived him of his First Amendment right to freely exercise his religion and his Fourteenth Amendment right to equal protection of the laws.*"[123]

Wicca is seen as a controversial religion to some based, in part, on ancient, northern European Pagan beliefs in a fertility Goddess and her consort, a horned God.[124] Although the religion is a modern creation, some of its sources pre-date the Christian era by many centuries. Most Wiccans do not believe that their religion is a direct, continuous descendent of this earlier religion. They see it as a modern reconstruction.[125]

Author Joanna Hautin-Mayer in *When is a Celt not a Celt?* who takes a peek into the Neopagan views of history, has written:

> *"We know tragically little about the actual religious expressions of the ancient Celts. We have a few myths and legends, but very little archeological evidence to support our theories. We have no written records of their actual forms of worship, and the accounts of their culture and beliefs written by their contemporaries are often highly biased and of questionable historical worth."*[126]

The above is part of the reason that Wicca is seen as a recently created, a Neopagan religion. The various branches of Wicca can be traced back to Gardnerian Witchcraft, which was founded in the UK during the late 1940s.[127] Wicca is based on the symbols, seasonal days of celebration, beliefs and deities of ancient Celtic society though. Added to this material were Masonic and ceremonial magical components from recent centuries. In this respect, it is a religion whose roots go back almost three millennia to the formation of Celtic society circa 800 BCE.[128]

A follower of Wicca is called a Wiccan. In the U.S., Canada and Europe and especially among the teen population, Wicca and Neopagan types of religions are experiencing continued growth. Since Wicca does not encourage autocracy, paternalism, sexism, homophobia, nor is it a religion that promotes insensitivity to the environment it is popular among the young who are more sensitive to these issues.[129] Many North Americans of European decent, who are keen to discover their ancestral heritage, are also being attracted to this religion.

Wiccans generally consider themselves to be Witches, Neopagans, and Pagans. However, not all Witches, Neopagans and Pagans are Wiccans. The terms *Witch, Neopagan* and *Pagan* can also refer to followers of many other faith traditions. Because of religious propaganda dating from the late Middle Ages, Wicca has often been incorrectly associated with Satanism.

Managing Workplace Diversity

Among those who research religion, it appears that Wicca became a religious movement in the 1950s in England. Wicca is currently one of the largest of the minority religions in the United States with estimates of membership at 750,000.[130] This estimate makes Wicca about the 5th largest organized religion in the United States, behind Christianity, Islam, Judaism, and Hinduism.

Because of the controversy or myths surrounding this religion many Wiccans hide their religious beliefs and practices. Those who allow their faith to be known publicly are often heavily persecuted in North America; on a per-capita basis, they are believed to be victimized more often than members of any other religious group.[131] Many physical assaults, arson, and economic attacks are reported yearly. There have even been shootings, one public mass stoning and a lynching in recent years.[132]

Some people believe that if others knew of the connection of this religion to Christianity that it would be better accepted. The first missionary to the Celts may have been St. Paul as he sought converts to Christianity in the Pagan Celtic land of Galatia (now part of Turkey) as recorded in his Epistle to the Galatians of the Christian Scriptures (New Testament).[133] Later Missionaries and the Roman army gradually spread Christianity across Europe, easily converting the rulers and the Druidic priesthood, but having less success in bringing the common folk to the new religion.

One holiday day celebrated by some Christians but also by Wiccans is the day of Halloween. The Halloween season of OCT-31 to NOV-2 each year is unique. It includes a Neopagan Sabbat, Samhain, which is usually celebrated on or near the evening of October 31.[134] It was originally a celebration of the final harvest of the growing season among the ancient Celts. According to research, the Celts believed that during this time of the year friends and relatives who were deceased would come back with souls resembling an animal--likely a black cat. This where the symbol of the black cat became associated with Halloween.[135]

Also during the Samhain which was a fire festival where bonfires were lit on hills in honor of the Gods, Celts would go door to door to gather food that they would offer to their Gods.[136] Thus, possibly creating the Halloween tradition of going "trick or treating."

Once the fires were put out at the fire festival the Celts would often feel afraid to walk in the dark due to any looming evil spirits. So instead they would try to scare the evil spirits themselves by dressing up in costumes.[137] The embers they held at the fires would also have carvings in them to scare the evil spirits.

Children continue to dress up today in various costumes and pumpkins get carved instead of embers.

Wiccan Beliefs

The main tenet of Wicca is the "Wiccan Rede" which states "And it harm none, do as ye will" and the Wicca law states that:

> *"All good that a person does to another returns three fold in this life; harm is also returned three fold."*[138]

It is this main belief that prevents Wiccans from doing harm to themselves or to others, or attempting to manipulate others, or taking harmful drugs, etc. Thus, many activities that have been attributed to Wiccans, from the laying of curses to conducting love spells, are strictly forbidden to them.

The following are other general beliefs of most Wiccans[139]:

- Everyone has the divine (or goddess) within.
- A creative force exists in the universe, called "The One" or "The All."
- The Goddess and the God represent the female and male aspects of the All.
- Divine forces or nature spirits are invoked in rituals.
- The Goddess, as either a symbol or a real entity, is the focus of worship.
- Nature and the earth are sacred manifestations of the Goddess.
- Everyone has his or her own spiritual path to follow.
- Rituals and celebrations are linked to the seasons and moon phases.
- One should develop natural gifts for divination or occult magic (often spelled 'magick' by occultists.)
- Meditation, visualization, invocation (calling on forces or gods/goddesses), chanting, burning candles and special rituals trigger a sense of the mystical, thus reinforcing the core belief system.

Wicca is also a religion of the natural grounded in the earth where it is believed that all living things like planets, humans, animals, plants, rocks and even stars have a spirit.[140] Sexuality is valued, and regarded as a gift of the Goddess and God, to be engaged in with joy and responsibility, and without manipulation.

Why learn about various religions?

After reading about all the religions in this chapter, no one would expect you to be an expert on these different religions or all the other religions that exist. However, what is important to know is that while there are many similarities amongst religions there are also differences that make each religion unique. These differences subsist of how many times the religious must pray, if at all; to the day of worship they observe, if at all. Because the Civil Rights Act of 1964 protects against discrimination based upon religion as well as requires accommodation of certain religious beliefs—it is important to be familiar with especially the largest religions in the United States. Because if you know very little about the various religions, how do you as a manager protect a person's rights or provide religious accommodation as required by law?

Religious Accommodation

It is up to the employer to determine when and if a religious accommodation is necessary as the employer cannot make the decision to "not" accommodate an employee. The first step is to determine if it is a sincerely held religious belief.

So, what is a sincerely held religious belief?

- A belief required of a recognized religious organization or
- Religious practices not just of a organized or recognized religion however;
- It is not a political, cultural or heritage belief as it must be based upon a religious practice. It is also not the person's preference but what is required.

How should the request be made by the employee?

The employee must clearly explain why an accommodation is needed indicating what religious belief would be broken or not adhered to. The following are some causes for a religious accommodation[141]:

- An employee needs their weekly Sabbath day off for religious observance. The Sabbath day is a holy day and there is no working on this day.
- An employee may need a particular day off each year for a religious holiday.

- An employee may be required to attend a religious pilgrimage and they have no vacation time.
- An employee may need to wear religious dress or maintain a certain physical appearance (not cutting facial hair) as a requirement of their religion.
- An employee may need to have a place to pray because a number of daily prayers are required and this will occur during work time.

Now once the sincerely held belief has been requested and established then there are a number of things that can be done to accommodate. For an employee who needs time off or can't work on Saturdays due to the Sabbath they can take an unpaid day, swap shifts or days with an employee, switch an off day or have flexible scheduling (work Sunday instead of Saturday or work Christmas instead of their religious holiday) and they could even be allowed to just work Monday through Thursday for those who have to observe a Friday-night Sabbath.[142]

You could also allow for voluntary assignment substitutions, lateral transfers to other departments or positions in the company, use of lunch or breaks in exchange for early departure.

After reading the above, you may now be thinking: do I have to provide the accommodation to the employees' specific request?

No. The employer can accommodate but not necessarily to the specific "desires" of the employee. For instance in the case of the employee who can't cut his facial hair, the employer could indicate that according to safety standards a beard must be a certain length and covered thereby allowing the beard but with specific requirements. In another instance, let's say the employer has a test scheduled for a Sabbath day but the employee would like to take it instead on the following Monday. If the same test or training is being given at another location on another day other than the Sabbath but not on the Monday the employee may be required to take it elsewhere--say on the following Wednesday not Monday. In addition, the employee may be required to use personal time to take the test or training.[143]

Now, your next thought could be: how does an employer allow for such things when there is a union mandated seniority system for job assignments etc. Do I have to accommodate every sincerely held belief?

No. If the employer can prove that by allowing the belief to be accommodated it creates an undue hardship then the employer does not have to accommodate. But, what constitutes an undue hardship?

This answer is not so "cut or dry" as there is not a concrete definition of undue hardship, but it was determined by the United States Supreme Court that a company does not have to incur more than "minimal" costs to accommodate an employees' religious belief.[144] For example, if time off is needed to participate in religious holiday this does not have to be paid time off--the United States Supreme Court indicated that a reasonable accommodation is nonpaid leave for a religious observance unless all other leaves in the company are paid.[145] This would mean the only unpaid leave was for religious observance, then this would not be fair. Other issues that can indicate undue hardship is seniority violation based upon union contracts as well as paying extra or overtime pay to accommodate.

Now, what if someone makes up a religion where they indicate that this religion does not allow them to work when it's raining outside?

The employer can deny the accommodation if it is not a sincerely held belief.[146] However, the worst mistake you can make as an employer is to assume that is not a bona fide religion or sincerely held belief. Instead it is important (when unknown) to research the religion or belief. Some religions have beliefs unlike your own, making them seem fictitious--but just because you think they are fictitious does not mean that they are. Always do your homework before saying no. Talk with your company's human resource department or lawyer to make sure you are doing everything possible to try to accommodate the employee--don't just say no.

Concluding Thoughts

Based upon the religious diversity in the U.S. it is critical for managers and employees alike to understand the religious differences of others so that they can work effectively, respect others beliefs and help to de-escalate potentially explosive situations that can occur from lack of understanding.

There are many different religious practices of the diverse communities that are represented in the workplace. Such as, there may be specific prayer times of Muslims depending on the month, day and location; another is that Sikhs may be required to wear five holy items at all times (including a small dagger); and that some Hindus do not shake the hands of strangers, particularly members of the opposite sex. While it is not possible to know all of the religious customs of various groups, it is possible to be open-minded so as to respect religious difference.

End of Chapter Questions

1. What are some basic beliefs of Christians, Muslims and Jews?

2. What are three things that are common amongst Christians, Muslims and Jews?

3. How does the Buddhist view of God differ from some other religions?

4. What practices of Wiccans and Hindus might require a religious accommodation?

5. What are four examples of religious accommodation that can be made for an employee and under what rationale?

Internet Exercise

Indicate what religion you practice in the space below. Now pick a different religion other than the one you practice (if any) or those discussed in the chapter. Find information on this chosen religion using the Internet or the library. Summarize the key beliefs about the religion and how it is similar or dissimilar to other religions that you have read about.

My religion is (if none, just leave blank)_____

End of Chapter Exercise

Do I Accommodate?

Case One:

I am a truck driver and have been on "light duty" for the past several weeks. Last week my supervisor told me to take one of the office girls to the bank to make a company deposit. The other employees made crude remarks about her and me. I then refused to take her. I explained to my supervisor that I felt it would be inappropriate for me (being married) to take her because of my religious beliefs. After yelling and swearing at me in front of the other employees he told me to go home without the overtime pay. Then he told another employee (with less seniority) to take her, which he did.

Was I wrong to say no? Was he wrong to send me home?

Case Two:

Mary Tiano sued her employer Dillard Department Stores for failure to make reasonable accommodation of her religious beliefs. Tiano was a top sales person for many years and a devout Roman Catholic. In late August of 1988, she learned of a pilgrimage to Medjugorje, Yugoslavia taking place between October 17 and October 26. Several people have claimed that visions of the Virgin Mary appeared to them in Medjugorje, although the Catholic Church has not designated Medjugorje an official pilgrimage site of the Church. Tiano testified that on August 22, 1988, she had a "calling from God" to attend this pilgrimage.

Tiano requested an unpaid leave of absence to attend. Dillard's vacation policy prohibited employees from taking leave between October and December, the store' s busy holiday season. As a result, Tiano's request was denied. She went anyway, and when she returned to work she was informed that she had voluntarily resigned and would not be offered reemployment. Was Dillard's correct? What rights did Tiano have?

References

Managing Workplace Diversity

1. Robinson, B.A. (n.d.). *Christianity: A Brief History*. Retrieved from: http://www.religioustolerance.org/chr_intr1.htm

2. American Academy of Religion. (1986). *Journal of Biblical literature*. Chicago, Illinois: American Theological Library Association.

3. Robinson, B.A. (n.d.). Christianity: A Brief History. Retrieved from: http://www.religioustolerance.org/chr_intr1.htm

4. American Academy of Religion. (1986). *Journal of Biblical literature*. Chicago, Illinois: American Theological Library Association.

5. Ibid.

6. Ibid.

7. Smart, N. (1998). *The world's religions*. Cambridge; New York: Cambridge University Press.

8. The History of Christmas. (n.d.). Retrieved from: http://www.thehistoryofchristmas.com/ch/in_america.htm

9. Aust, J. (2005, November/December). *Why Some Christians Don't Observe Christmas*. Retrieved from: http://www.gnmagazine.org/issues/gn61/christmas.htm

10. Robinson, B.A. (n.d.). *Christianity: A Brief Summary of Christianity*. Retrieved from: http://www.religioustolerance.org/chr_brief3.htm

11. Ibid.

12. Ibid.

13. Ibid.

14. Harris, I. (1992). *Contemporary religions: a world guide*. Harlow, Essex, United Kingdom: Longman Group, UK Ltd.

15. Major religions of the World. (n.d.). Retrieved from: http://www.adherents.com/Religions_By_Adherents.html

16. Harris, I. (1992). *Contemporary religions: a world guide*. Harlow, Essex, United Kingdom: Longman Group, UK Ltd.

17. Ibid.

18. Religions of the World: Christianity. Retrieved from:
http://www.gkindia.com/worldreligions/christianity.htm

19. Ibid.

20. Wikipedia. *Liberal Christianity*. Retrieved from: http://en.wikipedia.org/wiki/Liberal_Christianity

21. Hodge, D.R. (1985). *A test of theories of denominational growth and decline*. Pilgrim Press.

22. Holm, J. (1992). *Keyguide to information sources on world religions*. New York: JSOT Press.

23. Eliade, M. (1987). *The Encyclopedia of religion*. New York, N.Y.: Macmillan.

24. Mohammed. (n.d.). *Islamic Info and Dawah Page*. Retrieved from:
http://www.angelfire.com/ny/dawahpage/

25. Central Intelligence Agency. (n.d.). *The World Factbook*. Retrieved from:
https://www.cia.gov/library/publications/the-world-factbook/fields/2122.html

26. Major religions of the World. (n.d.). Retrieved from:
http://www.adherents.com/Religions_By_Adherents.html#Islam

27. Central Intelligence Agency. (n.d.). *The World Factbook*. Retrieved from:
https://www.cia.gov/library/publications/the-world-factbook/fields/2122.html

28. *Religion: a cross-cultural encyclopedia*. (1996). Santa Barbara, California: ABC-CLIO.

29. Khalifa, R. (2000). *Quran, Hadith, And Islam*. New York State: University Unity.

30. Major religions of the World. (n.d.). Retrieved from:
http://www.adherents.com/Religions_By_Adherents.html#Islam

31. Introduction to Islam. (n.d.). Retrieved from: http://www.al-islam.org/begin/intro/rizvi.html

32. Islam in Dearborn Michigan. (n.d.). Retrieved from: http://www.30-days.net/muslims/muslims-in/america-north/islam-in-dearborn-michigan/

33. Ibid.

34. Islam Answering. (n.d.). Retrieved from:
http://www.islamanswering.com/subpage.php?s=cat_open&cid=46

35. The Islamic Affairs Department, The Embassy of Saudi Arabia. (1989). *Understanding Islam and the Muslims*. Washington DC: The Islamic Texts Society.

36.   Ibid.

37.   Islamic Society of Michiana. (n.d.). Retrieved from: http://michianamuslims.org/faqs.html

38.   The Progress Report. (n.d.). Retrieved from: http://www.progress.org/islam01.htm

39.   An Introduction to Islam. (n.d.). Retrieved from:
http://userweb.port.ac.uk/~cve80345/oldpages/isintrod.htm

40.   Abu Qhodda, A. (n.d.). What is *Zakât*? Retrieved from: http://www.zpub.com/aaa/zakat-def.html

41.   Ibid.

42.   Khalifa, R. (2000). *Quran, Hadith, And Islam*. New York State: University Unity.

43.   Ibid.

44.   Ibid.

45.   Wikipedia. (n.d.). Retrieved from: http://en.wikipedia.org/wiki/Ramadan

46.   Ibid.

47.   Ibid.

48.   Khalifa, R. (2000). *Quran, Hadith, And Islam*. New York State: University Unity.

49.   Ibid.

50.   Ibid.

51.   Numan, F. (1992). *American Muslim History*. Retrieved from:
http://www.islam101.com/selections/muslim_us_hist.html

52.   Smart, N. (1999). *Atlas of the World's Religions*. USA: Oxford University Press.

53.   Ibid.

54.   Sharma, M. S. (2001). *Encyclopaedic dictionary of religion and ethics*. New Delhi: Mohit
Publications.

55.   Ibid.

56. Ibid.

57. Smart, N. (1999). *Atlas of the World's Religions*. USA: Oxford University Press.

58. Ibid.

59. Ibid.

60. Sharma, M. S. (2001). *Encyclopaedic dictionary of religion and ethics*. New Delhi: Mohit Publications.

61. Ibid.

62. Fischer-Schreiber, I. (1989). *The encyclopedia of Eastern philosophy and religion: Buddhism, Hinduism, Taoism, Zen / Buddhism & Taoism*. Boston: Shambhala.

63. Ibid.

64. Dhammanada, K. Sri. (n.d.). *What Buddhists Believe*. Retrieved from: http://www.buddhanet.net/pdf_file/whatbelieve.pdf

65. Ibid.

66. Fischer-Schreiber, I. (1989). *The encyclopedia of Eastern philosophy and religion: Buddhism, Hinduism, Taoism, Zen / Buddhism & Taoism*. Boston: Shambhala.

67. Ibid.

68. Ibid.

69. Prebish, C. S. (1999). *Luminous Passage: The Practice and Study of Buddhism in America*. California: University of California Press.

70. Ibid.

71, Ibid.

72. The different forms of Buddhism. (n.d.). Retrieved from: http://www.findingdulcinea.com/guides/Religion-and-Spirituality/Buddhism.pg_00.html

73. Ibid.

74. Ibid.

75. Hagen, S. (1998). *Buddhism: Plain and Simple*. New York: Broadway Publishing.

76. Ibid.

77. Ibid.

78. Gyatso, G. K. (1992). *Introduction to Buddhism.* New York: Tharpa Publications.

79. Ibid.

80. Ibid.

81. Soka Gakkai International. (2001). Retrieved from: http://www.sgi.org/prayer.html

82. Daishonin, N. (n.d.). *On Attaining Buddhahood in this Lifetime.* Retrieved from: http://www.sgilibrary.org/view.php?page=3

83. Wikipedia. (n.d.). *Rebirth (Buddhism).* Retrieved from: http://en.wikipedia.org/wiki/Rebirth_(Buddhism)

84. Ibid.

85. Smart, N. (1999). *Atlas of the World's Religions*. USA: Oxford University Press.

86. Subramuniyaswami, S. S. (2000). *How to Become a (Better)Hindu.* India: Himalayan Academy.

87. Ibid.

88. Ibid.

89. How to become a Hindu. (n.d.). Retrieved from: http://www.himalayanacademy.com/resources/pamphlets/BecomeHindu.html

90. Ibid.

91. Ibid.

92. Subramuniyaswami, S. S. (2000). *How to Become a (Better)Hindu*. India: Himalayan Academy.

93. Wikipedia. (n.d.). List of Jews in the African diaspora. Retrieved from: http://en.wikipedia.org/wiki/List_of_Jews_in_the_African_diaspora

94. Sacchi, P. (1990). *Jewish Apocalyptic and its History*. England: Sheffield Academic Press Ltd.

95. Ibid.

96. Cukierkorn, R. C. (n.d.). *Conversion to Judaism.*   Retrieved from: http://www.convertingtojudaism.com/Choosing-Judaism.htm

97. Ibid.

98. Ibid.

99. Sowell, T. (1983). *Ethnic America: A History*. New York, NY: Basic Books.

100. Kotkin, J. (1993). *Tribes: How Race, Religion, and Identity Determine Success in the New Global Economy*. New York, NY: Random House.

101. Sowell, T. (1983). *Ethnic America: A History*. New York, NY: Basic Books.

102. Ibid.

103. Ibid.

104. Rich, T. R. (n.d.). *Judaism 101*. Retrieved from: http://www.jewfaq.org/shul.htm

105. Ibid.

106. Ibid.

107. Ibid.

108. Steinberg, Rabbi M.. (1975). *Basic Judaism*. Florida: HBJ Publishing.

109. Ibid.

110. Ibid.

111. Wikipedia. (n.d.). *Bar and Bat Mitzvah.* Retrieved from: http://en.wikipedia.org/wiki/Bar_mitzvah

112. Smith, J. Z. (1995). *The HarperCollins dictionary of religion*. San Francisco: Harper San Francisco.

113. Wikipedia. (n.d.). *Bar and Bat Mitzvah*. Retrieved from: http://en.wikipedia.org/wiki/Bar_mitzvah

114. Ibid.

115. Smith, J. Z. (1995). *The HarperCollins dictionary of religion*. San Francisco: Harper San Francisco.

116. Ibid.

117. Ibid.

118. Ibid.

119. Sanders, J. A. (2005). *Torah and Canon*. Eugene, Oregon: Cascade Books.

120. Ibid.

121. Lewis, J. R. (1998). *The encyclopedia of cults, sects, and new religions*. Amherst, N.Y.: Prometheus Books.

122. EEOC Compliance Manual. (n.d.). Retrieved from: http://www.eeoc.gov/policy/docs/religion.html#_ftn35

123. Robinson, B.A. (n.d.). *Is Wicca a Religion*. Retrieved from: http://www.religioustolerance.org/wic_rel.htm

124. Basic Wicca. (1999). Retrieved from: http://www.journey1.org/basicj2.htm

125. Ibid.

126. Joanna Hautin-Mayer, J. (n.d.). *When is a Celt not a Celt*. Retrieved from: http://www.cyberwitch.com/wychwood/library/WhenIsACeltNotACelt.htm

127. Encyclopedia. (n.d.). Retrieved from: http://encyclopedia.kids.net.au/page/ne/Neopaganism

128. Ibid.

129. Robinson, B.A. (n.d.). *Teens and Wiccan*. Retrieved from: http://www.jesus-is-savior.com/False%20Religions/Wicca%20&%20Witchcraft/teens_and_wicca.htm

130. Retrieved from: http://www.wiqued.com/Wicca.htm

131. King, E. (n.d.). *Wicca/Paganism*. Retrieved from: http://www.masonicinfo.com/wicca.htm

132. Ibid.

133. Lewis, J. R. (1998). *The encyclopedia of cults, sects, and new religions*. Amherst, N.Y.: Prometheus Books.

134. A & E Television Networks. (n.d.). Retrieved from:
http://www.history.com/content/halloween/real-story-of-halloween

135. Ibid.

136. Ibid.

137. Ibid.

138. Lewis, J. R. (1998). *The encyclopedia of cults, sects, and new religions*. Amherst, N.Y.:
Prometheus Books.

139. Ibid.

140. Ibid.

141. Anti Defamation League. (n.d.). *Religious Accommodation*. Retrieved from:
http://www.adl.org/religious_freedom/resource_kit/religion_workplace.asp

142. Ibid.

143. Ibid.

144. Ibid.

145. Ibid

146. Ibid.

Chapter Ten

Understanding The Disabled

Whether we will philosophize or we won't philosophize, we must philosophize.

Aristotle

UNDERSTANDING THE DISABLED

Chapter Objectives

After reading this chapter, you should be able to:

- understand what a disability is.

- explain the myths regarding the disabled.

- identify what the ADA says about mental impairment.

- describe the cultural differences between various impairments.

- provide tools and tips for addressing numerous disabilities including cancer and HIV.

In 1954, the U.S. Supreme Court ruled that "separate" was not "equal" in the education of African American children. However, it took twenty more years to do the same for disabled children. In 1975, the Free Education for All Handicapped Children Act was enacted. It stated that disabled children must be taught in "the least restrictive environment possible."[1] Previously these children could only be taught at home or in restrictive separate environments.

But, of course laws don't change people's mindsets right away. In 1990, many children were still being regulated to special "resource rooms" rather than being integrated into regular classrooms. Should having a disability restrict you from the same opportunities as others?

What is a disability?

The most frequently applied framework of disability comes from Nagi (1969). Nagi concept of disability is that it is the difficulty associated with performing socially expected activities such as work for pay, and this definition explicitly recognizes the interaction of the environment and pathologies/impairments to cause disabilities.[2] The Americans with Disabilities Act (ADA) rests upon the Nagi framework and recognizes that improvements in the environment (access to public transportation, workplace accommodations, etc.) can reduce disability and thus improve the inclusion of all people.

First of all, a disability is a condition of impairment, physical or mental, having an objective aspect that can usually be described by a physician. This physical or mental condition limits a person's activities or functioning.[3] Although all people with physical disabilities are not handicapped, there is a tendency for others to think of them as being handicapped. Disabilities are really just deficiencies but some individuals look down on people who have them.

In addition, a disability is not an interchangeable term for handicap. The term handicapped should only be used when legally specifying life processes or social activities that are ADVERSELY affected.[4] A handicap is the cumulative result of obstacles, which a disability interposes between the individual and his/her maximum function level. Also, an individual can be handicapped in certain aspects of functioning and, at the same time, be fully functional in many others. Therefore a person may have a handicap, but is not himself or herself "handicapped." Therefore, we do not use the term handicapped to refer to individuals with disabilities.

But, even with this change in terminology, there are still common myths associated with the disabled as described below.

COMMON MYTHS

Myth: Workers with disabilities are not able to perform their jobs.

Fact: When a person applies for a job they should meet the requirements in order to do the job, so if someone disabled is hired then they must possess the necessary skills to accomplish the job with or without a reasonable accommodation. A Dupont Corporation study showed that 92 percent of their workers with disabilities were rated average or above average, compared with the 91 percent for the workers who did not have disabilities.[5]

While there are a number of studies that document the credibility of disabled employees, none are more extensive than the longitudinal studies done by the E.I. DuPont Company. The DuPont Company did its original study in 1973 and then followed with another in 1981. The 1981 study ("Equal to the Task") covered 2,745 disabled employees working for the company that year. In four categories (Safety, Performance of Job Duties, Attendance, and Job Stability/Turnover), disabled employees equaled or outdid their non-impaired co-workers.[6]

Furthermore, Robert B. Reich, a U.S. Secretary of Labor, has encouraged management and labor to make the necessary adjustments to train and retrain the most highly motivated people in our country; such adjustments Reich believes would include hiring one of the best-educated and most highly trained minority groups in the United States, persons with disabilities.[7]

Myth: Workers with disabilities are absent from their jobs a lot due to their problems.

Fact: Employees with disabilities are very much aware of the difficulty of finding work and they often work hard to maintain a good record. ITT discovered that the workers with disabilities in their Corinth plant had fewer absences than their non-disabled co-workers, and many other employers site the same outcome.[8]

Myth: Companies will have to spend a fortune to accommodate disabled workers.

Fact: The expenditures that most companies would have to make to accommodate disabled workers are minimal in comparison to their annual profits. Many smaller companies could receive assistance through the government.[9]

Myth: An on the job accident that, when added to a worker's prior disability, results in permanent total disability will make the company liable for permanent total liability.

Fact: The second injury fund that all states have assumes responsibility of compensation to people with physical disabilities that become totally disabled through industrial accidents allocating to the employer's expense only the single injury sustained at their company.[10]

The above facts prove that employing individuals with disabilities causes no "real" hardship to the companies that employ them. Rather these workers often become valuable employees due to their work ethics. Even still, this group has an unemployment rate three times larger than the unemployment rate of non-institutionalized civilians aged 18-64 who do not report a work limiting health problem or disability.[11]

Despite this outrageous unemployment rate, the following laws have caused gains to be made that improve the quality of life for the disabled.

- In 1956, Disability Insurance became a part of the Social Security Act.

- The Rehabilitation Act of 1973 stated that no otherwise qualified handicapped individual shall solely by reason of his handicap be excluded from participation in any program or activity receiving federal financial assistance. It also established the following: Interagency Committee on Handicapped Employees which will review annually the adequacy of federal hiring, placement and job advancement of persons with disabilities; Architectural and Transportation Barriers Compliance Board which monitors the construction of new federal buildings and remodeling of old federal buildings to ensure accessibility for those with physical disabilities; Affirmative Action Requirement (recruiting, hiring, rates of pay, apprenticeship, etc.) for those companies doing business with the federal government for more than $2,500.[12]

The 1990 American with Disabilities Act (ADA), eliminated discrimination against individuals with disabilities. It permits reasonable accommodation to be made for the disabled. It is important to note that in this act they no longer used the term "handicapped worker" but replaced it with individuals with a disability. Title II of this act provides public services for any qualified individual with a disability; Title III includes public accommodations and services operated by private entities whereas Title IV includes telecommunications. The ADA makes it unlawful to discriminate in all employment practices such as[14]:

- recruitment

- pay

- hiring

- firing

- promotion

- job assignments

- training

- leave

- lay-off

- benefits

- all other employment related activities.

- it prohibits an employer from retaliating against an applicant or employee for asserting his rights under the ADA. The Act also makes it unlawful to discriminate against an applicant or employee, whether disabled or not, because of the individual's family, business, social or other relationship or association with an individual with a disability.

Reasonable Accommodation

The term reasonable accommodation is defined by Title 29 of the Code of Federal Regulations, Part 1630[14]:

(1) Modifications or adjustments to a job application process that enable a qualified applicant with a disability to be considered for the position such qualified applicant desires; or

(2) modifications or adjustments to the work environment, or to the manner or circumstances under which the position held or desired is customarily performed, that enable a qualified individual with a disability to perform the essential functions of that position; or

(3) modifications or adjustments that enable an employee with a disability to enjoy equal benefits and privileges of employment as are enjoyed by its other similarly situated employees without disabilities.

Reasonable accommodation may include but is not limited to: (1) Making existing facilities used by employees ready accessible; and (2) job restructuring.

Reasonable accommodation may also include but is not limited to, making existing facilities used by employees readily accessible to and usable by persons with disabilities, such as: job restructuring; modification of work schedules; providing additional unpaid leaves; reassignment to a vacant position; acquiring or modifying equipment or devices; adjusting or modifying examinations, training materials, or policies; and providing qualified readers or interpreters.[15]

An employer is required to make a reasonable accommodation to a qualified individual with a disability unless doing so would impose an undue hardship on the operation of the employer's business. Undue hardship means an action that requires significant expense when considered in relation to factors such as a business' size, financial resources, and the nature and structure of its operation.

Workplace Assistance for Specific Disabilities

Mental Impairment in the Workplace

Mental impairment can affect any worker at any time in the workplace according to a report by the U.S. Surgeon General. The report indicated that "one of every two Americans alive today will suffer from a mental illness at some point in their lifetime."[16] But mental illness, unlike a physical illness or ailment has a negative connotation with it. In a *USA Today* article, it indicated that the age group of 15 to 44 has the highest amount of mental illness, that is, working teens and adults.[17] Yet, these people though they are working, they are working wounded.

When it comes to mental impairment in the workplace, the ADA covers workers with mental illness as long as their illness meets the definition of a disability. However, there are conditions that are not within the definition of a disability and some are as follows: kleptomania, pyromania, exhibitionism, voyeurism, other sexual behavior disorders, and psychoactive substance use disorders resulting from current illegal drug use; as well as common personality traits like poor judgment, a quick temper, or irritability, so long as the traits are not a symptom of a protected mental impairment.[18]

The ADA can provide what is and what is not included as mental impairment, but there are also some general work practices that should be adhered to when working with persons with these conditions. Just like with sexism, racism or any other ism when dealing with persons with mental impairment avoid generalizations, stereotypes and degrading the individual as this can not only be considered harassment but may prevent the employee from feeling comfortable asking for any necessary accommodation.

Also, if you find there is workplace problems always ask "any" employee if they are able to perform the essential duties of the job.[19] If the employee cannot perform the essential duties of the job then an accommodation may be needed. Any impairment at this time would need to be disclosed and validated by a medical professional, in order for the accommodation to be made. Furthermore, if the employee seems to have a non-work related issue that they want to discuss with management-refer them to the appropriate employee assistance program or professional. Managers are not qualified to heal or discuss any non-work related problems for any employee.

Learning Disabled Adults in the Workplace

Let's start by saying that learning disabilities have nothing to do with intelligence. Learning disabilities are instead problems that impact the brain's capacity to accept, manage, scrutinize, or gather information. Having these types of problems can affect "how" a person learns or how quickly they can process information. Children and adults with learning disabilities often learn differently than the mainstream.

So, what does this mean for learning disabled adults in the workplace? It means that if work procedures have been created for the mainstream someone with a learning disability may have some difficulty with the process. But, this just means an adjustment needs to be made which is an accommodation. It is important to remember when dealing with these issues in the workplace that where one person has a weakness that person also has an alternating strength. It therefore becomes just a matter of tapping into the strengths and accommodating any resulting weakness that affects the person's ability to earn a living.

Learning disabilities can also be diagnosed by a medical professional and therefore must be taken seriously in the workplace. But even with a medical diagnosis learning disabled adults face various issues in the workplace. One such issue is lack of understanding and support. There are also managers or employees who may make negative assumptions about the learning disabled adults' ability or manner of doing tasks. Both of these issues could affect their ability to be promoted. Also, depending on the type of learning disability suffered this worker could be forced into low-paying jobs. All of these instances could create low self esteem for the employee, where really all that was needed was some type of assistive technology or equipment to support their learning impairment.[20]

While adults may struggle with their learning disabilities, they should be given the opportunity to excel in the workplace just like any other person. Management must be supportive and provide the necessary accommodation(s).

Hearing Impairment in the Workplace

According to Wikipedia, a hearing impairment or hearing loss is a full or partial decrease in the ability to detect or understand sounds which can be caused by a wide range of biological and environmental factors, as loss of hearing can happen to any organism that perceives sound.[21] If there is an insensitivity to sound this is often referred to as a hearing impairment but there are varying degrees of severity in this insensitivity.

Hearing loss is therefore categorized by its severity and by the age of onset and this simply means that hearing loss at age 2 as opposed to age 42 will be a difference occurrence.[22] There is also an opportunity for the loss to be one sided or on both sides which affects the severity of the loss as well.

What Is The Difference Between a Deaf and a Hard of Hearing Person?

Hearing impaired individuals are often referred to as deaf or hard of hearing. According to the National Association of the Deaf *"the deaf and hard of hearing community is very diverse, differing greatly on the cause and degree of hearing loss, age at the onset, educational background, communication methods, and how they feel about their hearing loss. How a person "labels" themselves in terms of their hearing loss is personal and may reflect identification with the deaf community or merely how their hearing loss affects their ability to communicate. They can either be deaf (lower case "d") which often means they are unable to hear well enough to rely on their hearing whereas Deaf (capital "D"), or hard of hearing refers to a particular group of people who utilize the American Sign Language (ASL)."*[23]

Many Deaf people function bilingually and are able to utilize both ASL and the written English language as sign languages do not have written forms.[24]

Cross Cultural Differences

Deaf people communicate in a visual way. In addition to ASL, rules of behavior include visual strategies for attention-getting such as touching, waving, vibration or light signaling. Eye contact, body language and facial expression are all keys to effective communication. Communication discourse is direct and to the point, and written English may also seem terse and abbreviated by standards of hearing people.

The following are examples of how a Deaf person's activity could be misinterpreted by someone who is not familiar with Deaf culture[25]:

Example A:

A Deaf construction worker seems angry as he is putting away his tool because he is very noisy and has a stern look on his face. But what this means is the one he is just not aware of his noise level and two he is concentrating or thinking and not aware of how his facial expression appears to others.

Example B:

You are leaving a classroom and the person in front of you slams the door in your face as you are walking out too. However, this Deaf individual did not hear your footsteps behind them and were not aware that someone else was leaving.

Example C:

As the manager you are giving a Deaf employee work instructions. She frowns and seems disinterested in the instructions. As the manager, you take the nonverbal expressions to mean something negative when merely the Deaf employee is focusing on what is being told and thinking about it intently.

"This "frown" of concentration is often misinterpreted as disagreement or annoyance, when it is actually a common element of communication in Deaf culture. Hard of hearing people also commonly frown when listening, an indicator of the enormous amount of energy required to communicate when you have a hearing loss."

Facial expressions in someone who is Deaf does not always mean what we think they may mean just as well as behaving loudly does not mean the Deaf person is rude. That is why, when we deal with difference in the workplace--don't make negative assumptions. If you are going to assume, assume the best scenario—that is give the person the benefit of the doubt. You could also, in a polite fashion, ask the "why" so that you have the facts.

Managing Other Workplace Issues

On the Job with Cancer

For most people, work is a healthy part of life. Continuing to work during cancer treatment or returning to work after time has been taken off can make a person feel healthier and more productive. Working may give a person something to focus on besides their illness and can help an employee feel more in control while keeping them connected to people who care about them.[26]

Whether a person is returning to work after time off or continuing to work during a cancer treatment, these employees likely face some obstacles at their workplace. It is important that the cancer patient address these situations:

Decide who needs to know about the cancer

A cancer patient needs to decide whether they want their co-workers to know about the cancer and, if so, how open will they want to be. There's no right or wrong approach. They may want their supervisor to tell the co-workers about the cancer, or the employee may choose to do it themselves. It is important that the employee does what is comfortable for them and know their options. Actually they may choose not to tell anyone about the cancer if they're a private person. But, for practical reasons, it may make sense for them to tell their supervisor or human resources representative so they can receive reasonable accommodations if necessary.[27]

On the Job with HIV

During the early years of the HIV epidemic, returning to work after diagnosis just didn't happen. Because there were no early detection HIV tests, people were diagnosed only after they presented the gravest of opportunistic infections. People were too sick to work and sadly died soon after diagnosis. Today, early diagnosis and the advent of powerful HIV drugs mean people are living long, healthy and productive lives. After diagnosis, many HIV positive men and women continue to work.[28] For those too sick to work when diagnosed, HIV medications will get them back to health and back to work. While going back to work is a positive thing for many people, the workplace and employee must be aware of some things in order to make their return a positive experience.

Does the HIV employee have to inform their employer of their HIV Diagnosis?

Whether or not an employee discloses their HIV status to the employer is entirely up to them. They are under no legal obligation to disclose their HIV status that is in most cases they don't because HIV is not transmitted by casual contact.[29] So they are under no risk to their fellow employees (again in most cases).

Does casual contact with an HIV infected employee put others at risk?

Like every rule, there are some exceptions. For one, if an HIV infected employee works in a job that could expose others to their blood or bodily fluids, there should be some consultation with a local HIV advocacy group to help determine if telling the employer is necessary.[30] Some people that say an HIV infected employee has a moral obligation to tell their employer. Again, because casual contact is not a risk factor for transmitting HIV, there is no moral obligation to tell anyone in the workplace.[31] However, if being HIV infected makes it difficult to perform some expected duties (too fatigued to restock shelves for instance), the employee will need to notify their employer in order to receive reasonable accommodation.

What if the employee needs special accommodations in order to work?

In an article by *Registered Nurse*, Mark Cichocki states that, "in September 1994, Sidney Abbott visited the office of dentist Dr. Randon Bragdon. This routine visit would spark a controversy that would eventually involve the United States Supreme Court. On that day, Dr. Bragdon refused to fill Ms. Abbott's simple cavity because Ms. Abbott admitted to being HIV positive."[32] After four years of legal debate, the Supreme Court ruled that The Americans with Disabilities Act (ADA) did include people living with HIV. So, she was discriminated against when a reasonable accommodation such as the dentist wearing latex gloves was not provided. Since then, providers and employers by law have to make reasonable accommodations for their patients and employees, including those living and working with HIV.

The reasonable accommodations that must be made for any other disability must also be made for those with HIV or AIDS. However, the employee must seek the accommodation and of course medical documentation must disclose their HIV status. Once disclosure is made, this information must be kept in strict confidence according to the law.

Nine Facts about HIV Infection and AIDS:

1. AIDS stands for Acquired Immune Deficiency Syndrome, a condition in which the body's immune system is destroyed. While there are treatments that help people survive some of the diseases they get as a result of losing their immunity, there is no cure for AIDS.

2. AIDS is caused by infection with the Human Immunodeficiency Virus, or HIV. Infection with HIV is completely preventable. Prevent HIV infection and you will prevent AIDS.

3. HIV is spread through contact with blood, semen, vaginal fluids, and breast milk. This contact comes primarily through sexual relations and sharing needles when using illegal drugs.

4. When it comes to HIV infection, it doesn't matter who you are, it matters what you do. Make choices that are healthy.

5. HIV is not spread through casual contact. Shaking hands, hugging, sharing rest rooms, equipment, food utensils, and drinking fountains will not transmit HIV.

6. Medical tests detect antibodies to HIV. These antibodies are in the bloodstream, and are an attempt of the immune system to eliminate the virus. Antibodies are generally detectable six to 12 weeks after infection with HIV. When antibodies are present in someone's blood, that person is said to be "HIV-positive."

7. Most HIV-positive people live normal, active lives for years after infection. While everyone who is HIV-positive will not necessarily develop AIDS, many have. For some HIV-positive people, symptoms serious enough to constitute an AIDS diagnosis begin to appear eight to ten years after infection.

8. While many people associate the AIDS epidemic in America with gay men, (and while the first wave of the epidemic primarily centered in the gay community), the epidemic continues to affect all groups. Infections among women and adolescents are increasingly the fastest of all population groups.

9. Assessing and taking responsibility for sexual behavior and educating one's self about HIV and AIDS is key to protection from a HIV infection. When dealing with exposed blood of another ALWAYS have a safety kit available which includes latex gloves and wear them.

HIV/AIDS and the Workplace Law

The following entire section is copied with permission from the *U.S. Department of Justice Civil Rights Division Disability Rights Section* Questions and Answers regarding THE AMERICANS WITH DISABILITIES ACT AND PERSONS WITH HIV/AIDS:[33]

Are people with HIV or AIDS protected by the ADA?

Yes. An individual is considered to have a "disability" if he or she has a physical or mental impairment that substantially limits one or more major life activities, has a record of such an impairment, or is regarded as having such an impairment. Persons with HIV disease, both symptomatic and asymptomatic, have physical impairments that substantially limit one or more major life activities and are, therefore, protected by the law.

Persons who are discriminated against because they are regarded as being HIV-positive are also protected. For example, a person who was fired on the basis of a rumor that he had AIDS, even if he did not, would be protected by the law.

Moreover, the ADA protects persons who are discriminated against because they have a known association or relationship with an individual who is HIV-positive. For example, the ADA would protect an HIV-negative woman who was denied a job because her roommate had AIDS.

Does an employer always have to provide a needed reasonable accommodation?

An employer is not required to make an accommodation if it would impose an undue hardship on the operation of the business. An undue hardship is an action that requires "significant difficulty or expense" in relation to the size of the employer, the resources available, and the nature of the operation. Determination as to whether a particular accommodation poses an undue hardship must be made on a case-by-case basis.

Customer or co-worker attitudes are not relevant. The potential loss of customers or co-workers because an employee has HIV/AIDS does not constitute an undue hardship.

An employer is not required to provide an employee's first choice of accommodation. The employer is, however, required to provide an effective accommodation, i.e., an accommodation that meets the individual's needs.

HIV/Aids Reasonable Accommodation Examples

- An HIV-positive accountant required two hours off, bimonthly, for visits to his doctor. He was permitted to take longer lunch breaks and to make up the time by working later on those days.

- A supermarket check-out clerk with AIDS had difficulty standing for long periods of time. Her employer provided her with a stool so that she could sit down at the cash register when necessary.

- A secretary with AIDS needed to take frequent rest breaks during her work day. Her boss allowed her to take as many breaks as she needed throughout the day, so long as she completed her work before going home each evening.

- A machine operator required time off from work during his hospitalization with pneumocystis carinii pneumonia. He had already used up all his sick leave. His employer allowed him to either take leave without pay, or to use his accrued vacation leave.

- An HIV-positive computer programmer suffered bouts of nausea caused by his medication. His employer allowed him to work at home on those days that he found it too difficult to come into the office. His employer provided him with the equipment (computer, modem, fax machine, etc.) necessary for him to work at home.

- An HIV-positive newspaper editor who tired easily from walking began to use an electric scooter to get around. His employer installed a ramp at the entrance to the building in which the editor worked so that the editor could use his scooter at the office.

When is an employer required to make a reasonable accommodation?

An employer is only required to accommodate a "known" disability of a qualified applicant or employee. Thus, it is the employee's responsibility to tell the employer that he or she needs a reasonable accommodation. If the employee does not want to disclose that he or she has HIV or AIDS, it may be sufficient for the employee to say that he or she has an illness or disability covered by the ADA, that the illness or disability causes certain problems with work, and that the employee wants a reasonable accommodation. However, an employer can require medical documentation of the employee's disability and the limitations resulting from that disability.

What if an employer has concerns about an applicant's ability to do the job in the future?

Employers cannot choose not to hire a qualified person now because they fear the worker will become too ill to work in the future. The hiring decision must be based on how well the individual can perform now. In addition, employers cannot decide "not to hire" qualified people with HIV or AIDS because they are afraid of higher medical insurance costs, worker's compensation costs, or absenteeism.

Can an employer consider health and safety when deciding whether to hire an applicant or retain an employee who has HIV/AIDS?

Yes, but only under limited circumstances. The ADA permits employers to establish qualification standards that will exclude individuals who pose a direct threat -- i.e., a significant risk of substantial harm -- to the health or safety of the individual or of others, if that risk cannot be eliminated or reduced below the level of a "direct threat" by reasonable accommodation. However, an employer may not simply assume that a threat exists; the employer must establish through objective, medically supportable methods that there is a significant risk that substantial harm could occur in the workplace. By requiring employers to make individualized judgments based on reliable medical or other objective evidence -- rather than on generalizations, ignorance, fear, patronizing attitudes, or stereotypes -- the ADA recognizes the need to balance the interests of people with disabilities against the legitimate interests of employers in maintaining a safe workplace.

Transmission of HIV will rarely be a legitimate "direct threat" issue. It is medically established that HIV can only be transmitted by sexual contact with an infected individual, exposure to infected blood or blood products, or perinatally from an infected mother to infant during pregnancy, birth, or breast feeding. HIV cannot be transmitted by casual contact. Thus, there is little possibility that HIV could ever be transmitted in the workplace.

For example:

- A superintendent may believe that there is a risk of employing an individual with HIV disease as a schoolteacher. However, there is little or no likelihood of a direct exchange of body fluids between the teacher and her students, and thus, employing this person would not pose a direct threat.

- A restaurant owner may believe that there is a risk of employing an individual with HIV disease as a cook, waiter or waitress, or dishwasher, because the employee might transmit the disease through the handling of food. However, HIV and AIDS are specifically not included on the Centers for Disease Control and Prevention ("CDC") list of infectious and communicable diseases that are transmitted through the handling of food. Thus, there is little or no likelihood that employing persons with HIV/AIDS in food handling positions would pose a risk of transmitting HIV.

- A fire chief may believe that an HIV-infected firefighter may pose a risk to others when performing mouth-to-mouth resuscitation. However, current medical evidence indicates that HIV cannot be transmitted by the exchange of saliva. Thus, there is little or no likelihood that an HIV-infected firefighter would pose a risk to others.

Having HIV or AIDS, however, might impair an individual's ability to perform certain functions of a job, thus causing the individual to pose a direct threat to the health or safety of the individual or others.

For example:

- A worker who operates heavy machinery and who has been suffering from dizzy spells caused by the medication he is taking might pose a direct threat to his or someone else's safety. If no reasonable accommodation is available (e.g., an open position to which the employee could be reassigned), the employer would not violate the ADA by laying the worker off.

- An airline pilot who is experiencing bouts of dementia would pose a direct threat to herself and her passenger's safety. It would not violate the ADA if the airline prohibited her from flying.

As noted above, the direct threat assessment must be an individualized assessment. Any blanket exclusion -- for example, refusing to hire persons with HIV/AIDS because of the attendant health risks -- would probably violate the ADA as a matter of law.

When can an employer inquire into an applicant's or employee's HIV status?

An employer may not ask or require a job applicant to take a medical examination before making a job offer. It cannot make any pre-offer inquiry about a disability or the nature or severity of a disability. An employer may, however, ask questions about the ability to perform specific job functions. Thus, for example, the owner of an outdoor cafe could not ask an individual with KS lesions who was applying for the position of a waiter whether the applicant had AIDS. The owner could, however, ask the applicant whether he can be in the sun for extended periods of time.

An employer may condition a job offer on the satisfactory result of a post-offer medical examination or medical inquiry if this is required of all entering employees in the same job category. However, if an individual is not hired because a post-offer medical examination or inquiry reveals a disability, the reason(s) for not hiring must be job-related and consistent with business necessity. HIV-positive status alone, without some accompanying complication (e.g., dementia, loss of vision, etc.) can almost never be the basis for a refusal to hire after a post-offer medical examination.

After a person starts work, a medical examination or inquiry of an employee must be job-related and consistent with business necessity. Employers may conduct employee medical examinations where there is evidence of a job performance or safety problem, when examinations are required by other Federal laws, when examinations are necessary to determine current "fitness" to perform a particular job, and/or where voluntary examinations are part of employee health programs. For example, an employer could not ask an employee who had lesions on his face or who had recently lost a significant amount of weight, but whose job performance had not changed in any way, whether the employee had AIDS. An employer could, however, require an employee who was experiencing frequent dizzy spells, and whose work was suffering as a result, to undergo a medical examination.

What obligations does an employer/supervisor have if an employee discloses his or her HIV status?

The ADA requires that medical information be kept confidential. This information must be kept apart from general personnel files as a separate, confidential medical record available only under limited conditions.

What obligations does an employer have to provide health insurance to employees with HIV/AIDS?

The ADA prohibits employers from discriminating on the basis of disability in the provision of health insurance to their employees and/or from entering into contracts with health insurance companies that discriminate on the basis of disability. Insurance distinctions that are not based on disability, however, and that are applied equally to all insured employees, do not discriminate on the basis of disability and do not violate the ADA.

Thus, for example, blanket pre-existing condition clauses that exclude from the coverage of a health insurance plan the treatment of all physical conditions that predate an individual's eligibility for benefits are not distinctions based on disability and do not violate the ADA. A pre-existing condition clause that excluded only the treatment of HIV-related conditions, however, is a disability-based distinction and would likely violate the ADA.

Similarly, a health insurance plan that capped benefits for the treatment of all physical conditions at $50,000 per year does not make disability-based distinctions and does not violate the ADA. A plan that capped benefits for the treatment of all physical conditions, except AIDS, at $50,000 per year, and capped the treatment for AIDS-related conditions at $10,000 per year does distinguish on the basis of disability and probably violates the ADA.

Concluding Thoughts

According to recent studies, the number of employees with disabilities will increase. The current generation of Americans with disabilities is well prepared to be tapped for the job market and able to provide an added solution for the labor shortages that can face American business.

People with disabilities are the nation's largest minority crossing all racial, gender, educational, socioeconomic, and organizational lines. They are also one of few minority groups that any person can join at any time. If you do not currently have a disability, according to researchers in the field you have about a 20% chance of becoming disabled at some point during your work life.

Companies that include people with disabilities in their diversity programs increase their competitive advantage. People with disabilities add to the variety of viewpoints needed to be successful and bring effective solutions to today's business challenges. The American economy is made stronger when all segments of the population are included in the workforce and in the customer base.

End of Chapter Questions

1. What is considered a disability? Is this the same definition for handicapped?

2. Learning disabled is a form of mental impairment, what are forms of learning disabilities and why should these individuals be given equal employment opportunities.

3. What are some tips that could be utilized to interview a hard of hearing applicant?

4. Why is it beneficial for an employee with a terminal illness to work and what benefit is this for the workplace?

Internet Exercise

Part A: Using the Internet go to www.eeoc.gov then find information on disability discrimination. Go to the "Questions and Answers Series" and chose a topic. Summarize the information you found and how it relates to the chapter information.

End of Chapter Exercise

Complete Part A & B.

Part A: Famous Persons with Disabilities

Directions: Go to www.google.com and type in the five famous person's name below and the word "disability" or type "famous disabled persons" or go to http://www.tampagov.net/dept_Mayor/Mayors_Alliance/famous_persons/ AND in the space following each name indicate the disability of the following "important" people in society.

1.   CRUISE TOM, 1962-present has

_____.

2.   BELL Alexander Graham, 1847-1922 was

_____.

3.   TUBMAN Harriet, 1820-1913 was

_____.

4.   ROOSEVELT Franklin Delano, 1882-1945 had

_____.

5.   WALTERS Barbara, 1931-present has

_____.

Now answer the following questions:

(1) How did the above famous person's disability affect their success?
(2) What does this say about the disabled in the workplace?

Part B: Do you promote him?

Directions: Read the following scenario and answer the questions that follow.

Scenario
Let's assume as the manager you know that a worker has missed some days due to his HIV infection. Now he is asking you for a promotion (he has made you aware of his condition/illness). The days he missed occurred over a year ago and since that time he has doubled his production. His disease is not debilitating but the job he is applying for is a high stress position. Please answer the following questions regarding this scenario:

1. Do you recommend him for promotion, why or why not?
2. You know that in this new position he will be working on a team, if you recommend him should you or can you tell the other teammates of his condition?
3. If you decided that this critical issue of contagious disease was worth educating your workplace through training, would you include all contagious diseases or just focus on HIV training?
4. What type of reasonable accommodations would be allowable if ever needed?

References

1.   Rabasca, L. (November 1999). Knocking down societal barriers for people with disabilities. *APA Monitor*, 1, 29.

2.   Cornell University. (n.d.). *Disability Statistics*. Retrieved from: http://www.ilr.cornell.edu/edi/DisabilityStatistics/issues.cfm

3.   Pope, A. M. & Tarlov, A. R. (1991). *Disability in America: Toward a National Agenda for Prevention*. Washington DC: Institute of Medicine.

4.   Academic American Encyclopedia. (1994). *Handicapped Persons*.

5.   Disbility Mentoring Day. (n.d.). Retrieved from: http://www.dmd-aapd.org/toolkit/downloads/AppendixA_2006.doc

6.   Ibid.

7.   The Reemployment and Training Act of 1994: hearing of the Committee on Labor and Human Resources, United States Senate, One Hundred Third Congress, second session. (1994, March 16). Retrieved from: http://www.archive.org/stream/reemploymenttrai00unit/reemploymenttrai00unit_djvu.txt

8.   Chima, F. O. (2001). Employee Assistance and Human Resource Collaboration for Improving Employment and Disabilities Status. *Employee Assistance Quarterly*, 17(3), 79-94.

9.   Pope, A. M. & Tarlov, A. R. (1991). *Disability in America: Toward a National Agenda for Prevention*. Washington DC: Institute of Medicine.

10.   State of New Jersey. (n.d.). *Worker's Compensation Law*. Retrieved from: lwd.dol.state.nj.us/labor/forms_pdfs/wc/MSWord/wc_law.doc

11.   Cornell University. (n.d.). *Disability Statistics*. Retrieved from: http://www.ilr.cornell.edu/edi/DisabilityStatistics/issues.cfm

12.   Jette, A. M., & Badley, E. (2000). *Conceptual issues in the measurement of work disability*. Washington, DC: National Academy Press.

13.   The U.S. Equal Employment Opportunity Commission. (n.d.). Retrieved from http://www.eeoc.gov/facts/ada17.html

14.   U.S. Department of Treasury. (n.d.). *Reasonable Accommodation*. Retrieved from: http://www.ttb.gov/eeo/reasonable_accomodation.shtml

15. Ibid.

16. Sonnenberg, S. P. (2000, June). Mental Disabilities in the Workplace. *Workforce*.

17. Armour, S. (2006, August). Mental Illness on the Job. *USA TODAY*.

18. Sonnenberg, S. P. (2000, June). Mental Disabilities in the Workplace. *Workforce*.

19. Ibid.

20. Logsdon, A. (n.d.). *Learning Disabled Adults-Learning Disabled Adults in the Workplace*. Retrieved from: http://learningdisabilities.about.com/od/careerissues/p/LDAdultsatwork.htm

21. Wikipedia. (n.d.). *Hearing Impairment*. Retrieved from: http://en.wikipedia.org/wiki/Deafness

22. Ibid.

23. National Association of the Deaf. (n.d.). Retrieved from: http://www.nad.org/site/pp.asp?c=foINKQMBF&b=180410

24. The Canadian Hearing Society. (2003). Retrieved from: https://www.canadianhearingsociety.com/info/es/deaf.html

25. Ibid.

26. Roberts, E. (1995). *Prophet of Independence*. Berkeley: Center for Independent Living.

27. Young, J. (1997). *Equality of Opportunity: The Making of the Americans With Disabilities Act*. Washington D.C.: National Council on Disability.

28. Annan, K. A. (n.d.). Living in a World with HIV and Aids. *United Nations Paper*.

29. Ibid.

30. Ibid.

31. Ibid.

32. Cichocki, M. (2007). *Is HIV a Disability?* Retrieved from: http://aids.about.com/od/legalissues/a/disability.htm

33. U.S. Department of Justice. (n.d.). *Questions and Answers: The Americans with Disabilities Act and Persons with HIV/AIDS*. Retrieved from: http://www.ada.gov/pubs/hivqanda.txt

Chapter Eleven

Understanding Ageism, Sexual Orientation, Transgenderism & Classism

---

If you always do what you always did, you will always get what you always got.

Jackie "Moms" Mabley

Chapter Eleven

UNDERSTANDING AGEISM, SEXUAL ORIENTATION, TRANSGENDERISM AND CLASSISM

Chapter Objectives

After reading this chapter, you should be able to:

- understand ageism and it's laws.

- explain the myths surrounding homosexuals, gays and lesbians.

- rationalize why all people have the right to work.

- describe transgenderism and the workplace implications.

- determine what is classism and how this issue relates to workplace diversity.

AGEISM

In 1900, almost 70 percent of American men aged sixty-five and older were gainfully employed or seeking employment. In the 1990s, only 2.8 percent of the labor force (both men and women) was over sixty-five. This may partly be due to the myths that surround older workers. The systematized stereotyping of and discrimination against people because they are "old" is what is referred to as ageism.

The aged are often stereotypically described as slow, tired, ill, forgetful, defensive, withdrawn, and unhappier than younger people. The theme around older people is one of loss. Loss of hearing, sex drive, loved ones etc... But, again these are all myths that are unfairly attributed to aging. The truth is those who believe these myths unfortunately know very little about "healthy" aging. Common sense and myths say we grow old because we wear out, but actually no wear and tear theory of aging exists.[1]

Let's discuss a few of the other myths associated with older workers.

Myth One: Elders are often frail and ill.

Fact One: Harkness (1999) states that "the reality is that society, the media, and physicians—even gerontologists—have focused on the 6 to 15 percent of elders who are frail and ill."[2]

Myth Two: Elders have a loss of sexual desire.

Fact Two: Regarding the sexual decline of seniors, Bortz (1991) reports on a 1984 study by Edward Brecher titled "Love, Sex and Aging" and states that among the 4,246 participants, who ranged in age from fifty to ninety-three, the study found that the following percentages of people were sexually active[3]:

- 93 percent of women and 98 percent of men in their fifties
- 81 percent of women and 91 percent of men in their sixties
- 65 percent of women and 79 percent of men in their seventies

Myth Three: Elders experience a loss of productivity and creativity

Fact Three: Birren in a 1990 study of scientific publications of people in varying age groups, no one age was found to be the most productive, thus supporting the conclusion that age cannot be used as surrogate criterion for creativity and productivity.[4]

The above myths along with a fear of old age and death, reinforced by ageism often allow the younger generation to see older people as inferior beings.[5] But, the young don't realize that they are just setting in motion their own negative conditions in later life. The young if lucky to live long may become a victim of their own stereotypical belief systems.

These stereotypes no doubt contribute to age discrimination. Age discrimination is often subtle but despite this subtlety causes workplace issues. A lack of opportunities and a lack of promotions along with forced retirement are just a few of these issues.

In order, to guard against the ill fates that can occur to older workers there have been several laws enacted for their protection. The Age Discrimination in Employment Act (ADEA) was passed in 1967 and became effective June 1968 as discussed in chapter two. The purpose of ADEA is to promote employment of older people age 40 and older based on their ability rather than age; to prohibit arbitrary age discrimination in employment; and to help employers and workers find ways to solve problems arising from the impact of age on employment.[6]

There was an amendment to ADEA, which rendered legally unenforceable most mandatory retirement policies for people up to age seventy. Mandatory retirement after age 70 was abolished in a 1986 amendment to the ADEA.[7] Some other important Acts are as follows: The ERISA (Employee Retirement Income Security Act) gives greater protection for pension plans. The 1990 Older Workers Benefits Protection Act (OWBPA) effective in 1991 provides additional safeguards against employers pressuring workers to accept early retirement.

Understanding that it is not age but ability that affects what a worker can or can't do—goes a long way towards addressing age discrimination.

Why hire "older" workers?

Older workers are experienced in many cases and can have motivators that drive them to succeed.[8] Some older workers who had children later in life may still have

---

children in college which is cost that would need funding. Also, along with that motivation comes seriously focused workers with fewer distractions than some younger workers.[9] However, the point is not to pit younger workers against older workers but to show that every worker regardless of age has some advantage to offer the workplace.

Older workers while some may retire after a primary career, many workers in this group continue to work full-time or take contract and consulting roles to strengthen their own financial positions. They're looking at adding a few more years to their pensions, paying off mortgages and helping children purchase their own homes. Recruiters indicate that some companies still illegally but secretly acknowledge they simply want a younger applicant. "It's stated as a preference, but often companies are not examining their biases and the changing employment outlook so positions go unfilled and there's still reluctance to hiring older candidates."[10]

Not all employers feel this way. Those that don't have biases against older workers see the value in hiring this group and have found tremendous success in hiring what is referred to as an under-utilized workforce.

Generational Workforce Issues

While there are clearly benefits to having older workers, there are some issues that result from younger and older employees working side by side.

Currently, the workforce is made up of four generations:

- The World War II Veterans or Traditionalists,

- Baby Boomers,

- Generation X, and

- Generation Y

Each with its own beliefs, motivations and work ethics.

Never before in the history of the workforce has four generations existed with so many massive differences between them, the following chart illustrates some of these differences.

Information for the chart: Generational Characteristics of the U.S. Population is taken from American Management Association and University of Phoenix Generational Study and Wikipedia and is based on general characteristics of the population. However said characteristics are not applicable to all of the described population in question.

Generational Characteristics of the U.S. Population[11]

GENERATION	BORN	AGE NOW	BELIEFS	MOTIVATIONS	MGT STYLE	INCENTIVES
WWII	1928-1946	60's, 70's and 80's	Absolutes, Security, Strong Work Ethic, Team Players	Country/Patriotism Advancement Responsibility	Control Authority Thinkers Conformity Conservatism	Personal acknowledgement from mgt (birthdays)
Baby Boomers	1946-1964	40's and 50's	Few Absolutes Variety Freedom	Individuality Achievement Relatable	Cooperation Competency Doers	Acknowledgement of contribution
Generation X	1965-1980	Late 20's, 30's and early 40's	No Absolutes Lifestyle Concerns Fun	Own Community Self Discovery Relational Independent Informal	Consensus Creativity Feelers	Interesting projects and teamwork
Generation Y	1981-2001	20's and those just entering the workforce	No Absolutes Lifestyle Concerns Fun	Own Community Self Discovery Relational Cultural Diversity	Consensus Creativity Feelers	Feedback and interest shown by others

Companies are recognizing that leveraging the strengths of the above generations is a powerful competitive edge. In order to get everyone working together towards one goal, it is important to first understand the historical and social circumstances that shaped each group's work ethic, and then decipher what their strengths and weaknesses are.

Managing Workplace Diversity

Traditionalists & WWII

Let's begin with the oldest generation, the Traditionalists also nicknamed the "Greatest Generation." The Great Depression and both World Wars forced this generation to make great sacrifices in order to flourish. They have been perceived as having one of the strongest work ethics of any generation and they possess a fierce loyalty to the company they are employed with.[12] Traditionalists and WWII Veterans also have a rigid respect of authority and rules, therefore, typically do not rock the boat. This generation took pride in motherhood and was almost always available at home to raise the children.

Baby Boomers

The Baby Boomer generation became the center of attention due to their traditionalists parent's beliefs. However, enduring many cultural changes also influenced this generation to redefine the rules of the Traditionalists especially when it came to family roles.[13] The divorce rate increased dramatically. Although still influenced with the strong work ethic of their parents, Baby Boomers became driven achievers in their careers. Their perception of success has often been defined through material gains. This driven work ethic caused the Boomer's presence at home to be more vacant resulting in their children, Generation X's ability to become unusually self-reliant and extremely adept at multi-tasking.

Generation Xers

Xers were the popular latchkey children who often took care of themselves after school.[14] Their free time was filled talking on the phone and online, resulting in a lack of face to face social skills that their parents had. Witnessing their parents being laid off because of mergers, acquisitions, and cutbacks; their sense of security in the workplace was shaken and influenced them to approach life with a more sense of balance between work and home. Often they refuse to have anything interfere with their fun and adventure, therefore, marriage and children are delayed.

Generation Yers

The newest member of the workforce Generation Y have been the most protected from economic downturn until now—when they are graduating college.[15] They face higher social pressures than the previous generations and the pressure to excel in school has dramatically increased for them. The majority of this generation has endured the most divorces and is often raised by one parent.[16] They are accustomed to being an active member in making family related decisions and expect to contribute to decisions within the company as well. For these reasons, they will be the most likely generation to rock the boat like never before. Growing up during the boom of the Internet, they are the most technically proficient generation, highly intelligent, and confident.[17]

When it comes to these groups working together they each must acknowledge that each group's work ethic brings something different and valuable to the workplace. When it comes to management of these various age groups there is one consistent factor that all generations accept—the value of transferring their skills to another industry or job function. Therefore, companies should offer career advancement and development opportunities for all of the generations.

Programs That Appeal to All Generations

Programs that deal with flexibility and work life often appeal across generations. Following are programs found to be of interest to all ages of workers.

Rethink retirement plans.

By shortening the vesting time of a retirement program it allows for career mobility which could be a benefit for employees who may not be employed long due to entering the workforce later or those looking for flexible careers.

Flexible work schedule.

It allows employees to vary their arrival and/or departure times from the normal 9 to 5 work day. For those who have family or personal needs to attend, this can be a great benefit.

Create a career pattern.
Some employees are not seeking to advance to management but instead would like to try different options within the organization.[18] By having career opportunities that focus on learning new skills and building expertise with promotion possibilities provides additional incentives to those not seeking to climb the corporate ladder.

Telecommuting/Home Computers.

Having laptops available for employees to work at home provides or computers to purchase through a loan program can facilitate telecommuting and flexible work options.

Employee assistance program.

When employers offer this as a benefit it shows a commitment to the emotional and physical well being of its employees and their families. This free service can be of help to employees during their time of need which can occur regardless of age.

Floating holidays.

Floating holidays is an incentive that promotes the cultural diversity of the workplace.

Performance-based pay and Merit pay.

These are pay systems that allow for hard work and efficiency to be rewarded. Performance based pay often gives a lump sum bonus whereas merit can be an adjustment to the employee's salary base. Both of these compliment an employee for a job well done.

Workplace Culture and Communication.

Having a workplace climate or environment that supports the uniqueness in individuals and allow for freedom and expression of thought through feedback, use of all communication venues to keep employees informed are some motivators that are nonmonetary and often meet the needs of employees regardless of age.

The above are just a few examples that can work toward motivating workers of all ages. Companies that want to hire and retain the best employees must realize that this has very little to do with age but instead there being a good job match between the position and the employee. Retaining good employees has a lot to do with the workplace environment through the offering of benefits, addressing older worker stereotypes and generating a work environment that is appealing to members of each generation.

Sexual Orientation in the Workplace

First, let's begin this discussion by understanding what it means to be homosexual/gay or lesbian. Being homosexual/gay or lesbian is when a person is sexually attracted and drawn to members of one's own sex.[19] The only basis for deciding whether one is or is not gay/lesbian is a continuing sexual preference for partners of the same sex.

The key here is a continued preference. Some people think that just one sexual act toward the same sex, makes a person gay/lesbian. But, numerous boys and girls during early childhood and adolescence have homosexual experiences without lasting effects.[20] Also, under special circumstances, such as military service and prison life, homosexual behavior sometimes occurs on a temporary basis.

While many would like to ignore the different sexual orientations that exist in the world, several authorities have estimated that perhaps one out of every ten adults could be classified as homosexual/gay or lesbian translating to many millions.[21] So, let's see what you know about the gay life-style?

Directions: Please Read each statement below, indicate if you agree or disagree with the statement.

What do you know about gay and lesbians?

1. Gay and lesbian people can ordinarily be identified by certain mannerisms or physical characteristics (ie. Men who flick their wrists and women with male "butch" hairstyles).
2. Homosexuality is unnatural.
3. Homosexuals are mentally ill.
4. Most sex offenders are homosexuals.
5. Increasing the civil rights to homosexuals will just cause more people to choose this lifestyle.
6. Homosexuals make bad employees.

After reading the above statements did you find you agreed with many of the statements? If you did, you are like many people who have a lack of knowledge regarding Homosexuals/Gays and Lesbians. All of the statements above are false.

Sexual Orientation Facts

FACT ONE. Gay and lesbian people can NOT ordinarily be identified by certain mannerisms or physical characteristics (ie. Men who flick their wrists and women with male "butch" hairstyles).[22] The truth of the matter is that just like heterosexual people have various mannerisms and dress styles so do homosexuals. People who choose to love someone of the same sex cannot be identified by underlying characteristics as all races, socioeconomic status and genders represent the homosexual population.

FACT TWO. According to science, homosexuality is natural. University of Oslo zoologist Petter Böckman, indicates that about 1,500 animal species are known to practice same-sex coupling, including bears, gorillas, flamingos, owls, salmon and many others.[23] If we don't question this gene trait in animals why is it such a taboo in humans? Is natural being confused with "normal"?

Who defines what is normal, the Puritan's who came to this "new land" said that sexism was normal or acceptable behavior, they believed that killing the Natives for their land was normal or acceptable behavior based upon their religious or cultural views. So, who has defined what is normal? Does this viewpoint change from time period to time period--should it?

FACT THREE. Homosexuals as a group are not classified as mentally ill by the medical community. Mental illness has not been associated solely with sexual orientation but instead is diagnosed on an individual basis for both heterosexuals and homosexuals.[24]

FACT FOUR. Most sex offenders are NOT homosexuals. Over 80% of child molesters and sex offenders are heterosexual not homosexual.[25]

FACT FIVE. Does legalizing equal rights for gays/lesbians create more homosexual individuals? Seeming laws don't equate to the creation of a person's sexual orientation no more than it equates to a person's disability. People who think this way tend to believe that people make a choice to be homosexual. Being "in the closet" verse being out of the closet is what will probably be impacted if gays and lesbians receive equal rights. In countries like the Netherlands or other countries in Western Europe where same-sex marriages and acceptance of homosexuality have had legal freedom for many years--there has not been a rise in the number of homosexuals reported.[26]

FACT SIX. "There are no studies that show that one's sexual orientation causes them to be a "bad" employee."[27] Instead there are more statistics that show that homosexuals are fired just for being "homosexual" with excellent work records. In March 2004 during the Bush Administration, the White House removed information from government Websites about sexual orientation discrimination in the workplace. Why? Because federal employees could be fired for just simply being homosexual.[28]

Other Workplace Issues

Gays and Lesbians in the workplace is a touchy subject for some. One reason is because of the fears that people have regarding homosexuality. But, if you were to ask the question: Do you need to know someone's sexual orientation to know how well he or she will perform his or her job? I believe most people would answer no. Many people feel that they don't need to know about someone's sex life in order to work with them. But, when some people think about homosexuality as a lifestyle it invokes fear.[29] Rather than see homosexuals as people with many facets to their personality and character, they are judged by one factor and one factor alone—their choice of a love relationship.

Some people even go so far as to hate homosexuals because of this choice. These people are homophobic and often hypocritical. Because many will clearly see that it is wrong to discriminate against women or against religion but justify this type of discrimination. But, discrimination is wrong no matter what the reason. Understanding difference is about being empathetic (putting yourself in another person's shoes), even those situations that we don't fully understand or agree with. Always remember that people are the way they are (no matter what that way is) for a reason. Still, it is so much easier to judge what you see rather than be empathetic to what you don't see or know.

It would be much easier for management if workers could maintain a boundary between their personal and work lives. But more often than not, people's personal lives intertwine with their work environment.   Creating workplace climates that are truly inclusive means the freedom of lesbian, gay and bisexual employees to do simple things like putting their partners' picture on their desks, or being able to name who they went on vacation with, or not feeling a need to lie about whose voice is on the answering machine at home.

One area that management should be concerned with is the workplace myths that have been generated about gays and lesbians. Stereotyping occurs when one thinks of an individual as assigned to a group or category and the characteristics commonly associated with that group or category. One of the workplace myths circulating today is that gays and lesbians are found only in certain stereotypical professions.[30] There is a generalization that male hairdressers are gay and that female construction workers are lesbians. Other common misconceptions are that gay men are not aggressive and that lesbians are too aggressive, or that only gay employees have the AIDS virus.[31]

Stereotypes become harmful particularly when they manifest into discrimination. Discrimination against certain people in the organization is not only a violation of United States Labor Laws; it is also counterproductive because the contributions of people who are discriminated against and ignored are not fully utilized. For example, if a manager wrongly believes that homosexual male workers are too emotional and submissive, the manager may overlook these employees for tasks that require assertiveness. These kinds of ill-conceived decisions can result in companies losing the insights of what may have been very productive workers.

According to Bob Powers & Alan Ellis, *A Manager's Guide to Sexual Orientation in the Workplace*, Gay men and lesbians typically respond to discrimination in the workplace in several ways, they remain in the closet in workplaces that are homophobic or they are open and deal with any negative consequences, including possible expulsion in states that don't have discrimination laws addressing sexual orientation.[32]

The decision to come out in the workplace for a gay or lesbian individual can be one of the most stressful decisions of his or her life. Many experts say that hiding one's sexual identity on a daily basis is also very stressful.[33] This hiding takes a tremendous amount of psychological and physical energy.

Studies show that those who hide their sexual identity in the workplace often have feelings of fear, guilt and anxiety.[34] They can feel fearful of losing their jobs or being rejected by their co-workers. They can feel guilty for passing themselves off as heterosexuals, and they feel anxious in their constant vigilance to hide their sexual orientation.

Furthermore, this fear and discomfort of working with homosexuals in the workplace may not be as big an issue if we were told the truth about the sexual orientation of some of our society's most significant leaders. But, if you were told that some of these leaders were homosexual/gay or lesbian would it change what they've accomplished? No. So why should any other person's sexual orientation affect their ability to contribute in our society and the workplace?

TRANSGENDERISM

"Transgendered" is a broad term that encompasses cross-dressers, intersexed people, transsexuals and people who live substantial portions of their lives as other than their birth gender.[35] "Transgender" is a broad term used to encompass all manifestations of crossing gender barriers.[36] Generally speaking, a transgender person manifests a sense of self, the physical characteristics and/or personal expression commonly associated with a sex other than the one he or she was assigned at birth.

Just like sexual orientation there is no federal law that protects transgendered employees. Some people may even be concerned that organizations that provide legal protection from discrimination based on gender identity and gender expression will lead to further accounts of transexualism and cross-dressing. The fact remains that these issues exist to protect both the workplace say from an employee who may want to continually alternate his or her gender identity in the workplace and to protect employees who may need to consistently present themselves in a gender other than their birth gender.

Furthermore, when it comes to cross-dressing protecting transgendered people from discrimination does not mean that employers can no longer require their employees to present a neat and professional appearance.[37] Rather, such protections would only permit people to dress in a way that supports their gender expression.

Although transgenderism can be understood as a form of gender nonconformity, transitioning employees present workplace challenges that may significantly exceed those presented by certain more common manifestations of gender nonconformity.[38] A transitioning transgender person is one who is modifying his or her physical characteristics and manner of expression to -- in effect -- satisfy the standards for membership in another gender.[39] For instance, in some workplaces, a woman's decision to forgo skirts, blouses, jewelry and cosmetics and to begin dressing in a masculine style might result in little more than raised eyebrows or a few arch comments. Yet in almost any workplace today, deeply held beliefs about gender roles likely would be challenged by a woman's decision to modify her sex characteristics by taking male sex hormones and undergoing a double mastectomy, and to begin identifying, dressing and behaving as a man (thus transitioning).

Transitioning

According to *Managing transsexual transition in the workplace* by Janis Walworth as many as 200,000 people have gone through a transition from male to female or female to male during the last several decades in the United States and perhaps 10,000 more do so each year.[40] Transitioning in the workplace has not always been supported, when this first started with employees they were required to leave their jobs and start their new life with their new identity elsewhere.[41]

However, now there are workplace guidelines that don't require employees to leave but instead require the workplace to have sensitivity toward this procedure. There is a process to transitioning in the workplace. An employee does not just change overnight from one gender to another.

Transition Process

Notification of Transition
It is the employees' responsibility to let their supervisor or human resource department know that they are going to be transitioning and what their particular needs and concerns are and this should be done in advance of the planned transition date.[42] During this meeting, the manager must remain open-minded and ensure the employee that they will be supported by the organization during this time of transition.

Management Support
Once management knows of a transitioning employee, it is management's job to support this individual and provide a workplace free of harassment. If managers are unsure of how to support a transitioning employee they can seek assistance from support agencies like the Human Rights Campaign found at www.hrc.org or from their organization's Human Resource department. The manager can also ask the employee for suggestions on how to make this transition process easier. The

employee must determine if he or she wishes to inform their co-workers and clients themselves, or prefers that this to be done for them or not at all. Then determine the best timing for that process.[43] It should be noted that transsexual employees have the right to be who they are without unnecessary disclosure of medical information.

However, there will come a time where other employees will become aware of the transitioning employee. The employees' response will often be determined by the amount of education and knowledge they have regarding the transitioning process. Trainings or briefing sessions should be completed prior to the employee's transition. This information is necessary so that the organization can provide a supportive environment free from misunderstandings.

Managers in this situation must lead by example. Treating the employee with value, respecting the employee's choice in this matter and using the new name and pronouns in all official and unofficial communication.[44]

Medical Leave/Name Change
Discuss the expected timeline and anticipated time off required for medical treatment, if known and in most cases normal sick pay and leave policies will apply. The employee should be asked if they would prefer to be in a different position during their transition, they should be asked about name changes, they should also be asked what name or pronoun to utilize during and after the transition.

It should be noted that all employee records, like birth certificates, driver licenses and school and work-related documents should be under the original name until the employee informs the workplace of the legal name change. "Where a person's legal name does not match his or her new name, the new name should be used on all documentation, such as e-mail, phone directory, company identification card or access badge, name plate, etc., except where records must match the legal name, such as on payroll and insurance documents."[45]

Restroom Approach
The question can often become: during the transition what restroom will the transitioning employee utilize? The recommendation has been to provide a single-occupancy or unisex restroom for the transitioning employee. But once the new identity has been established, the employee must then utilize the restroom of their new gender.[46]

Overview of the Law
(as it relates to sexual orientation and transgenderism)

When it comes to the law there are various levels of the law that apply to discrimination. The Title VII of the Civil Rights Act of 1964 which provides federal protection to individuals from discrimination mandates the entire country. Yet, we know that sexual orientation is not covered under the federal law. What about gender identity, gender nonconformity or gender expression all of which covers transgenderism and its forms? The Civil Rights Act does cover "sex" but federal courts of appeals indicated this was not to include transsexuals or homosexuals however more recently they have held that sex discrimination can include gender stereotypes but how this is applied is not yet known.[47]

Along with the federal law, there are state laws that cover each state and provide protection from discrimination. There are currently many states that protect from discrimination on the basis of sexual orientation but fewer that protect against discrimination on the basis of gender identity. Lastly, there are local laws that govern particular districts and there are many local laws that protect against discrimination on the basis of both sexual orientation and gender identity.

As it relates to gender identity, the following states and local jurisdictions as of the writing of this text protect against discrimination:

Protections in the State Level[48]

Currently California, Minnesota, New Mexico and Rhode Island are the only states that explicitly include "gender identity" in the states' anti-discrimination laws, but the following states have law cases where the court or the administrative agency on human rights ruled that transgender people are protected from discrimination:

The State of Connecticut: Transsexuals may bring claims of sex discrimination under existing state law, based on Connecticut Commission on Human Rights and Opportunities ruling Nov. 2000.

The State of Massachusetts: Transgenders are protected under state law prohibiting sex and disability discrimination, based on Massachusetts Commission Against Discrimination ruling Oct. 10, 2001.

The State of New Jersey: Transgender workers are protected under state law prohibiting sex and disability discrimination, based on the 3rd U.S. Circuit Court of Appeals ruling in Carla V. Enriquez, M.D. v. West Jersey Health Systems, July 3, 2001.

The State of New York: Transgenders are protected under state law prohibiting sex discrimination, based on court ruling.

Protections in the Local Ordinances and Organizations[49]

Over fifty localities have adopted ordinances prohibiting discrimination against transgender people. Jurisdictions that have passed such laws include, among others: New York City, Boston, Chicago, San Francisco, Dallas, Philadelphia, Atlanta, and Seattle. They also include a number of smaller cities, such as Tucson, AZ; Santa Cruz, CA; Iowa City, IA; Louisville, KY; Ann Arbor, MI; Toledo, OH; and Tacoma, WA.

Protections in Public and Private Employers

More and more public and private institutions and organizations are adding transgenderism to their non-discrimination policies just as they have sexual orientation. Before assuming that your company, organization or school does not provide this coverage, the best thing to do is ask what "groups" are covered by your organizations' non-discrimination policy.

For those organizations that protect on the basis of gender identity, how do they create a workplace with "reasonable" dress and identity expectations?

The key word here is reasonable, is it reasonable for a man to come into work dressed as superwoman--maybe if they work in a costume shop but a superwoman costume may not be considered "reasonable" dress in a corporate environment. Therefore, a company has the right to require that employees' appearance and behavior in the workplace are reasonable as it relates to the company environment.[50]

How does this issue of dress impact sexual orientation or transgenderism issues?

For some gays, lesbians, bisexuals and transgendered people, sexual orientation and gender expression are not separate issues. For those who are gay or lesbian that identity far more with the gender they are not, there dress and behavior may reflect this. So, if the workplace or jurisdiction protects against sexual orientation discrimination but not gender identity would a lesbian who dressed in men suits and attire be protected if she were told that she could not wear men's dress or take on a man's appearance? No. From a legal standpoint, sexual orientation has not been considered the same thing as gender identity or expression.[51]

<u>What happens in those places where there is no protection from discrimination?</u>

Employees can be fired for gender identity issues. Why? Because employers who have non-unionized or non-contract employees then have employees who are defined as at-will. At-will employees can be fired at the employers "will" for whatever reason they like including discrimination that is not covered under any federal, state, local law or company policy.

Lastly, if you look at some of the laws above they utilize the terms "gender identity disorder" where disorder usually denotes a physical/mental condition in which there is a disturbance of normal functioning. So, when gender identity is labeled a disorder it is because according to the American Psychiatric Association transgenderism is considered a mental illness (homosexuality was once labeled this way but is no longer). This means that people who want to transition can in this case under those states that consider it a disorder come under disability laws and benefits; however, in order to received this disability status the person has to take on the label of being mentally ill.[52]

CLASSISM

What is Classism?

Classism is defined by many as a systematic oppression of poor and subordinated people where subordinated means without endowed or acquired economic power, social influence, and privilege.[1] Classism creates a grouping of people who work for wages by those who have the means by which to control the necessary resources by which other people make their living.[2]

Do you know any people like this?

Classism exist first because those affected by it, don't realize or believe that it exist. Classism also exist because there is a "system" in place that creates beliefs and knowledge that translates into economic opportunity which ranks people according to economic status, "breeding," job and level of education.[3]

According to *Wikipedia*[4]:

> *Like racism, classism can be divided into (at least) individual classism and structural classism. Individual classism is a matter of the prejudices held and discrimination practiced by individual people (such as making jokes or stereotypes at those of lower class).*

> *Structural or institutional classism is a passive form of classism that occurs when institutions or common practices are structured in such a way as to effectively exclude or marginalize people from lower classes, which can be due, in part, to widespread individual classism within the organization or society.*

According to Holly Sklar in her article, "Growing Gulf Between Rich and Rest of America" she indicates that most of us may see classism but not really realize what it is and one fact that indicates classism exist in America is that the United States has rising levels of poverty and inequality not found in other rich democracies.[5] It is hard for some people to imagine that their lack of wealth is due to systematized oppression of people of their kind, but how do you answer for the fact that in the richest country in the world we battle with literacy, with credit card debt, with unemployment and low paying jobs yet still manage to have a society of those who reap many of the benefits of capitalism?

Is it because so many in the U.S. don't desire to succeed economically?

Is it because we skipped the classes in school on wealth creation and entrepreneurship?

Is it because people have a desire to be poor so much so that they pass on poverty to their children?

Why, would some classify the United States as a society that operates under classism? Another reason is because the U.S. has very options to move people out of poverty. If you are struggling to feed yourself and your kids, to find a place to live that's decent and safe, to pay bills off minimum wage income how do you have the time or the mental energy to do what it takes to move out of that state of being? If you have never been poor then you might think it was simple to move from poverty to middle class. But ask those in the ranks of the poor, I am sure they will tell you something different.

Since 2000, America's billionaire club has gained 76 more members while the typical household has lost income and the poverty count has grown by more than 5 million people.[59] According to United States Senator Jim Webb in his *Class Struggle* article he states, "the most important-and unfortunately the least debated-issue in politics today is our society's steady drift toward a class-based system, the like of which we have not seen since the 19th century. America's top tier has grown infinitely richer and more removed over the past 25 years. It is not unfair to say that they are literally living in a different country. Few among them send their children to public schools; fewer still send their loved ones to fight our wars..."[60]

When you live in one of the riches countries in the world but don't have access to health care, adequate housing, child care etc. the issue becomes survival not wealth attainment. Also, when talking about the poor some don't realize how this is defined according to the census data that reports these numbers.

The 2009 Poverty Guidelines for the 48 Contiguous States and the District of Columbia[61]	
Persons in family	**Poverty guideline**
1	$10,830
2	14,570
3	18,310
4	22,050
5	25,790
6	29,530
7	33,270
8	37,010

Wealth Pyramid

Paul Kivel in his article, *Affirmative Action, Immigration, and Welfare: Confronting Racism in 1998* which was taken from his speech given at the University of Kansas he asks us to imagine a pyramid and he explains that this pyramid represents 100% of the population of the United States.[62] In the pyramid he discusses wealth or the accumulation of our assets, which can be referred to as our net worth.[62]

In author Paul Kivel's more recent book, *You Call This a Democracy* he discusses his economic pyramid as I have described below:

Economic Pyramid[63]

Top 1% of the pyramid
(the ruling class):
- controls 47% of the country's wealth,
- their net worth is over $3,000,000

Next 19% of the pyramid
(the managerial class):
- controls another 44% of the country's wealth,
- the net worth of each household is over $500,000

THESE TWO GROUPS EQUAL 20% OF THE POPULATION BUT THEY CONTROL 91% OF THE WEALTH OF THE RICHEST COUNTRY IN THE WORLD.

Last 80% of the pyramid
(made up of the middle class, working class & dependent and working poor):
- controls only 9% of the wealth, which must be divided among them,
- their "average" net worth is $38,000 (where many of the dependent and working poor are in the negative)

To make sure you completely understand what this represents, we must define Net Worth.

Net Worth = Assets – Liabilities

Where, assets are items you own of value like an automobile or home and liabilities are items that you owe like the car note or mortgage.

For instance, let's assume that you are like many Americans and have the following living circumstances: Your annual income is $28,000, you rent rather than own your home, have credit card debt, have a car but you owe on it. You don't participate in an IRA (Individual Retirement Account), you have no stocks or mutual funds (wealth building assets), no other investments and only a small savings in the bank.

Your assets & liabilities may look like this:

Assets	Liabilities
Car worth $10,000	Car loan $13,000
Savings $1000	Credit Card Debt $15,000
Total Assets $11,000	Total Liabilities $23,000

Your net worth would be calculated as 11,000 – 23,000 = (12,000) which means that you are in the red, because you have a negative net worth. Now where does this person fall in the pyramid? If you answered in the bottom of the 80th percentile, you answered correctly. Now you may ask, *what does this have to do with embracing diversity*?

Do you think that this 80% of the population fighting for 9% of the wealth would consist of women and men; African Americans, Caucasians, Latino, and other races/ethnicities; the disabled and the able-bodied; young and old and individuals with various lifestyles?

So then, it would make sense that these people would have a common ground: fighting together for policies and laws that would make access to wealth creation a reality. Instead, what is often going on amongst these groups?

Managing Workplace Diversity

If you answered *fighting amongst each other* you guessed right—like Blacks blaming all whites for slavery and racism, white men blaming people of color and women for their lack of job opportunities, Christians against Muslims, the young not hiring the old, etc. Now, how does this help anyone in this economic group to move ahead? If you answered, *it does not*, you guessed right again. But, the fighting that goes on because of differences, prejudices, and stereotypes helps who in the pyramid? If you answered, *the top 20%*, you guessed right. Why, because energy amongst the largest group (80th percentile) could be utilized to dismantle policies and programs and systematic isms that exist that benefit only the rich. Instead this energy is lost on issues that have nothing to do with gaining wealth and making sure capitalism works for everyone. It keeps those that think they are free, from experiencing the "real" opportunities that are available in one of the greatest countries on earth.

This all occurs while the rich get richer and the rest of the economy experiences large scale cutbacks in social services, tremendous corporate downsizing, exportation of jobs overseas, environmental dumping of toxic wastes (primarily in communities of the poor representing many people of color), hate crimes (including church burnings, physical assaults, and cross burnings), and public policy attacks on communities of low socioeconomic status. What results is a tremendous concentration of wealth and segregation in society along lines of class more so than any other category like race.[64]

Keeping these elements alive can keep the 80% fighting each other when they really should be embracing diversity. The fact is that many of "us" are in the same boat regardless of sex/gender, age, race and religion, etc. When you look at who is in the top 20th percentile, you find they are mostly protestant white males. However, there are many more white males in the 80 percentile of the wealth distribution than in this 20th percentile.

This further illustrates that the segregation that exist in society is not just about one race versus another. The fact is that those in the 80 percentile do not have economic prosperity. They often have lives that are focused on problems rather than at finding worthwhile solutions. Many in this group have lack of opportunities but will find it easier to blame this on another ethnicity, race or gender rather than take a close look at the economic policies that make the rich richer and the poor poorer.

We must understand that those in the 20th percentile did not just get "rich" but that the economically wealthy have been the beneficiaries of advantage, while others were disadvantaged. The 80th percentile, the tossed salad of America, has more in common than they realize wouldn't you think?

Now that we know the economic plight of numerous laborers in this country, we cannot leave this discussion until it is fully understood how such an unbalanced concentration of wealth occurs in a "free" society. We must understand the operation of the three economic systems.

Three Economic Systems

The economic resources (LAND, LABOR & CAPITAL) of a country can be categorized into one of the following categories or a mixture thereof:

Communism

- An economic system where all the economic resources are controlled by the government.[65]
- There is no opportunity for entrepreneurship since the government owns all industry.
- Lack of freedom and individual control.
- If resources were equally divided, citizens could live well cared for. However, since many governments in these countries have dictatorships, there is no check and balance and often greed becomes a very serious issue, which means all citizens are not cared for.

Can you name some countries that (now or previously) operated under communism? Are any of these countries places where you would want to live, such as China, Cuba, Poland (under communist regime until in 1985 when Mikhail Gorbachev became leader of the Soviet Union and relaxed Communist strictures), Vietnam, Laos, North Korea, etc...? Do many of the citizens from these countries migrate to the U.S.? Why would you think? If you guessed for freedom, you guessed right.

Socialism

- An economic system where most of the major economic resources are controlled by the government.[66]
- There are some opportunities for entrepreneurship.

- Individual freedom as well as government control is prevalent, how much may depend on the form of government. Political systems that operate under democracy in these countries often indicate a fairer distribution of economic resources amongst citizens.

Name some countries that operate (now or previously) under socialism? Are any of these countries places you would want to live, such as Canada, Switzerland, Sweden etc...? Do many of the citizens from these countries migrate to the U.S.? Why not? Well let's look at Switzerland for example.

Switzerland is among the world's most prosperous countries in terms of private income as in 2003, the median household income in Switzerland was an estimated 96,000 CHF or US$ 54,000, 26% higher than the 2003 U.S. median of $43,000, slightly less than that of the wealthiest U.S. state, New Hampshire.[67] In addition to a high standard of living, all Swiss citizens have health insurance that they pay for themselves with no help from their employer. An American in this situation might face tens of thousands of dollars in expenses. But under the Swiss health-care system, individuals pay about a third less on health care than the average American, in part because of government-enforced price controls.[68]

In addition, almost all Swiss are literate (it is estimated that 99% of the population age 15 and over can read and write).[69] Switzerland's 13 institutes of higher learning enrolled 99,600 students in the academic year of 2001-02 alone and about 25% of the adult population holds a diploma of higher learning.[70] The Swiss constitution guarantees freedom of worship and the different religious communities co-exist peacefully and Switzerland consistently ranks high on quality of life indices, including per capita income, concentration of computer and internet usage per capita, insurance coverage per individual and health care rates.[71] After the Second World War, Switzerland had absolutely no experience with unemployment until about 1990. But even now their unemployment rate is very low and they have one of the most stable economies.

So again I ask you why aren't the Swiss migrating to the U.S.? The answer should be simple.

Capitalism

- An economic system where very few of the resources are controlled by the government.[72]
- Entrepreneurship is the backbone of the economy.

- Individual freedom is prevalent, where you have the freedom (within the laws) to do what you want, live where you want, and fail or succeed based upon your opportunities.

Name a country that operates purely under capitalism? The United States is the answer. Now why do you think many people migrate here? Freedom of course. But how free are you if the majority people don't know how to or have the ability to build wealth?

So, let's go back to the original question: How does an unbalanced concentration of wealth occur in a "free" society like the capitalistic United States? Rather than give you my opinion, I ask you to think about the following questions.

Critical Thinking Questions

1. How in a free society like the U.S., can a small group of people continually control so much of the wealth?

2. Do you think if the people with the wealth, controlled the media, public school systems, and other systems where people gained many of their values and knowledge, the focus could be placed on issues that have nothing to do with gaining wealth?

3. Would it be possible to make certain "minority" groups the focus of society's problems?

4. Could the top pyramiders create (by using the media, etc.) hate amongst the bottom 80% in the pyramid, to keep the attention off them?

5. Can those in the 80th percentile be so burdened with day to day life that issues like wealth and net income become second place to finding health insurance, proper education for their children, a safe place to live (issues that would not be of concern if you had wealth)?

While I am not an advocate of the following fact: money or wealth will make life better, because it alone does not. However, I am an advocate for equal opportunity in the land of the free. If true equality does exist, then wouldn't this equality also exist in areas such as the wealth distribution? We have since the beginning of this text discussed many events that have occurred in the United States that should help you formulate answers to all of the above questions.

Answering these critical questions becomes important because as you address workplace diversity you need to know:

why discrimination occurs,
what history has to do with the U.S. cultural climate,
why the isms still plague the U.S. workplace,
why some people have opportunities and some don't,
and why a free society might be considered classist.

Despite whether you belief classism exist or not a few facts cannot be ignored.

For one, depending on the "breadth" of one's definition, 40-80% of the population can be considered working class.[73] This is true despite the fact that the individuals themselves might identify as or with the working class. These individuals, however, are not beneficiaries of middle class privileges because having a certain income does not equate to having wealth.

A second fact that cannot be ignored is that class issues affect people not only on an economic level, but also on an emotional level.[74] Classist attitudes have caused great pain by dividing people from one another and keeping individuals from personal fulfillment or the means to survive. Consequently, the process of rejecting such attitudes and their accompanying misinformation is an emotional one.[75] Since people tend to hurt each other because they themselves have been hurt, and since most forms of oppression are accompanied by economic discrimination, class overlaps with many other social issues, all of which move as we unravel how we've been hurt.[76]

Distrust, despair and anger are common consequences of oppression; this can be internalized or targeted toward others or self. To begin to undo the damage caused by issues like classism, it is useful for everyone to examine their own feelings about money, education, privilege, power, relationships, culture and ethnicity. This advice applies to organizations as well.

Concluding Thoughts

Ageism, Homophobia(ism), Transgenderism and Classism are all issues that can affect a person of any race or ethnicity. As we address these various "isms" that can plague the workplace remember—Martin Luther King's famous saying:

INJUSTICE ANYWHERE AFFECTS JUSTICE EVERYWHERE

Just because you may not be older, transgendered, gay/lesbian or at the bottom of the wealth pyramid doesn't mean that those that fit these categories should not have everyone fighting for their right to work free of discrimination.

End of Chapter Questions

1. What is ageism and does it exist in today's workplace?

2. What are some of the major differences between the four generations that exist in the workplace?

3. What does fear have to do with workplace equality and homosexuality?

4. What are the various forms of transgenderism?

5. Name four things a manager could do to help a transitioning employee?

6. Do you believe classism exist in America, why or why not? How can the facts known about this ism be utilized to unite various groups of people?

Internet Exercise

Part A: In the small space below **give one fact that indicates if the six individuals are or ever were speculated to be gay, homosexual or lesbian** along with the website address or source. To find this information go to www.google.com and type in the person's name along with the word "homosexual" or at the search box type "famous homosexuals in society."

1. Susan B. Anthony

   _____

   Source:

2. J. Edgar Hoover

_____

  Source:

3. President James Buchanan

_____

  Source:

4. Eleanor Roosevelt

_____

  Source:

5. Emily Dickinson

_____

  Source:

6. James Baldwin

_____

  Source:

Part B. Answer the following question: Let's assume that there are very famous people who were/are indeed homosexual, what way of thinking from chapter one is a person exhibiting when they talk so negatively about someone who loves differently than them and why would you choose this way of thinking?

End of Chapter Exercise

Net Worth Calculation

Net worth, investing, home ownership are all important concepts to understand in a Capitalistic economic system. Please complete the following:

> i. Calculate your net worth (on scrap paper not to be seen by others) and then indicate if your overall net worth is positive or negative.

ii. Now after reading the following information write out your own plan to improve your net worth (whether negative or positive).

Common Suggestions for Building Wealth

1. Pay off high-cost debt. The best investment most borrowers can make is to pay off consumer debt with double-digit interest rates. For example, if you have a $3,000 credit card balance at 19.8%, and you pay the required minimum balance of 2% of the balance or $15, whichever is greater, it will take 39 years to pay off the loan. And you will pay more than $10,000 in interest charges.

2. Buy a home and pay off the mortgage before you retire. The largest asset of most middle-income families is their home equity. Once these families have made their last mortgage payment, they have far lower housing expenses. They also have an asset that can be borrowed on in emergencies or converted into cash through sale of the home.

3. Participate in a work-related retirement program. Many employees turn down free money from their employer by not signing up for a work-related retirement program such as a 401(k) plan. If they did participate, with a dollar-for-dollar match they would likely receive an annual yield of greater than 100% on their investment.

4. Outside of work, save monthly through an automatic transfer from checking to savings. These savings will provide funds for emergencies, home purchase, school tuition, or even retirement. Almost all banking institutions will, on request, automatically transfer funds monthly from your checking account to a savings account, U.S. Savings Bond, or stock mutual fund. What you don't see, you will probably not miss.

5. Calculate your risk and return. If you earn 4% interest, your money will double in less than 15 years; at 7% it will double in about 10 years and at 10% it will double in 7%. Use Asset Allocation to reduce your overall risk.

Home Ownership is one way to build wealth—here are some tips to owning a home taken from home ownership manuals:

Since you most likely will need to get a mortgage to buy a house, you must make sure your credit history is as clean as possible. A few months before you start house hunting, get copies of your credit report. Make sure the facts are correct, and fix any problems you discover.

Aim for a home you can really afford.

The rule of thumb is that you can buy housing that runs about two-and-one-half times your annual salary. But you'll do better to use one of many calculators available online to get a better handle on how your income, debts, and expenses affect what you can afford.

Don't worry if you can't put down the usual 20 percent.

There are a variety of public and private lenders who, if you qualify, offer low-interest mortgages that require a down payment as small as 3 percent of the purchase price.

Buy in a district with good schools.

In most areas, this advice applies even if you don't have school-age children. Reason: When it comes time to sell, you'll learn that strong school districts are a top priority for many home buyers, thus helping to boost property values.

Get professional help.

Even though the Internet gives buyers unprecedented access to home listings, most new buyers (and many more experienced ones) are better off using a professional agent. Look for an exclusive buyer agent, if possible, who will have your interests at heart and can help you with strategies during the bidding process.

Choose carefully between points and rate.

When picking a mortgage, you usually have the option of paying additional points -- a portion of the interest that you pay at closing -- in exchange for a lower interest rate. If you stay in the house for a long time -- say five to seven years or more -- it's usually a better deal to take the points. The lower interest rate will save you more in the long run.

Before house hunting, get pre-approved.

Getting pre-approved will you save yourself the grief of looking at houses you can't afford and put you in a better position to make a serious offer when you do find the right house. Not to be confused with pre-qualification, which is based on a cursory review of your finances, pre-approval from a lender is based on your actual income, debt and credit history.

Hire a home inspector.

Sure, your lender will require a home appraisal anyway. But that's just the bank's way of determining whether the house is worth the price you've agreed to pay. Separately, you should hire your own home inspector, preferably an engineer with experience in doing home surveys in the area where you are buying. His or her job will be to point out potential problems that could require costly repairs down the road.

References

1.   Achenbaum, W. A. (1978). *Old age in the new land*. Baltimore, MD: Johns Hopkins University Press.

2.   Harkness, H. (1999). *Don't Stop the Clock: Rejecting the Myths of Aging for a New Way to Work in the 21st Century*. Palo Alto, California: Davies-Black Publishing.

3.   Brecher, E. (1984). *Love, sex and aging: a Consumers Union report*. Boston: Little Brown.

4.   Sternberg, R. J. (December 2005). Older but not wiser? The relationship between age and wisdom. *Ageing International*, 30(1).

5.   Boone, D. R. (1985). Ageism: A negative view of the aged. *ASHA*, 27, 51-53.

6.   Butler, R. N. (1969). Age-ism: Another form of bigotry. *The Gerontologist*, 9, 243-246.

7.   Fischer, D. H. (1978). *Growing old in America*. New York: Oxford University Press.

8.   What's happening with employment opportunities for the "older worker"? (n.d.). Retrieved from: http://www.employmentblawg.com/2007/whats-happening-with-employment-opportunities-for-the-older-worker/

9.   Ibid.

10.   Ibid.

11.   Zemke, R., Raines, C. & Filipczak, B. (1999). *Managing the Clash of Veterans, Boomers, Xers, and Nexters in Your Workplace*. American Management Association and Wikipedia. Retrieved from: http://en.wikipedia.org/wiki/Demographics

12.   Schuman, H. and Scott, J. (1989), Generations and collective memories, *American Sociological Review*, vol. 54, 1989, pp. 359-81.

13.   Freedman, M. (1999). *Prime Time: How Baby Boomers Will Revolutionize Retirement and Transform America.* New York: Public Affairs.

14.   Meredith, G., Schewe, C., and Haim, A. (2002). *Managing by defining moments: Innovative strategies for motivating 5 very different generational cohorts*. New York: Hungry Minds Inc.

15.   Ibid.

16.   Ibid.

17.   Ibid.

18. Billikopf, G. (n.d.). Promotions, Transfers & Layoffs. Retrieved from: http://www.cnr.berkeley.edu/ucce50/ag-labor/7labor/04.htm

19. Miller, M. (1971). *On Being Different: What It Means to be a Homosexual*. New York: Popular Library.

20. Bullough, V., Dank, B. M., Fradkin, H. E., Kepner, J. L., Legg, W. D. & Newton, R. E. (n.d.). *Commonly Asked Questions and Answers about Homosexuality*. Retrieved from: http://www.lhup.edu/diversity/studentlife/qanda.html

21. Ibid.

22. Marcus, E. (1993). *Is It a Choice?: Answers to 300 of the Most Frequently Asked Questions About Gays and Lesbians*. San Francisco: Harper San Francisco.

23. Moskowitz, C. (2008). Same sex couples common in the wild. *LiveScience*. Retrieved from: http://www.livescience.com/animals/080516-gay-animals.html

24. Fletcher, L. Y. (1990). *Lavender Lists: New Lists about Lesbian and Gay Culture, History, and Personalities.* Boston: Alyson Publications.

25. Bullough, V., Dank, B. M., Fradkin, H. E., Kepner, J. L., Legg, W. D. & Newton, R. E. (n.d.). *Commonly Asked Questions and Answers about Homosexuality*. Retrieved from: http://www.lhup.edu/diversity/studentlife/qanda.html

26. Eskridge, W. N. (2006). *Gay Marriage: For Better or For Worse? What We've Learned from the Evidence.* Oxford University Press.

27. Bullough, V., Dank, B. M., Fradkin, H. E., Kepner, J. L., Legg, W. D. & Newton, R. E. (n.d.). *Commonly Asked Questions and Answers about Homosexuality*. Retrieved from: http://www.lhup.edu/diversity/studentlife/qanda.html

28. Singh, B. (2004, March). Gay gov't employees lose their protection. *Yale Daily News*.

29. Winfield, L. (1995). *Straight Talk About Gays in the Workplace: Creating an Inclusive, Productive Environment for Everyone in Your Organization*. New York, NY: AMACOM.

30. Marcus, E. (1993). *Is It a Choice?: Answers to 300 of the Most Frequently Asked Questions About Gays and Lesbians*. San Francisco: Harper San Francisco.

31. Winfield, L. (1995). *Straight Talk About Gays in the Workplace: Creating an Inclusive, Productive Environment for Everyone in Your Organization*. New York, NY: AMACOM.

32. Powers, B. & Ellis, A. (1995). *A Manager's Guide to Sexual Orientation in the Workplace*. London: Taylor & Francis, Inc.

33. Baird, R. M. & Rosenbaum, S.E. (1997). *Same-Sex Marriage: The Moral and Legal Debate*. Amherst, NY: Prometheus Books.

34. Fletcher, L. Y. (1990). *Lavender Lists: New Lists about Lesbian and Gay Culture, History, and Personalities.* Boston: Alyson Publications.

35. Sullivan, L. (1990). *From Female To Male: The Life Of Jack Bee Garland*. Boston: Alyson Publications.

36. Transgender. (n.d.). Retrieved from: http://www.debradavis.org/gecpage/gectransinfo.html

37. Transgender Equality. (n.d.). Retrieved from: http://www.thetaskforce.org/downloads/reports/reports/TransgenderEquality.pdf

38. Griggs, C. (1996). *Passage Through Trinidad: Journal of a Surgical Sex Change*. London: McFarland & Company.

39. Ibid.

40. Walworth, J. (August 2003). *Managing Transsexual Transition in the Workplace*. Retrieved from: http://www.gendersanity.com/shrm.html

41. Workplace Gender Transition Guidelines. (n.d.). Retrieved from: http://www.hrc.org/documents/HRC-Workplace-Gender-Transition-Guidelines.pdf

42. Walworth, J. (August 2003). *Managing Transsexual Transition in the Workplace*. Retrieved from: http://www.gendersanity.com/shrm.html

43. Ibid.

44. Ibid.

45. Workplace Gender Transition Guidelines. (n.d.). Retrieved from: http://www.hrc.org/documents/HRC-Workplace-Gender-Transition-Guidelines.pdf

46. Ibid.

47. Human Rights Campaign. (n.d.). *Transgenderism and Transition in the workplace*. Retrieved from: http://www.ren.org/hrcwork.pdf

48. Minter, S. (2004). *Representing Transsexual Clients: Selected Legal Issues. San Francisco: National Center for Lesbian Rights*. Retrieved from: http://www.hawaii.edu/hivandaids/Representing_Transsexual_Clients__Selected_Legal_Issues.pdf

49. Ibid.

50. Ibid.

51. Ibid.

52. Ibid.

53. Brantley, C., Frost, D., Pfeffer, C., Buccigrossi, J. & Robinson, M. (2003). *Class: Power, Privilege, and Influence in the United States*. Rochester, NY: Wetware, Inc. Retrieved from: http://www.workforcediversitynetwork.com/docs/class_9.pdf

54. School of the Americas Watch. (n.d.). *Confronting Classism*. Retrieved from: http://www.soaw.org/article.php?id=532

55. Croteau, D. (1995). *Politics and the Class Divide: Working People and the Middle Class Left*. Philadelphia: Temple University Press.

56. Wikipedia. (n.d.). *Classism*. Retrieved from: http://en.wikipedia.org/wiki/Classism

57. Sklar, H. (2005, September). Growing Gulf Between Rich and Rest of America. *Knight Ridder/Tribune Information Services*. Retrieved from: http://www.ms.foundation.org/wmspage.cfm?parm1=305

58. Ibid.

59. Albelda, R. P. & Withorn, A. (2002). *Lost Ground: Welfare Reform, Poverty, and Beyond*. Cambridge: South End Press.

60. Webb, J. (2006, November 15). Class Struggle. *The Wall Street Journal*.

61. The United States Department of Health and Human Services. (2009). *The 2009 HHS Poverty Guidelines*. Retrieved from: http://aspe.hhs.gov/poverty/09poverty.shtml

62. Kivel, P. (1998, November 15). Affirmative Action, Immigration & Welfare: Confronting Racism in 1998. *In Motion Magazine*.

63. Kivel, P. (2006). *You Call this a Democracy?* New York: The Apex Press.

64. Payne, R. & Krabill, D. (2002). *Hidden Rules of Class at Work*. Highlands, TX: Aha Process Inc.

65. Pride, W. M., Hughes, R. J. & Kapoor, J. (2008). *Introduction to Business*. Florence Kentucky: Cengage Learning, Inc.

66. Ibid.

67. Economy of Switzerland. (n.d.). Retrieved from: http://www.absoluteastronomy.com/topics/Economy_of_Switzerland

68. Ibid.

69. CIA World Factbook. (n.d.). *Switzerland.* Retrieved from: https://www.cia.gov/library/publications/the-world-factbook/geos/SZ.html

70. Ibid.

71. Ibid.

72. Pride, W. M., Hughes, R. J. & Kapoor, J. (2008). *Introduction to Business*. Florence Kentucky: Cengage Learning, Inc.

73. Sennett, R & Cobb, J. (1993). *The Hidden Injuries of Class*. New York: Norton.

74. Ibid.

75. Zweig, M. (2004). *What's Class Got to Do With It?* Ithaca, NY: ILR Press.

76. Albelda, R. & Lapidus, J. & Melendez, Edwin M. (1988). *Mink Coats Don't Trickle Down: The Economic Attack on Women and People of Color*. Cambridge, MA: South End Press.

Chapter Twelve

Affirmative Action

Smooth seas do not make skillful sailors.

From an old African proverb

AFFIRMATIVE ACTION

Chapter Objectives

After reading this chapter, you should be able to:

- define Affirmative Action (AA).

- explain the common myths surrounding Affirmative Action.

- rationalize why it is necessary to right the wrongs of the past rather than just ignore them.

- describe ways to implement Affirmative Action initiatives.

- determine why preferences are not just associated with Affirmative Action.

Managing Workplace Diversity

AFFIRMATIVE ACTION

Affirmative Action is a set of public policies and initiatives designed to help eliminate past and present discrimination based on race, color, religion, sex, or national origin.[1] Affirmative action seeks to include those who have been formerly excluded and it covers recruitment, hiring, promotion and training policies. Much of what many people know about affirmative action is based on emotions, myths and not the real definition of affirmative action.[2]

Myths, the stories that often guide our lives, can be so deeply ingrained that we seldom consciously think of them. They are unconsciously inherited from our ancestors, our culture, and our society. Unfiltered, unproved, and unexamined, these collective beliefs are accepted without question and many times are used to justify unsound attitudes and practices. The media, in all formats, often presents biased information on Affirmative Action which helps to make this policy one of the most misunderstood of all times.[3] But despite all the controversy, affirmative action would not be in existence if civil rights were a reality for all people of the U.S.

It strikes me as strange that in the U.S. where there has been over hundreds of years of slavery, Willie Lynch values, Jim Crow Laws and stereotypes, laws against migration and equal treatment, that people would think that after only 40 years of affirmative action and enforcement of civil rights laws that the U.S. workplace would be an equal playing ground. As historian Roger Wilkins has pointed out, Blacks have a 375-year history on this continent: 245 involving slavery, 100 involving legalized discrimination, and only 30 involving anything else.[4] Change takes time and does not happen on its own.

Originally, civil rights programs were enacted to help African Americans become full citizens of the United States (remember slaves were not considered human just property). The Thirteenth Amendment to the Constitution made slavery illegal; the Fourteenth Amendment guarantees equal protection under the law; the Fifteenth Amendment forbids racial discrimination in access to voting. The 1866 Civil Rights Act guarantees every citizen "the same right to make and enforce contracts ... as is enjoyed by White citizens ..."[5]

The first time the actual term "affirmative action" was first used was in the 1965 Executive Order 11246 that was issued by President Lyndon Johnson. This executive order required federal contractors to "take affirmative action to ensure that applicants are employed, and that employees are treated during employment, without regard to their race, creed (beliefs that are not religious), color, or national origin." and in 1967 President Johnson included women in this order.[6]

Affirmative Action requires measures that are in align with cultural competence. Just "valuing diversity" without regard to action is not enough companies have to decide where they will fall on the continuum of competence.

Continuum of Competence

Individuals and organizations can measure their competence on a continuum developed by James Mason (1993). There are five progressive steps in his continuum. Cultural destructiveness is the first step and is the least effective toward addressing cultural competence. When an organization and its employees are exhibiting cultural destructiveness they have attitudes, policies and practices that don't value diversity purposefully.[7]

After cultural destructiveness there is incapacity which is when an organization and its employees are not intentionally devaluing diversity.[8] Instead the organization has a system that does not promote, respect or reflect the diversity of its organization. This seems easier to fix than cultural destructiveness because it requires fixing the organizational system rather than fixing individuals or organizations with prejudiced disposition.

Mason goes on to indicate that the third level in the continuum of competence is blindness.[9] Often times people believe that if I "don't see color" or "don't see difference" then I am not being biased. But, how do you ignore a component of a person that makes them who they are? How do you ignore systems that have not been created equally? Ignoring them won't get them fixed. Ignoring someone who is abusive does not make them less abusive, just like ignoring race won't make racism go away it just means you are ignoring the problem. Blindness or turning a blind eye to something just perpetuates the status quo whatever that is.

The next level of pre-competence is more about individuals and organizations being more proactive as it relates to cultural competence and in this phase, they are recognizing that cultural differences exist and they are making efforts to improve equality in the workplace.[10] The last stage and most effective stage is competence. This is not just the acceptance and respect of cultural differences with the organization and individuals but there is the exhibition of attitudes, policies and programs that actively work toward managing a diverse workforce.

Affirmative action can assist with cultural competency, this last step if handled appropriately. However, before acceptance of Affirmative Action initiatives occur the myths regarding this program must be addressed.

MYTHS AND FACTS

In recent years, affirmative action has been debated more intensely than at any other time in its 35-year history.[11] Yet many people and corporations support affirmative action and what it attempts to accomplish despite any imperfections that its interpretation as a policy may have. Whatever opinion you have or don't have, it is important that you base your view of Affirmative Action on facts not myths or propaganda. Here are some of the most popular myths about affirmative action, along with a brief commentary on each one.

Myth 1: Affirmative action mainly benefits Blacks.

Affirmative Action benefits many groups such as Blacks, Asian-Americans, Latinos, Veterans and Women of all races. Actually, the largest beneficiary of Affirmative action is not Blacks but Caucasian women. Breaking the glass ceiling in many male dominated professions, has been one of the highest priorities of the workplace as it relates to affirmative action initiatives.[12] When people assume that Affirmative Action only affects Blacks, they often provide blind support to initiatives that seek to shut down affirmative action efforts. "Attacks on affirmative action programs have included everything from English as a Second Language Programs to breast cancer screenings, from mentoring and after school programs to magnet schools, from programs that require Asian-owned businesses to be advised of possible government contracts to battered women shelters that create a safe space for victims of domestic violence and their children. In short, there are countless initiatives across the country that affirmatively use race and gender to address the unwarranted obstacles confronted by the beneficiaries of affirmative action."[13]

Myth 2: A large percentage of White workers will lose out if affirmative action is continued.

Fear. If the argument utilized against Affirmative Action is fear of loss-how easy is it to produce anger toward a program that seeks to redress the wrongs of the past that continue into today's workforce. Fear is an emotion and emotions are not always correct. So, let's address the facts. According to the U.S. Commerce Department, there are 1.3 million unemployed Black civilians and 112 million employed White civilians so, even if every unemployed Black worker in the United States were to oust a White employee this would only affect 1% of Whites.[14]

If managers tell employees that they were displaced because they had to hire a person of color or hire a woman then this could incite anger--when it is never that simple. First of all, remember anyone that a company hires must be qualified. Affirmative Action does not support the hiring of nonqualified workers. Yet, oftentimes someone will say the woman or person of color weren't the best qualified. But in someone's mind they have a definition of the "best qualified" which could be someone they feel more comfortable with.

But, what is best qualified? It is subjective at best. If someone meets the job description or job advertisement then they are qualified. If a qualified women or person of color is chosen over a qualified white male, to say that someone of color "had to be hired" is inappropriate unless there is a sense of entitlement. Instead let's just say that competition was in effect and a qualified person was hired.

This losing out to someone of color or women is not according to the research the major reasons for job loss among White men. Job loss among Whites and in particular white males has a lot more to do with factory relocations, computerization and automation, downsizing, and outsourcing (sending jobs overseas).[15] It is unfortunate that some managers attribute job loss to Affirmative Action—using affirmative action as a scapegoat in this manner is a cop out.

Myth 3: Reverse discrimination is the result of Affirmative Action.

Studies of reverse discrimination lawsuits show that there are more gender-related complaints (men saying they were discriminated against because of their gender) than race-related complaints.[16] In a third study (as cited in Reskin, 1998), less than 1% of the reverse discrimination EEOC complaints filed in 1994 were deemed credible.[17] These studies suggest that relatively few reverse discrimination court cases and EEOC complaints have legal merit.

The belief that the majority of white males are said to be victims of reverse discrimination is in itself a misuse of the word reverse discrimination. The concept when used in its broadest meaning suggests widespread victimization. Some writers and authors still use the language reverse discrimination and affirmative action interchangeably. In a thoughtful retrospective on affirmative action, Charles Fried, former Solicitor General in the second Reagan administration, uses the concepts of 'affirmative action' or 'preferential treatment' throughout the article and as he makes the argument that there should be time limits on affirmative action at the end of the article, he slips in another phrase: "But if 'all deliberate speed' was fast enough for desegregation, then surely nothing speedier is required for phasing out reverse discrimination."[18] Using these terms interchangeably infers that they are one in the same—when they are not.

Why Affirmative Action?

There have been various equal protection laws passed to make discrimination illegal. Laws are great but they only work when enforced.

How do you get a workforce that may be accustomed to employees of the same sex, race and work ethics to integrate their workforce with people they may not value, trust or just don't associate with?

In addition, think about all of the subliminal messages that have been fed into individual minds regarding stereotypes—this alone can create unconscious bias which results in a homogenous workplace. It is unfortunate that policies have to be written that say "let's level the playing field," let's get rid of the hidden and written policies and beliefs that keep the workforce (especially higher paying careers and management positions) still segregated. But, to let change happen on its own is like telling an alcoholic to just stop drinking—doesn't work in most cases.

Commonly held assumptions about Affirmative Action

Affirmative Action lower standards

The only way Affirmative Action can lower standards is when the company doing the hiring does not require the new employees to meet the standards. Why? Because they themselves are trying to take a shortcut. This is not Affirmative Action causing them to do this but the company blaming Affirmative Action and not putting forth the "right" effort. This often happens when companies need to diversify or hire a "token" but are less concerned about hiring the right multicultural person with the appropriate skills for the job, focusing instead on hiring a person of the right color or sex with no regard to qualifications.

This is not what Affirmative Action stands for. Affirmative Action seeks to include classes of people who have historically been excluded. These hiring standards need not be lowered to accomplish this goal. For instance, assume there is a position available and the job required three years of experience in the field, an Associate's Degree, and a score of at least 70 out of 100, lowering the standards would mean hiring someone without an Associate's Degree. However, it would not be lowering the standards by hiring someone with a score of 75 over someone with a score of 90, as they both meet the standard. Most qualified has nothing to do with discrimination—as "most qualified" is a very subjective standard as stated earlier. What is most qualified to me may be different for you. Either you are qualified according to the standards set forth or you are not.

Quotas and Affirmative Action go hand in hand

No, a quota implies a fixed number and sometimes does not indicate qualified in the legal definition. For this reason, quota has a negative connotation. But, Affirmative Action focuses on goals instead of quotas for two reasons: (1) goals imply something to strive for and are based on the needs of the organization and the marketplace we serve, (2) quotas once reached can then be abandoned, whereas goals can often be exceeded and continued.[19]

An Affirmative Action Analogy

At this point, before we get into any further discussion about affirmative action, let me tell you a story I read in a fiction book, *Always,* authored by Timmothy B. McCann. In it he illustrates what affirmative action is really about. This story can explain it better than any definition I can give you. The character in the book is describing his views as he debates a political opponent on issues, he states this to the debate the audience when asked about affirmative action:

I am sure you would agree that historically people of color in this country have been disadvantaged in many ways. Let's look at sports since the World Series just ended. In baseball you have one player from one team facing nine from the opposition on the field. Now, the batter must earn his way on base. If he hits the ball and does not make it to first, he's out. Point-blank, end of discussion. But if by chance there is a tie . . ." And then I paused and looked at my opponent. If there is a tie, Representative Edwards, since it was nine players on the field against one in baseball, the batter is viewed as being disadvantaged and the tie goes to the runner. The affirmative action laws as they are written will not—and I repeat this because this is often overlooked—will not give anything to anyone who has not earned it. But if there is a tie between two applicants in terms of qualifications, what it does give is an opportunity for women and people of color to simply stay in the game."[20]

Maybe you still aren't convinced of the worth of affirmative action or that affirmative action is only about leveling the playing field for qualified candidates. So, let me say this—affirmative action does work. It has produced opportunities for jobs, education, and training for tens of thousands of people of color, white women, poor and working class White men. Although not often enforced strongly, affirmative action programs have broken down long-standing barriers based on the persistent and ongoing discrimination that our society faces.[21]

According to author Paul Kivel, head of the organization "White Guys for Affirmative Action", Affirmative Action for White males is an old tradition in American society. Kivel indicates that veteran preferences, alumni preferences, homeowner preferences in the form of home mortgage deductions, student deferments during the Vietnam war, and hundreds of millions of dollars of subsidies for manufacturers, farmers, mining and logging companies, including a $300 billion bailout of the Savings & Loan industry are all forms of affirmative action for White men that have not been called that.[22] But, these are preferences—so why aren't they challenged?

The other issue that we must consider is that Affirmative Action is and has been necessary because there are still many elements in the workplace that create opportunities based on bias. People and organizations alike still have myths and stereotypes that they associate with groups of people. They believe these myths and create bias through self-fulfilling prophecies.

Now, let me explain how a self-fulfilling prophecy works. We belief something to be true, so we treat the person this way, then they respond the way we thought they would and then our belief is confirmed. For example, let's assume (only for the sake of this example) that I believe anyone reading this book is stupid since they don't already know this information. So, when I use this text to teach a class, I won't waste my time trying to teach stupid people. Instead, I discuss my travels and other issues that are not related to this text.

Again, remember I am treating the students like they are stupid and can't learn. So then, I give a 30-page essay exam based upon all the collected theories that went into the development of this book. After all, if you were smart you would know this material. How many students would pass the test? That's right, very few. Why wouldn't they pass? Well it wouldn't be because they were stupid. It would be because I treated them like they were and did not give them a chance to learn. I biased the process.

But guess what; since they did not pass the test what am I going to think? You guessed it, that they were stupid just as I thought. Mind you, my thinking has nothing to do with truth or knowledge but the fact that I thought something and acted on it and then got my belief confirmed. Therefore, when you create a self-fulfilling prophecy you create your own reality.

Can this be dangerous in the minds of people with power? Yes.

Furthermore, bias is created by unfair systems. You may think that most aspects of today's society are fair. But, what you have to understand is that many systems are still very biased.[23/24] If you have never experienced discrimination or unfair work policies then you really might not understand.

But, just common systems, such as college entrance exams are not fair. Would you think it unreasonable if I told you that the SAT/ACT Test is one of these?[25] SAT testing and getting high scores has been an issue coming into the 21st century where those students who get high scores get passed over and feel they are being discriminated against.[26] So, many people argue, sue and fight these types of issues that they have so little information about. My point is—is there are a lot of instruments in society that create disadvantage. Is the SAT one of these?

What if you knew that the author of the SAT developed this instrument to confirm his suspicions that people of color were intellectually inferior? Therefore, this author developed questions based on this racist premise. Then students of color take these tests and don't do well because the questions are not based on intelligence but are based on privilege and lifestyle. For instance, if they ask a simple question like: dressing is to ranch as flower is to_____? Just in my own culture I would think the answer was something that had nothing to do with a flower since dressing (something I eat at Thanksgiving that others call stuffing has nothing to do with the flavor Ranch). Now you may be of a different culture and understand dressing to mean a type of sauce you put on a salad so ranch is a type—this totally changes the answer that you chose. Who gets this right—the one whose culture it reflects. Does this mean I am stupid—no it just means that according to my culture we utilize terminology differently.

According to an article written by DiversityInc, students of color generally score higher on the harder questions of the SAT/ACT and poorer on the easier questions.[27] Why? One rationale is because the harder questions are not so easy to bias as is the simple questions. Now when these students don't pass because the test was not created for them to pass, it has confirmed this author's suspicions. So then is this really a test that should determine who gets admitted to college, when it creates a self-fulfilling prophecy based upon the authors' bias?

Now, let's take this a step further—let's say this racist author states to the proper people that he wrote a bogus test. He realizes that what he did was wrong and then wants people to know his intentions. But, the people who now author this test for whatever reason still choose not to change the test. Now how would you feel about the SAT if this were true?

If they changed the test, would you then think they were changing it (making it easier) in favor people of color to lessen the standards or to right a wrong?

Do you think the authors of the SAT would come out and tell you this truth or lead you to believe that the victim (students of color) are the ones at fault?

Would you believe that the students were "too stupid" too pass?

Do you think that if this were true the SAT administrators would come out and say "No, you are wrong, this really was a test based on racist misconceptions and we are now realizing that we were wrong to use this test"?

Can you imagine the lawsuits? So, when something like this happens it is often the victims that get blamed and no one in the general public gets the truth.

Well, let me tell you that all of this is a true story regarding the SAT and its author. The author, Carl Campbell Brigham, based the test on racial superiority. He later recanted the test as bogus and his comments were presented in an article in the *New York Times*.[28] But, still this test is utilized in its created format even though many understand the background of this test. Do you think there are more instances like this that you don't even know about?

When you begin to think that life is simple and unbiased and equal, remember that in the history of the U.S., nothing has ever been that simple and has not been in the favor of a lot of people for a long time.

Because of the isms, prejudices, and superiority issues that have prefaced our society since the arrival of the Pilgrims—we should know that systems in society are not going to be as fair as they seem. If you work in an area that is not multicultural, don't accept the excuse that there are no people of color or women who can do the job; don't accept the excuse that they don't test well; when your job makes the effort to change the test, don't be angry thinking that they have lowered the standards--understand that we have a long way to go until we have systems free of bias. There are so many hidden biases that unless you have done a substantial amount of research these biases just would not be obvious to the common person.

But even though hidden bias is not obvious there is one way to tell if a system or company is free of bias or to tell where they are on the competence continuum: look at the people that make-up your employee and management base.[29]

- Are all or majority of your employees of color in janitorial/housekeeping or low-level staff positions?

- Are all or majority of the women in management positions located in the human resource department?

- Are all or majority of the women in the organization support staff administrative assistants/secretaries—no managers.

- Are all or majority of the teachers or bank workers female and all or majority of the principals or loan officers male?

This is not to say that janitorial, human resource, secretarial positions, etc. are bad jobs, but they are positions that have been traditional areas for certain groups of people. If the diversity of an organization is represented in this manner this may not equate to equal opportunity. The doors are not being opened, at least not to all positions. So how do you open the door?

Implementing Affirmative Action

Even organizations with the best intentions may not accurately implement affirmative action without a plan. In an affirmative plan, there should be an assessment of the workplace, recruitment goals, and training opportunities that are free of bias. This ensures that those groups formerly excluded will have an open door through which to enter. This often requires different tactics to reach diverse groups.

See the sample affirmative action plan below.

SAMPLE AFFIRMATIVE ACTION PLAN (for disabled veterans)*

*taken from with permission from: http://www.jobs.bpa.gov/How_To_Apply/disabledaction.cfm

INTRODUCTION

In accordance with Title 5, of the Code of Federal Regulations, Part 720, subpart C – Disabled Veterans Affirmative Action Program (DVAAP), Bonneville Power Administration is required to develop an annual DVAAP Action Plan.

COMPONENTS OF THE PLAN

1. Statement of agency policy regarding the employment and advancement of disabled veterans

2. The name and title of the official assigned overall responsibility for the development and implementation of the plan

3. An assessment of the current status of disabled veteran employment within the agency (with emphasis on those veterans who are 30 percent or more disabled). *(Note: see attachment 1 "FY04 Veteran's Employment Status Report" for details).*

4. A description of recruitment methods which will be used to seek out disabled veteran applicants, including special steps to be taken to recruit veterans who are 30 percent or more disabled

5. FY Goals:

Managing Workplace Diversity

- Continue to build partnerships. We will continue to pursue partnerships within BPA, with other organizations, and in the local community to support Disabled Veterans programs and the hiring of veterans in the Federal Service. We will seek new ways to communicate employment information, and to provide resources to support Veterans in BPA's workforce.
- Continue to maintain the "Applicant Supply File" for 30% or more disabled Veterans and refer applications for consideration on open vacancies as appropriate.
- We will also be distributing appropriate vacancies to the following military Transitional Assistance Program (TAP) contacts.

6. A description of how the agency will provide or improve internal advancement opportunities for disabled veterans:

- Career Services Workshops and training for: "Understanding the Application Process", "Resume Writing", "and Development of KSA's", and "How to prepare for an interview".
- BPA encourages all employees, including disabled veterans, to complete an individual development plan with their manager, which is used to identify training needs necessary to be successful in their current position, and in possible future advancement opportunities.
- Individual Career counseling and application coaching.
- Attend workshops focusing on: Career Transition, Active Retirement, or Entrepreneurship in addition to receiving one-on-one career counseling.

In addition to having a plan, there are additional efforts that are required if an organization wants to have a diverse workforce. This effort starts first with recruiting.

Recruitment (Opening the door for all applicants)

Using word of mouth to spread information about employment opportunities while it may be cheap to the organization is not recommended in securing equal opportunity. Why? People will talk to who they know and if the organization using word of mouth is not diverse then assuming that birds of a feather flock together then what may result is a homogeneous workforce--not diversity. Advertising is the more likely vehicle that should be utilized to inform the public of a job opening or opportunity because it can spread across communities. But, even advertising through traditional channels like major newspapers and large-scale job boards may not target everyone in the community.[30]

To attract a diverse grouping of recruits you must do more. Advertise in ethnic/culture specific publications whose readership represents diverse groups or whose readership attracts a multicultural population. Diversity Recruitment advertising also serves two purposes: it attracts a diverse pool of applicants and it sends a message that the organization cares about diversity.[31]

Additional Suggestions & Tips

1. Create internship and co-op opportunities for members of diverse groups. Recruit from schools that have diverse student bodies such as women colleges and HBCUs (historically black colleges and universities) and Native American Colleges).

2. Emphasize competency-based credentials rather than past experience because some groups have not had the access to comply with the experience requirements.[32]

3. Require qualifications that are necessary and not just historical, such as stating that you need to lift 40 pounds when that really is not a requirement—it is just what has been mandated historically.[33]

4. Review your own beliefs and attitudes about the positions that you are filling and the populations that you are targeting so that your own bias is not found in the job description or interviewing process.

5. Nurture relationships with groups and organizations that accommodate the needs of people of color, women, various religious groups and the disabled.

6. Interview utilizing a group made up of diverse individuals (have a hiring committee) if possible so that there are a range of opinions in the interview process.

7. Make sure your company has a workplace climate that is welcoming to all people regardless of background. If not, then those you work so hard to hire won't stay if they find a non-supportive environment.

8. Make sure employees and managers alike have gone through diversity training so they are aware of the benefits as well as challenges of managing a diverse workforce.

9. Make sure everyone has equal access to training opportunities and that the same training materials and standards are being distributed to all employees.

After reading the above, you may be wondering: Despite what has been said this sounds like preferential treatment and it seems unfair in some cases?

What about preferences?

Preferences to those formerly excluded: people of color, women, veterans, etc. is sometimes a part of providing inclusion to an opportunity that was formerly closed. Colleges give preferences (other than racial) to all kinds of students—children of alumni, veterans, athletes, musicians, etc., so race/ethnicity preferences are just one more consideration in the effort to craft a diverse, well-rounded workforce and in the case of schools a well rounded class. So, what's the problem-legally, morally, politically, or otherwise when it comes especially to preferences?

It seems that when it comes to anything but racial preferences there isn't a problem. Where is the outcry against legacy preferences? Many private schools have a huge affirmative action program for the daughters and sons (and other relatives) of their alumni known as "legacy preference."[34] Even though it has been argued that this type of preference builds institutional loyalty for many private schools (not just colleges but even private high schools) does this make it okay?

If you were part of a group who were never permitted to attend in the past then this disadvantage continues as these people will never be in a position to receive the alumni/legacy preference. The problem with this is that you can read about individuals speaking out against affirmative action (as was such the situation with The University of Michigan case in 2003) when they felt it benefitted students/people of color but very rarely do you hear groups or individuals argue against legacy preference. It would seem that the complaint (no matter who it is from) should be against all preferences—not just the ones that deal with race. What do you think?

Concluding Thoughts

Affirmative action programs are just one method to right the wrongs of the past. It allows those doors that were formerly closed to now be open. Will this method rectify all past discrimination—of course not. The problem is just not that simple. But, it is a program that sets goals, recognizes that some in America have had advantages over others and recognizes that laws alone won't change mindsets or biased systems. Most Fortune 500 companies support Affirmative Action initiatives. Many managers will be responsible for implementation of the program objectives—therefore it makes sense to know what it is, what it does and who it really benefits. If we can get past scarcity thinking (believing that if someone gains someone else loses) and know that there is enough for all—then maybe we can get closer to a workplace that is inviting to the qualified who want to participate.

End of Chapter Questions

1. What is Affirmative Action?

2. Who has been Affirmative Action's largest beneficiary? Why?

3. What does quotas have to do with Affirmative Action?

4. Why does Affirmative Action expand recruiting and training techniques? What are some of these recruiting techniques?

5. Why do you think Fortune 500 companies support and implement Affirmative Action policies?

Internet Exercise

Go to http://www.projectimplicit.net/generalinfo.php and read about the Project Implicit test. After reading about the test go to http://implicit.harvard.edu and take the race, age and sex implicit test by clicking on the "research" box. Print your results. Now comment on any biases that the test may or may not have picked up on. Explain how having unknown biases can perpetuate discrimination in the workplace and why this is an argument in support of affirmative action.

End of Chapter Exercise

Is Affirmative Action the answer?
Read the following scenario to decide if it is a valid exercise of affirmative action powers. Find a teammate in order to formulate arguments for or against the hypothetical scenario below. After coming back together, articulate your arguments for the entire class.

Scenario
University A has a history of racial discrimination. In the last twenty years, new leadership at the University has tried to change past policies, creating a much more diverse, "minority-friendly" environment. However, minorities are still underrepresented at the University. As a result, the admissions committee decided to institute a new policy when choosing between undergraduate applicants for admission. The admission committee will consider the following factors:

- high school grades-10 points,
- standardized test scores-20 points,
- high school quality-10 points,
- curriculum choices-5 points,
- geography (rural-receives 10 points others less),
- alumni relationships (prior family who attended)-15 points,
- leadership-10 points and
- an additional 20 points to underrepresented students of color (the least represented group on campus).

This is a total of one hundred points. Students with the higher point values will be admitted into the undergraduate program. Not everyone will receive admittance.

What are the preferences in the situation? Is this a valid exercise of affirmative action?

References

1.   Kahlenberg, R. D. (1996). *The remedy: class, race, and affirmative action*. New York: BasicBooks.

2.   Goldberg, D. T. (1991). *Anatomy of Racism*. Minneapolis, MN: University of Minnesota Press.

3.   SFSU Public Affairs Press Release. (n.d.). *The Affirmative Action Debate- Is the Media Getting it Right?* Retrieved from: http://www.sfsu.edu/~news/prsrelea/fy98/092.htm

4.   Wilkins, R. (May 1995). Racism has its privileges: The case for affirmative action. *The Nation,* pp. 409-410, 412, 414-416.

5.   Sykes, M. (August 1995). *The Origins of Affirmative Action*. Retrieved from: http://www.now.org/nnt/08-95/affirmhs.html

6.   Goldberg, D. T. (1991). *Anatomy of Racism*. Minneapolis, MN: University of Minnesota Press.

7.   Mason, J. L. (1993). *Cultural competence self-assessment questionnaire*. Portland, Oregon: Portland State University, Multi-cultural Initiative Project.

8.   Ibid.

9.   Ibid.

10.   Ibid.

11.   Pious, S. (2003). Understanding Prejudice and Discrimination. *Journal of Social Issues*, 52, 25-31

12.   Bacchi, C. L. (1996). *The Politics of Affirmative Action: 'Women', Equality and Category Politics*. London: Sage.

13.   African American Policy Forum. (n.d.). Retrieved from: http://aapf.org/tool_to_speak_out/focus/myth-5-affirmative-action-is-an-african-american-entitlement-program/

14.   Ibid.

15.   Pious, S. (2003). Understanding Prejudice and Discrimination. *Journal of Social Issues*, 52, 25-31

16.   Pincus, F. L. (2003). *Reverse discrimination*. Boulder, CO: Lynne Rienner Publishers.

17.   Burstein, P. (1991). "Reverse discrimination" cases in federal courts: Legal mobilization by a countermovement. *Sociological Quarterly*, 32, 511-528.

18. Fried, C. (September/October 1999). Uneasy preferences: Affirmative action, in retrospect. *The American Prospect*, pp. 50-56.

19. Hill, T. E., Jr. (1995). *The message of affirmative action*. New York: Routledge.

20. McCann, T. B. (2000). *Always*. New York: Harper Perennial.

21. Curry, G. (1996). *The affirmative action debate*. Reading, Mass.: Addison-Wesley.

22. Kivel, P. (1998, November 15). Affirmative Action, Immigration & Welfare: Confronting Racism in 1998. *In Motion Magazine*.

23. Black, H. (1963). *The truth about college entrance exams and other standardized tests*. New York: Hart Pub. Co.

24. Barker, P & Pelavin, S. H. (1976). *Issues of reliability and directional bias in standardized achievement tests: the case of MAT 70*. Santa Monica: Rand Corporation.

25. Brigham, C. C. (1923). *A Study of American Intelligence.* Princeton, New Jersey: Princeton University Press.

26. Black, H. (1963). *The truth about college entrance exams and other standardized tests*. New York: Hart Pub. Co.

27. Cole, Y. (April 2007). Why the SATS are Failing America. *DiversityInc*, 37-42.

28. Selecting College Material. (1976, April 4). *New York Times*, E7.

29. Williams, P. (1991). *The Alchemy of Race and Rights.* Cambridge, MA: Harvard UP.

30. Recruiting News. (n.d.). Retrieved from: http://www.recruitersnetwork.com/news/2006/3.22.htm

31. Ibid.

32. Resource Handbook for Diversity Recruitment in the Fields of Engineering and Architecture. (n.d.). Retrieved from: http://www.sandiego.gov/eoc/pdf/recruithandbook.pdf

33. Ibid.

34. Danneberg, M. (2008, August 20). Opposing view: Ban legacy preferences. *USA Today, 3*.

Chapter Thirteen

Managing Diversity Strategies

It's no measure of health to be well adjusted to a profoundly sick society.

Krishnamarti

MANAGING DIVERSITY STRATEGIES

Chapter Objectives

After reading this chapter, you should be able to:

- understand what managing diversity means to the workplace.

- clarify managing diversity strategies.

- describe mentoring programs.

- determine how to handle diversity training.

- understand cultural audits and diversity councils.

- learn appropriate workplace terminology.

Managing Workplace Diversity

While, Affirmative Action focuses on opening the doors to organizations that formerly had their doors closed (either purposely or otherwise) does this mean the job of handling diversity is done? Oftentimes no. It is not enough to just get people in the door. The work atmosphere needs to be inclusive and offer support and opportunities for advancement. To really realize equal opportunity, we have to have an environment that manages diversity. Managing Diversity promotes fair and just work practices and policies that create equal opportunity in the workplace.[1]

Managing Diversity involves making sure there is an equal chance to progress through the company based on the systems in place. R. Roosevelt Thomas, Jr. the author and educator who created the concept of "managing diversity" indicated in *Beyond Race and Gender* that companies need to go beyond simple recognition of cultural diversity to active diversity management: "Managing diversity is a comprehensive managerial process for developing an environment that works for all employees."[2] Thomas indicated that diversity management must not be viewed as "an us/them kind of problem to be solved but as a resource to be managed."[3]

Managing Diversity can involve changing the system of promotion and recognition to making sure the workplace culture is inclusive. Completing these types of objectives would require some if not all of the following actions:

- Leaders and managers who lead by example. Managers who show through attitude, policies and practice that they value diversity establishing this basis for the rest of the organization.

- Designing a corporate environment that is inclusive. Old values based upon the good ole boy network may not take into account the diversity of the workforce where issues of access, work and family, and creativity instead of groupthink become essential components of the environment.

- Creation of nondiscrimination, non-retaliation and anti-harassment policies that strictly forbid discrimination and harassment in all forms. These policies need to have specific instructions defining what is not tolerated and what occurs when the policy is violated in accordance with any union or company contracts.[4]

- Formation of company policies that are written and carefully explained to employees so that they understand the policy and ramifications involved.

This type of information can be included in employee manuals, mission statements, and other written communications.[5]

- Requiring diversity training for the various levels in the organizations (management and employees alike).

- Building company goals and strategic plans that are aligned with diversity initiatives and tied to rewards and promotion.

- Providing systematic and careful evaluations where expectations were known by the employee in advance. Making sure that evaluations carry with them the opportunity to reward those who have met their goals, including any diversity initiatives. Those who have not been successful in meeting previously stated goals and objectives, would be provided any necessary training.

- Making sure managers handle conflicts in a timely fashion by using the following model:

One:	Listen with respect and openness.
Two:	Look at the situation from the other person's perspective.
Three:	Let the other person hear an explanation of your perspective.
Four:	Recognize similarities and differences.
Five:	Acknowledge any cultural differences.
Six:	Look for common ground.
Seven:	Recommend action and be creative.
Eight:	Determine what adaptations each person in the conflict is willing to make to find a satisfactory alternative.
Nine:	Negotiate an agreement.

Managing Diversity Strategies

In order to manage diversity it becomes important that workplace programs not only address the above suggestions but also concentrate on specific retention efforts.

Retention Suggestions & Tips

1. Change often won't occur from the bottom up. Therefore, to make sure diversity initiatives through recruiting, promoting, training and retaining employees from various backgrounds occur it is absolutely essential that senior management demonstrate a commitment to these objectives. Senior management should set strategic and long-term goals that promote diversity.[5] These goals should translate to company policies and initiatives.

2. Create "formal" mentoring programs.[6]

3. Make sure all employees have access to career development and training opportunities. Access what your management and "power" positions look like? Is there diversity? Don't overlook people of color and women when training and promotion opportunities are made available.[6] When there are "known career paths" necessary to moving into upper management make sure there is a diverse group walking this path.

4. Evaluations must be objective not subjective. Document employees' contributions, strengths and weaknesses with the same type of written standards. Utilize this information for evaluation, creating a formal process for performance and promotion decisions. Allow an evaluating group/team to make performance and promotion recommendations so bias errors are reduced.[7]

5. Conduct cultural audits and exit interviews so the organization is constantly aware of the cultural climate of the organization. This will

assist management with determining what they are doing right and wrong as it relates to diversity. Always provide cultural audit feedback and communicate to employees/managers any changes that need to be made as a result of the various analysis of the organization.[8] Provide a timeline for change.

6. Allow employees to make lateral moves.[9] This provides management exposure to employees and employees get access to the various corporate decision-makers. This also assists with dismissing stereotypical positions.[10]

7. Create support groups and other sponsored employee networks that will eliminate the isolation that many non-majority employees feel by being part of a minority group.[11]

8. Create diversity councils that will continuously address issues of diversity and report to senior management.[12] These types of groups made up of employees and managers with everyone holding equal status can get to the root of issues that may not make it through the communication channels. The council can also be utilized to find ways to highlight all the progress the organization is making in terms of diversity as this may get missed as well.

TOOLS FOR MANAGING DIVERSITY

The following section will address and explain some of the various tools that can be utilized to "manage diversity", these include:

❖ Mentoring
❖ Diversity Training
❖ Cultural Audits
❖ Diversity Councils
❖ Appropriate Workplace Terminology

Mentoring: A Model that Works

Formal Mentoring

Mentoring is a relationship between two individuals in which a wiser, more experienced person teaches a less knowledgeable individual. Formal mentoring is mentoring that has been initiated and supported by a third party; that is, someone other than the mentor and protégé or mentee, such as the organization for which the mentor and protégé work.[13] Typically organizations that formalize mentoring do the following:

- set program goals
- select mentors and protégés/mentees
- extensively train mentors and protégés/mentees for program effectiveness.

Why formal mentoring? A formal mentoring program can help ease turnover troubles by providing workers from varied backgrounds with information on the company's climate, unwritten values, norms, and career opportunities.[14]

Informal Mentoring

This type of mentoring is the development of relationships between individuals without organizational structure and interventions. Informal mentoring is the natural coming together of a mentor or protégé/mentee to meet each other's needs. This works easier when people have a common base--culture, beliefs, hobbies etc. that makes it effortless to make that type of natural connection.[15] However, natural connections won't work for everyone in the organization who needs it that is why formal mentoring is recommended over informal mentoring.

Coaching

Often confused with mentoring, coaching is a process that occurs when a person views and critiques another at work and offers ways to improve his or her practice. Although a mentor does some coaching, it is just one role of the relationship, whereas, coaching can be done by peers or even by a manager of an employee.

Of the three programs, the most effective has proven to be formal mentoring. While these programs can be designed for anyone, it is an important ingredient in the success of people of color, the disabled and women in the workplace.[16] Entrance into a new job or position can bring about unique challenges in itself, but when you add being a "minority" in a culturally different workplace you add a whole different set of issues. Having a structured mentorship program can address these issues and help the employee make the transition easier.

Mentoring can be a dynamic, reciprocal relationship in a work environment between an advanced career incumbent (mentor) and a beginner (protégé) aimed at promoting the career development of both. For the protégé, the object of mentoring is the achievement of an identity transformation, a movement from the status of understudy to that of self-directing colleague. For the mentor, the relationship is a vehicle for being able to give back as well as enhance your relationship building skills.

What are the stages to mentoring?

Phillips (1977) studied mentoring in the world of business surveying and interviewed women managers.[16] Phillips' research described six phases of mentoring: invitation, sparkle, development, disillusionment, parting and transformation:[17]

- Invitation stage occurs when the mentor invites the protégé to participate in a mentoring relationship.
- Sparkle stage, the mentor and protégé try to please each other.
- Development stage, the mentor shares the most information with the protégé.
- Disillusionment phase involves the beginning of the end of the relationship—the protégé begins to see mentoring as unnecessary.
- Parting stage is literally the breakup of the relationship.
- Transformation, the final stage involves a redefinition of the relationship, where the protégé is seen as an equal.

How do you ensure a successful mentoring program?

Train, Train and Train

It is important that both mentors and protégés train in order to understand the dynamics, responsibilities and goals of the program.[18] Each person needs to make a solid commitment with clear expectations of each other. They must understand that any long lasting relationship is built upon trust and this should be the backbone of the relationship. This can all be conveyed at the training session so the relationship is able to get off to a good start. If there are going to be cultural or gender differences within any of the pairs this needs to be addressed in some type of "sensitivity" training. It is important to understand differences so that we can start where we are and build upon that, to get to some common goals.

What can be learned from mentoring?

Bova and Phillips (1984) conducted surveys and interviews to determine what kinds of things protégés learned from their mentors and how they learned them.[19] Their results illustrate why mentoring is critically important in developing individuals. The following is a summary of what they found the protégés learned[20]:

- risk-taking behaviors,
- communication skills,
- survival in the organization,
- skills in their profession,
- respect for people,
- ways to set high standards and not compromise them,
- how to be good listeners,
- how to get along with all kinds of people,
- leadership qualities and what it means to be a professional.

In summary, formal mentorship programs result in several benefits for both the mentor and protégé, but more importantly it greatly benefits the organization in making sure they get the best out of each employee. Through mentoring, protégés acquire skills and knowledge that enable them to cope with various unwritten responsibilities in the organization that often revolve around the corporate culture. Mentors themselves, having learned the systems and culture, can be rejuvenated as they teach newcomers the tricks of the trade.

Diversity Training

Today, there is no question that diversity training can be of vital importance to the business strategy of corporations and organizations. Diversity training if conducted correctly can improve customer satisfaction, workplace productivity and reduce legal exposure. When an organization improves how they handle diversity it improves how employees relate to customers and each other, it also can help management understand the legal implications of the 1964 Civil Rights Acts. Organizations that don't make diversity a focus can be out performed by diversity-focused organizations and experience higher levels of employee dissatisfaction, higher turnover rates and lower productivity.

Organizations without wide-ranging diversity training and anti discrimination and harassment policies are in a more risky state when faced with a harassment or discrimination lawsuit.

Conducting Diversity Training

Although diversity training can provide some substantial benefits, anyone who has ever attempted to conduct diversity training in organizations of any size know they will encounter a "review." No matter how good the material, how engaging the exercises, how skilled the group process techniques, there is one obstacle even the most experienced and skilled facilitator cannot overcome... the unexamined negative reactions to the message.[21]

All an organization requires to become jittery about diversity intervention is to see a few bad evaluations or reviews, or listen to a few apocryphal stories, and diversity training can become the nucleus of all things negative with a half-life lasting sometimes several years. Often, the resolution is to avoid confronting anything, which smacks of diversity, or at least to insure the next facilitator does nothing to disturb the fragile dispositions of future trainees.[22]

When it comes to training, society issues and one's own experiences can work against attempts to teach value and respect for people's differences. The co-conspirators include[23]:

1. Inherited Social Systems which unfairly advantage some, and limit others;
2. Individuals who are reluctant to explore diversity issues;
3. Organizations who are unclear about diversity goals, and
4. Diversity professionals who have not prepared clients to engage in a process capable of achieving significant and abiding outcomes.

Below, are a few thoughts about the above in hopes of expanding access to diversity issues:

For one, there are many inequitable systems that have advantaged some and disadvantaged others. However, those in training while not the perpetrators of these societal ills they must understand that this does not preclude them from being part of the solution to solve these ills. The challenge is to get people to choose responsibility over guilt, to seek healing over shame, and to engage in a process capable of producing cooperation instead of conflict.

When individuals are confronted with their own involvement in refusing to challenge blatant systemic inequities, some may feel that those who claim to be victims just need to get over it and get on with today. However, perpetuating the status quo won't bring about change and this must be stressed with diversity training participants.

Secondly, when individuals refuse to explore diversity goals they rarely realize that successful diversity initiatives affect the company's bottom-line. Therefore when diversity training addresses the "business case" and the profitability of successfully managing a diverse workforce, it refutes the belief that diversity should just be ignored.

Also, on a ethical level the question which should be asked is: What does it say about individuals who, when exposed to ideas which propose fairness ... inclusion ... and the creation of new systems to replace biased and unfair ones ... can only manage the response that "it was a waste of time?" Further, what does it say about the character of an organization that would allow such responses to derail further exploration of these critical issues?

When top management makes it clear that they are committed to diversity by the creation of policies, programs and strategic goals it sends the message that diversity must not be ignored. Therefore, potential clients and diversity specialists must assess the strategies they will employ within the limitations of time, budget, and like considerations. One area that should never be compromised, however, is the integrity of either party to commit to the pursuit of clear diversity values and goals.[24] Working from a common understanding ensures the best chance for success. Successful programs rooted in integrity, compassion, and confidences are more than possible, but they come about by design, not by accident.

When designing diversity training, there are two commonly utilized diversity training techniques; they are role-playing and experiential learning. In these types of training, you can for example have participants take on the roles of someone different and provide them with a set of scenarios where they must respond and act as their new identity or you can have someone spend the day with an artificial disability. These types of training can provide invaluable insight that provides real-life situations, challenges and solutions while reviewing Human Resource policies, looking at career development issues, promotion procedures, leadership development opportunities, and other business practices.

Managing Diversity strategies like diversity training is a good step in the right direction when it comes to workplace difference.[25] The following programs work to make sure individuals easily adapt to the organization and its system. These programs can be implemented either through very structured programming or informal structures.

Cultural Audits

How do you recognize if a human relations problem is present in your department or area? What are the perceived barriers to enhanced working relationships? What are people in your department/area proud of, and why? These questions are addressed by conducting an internal cultural audit, with information provided by surveys and individual and focus group interviews.

A cultural audit is an assessment of the work climate of an organization or department, providing a current "snapshot" of the area. The purpose of the audit is to describe the overall working environment, identify the unwritten "norms" and rules governing employee interactions and workplace practices, determine possible barriers to effective work practices and communication, and make recommendations to address identified problems.[26] Race, gender, and class issues are also often examined.

The objectives of an audit are to:

- Determine an organization's "climate,"
- Establish how the current status of each department aligns with the company's vision,
- Provide a planning tool, and
- Provide a baseline for future comparisons.

Individual interviews with persons representing a "vertical slice" of the total organization population can be conducted. These individual assessments, along with the survey used to get a snapshot of the organization as well as group interview data help to provide a corroborative balance of the organizations cultural climate.

Data from the survey, along with group and individual interviews, are compiled and analyzed. The results are then presented to Senior Staff, and Organizational Development and/or Training representatives. They must then determine how to communicate the results and corresponding actions to all employees, as well as to determine if any training is necessary. The appropriate staff must then ensure the proper customization of any training program. After delivering the training, the findings are documented and recommendations to the organization in a formal, written report are developed.

The Cultural Audit is an ideal tool to measure program effectiveness. The Cultural Audit is the key to answering the frustrating question, "*Where do we go from here?*"[27] Since audit data clearly pinpoints and quantifies general population and group-specific issues, the process of developing a viable strategic plan for diversity and other types of training is made much easier.

People need to be both empowered and motivated in order for real change to take place. That is, you need to achieve a situation where all of management and staff are both *able* and *willing* to change. "A Cultural Audit will in itself facilitate change - 'if you measure it, you change it'. A very powerful form of measurement is to obtain customer feedback on the service provided - this provides a significant motivation for change across all levels of management and staff."[28]

Diversity Councils

An employee diversity council is a group of people joined by a common interest and a vision in which employee differences are accepted and valued. A diversity council usually consists of 10 to 24 employees from various organizational levels and groups. White men--especially senior white men--need to be included.[30]

The effectiveness of diversity councils varies considerably from organization to organization, and there is no consistent approach to making them work. The effective use and application of a diversity council strategy is one of the critical challenges and opportunities facing organizations. However, with careful planning and implementation process diversity councils can be a welcoming unit to the diversity process.[29]

Diversity Councils Work as a team to:

- review data from cultural audits,
- create a diversity plan,
- offer ideas and recommendations,
- implement agreed upon changes, and

- recognize and track progress.

Activities may include:

- orientation and training programs,
- career development systems, mentor programs, and internal job fairs,
- policy development,
- lunch discussion or feedback sessions,
- recruitment and retention programs.

A diversity council can provide a way to reinforce justice and reverence for diversity by "walking the talk." Diversity councils also provide an opportunity for continuous learning about diversity that should contribute to the cultural competence of the organization by enhancing attitudes and behavior, team and workforce development, and strategic planning as it impacts diversity.

Strategies, policies and work groups like diversity councils are important tools in aiding to manage diversity. But these are without value if people in the workplace aren't able to communicate with each other effectively. Sometimes we can offend others without even meaning to, simply because we utilize inappropriate terminology.

Politically Correct and Incorrect Workplace Terminology

It is very important to incorporate understanding and respect of differences in the workplace—as tolerance is not a concept that is always learned early on. But, there are very simple ways to acquire this skill. One such way is by being aware of the language we accept as part of our corporate culture. Making sure we use the most politically correct terminology in addressing individuals in the workplace shows respect to others. In having an understanding of cultural knowledge you can begin to understand why some terminology is offensive due to the history associated with the word.

The following terms should therefore be examined as either politically correct and appropriate to use or not politically correct and inappropriate to use in the workplace:

African (politically correct term)
These are the people who currently migrate from the continent of Africa. Africa is often mislabeled as a country when it is a continent full of various countries. Africa, the second largest continent in the world in both physical size and population, has for the most part been "under" taught, marginalized and often grossly misrepresented in our classrooms as well as in our media and popular culture. There is no such language as "African." Africa is the home to many languages and dialects.

African American (politically correct term)
These are Americans of primarily African descent. Sometimes used interchangeably with "black" (a preferred term of some because not every brown person is of African descent.) Both of these terms, like other racial descriptors, are adjectives as in "a black person," not nouns as in "a black." Objectionable terms are "colored," "Negro," "Negroes," "nigger—in any form is not acceptable by use by anybody," "pickaninny," "spade," "giggaboo."

American Indian (politically correct term)
These are the native people of America. Sometimes called "Native American"—the more appropriate term. Some object to the universal classification of "Indian" in favor of tribal designations, such as Cherokee, Cheyenne, Hopi, etc. Others consider "Indian" a misnomer dating back to when Columbus landed in America, mistook his location to be India, and designated the natives "Indian."

Anglo (politically correct term)
These are people of Anglican descent. Sometimes used interchangeably with "white."

Articulate (NOT a politically correct term)
Sometimes this expression is used to describe people of color and is often seen as a compliment when really it is derogatory. It means the person had the unanticipated ability to express oneself verbally. Why assume certain people would not be articulate and then get surprised when they are.

Asian American (politically correct term)
It is the preferred term for describing Americans of Asian descent. Not interchangeable with "Asian." Objectionable terms are "chink," "coolies," "gook," "nip," "slant," "slant-eye," "chinaman," "china doll," "dragon lady."

Banana (NOT a politically correct term)
It is an offensive term referring to Asian Americans who are considered to have abandoned their culture. Other similar terms: "Oreo" for Black Americans, "coconut" for Mexican Americans.

Bisexual (politically correct term)
This is a person who is attracted to members of both sexes. Objectionable term is "bi."

Boy (NOT a politically correct term for males age 18 and over)
An offensive term used to refer to Black men, those over the age of 18. This is a reference to times of slavery when black men were not addressed in terms of respect.

Buck (NOT a politically correct term)
This is an offensive term used to describe an American Indian or African American male.

Caucasian (politically correct term)
It is the classification of a race of people. Used interchangeably with "white" this applies to some light skinned Hispanics as well.

Chief (NOT a politically correct term)
This is offensive when used to describe an American Indian.

Cracker (NOT a politically correct term)
A term of offense used to refer to low-income white people.

Flip (NOT a politically correct term)
It is a racial slur referring to Filipinos and Filipino Americans.

F.O.B. (NOT a politically correct term)
This is an acronym for "fresh off the boat," a derogatory term for immigrants.

Hispanic (politically correct term)
This is people of Latin American or Spanish descent. This does not include everyone who speaks Spanish. A term that is more inclusive and interchangeable with Hispanic is Latino.

Homosexual (politically correct term)
This is a person who is sexually attracted to members of his/her own sex. Objectionable terms are "Faggot," "Fruit," "homo."

JAP (NOT a politically correct term)
This is an objectionable term applied to Jewish women, stands for Jewish American Princess.

Jew Down (NOT a politically correct term)
An offensive term used to suggest bartering for a lower price.

Oriental (NOT a politically correct term when used to describe people)
This should be used to refer only to objects such as art and rugs. Most activists consider this term to be outdated and dislike it because it was imposed on them for easy classification by whites. Instead, use the terms Asian American, Chinese American, etc.

Person with Disability (politically correct term)
This is a preferred term along with mentally or physically challenged. Objectionable terms are cripple, handicapped.

Raghead/Towelhead (NOT a politically correct term)
This is a derogatory term used to describe Sikhs, referring to the custom of wearing turbans.

Speech/Hearing Impaired has been replaced by Hard of Hearing (politically correct term)
This is the preferred term as opposed to using the objectionable term "deaf and dumb."

Uncle (NOT a politically correct term)
This is offensive when used as a substitute for Mr. in addressing a black man. This is a reference to times of slavery when black men were not addressed in terms of respect.

Senior Citizen (politically correct term)
This refers to people over the age of 65 or an elderly person who is retired. Objectionable terms are codger, geezer, old fart, old fogy.

Whigger (NOT a politically correct term)
This is a derogatory term that refers to white people who act black in other words a "white nigger."

White Trash (NOT a politically correct term)
This is a derogatory term for whites, usually used to refer to those in low-income brackets.

Woman (politically correct term)
This is the term that should be used to refer to an adult female (over the age of 17). Objectionable terms are babe, bimbo, broad, chick, girl, gal, sweetie, dear, honey, wench.

Remember the saying: Sticks and stones will break my bones but words will never hurt me? Well, words do hurt and often are used to demean another. The derogatory terms described above should not be of use in the workplace. If you are not sure what to call a person, the easiest thing to do is ask them. Using appropriate terminology can help to effectively address workplace diversity.

Concluding Thoughts

Organizational culture can be defined as "a system of informal rules about how people should behave most of the time." These rules--or values--can involve "the way we do things," "how people dress and interact," "taken-for-granted points of view," "workplace humor," and "what happens at lunchtime." A commitment to strengthen cultural diversity can grow out of a vision of equality, a sense of social responsibility, valuing the role of diversity in nature and in life, or legal mandates.

In summary, we want to make sure that the corporate or organizational culture values differences, creates open doors for all to participate in the workplace, embraces practices and procedures like diversity training, cultural audits, mentoring and diversity councils to make sure policies and procedures work for everyone. This helps to eliminate a revolving door, low employee morale or lawsuits that can occur when a workplace is not providing equality and access.

End of Chapter Questions

1. How does Managing Diversity as a tool to help with workplace equality differ from Affirmative Action?

2. Who are difficult people and what are some tips for dealing with difficult people.

3. Under what corporate conditions would a Mentorship Program benefit the organization?

4. Why would a company conduct a cultural audit and have a diversity council?

Internet Exercise

Go to www.google.com and type in "mentoring tips" and choose an article on workplace mentoring. Summarize this article along with answering why and how mentoring can work in organizations.

End of Chapter Exercise

Take the Pretest/Posttest Challenge

Post test

Directions: Answer questions 1-17 utilizing your "best" guess. Now compare these answers with your pre test taken in chapter one. Explain what answers changed. Now once you have received the correct answers, determine if the cultural knowledge you gained changed your answers for the better/worse or if there was no change.

True/False

1. Thanksgiving is a celebration that everyone enjoys. Native-Americans especially enjoy this holiday because of the peace it represented to their community.

2. Gay and lesbian people are a threat to the workplace and have few leaders who have contributed to our society.

    _____

3. African-Americans even though they started as slaves in this country now have equal opportunity.

    _____

4. Disabled employees can be a liability to a company due to missed work time.

    _____

5. Caucasian men are accepted in Corporate America because they all belong to the "old boys network."

    _____

6. For every job that a man can do, there is a woman able to do the same job.

    _____

7. Most people on welfare (a government transfer system where tax payer dollars are given to the poor for housing etc.) are Black and Hispanic women who live off the system forever.

    _____

8. Arabs come to this country and are given government subsidies (free money that is not to be paid back) this is why they are able to buy their own companies.

    _____

9. Asian-Americans have always been privileged minorities because of their higher intelligence and because they do not suffer from discrimination or illiteracy.

    _____

10. Hispanics are the poorest minority because they are lazy.

    _____

11. Cultural knowledge of various groups is not necessary to preventing discrimination in the workplace.

    _____

12. I believe that most people are treated fairly in the workplace and history plays no factor in how people treat each other.

    _____

13. It is not necessary to have diversity training in the workplace as most people understand diversity and its implications.

    _____

Multiple Choice

14. I belong to the following group: a. male or b. female

15. I belong to the following group:
    a. Asian American
    b. African American/Black
    c. Caucasian
    d. Latino/Hispanic
    e. Native American
    f. Other

16. I belong to the following age group:
    a. Under the age of 18
    b. age   18-25
    c. age   26-45
    d. age   46 and older

17. The following is a true statement:
    a. I have had previous diversity training that relates to culture
    b. I have never had diversity training.
    c. I have had sexual harassment training only.
    d. I have had diversity training and sexual harassment training.

References

1. Thomas, R. R. (1996). *Redefining Diversity*. New York: Amacom.

2. Thomas, R. R. (1991). *Beyond Race and Gender: Unleashing the Power of Your Total Workforce by Managing Diversity*. Atlanta, GA: American Institute for Managing Diversity.

3. Ibid.

4. Curtice, J. (2005). Want to motivate your employees? Keep your company safe and you will. *Handbook of Business Strategy, 6*(1), 205-208.

5. Loden, M. & Rosener, J. B. (1991). Workforce America!: Managing Employee Diversity as a Vital Resource. Columbus, OH: Irwin Professional Publishing.

6. Larkins, D. (2000). *Issues of recruitment and retention*. Lincoln: University of Nebraska: People of Color in Predominantly White Institutions-Fifth Annual National Conference.

7. Ibid.

8. Loden, M. (1995). *Implementing Diversity*. Columbus, OH: Irwin.

9. Larkins, D. (2000). *Issues of recruitment and retention*. Lincoln: University of Nebraska: People of Color in Predominantly White Institutions-Fifth Annual National Conference.

10. Ibid.

11. Ibd.

12. Gardenswartz, L. & Rowe, A. (1995). *Diverse Teams at Work: Capitalizing on the Power of Diversity*. Columbus, OH: Irwin Professional Publishing.

13. Burke, R. J. & McKeen, C. A. (1990). Mentoring in Organizations: Implications for Women. *Journal of Business Ethics*, 9.

14. Ibid.

15. Foster, J., & Cross, J. (1988, April). *Workforce Diversity and Business*. Training and Development Journal.

16. Lee, J. H. & Nolan, R. E. (1998, December). The relationship between mentoring and the career advancement of women administrators in cooperative extension. *Journal of Career Development*, 25(1), 3-13.

17. Portner, H. (2005). Teacher mentoring and induction: the state of the art and beyond. Thousand Oaks, CA: Corwin Press.

18. USDA Career Intern Mentoring Handbook. Retrieved from: http://www.da.usda.gov/employ/MentorProtegeHandbook.pdf

19. Bova, B. M. & Phillips, R. R. (1984). Mentoring as a Learning Experience for Adults. *Journal of Teacher Education*, 35(3), 16-20.

20. Ibid.

21. Delatte, A.P., & Baytos, L. (1993). Eight Guidelines for Successful Diversity Training. *Training*, 30, 55-60.

22. Karp, H.B., & Sutton, N. (1993). Where the Diversity Training Goes Wrong. Training, 30, 30-34.

23. Ibid.

24. Ibid.

25. Ghiselin, B. W. (1995). *Work Teams and Diversity*. Center for Creative Leadership.

26. Gallos, J. (1994, January/February). Competitive advantage through managing diversity. *Franchising World*, 26(1).

27. Wagner, C. & Madsen-Copas, P. (2002, Summer). An audit of the culture starts with two handy tools. *Journal of Staff Development*, 42-53.

28. Ibid.

29. Etsy, K., Griffin, R. & Hirsch, M. S. (1995). *Workplace Diversity*. Holbrook, MA: Adams Media Corporation.

30. Tuohy, J. (2002, December). *Setting the Bar....Diversity Leadership Practices*. VPA Diversity Council Handbook.

Appendix A

Diversity Journal & Index

Evaluation - the only reliable road to knowledge.

Mohandas Karamchand Gandhi

Diversity Journal

This Diversity Journal is a place to express all your inner thoughts and feelings concerning the deep and somewhat controversial subject matter that relates to diversity in the workplace. The goal of this writing assignment is for you to begin to understand yourself through writing. You can then move closer to knowing who you are and what adjustments you may need to make in order to better value diversity. Your feelings, your breakthroughs, your desires — record them all here. Discover yourself.

Why Journal?

Journaling as you complete this course can help you with:

1. Understanding your own feelings about the issues discussed and connect you to why you feel as you do.

2. Provide you with an opportunity to release the stress you might feel as we discuss the various topics. Putting your thoughts on paper, can take them off your heart and mind.

3. Journaling can help you address issues that you may feel angry about and help you get to a place of forgiveness and healing.

4. Connecting with your inner thoughts, no matter what they are as we address these controversial topics, can provide you with insight and peace. Also, providing you an opportunity to see how your own perspectives may change as we move through the topics presented in the text.

General Directions are to write out your response to the statements that correlate with each chapter. The amount of detail will vary depending upon your writing style and views. Please utilize complete sentences to translate your thoughts.

Chapter One Thinking Journal

Name_____

Think about two positive messages you have been told through out your life or when you were a kid or two positive things you believe about yourself. Now indicate below how these messages have manifest themselves in your life.

_____

_____

_____

_____

_____

_____

_____

_____

_____

_____

How does thinking negative instead of positive impact you when you encounter someone different than yourself?

_____

_____

_____

_____

_____

_____

_____

_____

_____

_____

_____

Chapter Two Thinking Journal

Name_____

Directions: After reading this chapter, indicate your feelings, viewpoint or question on the following topic:

How to change your own ways of thinking to positively impact dealing with diversity

_____
_____
_____
_____
_____
_____
_____
_____
_____
_____
_____
_____
_____
_____
_____
_____
_____
_____
_____
_____
_____
_____
_____
_____
_____

Other comments:

_____
_____
_____
_____
_____
_____
_____
_____
_____
_____
_____
_____
_____
_____
_____
_____
_____
_____
_____
_____
_____
_____
_____
_____
_____
_____
_____
_____

Chapter Three Thinking Journal

Name_____

Directions: After reading this chapter, indicate your feelings, viewpoint or question on the following topic:

Discrimination And Tolerance

_____
_____
_____
_____
_____
_____
_____
_____
_____
_____
_____
_____
_____
_____
_____
_____
_____
_____
_____
_____
_____
_____
_____
_____

Other comments:

_____
_____
_____
_____
_____
_____
_____
_____
_____
_____
_____
_____
_____
_____
_____
_____
_____
_____
_____
_____
_____
_____
_____
_____
_____
_____
_____

Chapter Four Thinking Journal

Name_____

Directions: Read the passage below and indicate whether or not you/your culture agree with the statement. State why you believe this way and if you do not believe this way indicate what your belief is regarding the issue. Lastly indicate if you think your viewpoint on this statement can interfere with diversity if others don't feel like you.

Patriotism, Loyalty To Country, And Political Involvement: We believe that we are to be good citizens. This means we are loyal to our nation: we are to support our Armed Forces, law enforcement officials, and we should participate in the political process. We live in a free country but we must all be loyal and not question authority in order to be patriotic.

Other comments:

_____
_____
_____
_____
_____
_____
_____
_____
_____
_____
_____
_____
_____
_____
_____
_____
_____
_____
_____
_____
_____
_____
_____
_____
_____
_____
_____
_____

Chapter Five Thinking Journal

Name_____

Directions: After reading this chapter, indicate your feelings, viewpoint or question on the following topic:

Women in the workplace

_____
_____
_____
_____
_____
_____
_____
_____
_____
_____
_____
_____
_____
_____
_____
_____
_____
_____
_____
_____
_____
_____
_____
_____
_____
_____
_____

Other comments:

_____
_____
_____
_____
_____
_____
_____
_____
_____
_____
_____
_____
_____
_____
_____
_____
_____
_____
_____
_____
_____
_____
_____
_____
_____
_____
_____
_____

Chapter Six Thinking Journal

Name_____

Directions: After reading this chapter, indicate your feelings, viewpoint or question on the following topic:

Stereotypical Mascots & Native American Respect

_____
_____
_____
_____
_____
_____
_____
_____
_____
_____
_____
_____
_____
_____
_____
_____
_____
_____
_____
_____
_____
_____
_____
_____

Other comments:

_____

_____

_____

_____

_____

_____

_____

_____

_____

_____

_____

_____

_____

_____

_____

_____

_____

_____

_____

_____

_____

_____

_____

_____

_____

_____

_____

Chapter Seven Thinking Journal

Name_____

Directions: After reading this chapter, indicate your feelings, viewpoint or question on the following topic:

Blacks & Whites Uniting during slavery

_____
_____
_____
_____
_____
_____
_____
_____
_____
_____
_____
_____
_____
_____
_____
_____
_____
_____
_____
_____
_____
_____
_____
_____
_____
_____
_____

Other comments:

_____
_____
_____
_____
_____
_____
_____
_____
_____
_____
_____
_____
_____
_____
_____
_____
_____
_____
_____
_____
_____
_____
_____
_____
_____
_____
_____
_____
_____

Chapter Eight Thinking Journal

Name_____

Directions: After reading this chapter, indicate your feelings, viewpoint or question on the following scenario:

You have moved to a new country (very different from your own culture) indicate how you would feel as a minority—answer this if you are part of the majority in your current country. If you are currently a minority in your current country indicate how you would handle being the majority in your own country.

Other comments:

_____
_____
_____
_____
_____
_____
_____
_____
_____
_____
_____
_____
_____
_____
_____
_____
_____
_____
_____
_____
_____
_____
_____
_____
_____
_____
_____
_____
_____

Chapter Nine Thinking Journal

Name_____

Directions: After reading this chapter, indicate your feelings, viewpoint or question on the following topic:

Religious Freedom

_____
_____
_____
_____
_____
_____
_____
_____
_____
_____
_____
_____
_____
_____
_____
_____
_____
_____
_____
_____
_____
_____
_____
_____

even Thinking Journal

After reading this chapter, indicate your feelings, viewpoint or question
wing scenario:

born an Intersexed person. This is the state of a person whose sex
mes, genitalia and/or secondary sex characteristics are determined to be
xclusively male nor female. A person with intersex may have biological
istics of both the male and female sexes. **At the age of five your
changed your biological sex to what you have determined as an
be the wrong gender. What do you do?**

_____
_____
_____
_____
_____
_____
_____
_____
_____
_____
_____
_____
_____
_____
_____
_____
_____
_____
_____
_____
_____
_____
_____

Other comments:

_____
_____
_____
_____
_____
_____
_____
_____
_____
_____
_____
_____
_____
_____
_____
_____
_____
_____
_____
_____
_____
_____
_____
_____
_____
_____
_____
_____
_____
_____
_____

Chapter Ten Thinking Journal

Name_____

Directions: After reading this chapter, indicate your feelings, viewpoint or question on the following scenario:

You have just learned that you have HIV. Now indicate how you would want to be treated at work/school by your supervisor/colleagues/peers.

_____
_____
_____
_____
_____
_____
_____
_____
_____
_____
_____
_____
_____
_____
_____
_____
_____
_____
_____
_____
_____
_____
_____

Other comments:

_____
_____
_____
_____
_____
_____
_____
_____
_____
_____
_____
_____
_____
_____
_____
_____
_____
_____
_____
_____
_____
_____
_____
_____
_____
_____
_____

Chapter El

Name_____

Directions:
on the follo

You were
chromoso
neither e
character
parents
adult to

Other comments:

_____
_____
_____
_____
_____
_____
_____
_____
_____
_____
_____
_____
_____
_____
_____
_____
_____
_____
_____
_____
_____
_____
_____
_____
_____
_____
_____
_____
_____
_____
_____

Chapter Twelve Thinking Journal

Name_____

Directions: Read the passage below and indicate whether or not you/your culture agree with the statement. State why you believe this way and if you do not believe this way indicate what your belief is regarding the issue. Lastly indicate if you think your viewpoint on this statement can interfere with diversity.

Racism a disorder: Extreme bias can be an illness. Extreme forms of racism, homophobia and other prejudices should be addressed by a psychiatrist in the course of therapy because some patients are disabled by these beliefs.

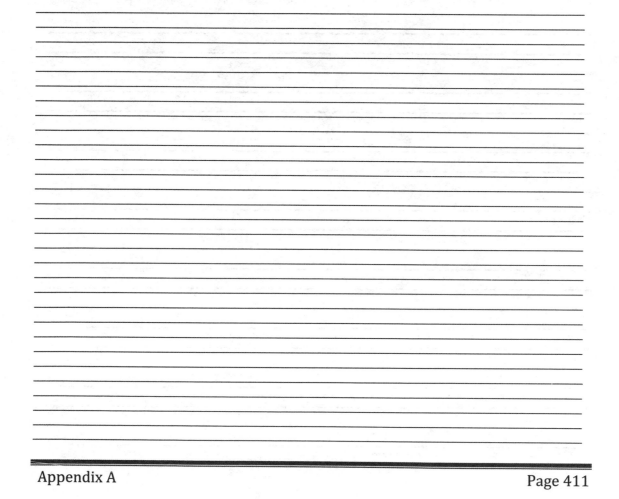

Other comments:

_____
_____
_____
_____
_____
_____
_____
_____
_____
_____
_____
_____
_____
_____
_____
_____
_____
_____
_____
_____
_____
_____
_____
_____
_____
_____
_____
_____

Chapter Thirteen Thinking Journal

Name_____

Directions:

After reading this chapter, indicate what tool you would utilize in the workplace.

_____
_____
_____
_____
_____
_____
_____
_____
_____
_____
_____

Indicate what topic(s) in the entire course touched you most.

_____
_____
_____
_____
_____
_____
_____
_____
_____
_____
_____
_____
_____
_____
_____
_____
_____
_____
_____
_____

INDEX